The Venal Origins of Development in Spanish America

Venal Origins is a comparative and historical study of the roots of spatial inequalities in Spanish America. The book focuses on the Spanish colonial administration and the eighteenth-century practice of office-selling – where colonial positions were exchanged for money – to analyze its lasting impact on local governance, regional disparities, and economic development. Drawing on three centuries of rich archival and administrative data, it shows how office-selling exacerbated venality and profit-seeking behaviors among colonial officials, fostering indigenous segregation, violent uprisings, and the institutionalization of exploitative fiscal and labor systems. The enduring legacies from their rule remain visible today in the form of subnational authoritarian enclaves, localized cycles of violence, and marginalized indigenous communities, which have reinforced and deepened regional inequalities. By integrating perspectives from history, political science, and economics, *Venal Origins* provides a nuanced and empirically grounded analysis of how colonial officials shaped – and still influence – subnational development in Spanish America.

Jenny Guardado is Assistant Professor at Georgetown University's School of Foreign Service. Her research, featured in top academic journals, has received the *Pi Sigma Alpha* and *Oliver E. Williamson* awards. She previously served as a postdoctoral scholar at the Harris School of Public Policy.

CAMBRIDGE STUDIES IN ECONOMICS, CHOICE, AND SOCIETY

Founding Editors

Timur Kuran, *Duke University*
Peter J. Boettke, *George Mason University*

This interdisciplinary series promotes original theoretical and empirical research as well as integrative syntheses involving links between individual choice, institutions, and social outcomes. Contributions are welcome from across the social sciences, particularly in the areas where economic analysis is joined with other disciplines such as comparative political economy, new institutional economics, and behavioral economics.

Books in the Series:

PAUL DRAGOS ALIGICA *Public Entrepreneurship, Citizenship, and Self-Governance*

TERRY L. ANDERSON and GARY D. LIBECAP *Environmental Markets: A Property Rights Approach*

ADAM CREPELLE *Becoming Nations Again: The Journey Towards Tribal Self-Determination*

SHELBY GROSSMAN *The Politics of Order in Informal Markets: How the State Shapes Private Governance*

MORRIS B. HOFFMAN *The Punisher's Brain: The Evolution of Judge and Jury*

RANDALL G. HOLCOMBE *Political Capitalism: How Political Influence is Made and Maintained*

ROGER KOPPL *Expert Failure*

PETER T. LEESON: *Anarchy Unbound: Why Self- Governance Works Better Than You Think*

MICHAEL C. MUNGER *Tomorrow 3.0: Transaction Costs and the Sharing Economy*

JENNIFER BRICK MURTAZASHVILI AND ILIA MURTAZASHVILI *Land, the State, and War Property Institutions and Political Order in Afghanistan*

ALEX NOWRASTEH AND BENJAMIN POWELL *Wretched Refuse?: The Political Economy of Immigration and Institutions*

BENJAMIN POWELL *Out of Poverty: Sweatshops in the Global Economy (First Edition)*

BENJAMIN POWELL *Out of Poverty: Sweatshops in the Global Economy (Second Edition)*

JEAN-PHILIPPE PLATTEAU *Islam Instrumentalized: Religion and Politics in Historical Perspective*

JARED RUBIN *Rulers, Religion, and Riches: Why the West Got Rich and the Middle East Did Not*

VERNON L. SMITH AND BART J. WILSON *Humanomics: Moral Sentiments and the Wealth of Nations for the Twenty-First Century*

CASS R. SUNSTEIN *The Ethics of Influence: Government in the Age of Behavioral Science*

ANDREAS THIEL, WILLIAM A. BLOMQUIST AND DUSTIN E. GARRICK *Governing Complexity: Analyzing and Applying Polycentricity*

CAROLYN M. WARNER, RAMAZAN KILINÇ, CHRISTOPHER W. HALE and ADAM B. COHEN *Generating Generosity in Catholicism and Islam: Beliefs, Institutions, and Public Goods Provision*

TAIZU ZHANG *The Laws and Economics of Confucianism: Kinship and Property in Preindustrial China and England*

TAISU ZHANG *The Ideological Foundations of Qing Taxation: Belief Systems, Politics, and Institutions*

The Venal Origins of Development in Spanish America

JENNY GUARDADO
Georgetown University

Shaftesbury Road, Cambridge CB2 8EA, United Kingdom

One Liberty Plaza, 20th Floor, New York, NY 10006, USA

477 Williamstown Road, Port Melbourne, VIC 3207, Australia

314–321, 3rd Floor, Plot 3, Splendor Forum, Jasola District Centre, New Delhi – 110025, India

103 Penang Road, #05–06/07, Visioncrest Commercial, Singapore 238467

Cambridge University Press is part of Cambridge University Press & Assessment, a department of the University of Cambridge.

We share the University's mission to contribute to society through the pursuit of education, learning and research at the highest international levels of excellence.

www.cambridge.org
Information on this title: www.cambridge.org/9781009635127

DOI: 10.1017/9781009635134

© Jenny Guardado 2025

This publication is in copyright. Subject to statutory exception and to the provisions of relevant collective licensing agreements, no reproduction of any part may take place without the written permission of Cambridge University Press & Assessment.

When citing this work, please include a reference to the
DOI 10.1017/9781009635134

First published 2025

Cover image: The royal administrator and his low-status dinner guests; the mestizo, the mulatto, and the tributary Indian. by Felipe Guamán Poma de Ayala (1535–1616) – Alamy Stock Photo

A catalogue record for this publication is available from the British Library

A Cataloging-in-Publication data record for this book is available from the Library of Congress

ISBN 978-1-009-63515-8 Hardback
ISBN 978-1-009-63512-7 Paperback

Cambridge University Press & Assessment has no responsibility for the persistence or accuracy of URLs for external or third-party internet websites referred to in this publication and does not guarantee that any content on such websites is, or will remain, accurate or appropriate.

For EU product safety concerns, contact us at Calle de José Abascal, 56, 1°, 28003 Madrid, Spain, or email eugpsr@cambridge.org

To Steven, Georgie and Nicholas
For always making me smile

Contents

List of Figures		page xi
List of Tables		xv
Acknowledgments		xvii
1	Introduction	1
2	The Eighteenth-Century "Market" of Offices	22
3	Why Sell Offices?	47
4	Office-Selling-Turned-Venality	72
5	Captured Administration: Eighteenth-Century *Audiencias and Corregidores*	94
6	To Flee or to Fight: Indigenous Responses to Venality	124
7	Colonial Venality and Nineteenth-Century State-Building	160
8	Conclusion: *Corregimientos* and *Alcaldías* in Spanish America Today	195
	Epilogue	218
Appendices		221
Bibliography		241
Index		261

Figures

1.1	*Gobiernos, corregimientos,* and *alcaldías mayores* sold (1670–1751)	page 6
1.2	The short- and long-run effects of office-selling	12
1.3	*Audiencias* and population prior to independence	14
1.4	Population persistence versus territorial shifts: Mexico 1808 and today	15
1.5	Country-level rankings of GDP per capita in 1800 and 1900 (selected countries)	16
2.1	The Spanish Empire ca. 1700	25
2.2	Spanish *audiencias* ca. 1700	26
2.3	Frontiers and military governors (*gobernaciones*) ca. 1700	29
2.4	Treasury *cajas* in Spanish Empire ca. 1700	30
2.5	Provincial *corregimientos* and *alcaldías mayores* ca. 1700	31
2.6	Office prices and *repartimiento* quotas in Peru and Bolivia	42
2.7	Probability of appointment by social status: *corregimientos* and *alcaldías*	45
2.8	Prices paid by social status: *corregimientos* and *alcaldías*	45
3.1	Total offices sold and revenue collected (1670–1751)	53
3.2	Total revenue and military expenditure by the Crown (1670–1751)	55
3.3	Total revenue collected by type of position (1670–1751)	59
3.4	Share of tax income by different sources (1680–1810)	61
3.5	Type of officials: Spanish members in the *audiencia* (1687–1800)	67
3.6	Military and nobility officials in *corregimientos* and *alcaldías*	68

List of Figures

4.1	Depictions of *audiencia* council members and *corregidores* in sixteenth-century Peru	76
4.2	Key wars and characteristics of *audiencia* members (1687–1751)	87
4.3	Key wars and social status of *corregidores* and *alcaldes* (1670–1751)	88
4.4	Key wars and social status of purchasers by office profitability	89
5.1	Share of purchasers across Spanish American *audiencias* (1687–1800)	97
5.2	Price growth and purchaser presence in the *audiencia*	104
5.3	Geopolitical concerns based on the positions excluded from sales	105
5.4	Mean share of purchasers in *audiencias* by foreign threat status	107
5.5	Price growth and purchaser presence in the *audiencia* by geopolitical threat	107
5.6	Price growth and purchaser presence in the *audiencia* by individual traits	110
6.1	Uprisings and the end of the *Pax Hispannica* (1680–1808)	135
6.2	Yearly uprisings and *audiencia* composition (1680–1780)	137
6.3	Venality and postsales uprisings: Mexico, Peru, and Bolivia	140
6.4	Weather anomalies and uprisings in Mexico, Bolivia, and Peru	143
6.5	Subsistence crises, uprisings, and venality: Mexico, Bolivia, and Peru	144
6.6	Late eighteenth-century *intendencias* and *subdelegados* reform and office-selling	146
6.7	Ethnic composition of parishes ca. 1770 and distance to provincial *cabecera*	156
6.8	Indigenous segregation ca. 1770 and histories of venality: Mexico and Peru	157
7.1	Venality and coffee wage laborers in Guatemala (1881 and 1893)	169
7.2	Colonial venality, public good provision, and voter registration	170
7.3	Eighteenth-century price spread poll tax payers and *concertaje* in Ecuador	173

7.4	Colonial *repartimiento* and size of population paying *tributo* in Bolivia	176
7.5	Timing of *municipio* creation and colonial venality in Peru and Mexico	179
7.6	Insurgency, rural unrest, and revolution in rural Mexico (1810–1920)	183
7.7	Nineteenth-century and early twentieth-century historical conflicts in Peru	185
7.8	Indigenous presence by distance to former colonial capitals	189
8.1	Summary of argument: the contemporary legacies of colonial venality	196
8.2	Indigenous segregation by venality status today	198
8.3	Subnational undemocratic regimes index by colonial venality status	200
8.4	Provincial stunting in children by colonial venality status	204
8.5	Bordering *centros poblados* in Pacages, Sicasica, and Omasuyos (Bolivia)	208
8.6	Price spread and educational outcomes among bordering settlements	209
8.7	Price spread, public goods, and poverty rates across bordering settlements	211
A.1	Distance to the colonial *cabecera* prior to office-selling	233
A.2	Stunting among indigenous children by colonial venality status	236
A.3	Contemporaneous indigenous presence along colonial jurisdictional borders	240

Tables

2.1	Summary of key offices for sale in 1670–1750	page 32
2.2	Mean price and quantity of sales by office type (1670–1751)	39
2.3	Rankings and prices of *alcaldías* and *corregimientos* by anonymous *Yndize*	43
3.1	Share of total contribution from Indies	57
3.2	List of positions excluded from sales since 1717 and their reason	63
3.3	Place of birth of purchasers versus appointees	65
6.1	Mean differences in uprisings before and after sales: Mexico, Peru, and Bolivia	139
7.1	Postindependence shares of indigenous taxation to total revenue: Bolivia	175
7.2	Number of *municipios* by date of creation in Peru (1525–2010)	178
8.1	Price spreads and living standards in Spanish America: pooled results	205
A.1	Mean real price and quantity of sales by office type (1670–1751)	221
A.2	Probability of appointment by social status: *corregimientos* and *alcaldías*	222
A.3	Prices paid by social status: *Corregimientos* and *Alcaldías*	222
A.4	Key wars and official's characteristics in the *audiencia* (1687–1751)	224

A.5	Key wars and social status of *corregidores* and *alcaldes* (1670–1751)	224
A.6	Price growth and purchaser presence in the *audiencia*	226
A.7	Price growth and purchaser presence in the *audiencia* by geopolitical threat	227
A.8	Price growth and purchaser presence in the *audiencia* by individual traits	227
A.9	Venality and postsales uprisings: Mexico, Peru, and Bolivia	229
A.10	Subsistence crises, uprisings, and venality: Mexico, Bolivia, and Peru	230
A.11	Uprisings in Guatemala, Ecuador, and Colombia (1680–1808)	231
A.12	Data sources and variables of indigenous presence by locality	234
A.13	List of data sources for biological living standards at the individual level	235
A.14	Variables and sources for *centro poblado*/locality outcomes	236
A.15	Geographic differences along jurisdictional borders	237

Acknowledgments

Unbeknownst to me at the time, the research behind this book started in my fourth year of graduate school, almost fifteen years ago. At the time I was interested in Spanish fiscal policy, such as the issuance of debt in the form of *juros*. Soon I discovered the lengths the Spanish Crown went to secure revenue in the late seventeenth century, including by selling high-level offices across its empire overseas. After some initial archival evidence gathering, it became clear to me that this policy was extensive: There seemed to be very few places that sales did not touch. The question was, how did this policy shape the governance of the places where it was implemented? The subject of this book.

Key to this academic journey has been the valuable advice of my PhD advisors: Adam Przeworski, Leonard Wantchekon, David Stasavage, Oeindrila Dube, and Pablo Querubin. I am thankful for Adam's probing questions ("Can we really say this is corruption?") and for Oeindrila's frankness in telling me to not pursue an alternative project – advice without which I would not have embarked on this one. Together with Pablo, I thank them both for their suggestions on the empirical approach. I am particularly grateful for David's continuous mentoring and guidance and in helping me shape vague notions of premodern fiscal policies into a workable project. Finally, I am indebted to Leonard's support from our first conversations about this project idea, his suggestions on how to expand it, and his unflagging mentorship.

I am particularly indebted to my book readers – Leticia Arroyo-Abad, Maria Alejandra Irigoin, James Mahoney, Hillel Soifer, Mark Koyama, Joel Simmons, Erick Langer, and Julio Rios-Figueroa – who, each from their own disciplines, deeply engaged with the manuscript and provided chapter-by-chapter feedback. Their deep knowledge of the regions' history, society, fiscal, and monetary policies has enriched this manuscript. Leading to a better version from what they read. In addition to their critical reading of the manuscript, their encouragement and support were particularly important to keep the project going. Together with the editorial work at Cambridge – Robert Dreesen – and the *Economics, Choice and Society Series* editors, Peter Boettke and Timur Kuran, and the invaluable comments of two anonymous reviewers were all key for bringing this work to life.

I also thank other faculty at New York University (NYU), The University of Chicago-Harris and Princeton, who provided important support either by attending my talks, providing feedback, or guiding me in other projects that indirectly fed into this one: Michael Gilligan, Shanker Satyanath, James Vreeland, and John Londregan. A postdoctoral year at the Harris School of Public Policy at the University of Chicago also gave me time to pursue this research and other work on conflict; Chapter 6 would not have been possible without that time and the discussions I had there.

This project also benefited from my peers at NYU and other universities, which saw the start of the idea and provided valuable feedback (and pushback!). Particular thanks to Jean Hong, Ben Pasquale, Kongjoo Shin, Pedro Nunes Da Silva, Parashar Kulkarni, Jorge Gallego, and Tianyang Xi. I also benefited from a New York City Area group of graduate students interested in historical political economy (even though it did not have that name at the time): Ali Cirone, Scott Abramson, Volha Charnysh, Pavithra Suryanarayan, Carlos Velasco, Emily Sellars, and Maria Paula Saffon, with whom I shared manuscript drafts, presented versions of this project, and exchanged feedback. I also thank my coauthors on other papers, Daphne Álvarez-Villa, Steven Pennings, and Edgar Franco-Vivanco, whose insights and discussions have deeply shaped my view of Mexican colonial history and of economics.

In terms of venues to present this research, I am especially grateful to the Stanford-LSE-Uniandes Long-Range Development in Latin America Conference, organized by Alberto Díaz-Cayeros, Jean-Paul Faguet, and Maria del Pilar López Uribe, who put together an amazing set of scholars to discuss the topics most germane to this book: development, persistence, and Latin America's colonial history. A similar role was that of the Washington Area Economic History and Development organized by Mark Koyama and Noel Johnson, whose feedback has been key to develop some of the arguments of this book. More recently, conferences, workshops, and edited volumes, organized by the historical political economy networks by Jeff Jenkins, Jared Rubin, and Felipe Valencia Caicedo, have been helpful in refining the main themes of this book.

At Georgetown I have benefited enormously from the expertise on Latin American history and the political economy group. Informal conversations with John Tutino, Erick Langer, and Kevin Haley have been hugely beneficial to understand indigenous populations in Mexico, Peru, and Bolivia. The monthly Americas Initiative workshop has been instrumental in workshopping chapters of the book and bridging the gap between political science and other disciplines. This project would not have been possible without the support of the Center for Latin American Studies at SFS and its members, particularly Matt Carnes, Diana Kapiszewski, Angelo Rivero Santos, and Julie McMurtry, who made all the other aspects of academic life run smoothly. The Mortara Seminar generously sponsored my book conference and served as a key venue to discuss some of the ideas of this book with input from Nita Rudra, Eric Voeten, Abe Newman, Kate McNamara, Irfan Nooruddin, Diana Kim, Laia Balcells, Dennis Quinn, and Rod Ludema.

The last but not least acknowledgment is to family: my husband, Steven Pennings, for holding the fort and keeping the companionship, love, and support while writing this book. To my kids, Georgie and Nicholas, who think I am writing a very long children's book, I hope you are not too disappointed when you read this. To my parents and sister, Leonardo, Rosario and Susana, for always being there for me. Finally, to my late grandfather, who would have been the most avid but critical reader of this manuscript.

1

Introduction

As the bicentennial celebrations for independence in 2021 neared, the president of Mexico requested an apology from the King of Spain, Phillip VI, citing the sixteenth-century abuses committed against the indigenous populations during the conquest of Mexico.[1] The Spanish government summarily rejected the idea, leading to a pause in diplomatic relations between the two countries at the time.[2] Yet, the impasse did not stop the president of Venezuela from joining-in the effort and creating a national commission to unearth the "truth about European colonialism" and seek justice and economic reparations.[3]

At the core of both cases is the idea that the 300-year colonial experience in Spanish America – roughly from the sixteenth to the nineteenth century – is somewhat responsible for current inequities and lagging economic performance in the region.[4] Particularly salient are the onerous fiscal demands; the trade restrictive policies; the vast mineral extraction; and the creation of racial hierarchies, to name a few. Clearly, this explanation still resonates with voters, as shown by Pedro Castillo's presidency, aimed to redress the "deep Peru" from centuries of neglect. It is also reflected in the people's anger in Chile,[5] where more than 400 public monuments associated with its colonial past were destroyed during the massive protests of 2019–2020. But how can this be the case?

---

[1] See Minder and Malkin (2019).
[2] Disagreements with energy companies also contributed to this pause. See Associated Press (2022).
[3] See Libertad Digital (2022).
[4] This sentiment appears more elite driven, as public opinion data show that globally, citizens seem to have little animosity to their former colonizer (Baker and Cupery 2023).
[5] See Huenchumil (2021).

After all, until very recently, the economic fortunes of the colonizer (Spain) and the colonized were not very different. In 1960, Mexico and Spain had practically the same GDP per capita, both below that of Chile in the same year.[6] Yet today Spain's GDP per capita doubles that of Chile and triples that of Mexico. Is this divergence even attributable to colonialism? Unlike more recent cases of decolonization in Africa and Asia, most Spanish American countries have ruled themselves for more than 200 years now – certainly enough time to scrape and reverse the most noxious colonial policies – why would they still matter?

While some legacies of Spanish rule are clear and indisputable – language, architecture, religion, and cultural traits – others are less so. Particularly at the *local* level – at or below the level of current municipalities[7] – it is unclear that colonial policies 200 years ago can help explain today's variation in the distribution and quality of public services and infrastructure, ethnic and authoritarian enclaves, or overall differences in governance, for example. This book shows a way in which it does – once we factor-in the administrative organization and personnel policies of the Spanish Empire.

Unlike other colonial Empires in the Americas – Portuguese, British, French, or Dutch – the Spanish one was by far the largest and most sophisticated one as of 1700 (Burkholder 2018).[8] It also had large distributional consequences where in place: Administrative decisions determined the trade monopoly rights of certain ports; the tax-rates to be levied across its territories; the political status of cities and provinces within the administrative hierarchy; as well as the legal standing of indigenous communities. All of which came both with political rights, fiscal obligations, and economic opportunities.[9]

Yet, this highly developed administrative apparatus came with a cost: As areas at the core of the Empire became more exposed to Spanish administrative pathologies. Namely, to the eighteenth century practice

---

[6] In 1960, Mexico's GDP per capita was 360 in current USD; that of Spain was 408 USD and Chile 504 USD (World Development Indicators). See https://databank.worldbank.org/source/world-development-indicators (accessed August 8, 2024).

[7] Namely, administrative level 3 such as *municipios* in Mexico, *comunas* in Chile, *parroquias* in Ecuador, and *distritos* in Peru.

[8] Although the administrative organization of colonial Brazil is similar, its development was "slower and far smaller in scale" than that of Spanish America (Burkholder 2018, xvi). Furthermore, "[T]he English and French colonies had even smaller and less sophisticated administrations" (Burkholder 2018, xvi).

[9] For example, long-gone Spanish colonial jurisdictions continue to shape the distribution of indigenous settlements in Mexico today (Guardado and Franco-Vivanco 2024).

of office-selling – the exchange of colonial offices for money – and to its noxious consequences in the short and long run. It is not coincidental that where more intensely practiced, office-selling and its ensuing venality led to a host of local-level distortions today: ethnic segregation, authoritarian enclaves, limited representation, and recurrent violent conflict, factors that underpin the region's spatial inequalities.

Indeed, this book shows that rule by certain types of colonial officials – *venal* ones – led to differences in local governance at the time, even among otherwise similar areas. Because postcolonial states only partially erased these differences (if at all), these early administrative roots contributed to glaring regional inequalities today. As any observer can attest, Spanish America exhibits the whole gamut of development: Cities and municipalities with living standards of high-income countries coexisting with areas where the population lives in abject poverty. While frequently attributed to general "historical reasons," this book is an in-depth study of *which* and *how* they got us here.

In a sense, the answers here vindicate the Presidents of Mexico and Venezuela's claims of abuses suffered the indigenous population in colonial times. Yet, it also shows that the most enduring, intractable, and economically costly legacies of colonialism are often the ones less publicly discussed – the economic geography inherited, the limits to political representation, or the unequal provision of public goods. Legacies these presidents have not erased, even from their positions of power.

However, to understand the role played by the particular Spanish administrative organization and its policies, one must go back to the late seventeenth century. A time of institutional consolidation and projection of royal power as the challenges from settlers and fears of demographic collapse in the Americas start to recede.

1.1 OFFICE-SELLING IN SPANISH AMERICA

The starting point of this book is the 1670 decision by the King of Spain, Charles II, to systematically sell high-ranking government positions in its American Empire. This decision was unprecedented in that it drastically expanded the set of offices normally sold by the Crown. Since at least the reign of Phillip II (1556–98), the Spanish Crown had only sold minor posts that carried no judicial or executive powers such as seats in local councils (*regidores*), notary posts, or municipal ensigns. Charles' decision opened up the most important positions in the colonial government – in charge of ruling the local population, administering justice, and collecting taxes – for purchase.

The main justification for sales was the need for revenue due to Spain's military conflicts.[10] In fact, in 1670, the Crown had just lost the War of Devolution and was about to enter the six-year Franco-Dutch War. Fifty-one of the following eighty years would be spent in one conflict or another, a drain to the royal coffers. The lack of funds was so dire that at the time of Charles' II death in 1700, the royal household did not have enough money to pay for his funeral (Swart 1949: 38). Yet, unlike liquidity crises of the previous centuries, the Crown was much more reluctant to contract foreign debt to meet its needs, even under favorable loan conditions (i.e., interest rates). Instead, it relied on more *ad hoc* remedies such as office-selling.[11] Sales would remain officially in place throughout the next eighty years: The last thirty years of the Habsburgs' reign and the first fifty years of the Bourbon reign (until 1751), albeit with some interruptions.

Key to the durability of office-selling was its success in raising revenue for the Crown due to the ample supply of offices in Spanish America and the high demand for them. As the most extensive and administratively sophisticated bureaucracy in the Americas (Burkholder 2018, xvi), it had a large number of positions potentially for sale each year. The offices sold also carried high political, economic, and social values at the time, which, together with the vast distances and communication challenges within the empire – effectively decentralizing governance – meant that officials were *de facto* autonomous and faced minimal oversight. Demand for certain offices was so high that individuals even bought them decades in advance (*futuras*), which they then used as financial instruments or to settle debts in the secondary market – a true testament of its value.

A second factor behind the longevity of office-selling was that the seller (the Crown) did not fully internalize the negative consequences caused by the sales, therefore making them more prevalent than optimal. Although the Crown openly worried about the suitability and motivation of many of the purchasers, it could pass through many of its costly consequences to the colonial population while still reaping the

---

[10] A list of wars involving Spain during this period were: the Franco-Dutch War (1672–78), War of the Reunions (1683–84), Nine Years' War (1688–97), War of the Spanish Succession (1701–14), War of the Quadruple Alliance (1718–20), Anglo-Spanish War (1727–29), War of the Polish Succession (1733–38), War of Jenkins' Ear (1739–42), and the War of the Austrian Succession (1740–48).

[11] Some historians attribute it to a new anti-debt mentality (Gonzalez Enciso 2007).

benefits, at least in the short term. For example, if unsuitable officials caused discontent and rebellions overseas, the local treasury and population bore the cost of squashing the uprising, not directly the Crown. It also viewed office-selling as a way for the colonies to bear some of the enormous expenses needed to defend them from foreign attacks. Thereby justifying them.[12]

In all, the ample supply, high demand, and relatively few (short-term) consequences made office-selling an attractive way for the Crown to smooth its consumption when money ran out.

Sales would only end in 1751, a time of more balanced budgets and peace in Spain. Yet, by then, more than 2,600 positions had been sold throughout the Empire: primarily provincial[13] ruling positions (*corregimientos* and *alcaldías mayores*[14]) but also seats in the top judicial governing councils (*audiencias*) in the Americas, treasury posts (*cajas*), and key military-governor positions in strategic areas (*gobernaciones*). Moreover, despite officially stopping, many purchasers would remain in their posts for years (and decades) to come – until the backlog of sold appointments cleared or those with lifetime appointments perished.

To illustrate the geographic dimension of office-selling at the time, Figure 1.1 maps the territorial organization of two administrative layers of the Empire as of 1700: that of *gobernaciones* together with that of *corregimientos* and *alcaldías mayores*. Panel (a) presents the jurisdictional borders of these units and whether sold between 1670 and 1751, while panel (b) displays the average prices they fetched throughout the period under study.

The first notable feature of Figure 1.1 is the vast territorial extension of the Spanish Empire ca. 1700. Counting frontier territories (*fronteras*) – areas nominally in the Empire but not yet conquered and directly ruled by the Crown – it extended from Alaska to Patagonia. But even if only considering the territory ruled directly by royal officials (solid lines in panel a), it still encompassed parts of what today is the United States

---

[12] Letter from the Minister Villarias to the King. Source: AGI, Mexico 1970. *Marques de Villarias a Su Majestad*. Buen Retiro, Diciembre de 1739. Throughout the text, AGI stands for *Archivo General de Indias* (colonial archives).

[13] Throughout the book I use the term provincial rulers, *corregidores*, and *alcaldes mayores* interchangeably.

[14] The same position of local tax collector and judicial authority would be called *alcaldes mayores* in the Viceroyalty of New Spain (Mexico, Central America, Caribbean, and the Philippines) while *corregidor* in the Viceroyalty of Peru (Peru, Bolivia, Chile, Ecuador, and Colombia). What is today Venezuela, Uruguay, Paraguay, and most of Argentina had no *corregimientos* or *alcaldías* at the time.

6   *The Venal Origins of Development in Spanish America*

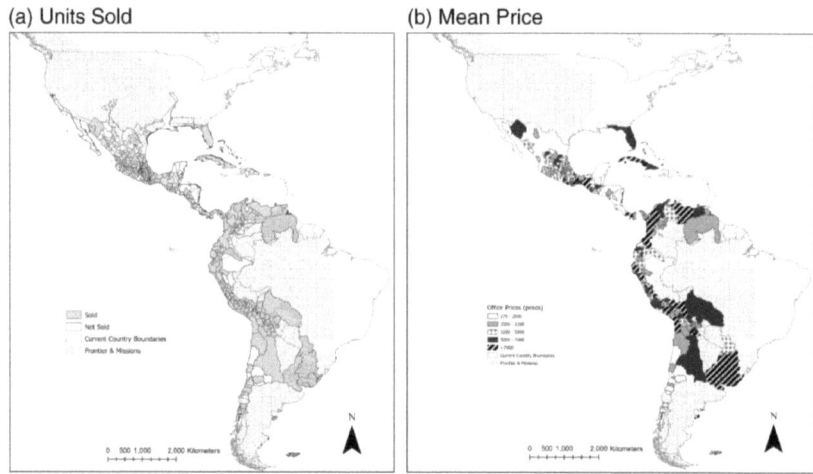

FIGURE 1.1   *Gobiernos, corregimientos,* and *alcaldías mayores* sold (1670–1751).

Sources: Own elaboration combining sales and price data and the boundaries of *gobernaciones, corregimientos,* and *alcaldías* come from Stangl (2019a). Dotted areas are those with no *gobernaciones, corregimientos,* or *alcaldías* mayores, for example, fronteras, or misiones, or those that have not yet been assigned to an administrative authority as of 1700 (e.g., unconquered territories of the Amazon).

(La Florida, Alta California, and Nuevo México to central Chile – north of the Biobío river.

The second significant feature is the geographic reach of office-selling: from north Mexico to southern Chile, the sale of *corregimientos, alcaldías,* and *gobernaciones* touched every corner of the areas directly administered by the Crown. Very few units would be spared, mainly those sparsely populated or with high geopolitical value to the Crown along coastal areas and frontiers.

In terms of prices, panel (b) depicts the high degree of variation in the monetary value positions fetched over time. With prices determined by their type and (or) location. On average, a buyer of a *corregimiento* or *alcladia mayor* position paid to the Crown around 4,000 pesos de a ocho, equivalent to 16,000 days of labor (forty-four years) at the daily wage an indigenous person received at the time (two *reales*),[15] a non-negligible amount.[16] Yet, many positions actually exceeded the

---

[15] One *peso de ocho* was equivalent to eight *reales*.
[16] At the current federal minimum wage in 2024 ($7.25) and assuming a workday of eight hours, this would be equivalent to 3.7 million dollars.

average. As shown, the price paid to serve as *Gobernador* of Buenos Aires, Cartagena, or Havana was well above 7,000 pesos. This was also the case of some *corregimientos* in Peru and Bolivia and some *alcaldías* in Mexico and Guatemala. Elsewhere, such as the current territories of Ecuador, Colombia, and Chile, prices were not as exorbitant but still sizeable.

The policy of office-selling – its origin, functioning, and ultimately its consequences – is the subject of this book. What motivated individuals to purchase these officials? What was the logic of the Crown to engage in sales? How did this policy affect the governance of the Spanish Empire? More importantly, how did it contribute to the quality of local governance and spatial economic inequality observed in the region today? Through the analysis of individual buyers' traits and provincial administrative records spanning three centuries, I trace the local consequences of this practice in Spanish America. But first, why would this policy "matter" in the first place?

1.2 DOES OFFICE-SELLING LEAD TO VENALITY?

In principle, exchanging appointments for money need not lead to any tangible changes in the quality, incentives, and performance of the Spanish colonial officials in the Americas. In fact, compared to other forms of appointing officials at the time, such as those by "favorites", office-selling was superior according to Montesquieu, a contemporaneous of the practice in France (Montesquieu [1748] 2001). Similarly, for Jeremy Bentham, also familiar with it, officials who purchased their positions would take better care of them, provided they were compensated with salaries (and not fees).[17] If anything, office-selling represented a more "modern" notion of merit, not bounded by the idea that the nobility were the most deserving class to hold offices. Rather privileging more instrumental and utilitarian views of public administration (Rosenmüller 2016).

Even recent works find that the exchange of appointments for money need not be socially inefficient, particularly in two scenarios (see Weaver 2021; Banerjee et al. 2013). The first case is if there are few (if any) opportunities for self-dealing – and the office in question has a fixed

---

[17] See Bentham (1825: 247). The distinction was important as otherwise purchasers would be incentivized to raise more fees in compensation.

wage, in-line with Bentham (1825). The second case is if the ability to pay for the position (wealth) is correlated with desirable traits to perform in office, such as ability or education. For example, in nineteenth-century Qing-China, there were little differences among individuals who entered office via purchase or via examination (Zhang 2013). In these circumstances, the exchange of money for appointments may not lead to worse performance than usual.

Yet, these conditions were exactly the opposite in Spanish America. First, positions often had high profit potential, allowing for greater appropriation of economic surplus from the population. Historians estimate that a provincial position of *corregidor* or *alcalde* could net between 60,000 and 150,000 pesos, depending on the ability of the official in question. Second, unlike nineteenth-century China, where purchasers and nonpurchasers did not differ significantly, I show that office-buyers in Spanish America had lower social status and career connections to the Crown than those who were appointed. Therefore, less in need to maintain the Crown's favor, perform in office and/or limit their appropriation of economic surplus. This is not to say that officials prior to sales were paragons of good governance. Rather, that the introduction of office-selling worsened existing structural weakness and increased opportunities for self-dealing at the time.

Evidence of the change in the quality of the colonial administration comes from various sources. Already in the 1740s the Crown was aware of a scathing report on the state of the colonies, known as the Secret News (*noticias secretas*). In them, two undercover Spanish officials described the colonial government as rife with "abuses, excesses, graft, corruption, mismanagement, and cruelty," a view the authors gathered from their years long undercover mission throughout what is now Ecuador and Peru (Juan and Ulloa 1978 [1749]: 25). While the report is not limited to colonial officials – it also decries the activities of landowners, priests, and social elites – the report singled out the role of office-selling in undermining the colonial administration.

The exploitative practices of these *corregidores* and *alcaldes* continued even after office-selling ended in 1751. Letters from the Bishop of Arequipa (southern Peru) to the King in the 1770s decried exactly the same abuses as those in the *noticias secretas* thirty years earlier. Similar worries appear in high-level correspondence between the Crown and royal inspectors of what is now Mexico (José de Gálvez) and Peru (José Antonio Areche). This correspondence revolved around the extreme concern over the extent of graft and exploitation in the colonial administration, which endangered the Crown's hold of this territory.[18] Finally, anonymous documents circulating in the 1770s highlight many of the same practices that made purchasing offices attractive decades earlier as seen in its strong correlation with office prices (see Chapter 2).[19] Parallel to this high-level discussion, there was also visible discontent among the population, evident from the proliferation of *pasquines*, a form of anonymous satirical political manifestos, in which the public spoke frequently of the prevailing corruption among colonial officials.

The deterioration in the colonial administration is also visible quantitatively. Analysis of a wealth of primary data collected from archival sources reveals that office-selling led to a drastic reduction in the traits associated with good governance. In particular, it led to an influx of "unconnected" officials by social status or profession to serve in the most productive and profitable positions across the Empire. Prior to 1670, appointments were limited to those of a particular social background, namely, those of aristocratic origin and connected to the Crown. With sales, a more diverse set of aspirants – outside the classes connected to the Crown by social origin (nobility) or in their career prospects (military) – entered the colonial administration. Being outside of the closest circles of the Crown did not mean they were inherently dishonest. Yet, it did mean that their performance in office would be less constrained by social and reputational costs than if their careers or fortune depended on the Crown's favor.

Second, in addition to bringing about a new class of socially unconnected officials, sales made it easier for them to enter the positions that most favored their skills and connections for profit (sorting). For example, those with merchant connections could bid for positions overseeing ports – and benefit from contraband – or bid for positions that could sell goods to the indigenous population. Before office-selling, interested candidates would have to wait for their desired position to vacate, make sure no one else was vying for the post, and hope the Crown indeed favored them (and no one else). Buying a specific position ensured that positions would better match buyers' skills, interests, and networks.

Finally, office-selling also changed the incentives of individuals to profit from their position. This was the chief concern of many jurists and advisors to the King, such as the Council of Indies, who openly worried

---

[18] Chapter 6 examines in the correspondence between these officials at the time.
[19] See *Yndize comprehensibo de todos los gobiernos, corregimientos y alcaldías mayores* (Anonymous 1777).

that the exchange of positions for money was akin to sanctioning profiteering from office. The transactional nature of these appointments also made it more difficult to dismiss or remove officials, even in the face of known malfeasance, because it would require refunding their purchase money, which a cash-strapped Crown was always reluctant to do.[20]

In sum, this class of officials – bent on recouping their investment, unconstrained by social or reputation costs, undeterred by potential sanctions, and selectively occupying positions that best maximize their profits – epitomizes what I call *venality* in the colonial administration. While office-selling per se was not corruption at the time, and need not lead to "worse" officials, in Spanish America it did. What started as a policy to raise revenue in Madrid had turned into venality in the Americas.

1.3 THE CONSEQUENCES OF VENALITY

What were the consequences of this new class of officials? The most visible one was the increase in the number of uprisings targeting colonial authorities, particularly where office-selling had been more intense. The frequency and intensity of these rebellions effectively spelled the end of the last 200 years of *Pax Hispannica* in the Americas. While the immediate causes of rebellion always varied,[21] uprisings were more likely precisely where venal officials ruled: Fuses were shorter and responses more violent in these locations vis-à-vis others. For example, Chapter 6 shows that historical exposure to venality exacerbated subsistence crises created by drought or El Niño/a weather patterns throughout the eighteenth century in Mexico, Peru, and Bolivia.

In addition to violent uprisings, more venal officials exacerbated the displacement of the indigenous populations away from majority-Spanish and mestizo[22] settlements, changing the economic geography in the region. Already in the 1770s, the displacement of the indigenous population away from areas they had previously inhabited is evident, particularly where venality was stronger. The political and economic consequences of this segregation will be wide-ranging: from hindering state formation

---

[20] This was the case of several *audiencia* members, who, after being removed from their post for self-dealing, had to be reinstated by the Crown due to a lack of funds to reimburse them (Burkholder and Chandler 1977).

[21] For example, legitimacy or subsistence crises due to demographic pressure, or abuses by particular officials.

[22] Individuals of mixed origin – Spanish and indigenous.

by exacerbating regional heterogeneity,[23] to limiting market access and political representation for indigenous populations, to worsening spatial inequality today.

Attempts to reform the administration, such as stopping the sale of offices in 1751, had limited effects at the local level. By then, practices over the previous eighty years – such as overtaxing, labor coercion, and surplus appropriation – were entrenched. In some cases, these practices actually became law. For example, the reviled *repartimiento*[24] – a commercial monopoly managed by colonial officials – reached its peak as an illicit (but profitable) activity during the office-selling period, but was eventually legalized due to its effectiveness in procuring revenue for officials and merchants alike. In other cases, networks of interests helped keep these activities in place, particularly in the absence of wage increases, clear career paths as well as "venal" holdovers in other parts of the administration. Finally, the news of large profits developed in the last decades continued to help appointees sort into the positions that best matched their thirst for riches.

The dire situation led to a series of administrative reforms from the 1780s onward – known as the Bourbon Reforms – to improve governance in the colonies, particularly in the fiscal realm. Despite increasing overall tax collection (Chiovelli et al. 2024), the reforms could not undo the local practices associated with the previous period. For example, at the level of *corregimientos* and *alcaldías*, they renamed the officials and units into *subdelegaciones* without changing many of the underlying incentives of those responsible for collecting taxes and administrating justice.[25] In other cases (i.e., Guatemala, Ecuador), the reforms were never implemented and *alcaldes* and *corregidores* continued to be appointed from Madrid until the nineteenth century.

With independence in the first quarter of the nineteenth century, the new states proved unable or unwilling to abolish many of the existing colonial policies. To start, the roughly first fifty years of independent life were spent in conflict over the organization of the new states such

---

[23] See Mazzuca (2021).
[24] This practice would take different forms across Spanish America. In some cases, it was the practice of giving cotton to be woven by women in Guatemala (Solórzano Fonseca 1985), monopolizing the trade of cochineal in Mexico (Baskes 1996, 2000), or monopolizing consumption goods in Peru and Bolivia. Yet, in all cases, it was carried out by *corregidores* or *alcaldes mayores*.
[25] Specifically, an additional layer of administration was created, that of the *intendentes*, and generally, former *corregidores* and *alcaldes* were repurposed as *subdelegados*.

that few (if any) policies were consistently pursued. Moreover, even after the conflict ended, nominally "liberal" governments came to rely on the same policy instruments and practices of the regime they were supposedly vanquishing (colonial), particularly in territories with a stronger venal administration. Examples include the continuation of colonial taxes and labor coercion practices in Bolivia, Ecuador, and Guatemala; the further spatial segregation of the indigenous population in almost all countries; and the delayed formation of new politically representative bodies (*municipios*) in countries such as Peru and Mexico. Even though colonial officials had been long gone, the economic geography, labor and fiscal policies, and political underrepresentation they left behind remained.

Today, provinces that saw their governance particularly deteriorate in the eighteenth century exhibit lower living standards in the form of childhood stunting and low birthweight. In Mexico, areas with high colonial venality are also more likely to serve as enclaves of subnational authoritarianism. Across Peru, Bolivia, Guatemala, and Mexico, indigenous geographic segregation has not only remained but also in some cases worsened from its nineteenth-century version. Finally, across all countries, areas with a venal past exhibit lower provision of public goods in the form of schools and basic public services. These differences are visible even among areas that are similar in every other aspect but were part of different colonial jurisdictions in the past.

Figure 1.2 visually summarizes this chain of events: from a late seventeenth-century policy to supplement expenses in Madrid to current spatial inequalities in Spanish America. In the short term, office-selling – combined with the preexisting jurisdictions and local characteristics – undermined local governance in two ways. First, by facilitating elite collusion across administrative layers and, second, by reducing

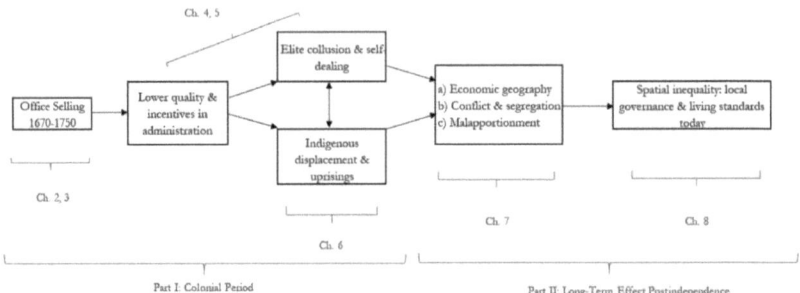

FIGURE 1.2 The short- and long-run effects of office-selling

indigenous economic surplus – leading to more uprisings and displacement. These changes to the economic geography, propensity to conflict, and political representation in colonial times then persisted until today through a combination of political (malapportionment) and economic mechanisms (regional heterogeneity), to name a few.

1.4 ALTERNATIVE EXPLANATIONS

The main alternative accounts to explain local differences in governance are that they are instead the result of more recent events – or that even if colonial, unrelated to administrative venality. For example, the nineteenth century is often regarded as the critical juncture that shaped the state-building trajectories of former Spanish American countries (e.g., Centeno 2002; López-Alves 2000; Soifer 2016; Saylor 2014; Kurtz 2013; Mazzuca 2021). It is also possible that these differences instead emerged from the region's transition to democracy in the late twentieth century. For example, subnational inequalities may arise due to the level of subnational political competition (Alves 2015; Chibber and Nooruddin 2004), civic engagement (Cleary 2007), and national-level technocratic autonomy (Otero-Bahamón 2016), to name a few.

Moreover, even if these patterns do have colonial origins, they need not be attributed to more or less exposure to venality. They could instead reflect the production conditions colonizers encountered upon their arrival, such as the disease environment, population levels, or factor endowments (mineral or agricultural), which in turn influenced existing institutions and the prevailing political economy (Acemoglu, Johnson, and Robinson 2001, 2002; Engerman and Sokoloff 1997; Mahoney 2010). I discuss each possibility in turn.

1.4.1 Postindependence Divergence?

The period immediately after independence in the nineteenth century[26] is often seen as formative for the long-term economic and political trajectories of Spanish American countries. As the time of the first truly national and independent state-building projects across the region, its success (or failure) was key to unleashing economic growth and political stability among these new states.

---

[26] Most Spanish American countries were independent by 1850. Exceptions include Cuba, the Philippines, Puerto Rico, and territories colonized by other powers.

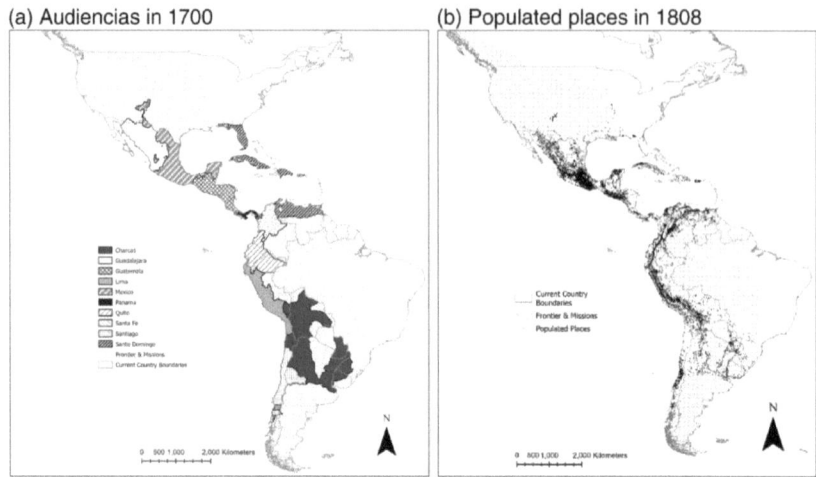

FIGURE 1.3 *Audiencias* and population prior to independence.

Sources: Own elaboration using geographic data from the Historical Geographical Information System of Las Indias www.hgis-indias.net (Stangl 2019a). *Audiencia* borders and populated settlements are those as of 1700 superimposed on current country borders.

Certainly, the postindependence period was one of change. Viceroys fled, colonial *audiencias* dissolved, and wars against Spain were fought and won. New national borders were drawn (sometimes more than once), and new institutions, foundational myths, and heroes emerged, replacing the old colonial regime. From a pure territorial perspective, the Spanish colonial organization seems inconsequential relative to the new configurations that emerged. For example, the system of *audiencias* depicted in panel (a) of Figure 1.3 only vaguely resembles the country borders we observe today. Some countries rose from fragmented *audiencias* (e.g., Central America), while others unified what used to be more than one *audiencia* (e.g., Mexico, Peru).

Yet, a pure focus on the territorial aspect of state formation could underestimate the administrative legacies of the Spanish Empire. In fact, a comparison of *where* most of the population was located at the eve of independence in 1808 (panel b) vis-à-vis current borders supports the idea of high degrees of *population persistence*. In other words, while borders shifted widely in Spanish America throughout the nineteenth century, populations barely changed the political unit that ruled them prior to independence.[27]

---

[27] See Guardado (2025) for the territorial legacies of the Spanish Empire.

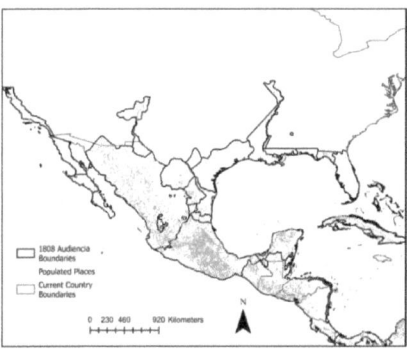

FIGURE 1.4 Population persistence versus territorial shifts: Mexico 1808 and today

Note: Each gray dot represents a populated place or settlement from Stangl (2019b), which as of 1808 would be concentrated in central Mexico. Sources: Geographic data comes from Historical Geographical Information System of Las Indias www.hgis-indias.net (Stangl 2019a). Borders and populated settlements are those as of 1700 superimposed on current country borders.

I estimate that 75 to 80 percent of the population of Spanish America in 1808 would be ruled from the same capital it did in colonial times. Moreover, in many cases, the new independent governments would rule from the same building as the viceroys and the *audiencias* had done in the past (i.e., *Palacio Nacional* in Mexico). Borders shifted more than population did.

This is clearly appreciated in Figure 1.4 for the case of Mexico. Despite the new Mexican state unifying what was previously two *audiencias* and several *gobernaciones* depicted by the solid lines (e.g., Yucatán, Nuevo León) as well as losing half of its territory to the United States by 1850, the overwhelming majority of the population that existed in 1808 (81 percent to be exact) would have still been ruled by Mexico City.

In sum, notwithstanding the novelty of the territorial configuration, these states' population – along with its practices, customs, social structure, and collective memories – was not new. In fact, massive migratory movements of the nineteenth century had transformative effects in Argentina, Uruguay, Brazil, and to some extent Chile, but would largely bypass the core of the Spanish administrative empire.

In addition to population persistence, the nineteenth century also witnessed a remarkable degree of stability in GDP rankings among them.

16   *The Venal Origins of Development in Spanish America*

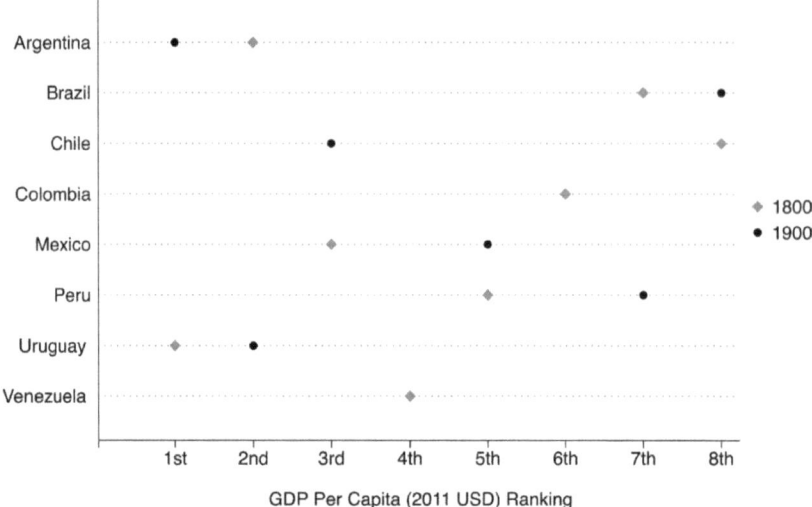

FIGURE 1.5 Country-level rankings of GDP per capita in 1800 and 1900 (selected countries)

Own elaboration based on 2011 real GDP per capita (USD) from Maddison (Bolt and Van Zanden 2020). Sources used in the dataset for Argentina and Colombia: Prado de la Escosura (2009), Bértola and Ocampo (2012). Brazil: Prado de la Escosura (2009), Barro and Ursua (2008). Chile: Díaz, Lüders, and Wagner (2007). Mexico: Arroyo-Abad and van Zanden (2016), Prado de la Escosura (2009), Barro and Ursua (2008). Peru: Arroyo-Abad and van Zanden (2016), Seminario B. (2015), Bértola and Ocampo (2012). Uruguay: Prado de la Escosura (2009), Bértola (2016) and Venezuela: De Corso (2013).

As shown in Figure 1.5, at the end of the colonial era in 1800, countries already at the top of the income distribution (Argentina and Uruguay) or clearly at the bottom (Brazil,[28] Colombia, and Peru) were roughly in the same position 100 years later (1900), with the only exception of Chile. As noted, Mexico, Brazil, and Peru hovered around the same position throughout the century – "pushed" around in the rankings by Chile's ascent – while Colombia and Venezuela remained in exactly the same spot.[29] This lack of dramatic reversals in economic development – already noted by Mahoney (2010) – suggests either a stability in the structural causes of long-run development after independence or changes in a way that did not alter the countries' relative incomes. It also supports the idea of looking at the colonial era as the critical historical

---

[28] While not part of the analysis, the case of Brazil serves as a reference point in this figure.
[29] Colombia and Venezuela actually had the same ranking, 6th and 4th respectively, in 1800 as in 1900.

moment for understanding the region's subsequent economic performance (Mahoney 2010).

Together, the stability of economic performance rankings and that of population suggest *less* change in this era than commonly thought. Particularly for the territories at the imperial administrative core and more exposed to office-selling. In fact, the most compelling accounts of successful nineteenth-century state transformation come from countries that the Spanish direct administration barely "touched" – Chile, Uruguay, Costa Rica, Argentina, or Paraguay. One contribution of this book is thus to show that this is not coincidental: Certain subnational legacies – economic geography, ethnic segregation, political representation, and conflict – can help us understand why some countries did not change rankings after independence.

1.4.2 Factor Endowments, Institutions ... and Venality?

Yet, even if one agrees that many of the inequities we observe today originated in the colonial era, they need not be related to the practice of office-selling or to the administrative organization of the Spanish Empire. Instead, the initial conditions colonizers encountered upon their arrival clearly shaped the type and quality of the institutions they brought about (Acemoglu and Robinson 2001; Engerman and Sokoloff 1997; Mahoney 2010). For instance, a consistent finding in the literature is that countries with high levels of precolonial indigenous populations tend to have lower GDP per capita today (Acemoglu and Robinson 2002). This is attributed to institutions designed to exploit indigenous labor, perpetuating inequality and stifling long-term growth.

1.4.2.1 *Subnational Institutions and Development*

While this argument aligns well with cross-country aggregate patterns, this is less so *within*-country in the Americas. As first shown by Maloney and Valencia (2016), subnationally, fortunes tend to persist rather than reverse. That is, some areas, despite having the "wrong" endowments in colonial times, remain some of the richest areas of their respective countries. Two somewhat extreme cases illustrate this point. The first is that of Mexico City, the former capital of the Aztec Empire, which has an average GDP per capita of 47,924 PPP dollars, far above the country's one of 20,634 in 2018.[30] Similarly, the region of Cusco, Peru – capital

---

[30] Regional OECD Statistics (2018).

of the Inca Empire and later the seat of the Cuzco *audiencia*[31] – exhibits the highest GDP per capita among the areas with the highest precolonial population density. Why are they not the poorest today?

The book provides three complementary reasons. The first is the ability of certain administrative policies to "blunt" the effect of factor endowments.[32] As said earlier, administrative decisions in colonial times had large distributional effects, ranging from which and whether territorial units would be granted the ability to form a representative body (*cabildo*), the exclusivity of their rights to trade (*royal ports*), or the rights to communal land (*pueblos*). Álvarez-Villa and Guardado (2020) show that the administrative designation of "royal ports" in colonial Mexico has led to higher levels of trade and local development in the long run than would have been predicted based on their disease environment, population levels, or geographic advantages. Similar findings emerge from China, documenting how changes in the administrative status of certain provinces promoted greater urbanization and population growth than would have been expected by location fundamentals alone (Bai and Jia 2020).

Second, beyond the cases of Cuzco and Mexico City, the variation in subnational development experiences observed today far exceeds the variation in the initial endowments found by colonizers. While some studies find broad differences in historical institutions driven by geographic and population endowments (Bruhn and Gallego 2012), other works find that the barriers to productivity in the Americas operate at a much more *local* level. For example, by shaping the provision of public goods and the security of property rights across municipalities (Acemoglu and Dell 2010: 187). Thus suggesting that for the same endowments encountered by sixteenth-century colonizers, we may expect different economic performance today.

This book argues that administrative features of the Spanish Empire – such as the mechanisms for selecting and appointing colonial officials, and the characteristics of the latter – played a significant but often overlooked role in local economic productivity differences. In the case of office-selling, it is true that certain endowments might have helped attract certain types of officials. Yet, which endowments led to more or less returns to colonial officials was not obvious *ex-ante*. Provinces with

---

[31] The short-lived *audiencia* of Cuzco was formed in 1787 until ca. 1827.
[32] These policies often have a "place-making" role, see Glaeser and Gottlieb (2008), Grossman and Lewis (2014), and Bluhm et al. (2021).

similar levels of indigenous population, but with different levels of social organization or bellicosity, would lead to different development outcomes today, depending on the type of officials that ruled them. In fact, Chapter 8 illustrates this phenomenon by showing how areas sharing similar initial conditions (endowments) but facing different jurisdictions and personnel in colonial times have divergent economic and political outcomes today.

Finally, and third, this book points to the importance of personnel policy in shaping the quality and incentives of colonial officials and their performance in office. For example, social and personal connections of members of the *audiencias* in the Americas with the Crown actually improved the formers' performance in office (Salgado 2021). Evidence from the nineteenth-century British Empire also shows that personnel policies (patronage) reduced the long-term fiscal development of the territories more exposed to it vis-à-vis those where merit criteria prevailed (Xu 2018; 2019). To the best of my knowledge, this is the first study to systematically link the sales of these positions across the Spanish Empire with the long-run economic trajectories of the places they ruled.[33]

1.4.3 Connecting the Spanish Colonial Administration and Development

Altogether, this book is a region-wide study of the short- and long-term effects of office-selling for local development. Most existing work on Spanish venality focuses on the Crown's motivations to sell positions (Parry 1953; Lejonagoitia 2015; Sanz Tapia 2009), on how office-selling changed the composition and quality of *audiencias* (Burkholder and Chandler 1977; Phelan 1960), or on how it led to the inefficient management of the royal treasury (Andrien 1982) and *corregimientos* in Peru and Bolivia (Moreno Cebrian 1977). Yet, much less is known about how these effects changed the individual characteristics and incentives of colonial bureaucrats, particularly across a broader set of positions.

Part of the reason behind the gap in the literature is the dearth of data. The secrecy inherent to corrupt activities of colonial officials, and the "fragmentary and impressionistic" nature of the available evidence (Andrien 1984: 1), have made it difficult to characterize systematically. Moreover, until recently, there has been a lack of information on the organization of the Spanish Empire, including basic data such as its territorial

---

[33] Guardado (2018) had only focused on the Peruvian case.

organization, particularly at the subnational level.³⁴ Furthermore, when studies do examine the empire's administrative organization and policies, by collecting data on the identities and characteristics of those in power, the focus has generally been on the higher levels of the administration (viceroys, *audiencias*), thus overlooking lower-ranked officials, such as those in direct contact with the colonial population (*corregidores, alcaldes mayores*).

Finally, much attention has been drawn to the Crown's policies of the last thirty years of colonial rule, known as the Bourbon Reforms. These reforms, successful in raising revenue, also led to discontent among certain sectors of colonial society, namely the *criollo* elites, key for the subsequent push for independence (Garfias and Sellars 2022). However, the success (or failure) of these policies have little correlation with postindependence outcomes at the local level. As noted by Soifer (2015) and Chiovelli et al. (2024), territories that were most successful in increasing revenue for the Crown during the Bourbon Reforms tend to exhibit some of the lowest levels of fiscal capacity today. Why? A missing factor could be the regions' historical exposure to venality. If areas with greater revenue collection also had greater exposure to venality, it would explain the short-term increase in collection but overall worse long-term governance.

This book thus revolves around the empirical question of *whether* and *how* office-selling-turned-venality shaped the economic trajectory of countries in the region. Evidence from outside Spanish America provides some clues. In France, the excessive reliance on office-selling in the seventeenth century likely had negative consequences for economic activity by diverting productive resources to the bureaucracy (Swart 1949: 14)³⁵ and limiting its fiscal options to deal with crises (Root 1994: 19). Office-selling also contributed to a culture where security in public sector employment is still highly esteemed (Doyle 1984: 831), potentially at the expense of the private sector. In China, reliance on nineteenth-century office-selling reduced the incentives to implement much-needed reforms to the bureaucracy and the system of public finance (Kaske 2008: 299, 300). In the case of Spanish America, whether this policy had any discernible impact (or not) is an open empirical question.

---

³⁴ This gap has been now filled by the HGIS Historical Geographic Information System Project, published in 2019, which provides many of the map base layers examined throughout the book.

³⁵ Swart (1949: 14) claims that nearly one-third of the population in France was linked one way or another to office-holders (*noblesse de robe*) of the seventeenth century.

1.5 ROADMAP

The rest of the book unfolds chronologically, with Part I examining the origins and consequences of office-selling throughout the colonial period. Namely, how office-selling led to *venality* in the colonial administration. Part II then traces the consequences of *venal* officials throughout the postindependence period until the present. While each chapter is organized around a set of empirical claims, they also provide a building block to the overarching argument of the relationship between venality, governance, and long-term development in Spanish America.

Part I opens with a brief description of the territorial and administrative organization of the Spanish Empire in the Americas (Chapter 2). Chapter 3 then explores why the Crown sold key positions of judicial, fiscal, legislative, and economic significance in the Americas, challenging existing accounts. Chapter 4 provides quantitative evidence of how office-selling changed the profile of colonial officials – by facilitating the entry of officials with different traits from those of appointed officials (selection) – likely for the purposes of self-enrichment at the expense of the local (mainly indigenous) population. A first consequence of this change in the quality of the administration is evident in the collusive behavior between high-level *audiencia* members and lower-level ones, documented in Chapter 5. In terms of the welfare of the population, Chapter 6 traces how exposure to venality increased the number and intensity of violent uprisings as well as the displacement of the indigenous population. Altogether, Chapters 2 to 6 document the short- and medium-term consequences of office-selling on local governance in Spanish America.

Part II then explores how these effects play out after independence in the nineteenth century. Building on previous findings, Chapter 7 uses evidence from postindependent Peru, Bolivia, Guatemala, Ecuador, and Mexico to show the different mechanisms through which early eighteenth-century venality lived on: by reinforcing geographic segregation, limiting political representation, and recreating forms of labor coercion and taxation from colonial times. Chapter 8 then shows that the combined effect of these policies contributed to the glaring levels of spatial inequality through the presence of ethnic enclaves, subnational authoritarianism, and underprovision of public goods that characterize the region today.

2

The Eighteenth-Century "Market" of Offices

In 1670, the King of Spain, Charles II – known as The Bewitched[1] for his absent and bizarre manners – inaugurated the sale of high-level positions across its American territories. This policy was a stark departure from precedent, as only minor offices – tax farming posts, notary publics, scriveners, among others – had been sold before in Spain and its American territories (Tomás y Valiente 1972; Swart 1949). While globally prevalent at the time,[2] the sale of positions tied to administering justice or overseeing key geopolitical and strategic locations was traditionally off limits for Spanish monarchs.

This changed with Charles' decision in 1670 to expand the market of offices to include provincial governorship positions known as *corregidores* in the viceroyalty of Peru and *alcaldes mayores* in that of New Spain (see Figure 2.1). Positions responsible for tax collection and justice administration across the more than 300 provinces of the Empire at the time. This expansion was soon followed by the sale of positions[3] managing fiscal accounts of the colonial treasuries known as *cajas* in 1672, military governorships in 1682 and[4] culminating in 1687 with the sale of *audiencia* seats.

---

[1] *El Hechizado*, in Spanish. The nickname likely arose from Charles II's sickly constitution and impaired cognitive abilities. He is often characterized in the literature as "imbecile" (Woods 1906) and "diseased in mind and body" (Hamilton 1938, 174), likely due to the high degree of inbreeding among the Habsburgs (Ottinger and Voigtlander, 2025, 8–9).

[2] For example, in countries such as France, England, the Ottoman Empire, and China under the Qing dynasty. See Swart (1949).

[3] In 1672, the Crown sold the position of accountant in the *caja* of Zaragoza (Antioquia, now Colombia) to Juan de Porras y Santa María for 875 *doblones*.

[4] One of the first positions sold was that of captain and *gobernador* of the island of Trinidad (now Trinidad and Tobago) to Don Tiburcio de Arce y Zúñiga. However, the position will not be sold again.

2 The Eighteenth-Century "Market" of Offices

Office-selling was generally opposed by distinguished jurists and the Council of Indies (*Consejo de Indias*) – the Crown's advisory body on all matters related to the Indies – for three main reasons.[5] First, selling justice-administration positions went against the divine mandate of the sovereign to impart justice. It also undermined the long-term fiscal interests of the Crown and ran against the laws governing the Indies. Second, sales worsened governance by promoting negative selection: Only the most ambitious individuals would ever purchase these positions, resulting in the oppression of their subjects. As put in a 1643 decree by Philip IV – Charles' own father – "those obtaining positions via sales were actually unfit to serve in them." Finally, quoting Roman Emperor (Marcus Aurelius) Alexander Severus, the Council made the case that those who sold justice (i.e., the Crown) would be hard pressed to punish those who sold justice themselves (i.e., purchasing officials), leading to the unhappiness of Republics.

Nevertheless, sales continued. This chapter outlines the "market" of offices, which started under Habsburg rule and continued through the first fifty years of Bourbon rule. First, it describes the "goods" transacted – namely, the type of positions sold and their frequency. Second, it examines the sale process and how each of the parts agreed on prices. Finally, it explores the drivers of demand: Why were some positions highly demanded *vis-à-vis* others?

2.1 TYPE OF OFFICES FOR SALE

One key precondition for the development of this market was the high degree of institutionalization and economic complexity of the Spanish Empire at the time. Although for some historians the seventeenth century was one of crisis in Spanish America – the period when the indigenous population hit its "nadir" (Borah 1951), trade volumes were at their lowest (García Fuentes 1980), and silver production was practically halted (Hamilton 2000) – this view has been recently revisited. In particular, the rapid growth of local industry, the presence of sizable interregional transfers (*situado*), the extensive construction of hospitals and churches, and the high demand for all types of offices in the Americas

---

[5] For the main arguments of the Council, see: AGI, Mexico 1970. *Extracto de Consulta hecha por el Consejo de Indias en 21 de Agosto de 1737, y ordenes del Ministerio de Hazienda sobre Venefizios de Empleos de Indias.*

cast doubt on the idea of a "crisis" altogether (Klein and Serrano 2019; Klein 2024).

Administratively, the Spanish Empire of 1700 had the largest and most sophisticated apparatus of all the other colonies in the Western Hemisphere – British, French, Dutch, or Portuguese (Burkholder 2018, xvi). Potential challenges to Crown rule from private settlers (known as *encomenderos*) had largely receded by this time. Instead, strategic and geopolitical threats arising from the need to protect this vast empire from foreign powers became its main concern. Including frontier territories, the Spanish Empire nominally extended from what today is Alaska to the Strait of Magellan in southern Chile and Argentina.

To govern this sizeable territory, encompassing continental North and South America, the empire was organized into two viceroyalties: that of New Spain (*Nueva España*) and that of Peru, each ruled by a viceroy personally appointed by the King. Later in the colonial period, the Crown would create two additional viceroyalties: that of Nueva Granada in 1739[6] (roughly what today is Colombia, Venezuela, Ecuador, and Panama) and the short-lived viceroyalty of Rio de la Plata,[7] centered in what today is Argentina and Uruguay. Figure 2.1 presents the approximate division of the two viceroyalties at the time.

On paper, viceroys were personal representatives of the King overseas. In practice, their power was never as absolute. For example, any change to legislation required approval from the royal *audiencia* council, which were eleven at the time.[8] However, viceroys and *audiencias* often held divergent policy preferences, resulting in acrimonious jurisdictional conflict that the King ultimately had to adjudicate. Viceroys also served at the King's discretion, their position tied to the success (or lack thereof) in furthering the Crown's agenda or their popularity in court.

Slightly below the viceroy stood the royal *audiencias*, with each council ruling an area similar in size to that of current countries. In fact, most seats of the former colonial *audiencias* are today the capital of their contemporary country.[9] As of 1700, the *audiencias* were those of Guadalajara (northwest Mexico); Mexico (central-south Mexico); Guatemala (Central America, excluding Panama); Panama; Santa Fe

---

[6] It had an earlier stint, from 1717 to 1723, and encompassed the current territories of Colombia, Venezuela, Ecuador, and Panama.
[7] From 1775 to 1825, covering the current territories of Argentina, Uruguay, and Paraguay.
[8] Known as *Real Acuerdo*.
[9] In Bolivia, the old *audiencia* capital (Sucre) is still the constitutional capital and seat of the judicial branch.

2 *The Eighteenth-Century "Market" of Offices* 25

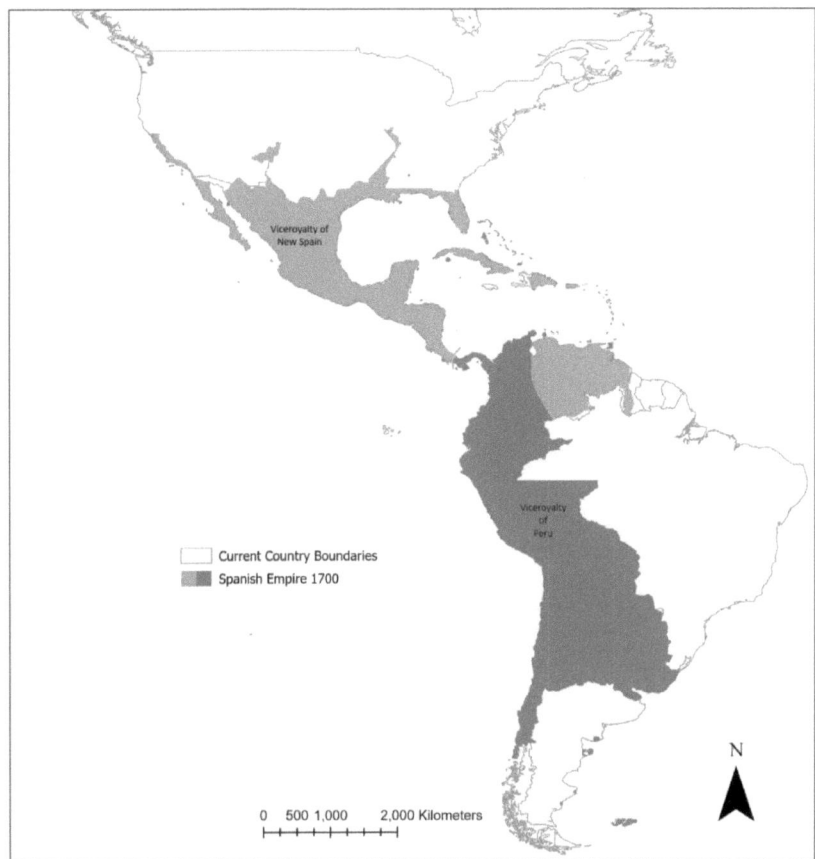

FIGURE 2.1 The Spanish Empire ca. 1700

Sources: Geographic data comes from Historical Geographical Information System of Las Indias www.hgis-indias.net (Stangl 2019a). Administrative units are those as of 1700.

(Colombia and Venezuela); Santo Domingo (Spanish Caribbean, coast of Venezuela, and the Florida Peninsula); Quito (Ecuador); Lima (Peru); Charcas (Bolivia); Santiago (Chile); and Manila (the Philippines).[10] To ease exposition throughout the book, I will generally refer to specific *audiencias* by its (rough) contemporaneous match, unless otherwise specified. Figure 2.2 illustrates the approximate boundaries of *audiencias* in the Americas, mapped onto present-day countries.

[10] Toward 1800, three more *audiencias* were formed: that of Cuzco in Peru; Caracas, representing the current territory of Venezuela; and Buenos Aires, centered around the homonymous port. The *audiencia* of Panama would be suppressed in 1752.

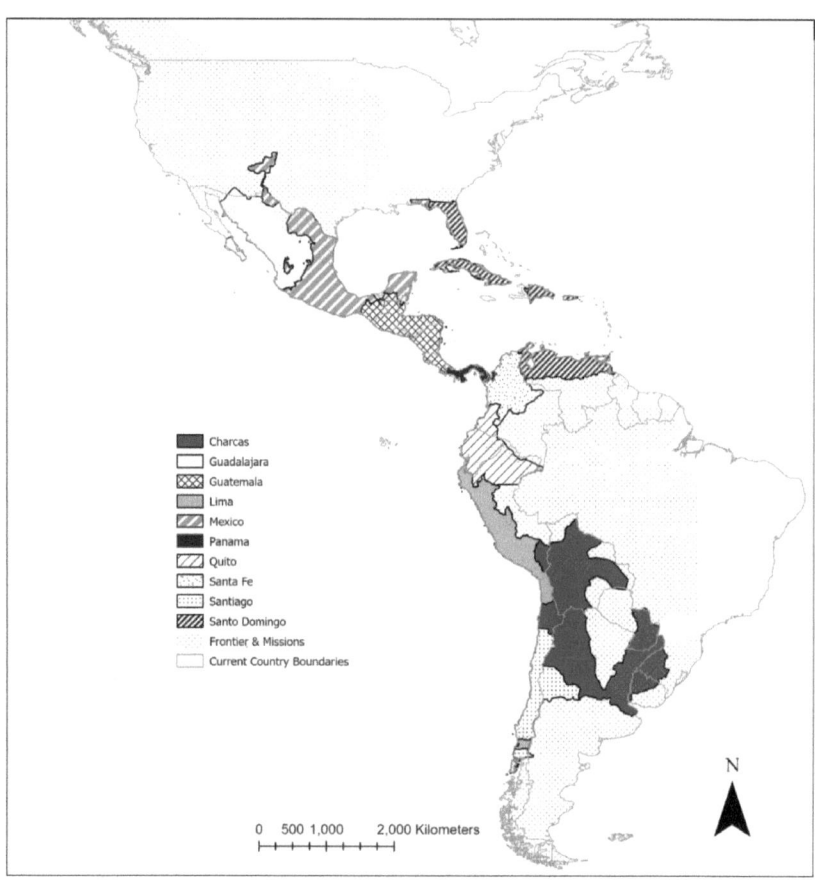

FIGURE 2.2 Spanish *audiencias* ca. 1700

Sources: See note to Fig. 1.

Audiencias can be best described as collegiate tribunals (councils) consisting of five to fifteen members, depending on the location. Important *audiencias* – Mexico and Lima – had fifteen members, and smaller ones had only five (Guatemala, Manila, and Santiago). Although they were nominally below in hierarchy to viceroys, *audiencias* served as an effective counterweight to the latter, particularly in topics related to taxation, land rights, mining, civil and criminal lawsuits, military defense, and oversight of other officials. Unlike viceroys, tenure in the *audiencia* was for life, meaning that officials had to either retire, be removed (rare), promoted, or perish in office to leave their seat. Given this longer time horizon, the *audiencia* could often afford to wait out viceroys to achieve their desired policy.

2 The Eighteenth-Century "Market" of Offices

In fact, away from the viceroyalties' capitals (Mexico City, Lima), *audiencias* served as the *de facto* highest authority. In their oversight role, they monitored officials from fiscal districts (known as *cajas*[11]) in their jurisdiction, thus helping account for taxes, revenues, and expenditures. They also oversaw all the provinces in their districts, that is, *corregimientos* and *alcaldías mayores*, putting them in direct contact with these officials. Judicially, they were the highest court in all civil and criminal cases in their territory, having the last say on high-profile cases.

Socially, members of the *audiencia* also represented the pinnacle of social hierarchy, sharing a similar status only with Church authorities and the viceroy (if present). For example, *audiencia* members led all public processions at major events, and Sunday Mass could not start without their presence. *Audiencia* members were also subject to specific sumptuary laws as established in a royal ruling of 1583: They had the exclusive right to wear the white ruffled collar known as "garnacha" (white neck flock) together with a dark cloak and cape, which distinguished them from other members of society (Bridhkina 2007). Such social status and policy influence, coupled with the Crown's conscious policy of not appointing local settlers (known as *criollos*[12]) to the *audiencia*, meant they were particularly attractive and sought after by the latter.

On par with the prestige of the *audiencias* but serving a different function were the military governors (*gobernadores* or *capitanes-generales*). As their titles indicate, these positions focused heavily on defense and security. They were generally deployed to high-value strategic and geopolitically sensitive areas, requiring individuals with military degrees and experience. Key locations included the islands of Cuba, Hispaniola, and Puerto Rico; the Florida Peninsula; and the ports of Cartagena and Veracruz, to name a few. These islands and ports played a vital role for maritime and trading routes but were also vulnerable to foreign powers stationed in nearby territories, such as the Dutch in Guyana or the British in Jamaica. Beyond ports and islands, threats to Spanish rule in frontier territories also came in the form of raids by unconquered populations that would destroy advanced settlements or thwart attempts at evangelization by missions. An example of this is Paraguay, which was ruled by military governors rather than an *audiencia* for most of the colonial period.

Due to their strong defense and strategic nature, the Crown often refused to sell many of these positions. Indeed, of the few occasions where

---

[11] Name comes from the "box" where the treasure/monies were held.
[12] These were direct descendants of Spanish individuals but born in the Americas.

purchase offers were outright rejected, it was typically for these posts. For example, attempts to buy an administration position at the port of San Juan de Ulúa in Veracruz or in Puerto Rico were frequently denied despite numerous bids.[13] Similar restrictions were placed on the positions of captain general of Cuba, government of Havana, treasurer or accountant of Isla Margarita, and governor of Portobelo (Panama) or Cartagena (Colombia). In fact, a unique document drawn by the Crown lists all the positions that should not be sold due to their critical roles in defense and trade within the empire.[14] Still, some of these positions were put for sale, particularly by Charles II, but not with the same intensity as others.

Figure 2.3 depicts the distribution of military governorships, *gobernaciones*. As shown, they predominate in coastal and frontier areas. Although their territories appear larger than those of the *audiencias*, military governors actually ruled over fewer people (by design).

Below the level of the *audiencia* and *gobernadores* stood royal officials in charge of the various regional *cajas* or treasuries. Each *caja* had two officials (a treasurer and an accountant) to manage the royal treasury, while larger *cajas* also had an assayer (*factor veedor*). *Caja* officials did not exert executive or judicial functions per se, but they did play a vital role in implementing the Crown's fiscal policies. For instance, it had the ability to determine the amount of revenue to be used to pay for administrative and other local costs and the income to be sent to other *cajas*, for example, for defense purposes (Andrien 1982).

Cajas were strategically deployed in prosperous areas to facilitate tax collection for the Crown. This was the case of mining areas where the Crown taxed silver at 20 percent (known as the *Quinto Real*). *Cajas* were also located close to ports, as the import-export of goods was taxed via the *almofarijazgo* and merchants had to pay for the Crown's protection, known as the *averia*. Commercial centers and major indigenous areas also had their own *caja* to collect revenue from sales taxes (*alcabalas*) and head taxes (*tributo*), respectively. The role of *caja* officials was thus to receive and tally these sources of income, which indirectly meant making sure other officials accurately and collected them.

In terms of disbursements, *cajas* were in charge of paying salaries, debts, and remitting resources to other treasuries to cover expenses there (*situado*). For example, revenue in the Empire typically flowed from the richest areas (i.e., Peru) to strategic ones that did not generate enough

---

[13] AGI, Mexico 1970, *Relacion de los Beneficios que no se han Admitido*, March 4, 1712.
[14] See Chapter 3.

2 *The Eighteenth-Century "Market" of Offices*   29

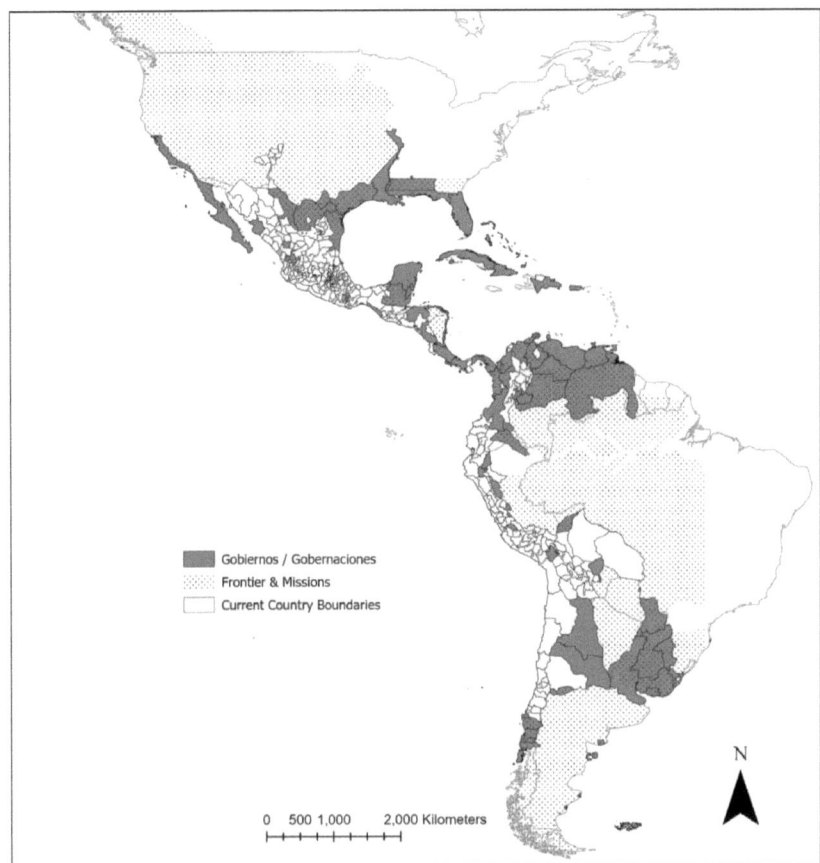

FIGURE 2.3 Frontiers and military governors (*gobernaciones*) ca. 1700

Sources: See note to Fig. 1. Note: Some *gobernaciones* that overlap with *corregimientos* or *alcaldías* are not depicted in this figure.

of their own income (i.e., Buenos Aires).[15] Additionally, *cajas* held in escrow the bonds (*fianza*) that *corregidores* and *alcaldes mayores* were required to pay to the Crown as insurance against uncollected taxes. As in the case of the *audiencia*, *caja* officials were appointed for life, and their role was considered vital for the fiscal health of the overseas territories. Territorially, the jurisdiction of *cajas* was smaller than *audiencias* but generally larger than that of a province. Figure 2.4 presents the location of the roughly 80 *cajas* in the empire as of 1700.

[15] See Von Grafenstein and Marichal (2012) and Grafe and Irigion (2012).

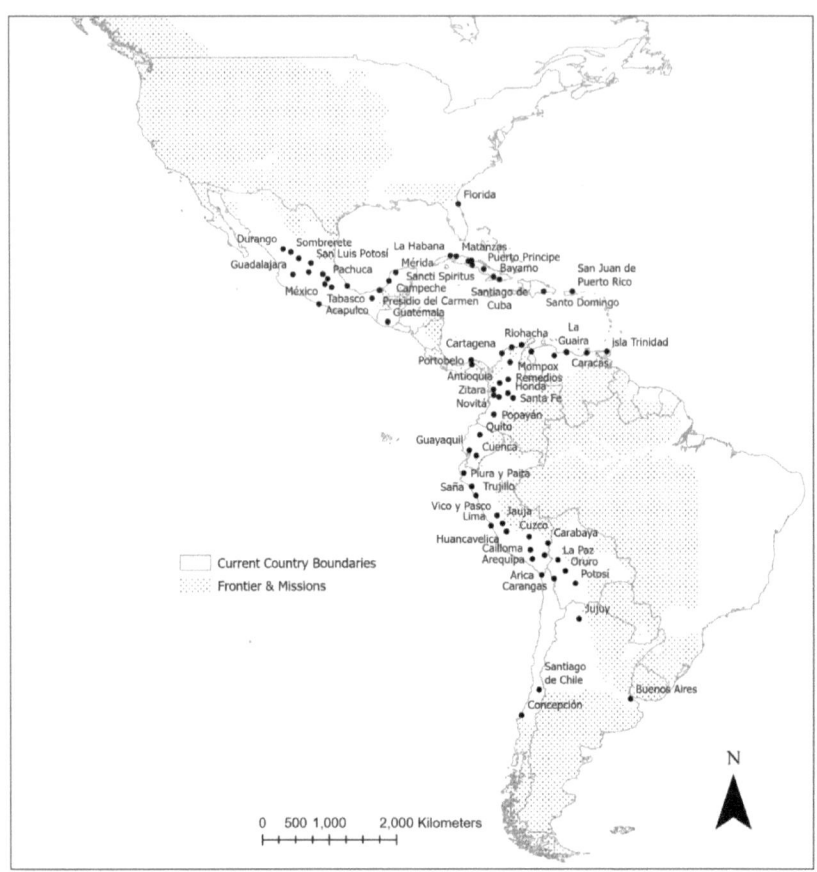

FIGURE 2.4 Treasury *cajas* in Spanish Empire ca. 1700
Sources: See note to Fig. 1.

Finally, within each of the *audiencias*, *gobernaciones*, and *cajas*, territories were further divided into *corregimientos* and *alcaldías mayores*. Although nominally at the bottom of the hierarchy, they were of great importance for the welfare of the general population due to their roles as tax collectors and first-instance judges. As the royal replacements of the early *encomenderos*, they served as direct representatives of the Crown where deployed. Institutionally, these officials were overseen by *audiencias*, viceroys, and *gobernadores*, and their appointment was in the hands of the King or Viceroys, depending on the province and period in question.

Provincial governors were also the most numerous of all the high-level positions. In 1700, there were around 320 *corregimientos* and *alcaldías*

2 The Eighteenth-Century "Market" of Offices

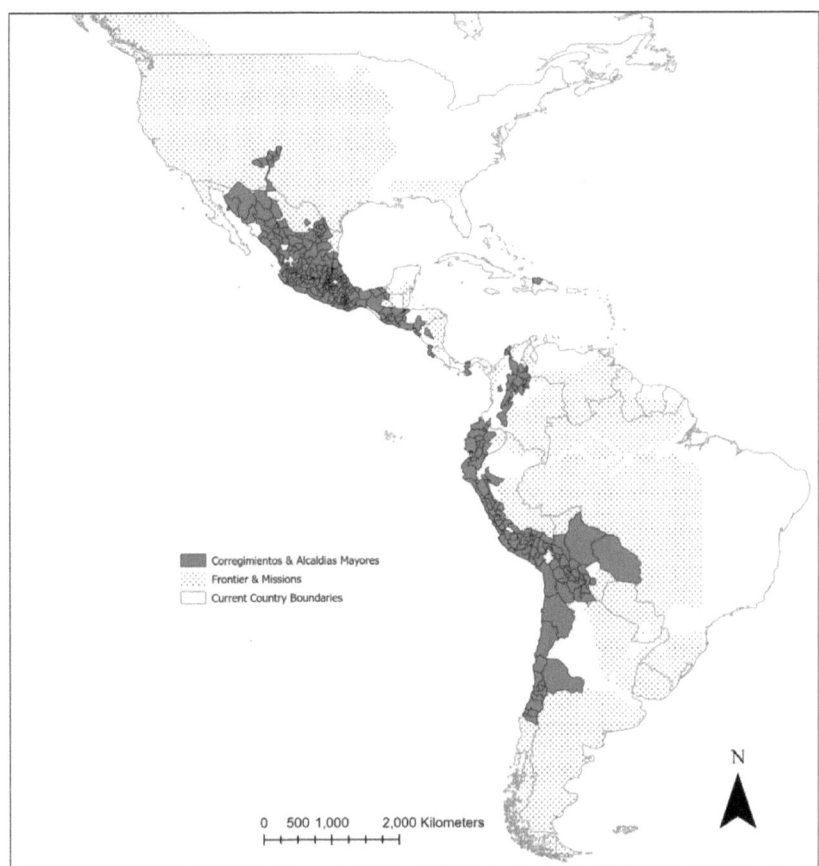

FIGURE 2.5 Provincial *corregimientos* and *alcaldías mayores* ca. 1700
Sources: See note to Fig. 1.

mayores (provincias).[16] Figure 2.5 shows all such provinces in the empire. As the figure illustrates, these positions are denser in regions with large indigenous populations – Central Mexico, the Andean Altiplano, and the Colombian highlands – while being sparser in the frontier areas of northern Mexico, southern Chile, and around the Amazon. The latter, being unexplored or not yet conquered, were instead administered by missionaries or military governors as described earlier. Figure 2.5 also highlights the virtual absence of *corregimientos* and *alcaldías mayores* in what is now Argentina, Paraguay, and Uruguay, indicating their lighter administrative presence.

---

[16] Either the *provincia mayor* or *menor* in which the empire was organized around 1700. This figure excludes minor *partidos* and other jurisdictions.

TABLE 2.1 *Summary of key offices for sale in 1670–1750*

Position	Function	Term	Jurisdiction	Number ca. 1700
Alcalde Mayor or *Corregidor*	Judicial, fiscal	2 to 5 years	Province	Approx. 320
Treasurer or accountant	Fiscal	Lifetime	*Cajas* (1–4 provinces)	Two or three officials per *caja*; 81 *cajas* approx.
Gobernador	Military, policymaking	Varied	Key ports, islands, frontiers	Approx. 50
Audiencia member	Judicial, policymaking	Lifetime	Several *Cajas* and provinces	Five to fifteen members per *audiencia*; eleven *audiencias*

Unlike other officials, provincial governors had a term limit of two to five years, as well as a limited career path within the colonial administration. For example, of the forty-nine individuals who had purchased their post at the *audiencia* of Lima in Peru, only one[17] had previously served as a provincial *corregidor*, showing that the position of provincial officials was not the typical path to obtaining higher-ranking positions. Finally, their wages, while sizable, barely covered the costs associated with their duties (Moreno Cebrian 1977).

In all, this position was one of high responsibility but often came with poor pay. As judicial authorities, these officials administered the local jail and set punishments for law infringements. As tax collectors, they established labor quotas for public works, collected taxes, maintained population and taxation records, and administered communal funds. They also served as trade authorities within their province, a source of much of their rents. Finally, they also had miscellaneous duties including guaranteeing the supply of maize in the province by overseeing public granaries in their jurisdictions and heading the local council (*cabildo*) in the province's capital (*cabecera*), to name a few. In all, they had important distributional consequences for the welfare of the colonial population.

Table 2.1 summarizes the main institutional characteristics of the four primary positions sold by the Crown.

---

[17] Conde de las Torres Juan Fernando Calderón de la Barca, in the *audiencia* from 1690 to 1718. Other five members of the *audiencia* were sons or sons-in-law of former *corregidores* but had not directly served as one.

2.2 HOW SALES TOOK PLACE

In addition to expanding the set of offices for sales, Charles II also changed the process through which sales took place. Before 1670, offices known as "salable and renounceable" were sold in public auction, with upcoming vacancies announced through public edicts and town criers in both the Americas and Spain. This was the case of municipal positions, for example.

For high-level positions – *audiencias*, military governors, *caja* officials,[18] *corregidores*, and *alcaldes* – these were in principle appointed due to "merit." Namely, a reward for "services" provided to the Crown. Candidates interested in these posts would submit long lists of their achievements, qualifications, and assistance to the Crown along with their requested position(s). The Council of Indies would then review these submissions to create shortlists for the King's final selection (typically favoring the first-ranked one). In other cases, they were also given to "favorites." For example, servants (*criados*) of Queen Mariana (regent and mother of Charles II) were often rewarded with these offices. In principle, these did not involve the payment of money, at least not openly or systematically.

This process changed with sales. Instead of appointment based on "merit," high-level positions were to be negotiated within the king's closest circle of advisors (*cámara*) on a case-by-case basis, often sidelining the full Council of Indies.[19] The process initiated when a buyer (or their agent) approached the Crown with a price for a particular position in the colonial government. At this point, prospective buyers had already assessed the position they sought, the Crown's price expectations, and when they might assume office. Once the offer was made, the Crown would decide whether or not to accept it or, though relatively rare, request a higher price. Generally, bidders made offers they knew the Crown would accept, either because they were in line with, or higher than, those of other contenders or previous payments for the position.[20]

Examples of these negotiations can be gathered from internal memos (*memoriales*) available at the colonial archives. For example, Don José de Toca y Herrera, an official of the Armada of Barlovento, offered

---

[18] There was an earlier stint of sales of *caja* officials that Philip IV later regretted as quoted by the Council of Indies.
[19] Thus, resembling a first-price closed bid auction.
[20] AGI, Mexico, 1970, Don Bernardo Tinajero, August 2, 1712.

the King 400²¹ pesos for the appointment to the *alcaldia mayor* of San Andres de Tuxtla, in Mexico. The internal discussion recognized that while this position had not been sold before and was not very profitable, if Don José were to offer 500 (instead of 400), the King should accede to the purchase. Similarly, a bid of 1,000 pesos for the *alcaldia mayor* of Tacuba in the area surrounding Mexico City was recommended for acceptance given that the position had only fetched 600 pesos in 1707 and 500 pesos in 1710. In contrast, an offer of 800 pesos for the position of *alcalde mayor* of Tecali in Mexico, from Don Juan de la Lastra, was advised to be rejected as it was much lower than the 3,000 pesos it had previously fetched.[22] It is through this negotiation and back and forth that the Crown and the buyer reached a mutually satisfactory price.

The second consideration for the purchase was whether the buyer was well-known in Court – namely whether someone could vouch for them. In the examples mentioned earlier, Don Bernardo Tinajero, a royal advisor who later became the first secretary of the Indies, was such a person. He could relay details to the King of the buyer, Don José, noting that he was a man of "mature age," born in Spain, and known in court for his good behavior ("de buen proceder y sanidad"). Tinajero also knew that Don José had lost all his fortune in the Armada ship that recently capsized in Havana, thus advocating for the sale. However, in many cases, the Crown was unable to obtain detailed information on the buyer, so it was left with second- to third-hand information of these purchasers.

2.2.1 *Futuras* and the Secondary Market of Offices

Facing high demand for certain positions, the Crown also started selling appointments in advance, known as *futuras*. In these cases, the buyer bought a "spot" in the queue to occupy the position when it became available. Because *corregimientos* and *alcaldías* had a five-year term, and the buying process took some time, purchasing in advance made sense. However, in the case of *audiencias* and fiscal offices (treasuries, assayers),[23] which had lifetime appointments, it was often unclear when the purchaser would enter office. For this reason, the purchasing titles

---

[21] Each peso is equivalent to four days of work at the daily wage paid to an indigenous person (2 reales).
[22] AGI, Mexico, 1970, Don Bernardo Tinajero, August 2, 1712.
[23] Known as *tesorero* or *factor veedor*, respectively.

(contracts) often specified a list of individuals who could enter in case the original purchaser could not occupy it.

The most common reason for not taking possession of their post is if the title bearer died or was in poor health. In these cases, the Crown allowed the appointment to be "transferred" to someone on the list in lieu of the original buyer, albeit subject to the approval of the viceroy and payment of a fee (usually one-third of the original price paid). While these substitutes were often family, this was not always the case, suggesting that their connection might have been commercial or financial. For example, Don Juan Fernandez de Ceballos bought the position of *alcalde mayor* of Huatusco in the *audiencia* of Mexico. Among the prerogatives of his purchase, he was allowed to name three individuals to take over his position in the event of his death or another "accident" (often health related), for which he paid 2,400 pesos to the Royal Treasury of Madrid.[24]

The ability to "transfer" the appointment by claiming they were unable to serve (e.g., due to health reasons) gave rise to a secondary market that the Crown strongly condemned. For example, an investigation by the Peruvian *audiencia* in 1698 discovered that individuals who had been granted *futuras* of *corregidores* in Peru by the Crown had subsequently sold them at exorbitant prices – approximately ten times more than they had paid the Crown for them. The report estimated the loss in revenue for the Crown in around 136,000 pesos.[25] The Crown swiftly declared these secondary appointees invalid and ordered the official to collect the difference in prices (however difficult) and to enter it in the royal *cajas*.

Yet, the Crown was also complicit in creating this secondary market by allowing these transfers in the first place. Transferability is what allowed colonial offices to serve as a financial instrument and storage of value. Offices were purchased several years in advance, and buyers could bequest it or use it as a dowry for whomever married their daughters or nieces. For example, the title of *alcalde mayor* of Jalapa y Jalacingo in the *audiencia* of Mexico could be transferred to whomever married

---

[24] AGI, Mexico 1221, *Título de Alcalde Mayores de Don Juan Fernández de Zeballos*, February 9, 1719.

[25] See AGI, Escribania 566A, *Lima Año de 1700, Autos sobre el Beneficio del Oficio del Corregimiento de Cajatambo que hizo Don Tomás Casimiro de Rosas, traspasándola a Don José Ordóñez*. The prices documented range from 15,000 to 56,000, totaling 136,000 pesos in fraud committed against the Crown.

any of the two daughters of Don Juan de Echagaray (Doña Antonia or Doña Juana) thanks to a fee of 1,500 pesos paid to the Royal Treasury.[26] Yet, not allowing transfers would place all the risk onto the buyer, likely reducing the price and profits to the Crown.

2.2.2 How Prices Were Set

As might be expected, the price paid for these positions, its denomination,[27] and the terms of disbursement were central to each transaction.[28] This was crucial for several reasons. First, it helped the buyer seek reimbursement if the Crown reneged on the promised appointment (which did happen in the early 1700s). Second, having accurate prices allowed the Crown to track which positions had been sold, what could be sold, and the acceptable price for each position. Therefore, every title and all related internal correspondence and accounting records included this information.

As noted earlier, prices were subject to negotiation in the buying stage. Yet, from the Crown's perspective, how did it know how high or low to go?

Archival evidence shows that internal lists of "acceptable" or "expected" prices were drawn for the first round of sales (1670–1700), which then became a reference point for later ones. For example, at the start of the office-selling period, the Crown estimated the value of the treasurer or accountant position at 8,000 pesos in the Guayaquil *caja*, 6,000 pesos in Chucuito and 4,000 pesos in Arequipa – other *cajas* in Southern Peru.[29] Actual prices seem to have superseded these estimates: The treasurer position for Arequipa was eventually sold for 5,000 pesos in 1712, 5,000 pesos in 1740, and 5,500 in 1745 – higher than predicted. Similarly, after being estimated in 6,000 in 1692, the treasury positions in the Chucuito *caja* fetched significantly higher prices: 12,000 pesos in 1700, 8,000 pesos in 1702, and 14,000 pesos in 1711, well above the

---

[26] AGI, Mexico 1222, *Persona que Casare con una de dos Hijas de Don Juan Echagaray*, July 21, 1730.
[27] Whether in pesos de a ocho, pesos de a diez, pesos fuertes, reales de vellon, or maravedíes, for example. See Appendix for prevailing exchange rates.
[28] There is at least one instance (sale of the *alcaldia mayor* of Temascaltepec and Sultepec to Don José Carrillo de Viezma in the year 1712) in which the buyer asked to not have the price put in the title. However, there is still evidence of the sale through other internal correspondence.
[29] AGI, Lima 89, *Recomendacion de Precios de Oficiales Reales*, 1692.

Crown's predictions.³⁰ These discrepancies suggest that the Crown may have underestimated the true returns for each of these positions due to limited or outdated information.

For the case of *corregimientos* and *alcaldías mayores*, estimates of their returns (*utilidades*) were less clear, as the Crown relied on information from viceroys and *audiencia* members overseas to gauge local conditions and the profitability of each of its provinces. However, the first reference point for the Crown was the wage – as one should expect higher prices if receiving higher wages. Beyond wages, the Crown did not always know the local conditions across all its territories. Instead, it is likely that buyers – who were typically better informed – generally underpaid the Crown for their positions. Therefore, the next section centers on the main considerations behind buyers' willingness to pay.

2.2.3 The End of Sales

The systematic sale of colonial offices would continue all throughout Charles II's reign. With the ascent of Philip V in 1700, the first Bourbon King, office-selling appeared to temporarily stop. In 1701 Philip V decreed an end to all sales of positions and initiated a "reform" by voiding all sales conducted in the previous ten years. According to the decree, buyers who had not yet occupied their position would be reimbursed.³¹ Furthermore, all newly appointed officials would now on be of "trustworthy character": individuals with military training or noble lineage, born in Spain, and with established connections to the court. However, Philip's intentions were short-lived, as Philip himself began to sell offices as early as 1705, in the midst of the Spanish Succession War. This led future purchasers to include clauses in their sale titles exempting them from any future reforms of this sort.

Office-selling continued mostly uninterrupted until 1751, when the last sale was recorded. By then, the Crown had sold 106 *audiencia* seats, 218 military governor positions, 416 *caja* offices (treasurer, accountant, or assayer), and 1,856 provincial governorships (*corregidores* and *alcaldes*).

---

³⁰ AGI, Contaduria, 235.
³¹ Because many individuals purchased positions in advance of the seat being vacated (*futuras*), it is possible that after ten years, some buyers may not have yet taken possession of their office.

2.3 MAIN DRIVERS OF DEMAND

From the buyer's perspective, there were three main reasons that made a position attractive. First, the institutional traits associated with the office. Second, its profitability ("how much could they make above and beyond what they paid for it") and third, their own individual characteristics.

2.3.1 Institutional Traits

The first driver of prices were the institutional traits, which included the powers and responsibilities that came with a certain position, its rank within the administration, its term length, and the wages attached to it. Albeit all positions studied here are "high-ranked," there were institutional differences between them.

Higher-ranked positions had more institutional power and social value and therefore drew higher prices. To exemplify, the average price of *audiencia* seats, although sold a mere 106 times in the eighty-year period, were the highest at around 13,000 pesos de *a ocho*, consistent with their lifetime tenure, greater social prestige, and policy influence. Nonetheless, there is still significant variation between seats, mainly driven by location, power, and wages. For example, a seat in the *audiencia* of Manila could cost as little as 2,000 pesos[32] or as much as 47,500 pesos, which Domingo de Orrantia paid for a seat in the Lima *audiencia* in 1749. On a similar institutional level were the positions of *gobernador* – a military appointment reserved for ports and strategic locations in the empire. Although their sales were less frequent vis-à-vis their number, when sold, they fetched around 9,385 pesos on average due to their rank, prestige, and sensitive nature.

Lower in the hierarchy (and in prices) stood the fiscal or *caja* offices. These were more numerous and appointed for life, of relatively high social status, but their policy influence was limited to the fiscal realm and to a much smaller territorial jurisdiction. On average, these positions were valued at 6,993 pesos. However, they could also cost as little as 500 pesos, as was the case of Francisco Martinez, who in 1673 sought a position of treasurer in the *caja* of Comayagua, Honduras. A particular, but rare, type of fiscal office were seats in the *tribunal de cuentas* of Mexico and Lima – a treasury overseeing all other regional treasuries within the viceroyalty. These fetched the highest prices of all: 95,000

---

[32] Paid in 1710 by Gregorio Manuel de Villa Barreda, in real terms it is 1,711.

TABLE 2.2 *Mean price and quantity of sales by office type (1670–1751)*

Type	Total sold	Avg. price	Std. dev.	Min.	Max.
Audiencia seats	106	13,294	8,444.8	2,000	47,500
Military-governors	218	9,385	10,111	500	60,000
Treasury official	415	8,206	10,153.6	500	95,000
Alcaldes & *corregidores*	1,856	4,702	4,810	150	42,952

Note: Nominal price in *pesos de ocho*. Table A.1 in the Appendix shows the result accounting for inflation in Spain.

pesos for serving as head (*regent*) of this tribunal in Mexico in 1740 and 65,000 pesos for that of Peru (Lima) in 1734 (nominal prices).

Finally, the position of *alcalde mayor* or *corregidor*, the most numerous and frequently sold, was also the relatively "cheapest" on average, at 4,000 pesos. This lower price was consistent with their lower rank, lower wage, and short term in office. However, this lower desirability is only relative; 4,000 pesos still represents around forty-four years of labor at the daily wage of an indigenous worker at the time (2 reales). In fact, some *alcaldías* and *corregimientos* could cost as much as the 42,952 pesos,[33] paid in 1748 for the *alcaldia mayor* of Jicayan in Mexico. Others were much cheaper, such as the *corregimiento* of Acasaguastlan in Guatemala in 1712, which sold for 150 pesos (nominal prices). Table 2.2 summarizes the prices paid for each position based on their institutional rank.

2.3.2 Profit Opportunities and Prices

The second – and most important – driver of demand were the financial gains to be made in office. Specifically, how much an individual could profit from their position beyond what they had paid for access. Spanish America offered plenty of such opportunities at every level of the colonial administration.

For *audiencia* members, the power and prestige of their position came with broad jurisdiction over political, economic, and judicial matters. It was not uncommon for unscrupulous *audiencia* members to partner with private merchants, turning a blind eye to illicit contraband, or to enter into joint ventures with provincial *corregidores*

---

[33] Or more than 17,000 *pesos fuertes*.

and *alcaldías* to secure (indigenous) labor for their haciendas. They might also "bury" lawsuits against close business associates, friends, or family members. Or make sure they receive favorable judicial outcomes. In their policy and judicial role – that is, settling disputes over land, mining, or labor – *audiencia* members had large distributional consequences within colonial society. This is particularly true of well-connected local elites (*criollos*), who had better knowledge of local conditions and were better positioned to reap the rewards from belonging to the *audiencia*. While this does not mean all necessarily did, the opportunities were still there.

Caja and treasury officials enjoyed their own opportunities to profit, albeit within the narrower realm of treasury management. The role of treasurer or accountant was to serve as a "political broker" or mediator "between the financial demands of the Crown and the resistance of taxpayers in the viceroyalty [of Peru] to new government levies" (Andrien 1982: 49). As such, they often had a say in what was collected, from whom, and how. They also decided which debts to be paid first from incoming revenue, another role prone to favoritism. Finally, when deployed in ports, they directly oversaw the collection of taxes from foreign trade, ripe for contraband. In fact, from the viewpoint of the Council of Indies, fiscal officials were key to the proper administration of justice and the management of royal tax receipts.[34]

Finally, the attractiveness of purchasing *corregimientos* and *alcaldías mayores* lay in their direct jurisdiction over the indigenous population, which they could extort. Examples of the latter include overtaxing and expropriating community savings (*cajas de la comunidad*) intended for public goods. In fact, the latter was so ubiquitous that the Crown explicitly forbade *corregidores* from using these funds for personal dealings.[35] These officials were also in charge of mobilizing labor for private and public works, another role prone to abuse. Known as the mit'a (*mita*) in Peru and Bolivia, or the *repartimiento de indios* (indigenous labor drafts) in Guatemala or Mexico, the goal was to ensure a steady supply of labor for public or private use.

Another key source of profits was the practice of *repartimiento*, distinct from the labor drafts. *Repartimiento* took different forms across the

---

[34] AGI, Mexico, 1970, *Extracto de Consulta Hecha por el Consejo de Indias en 21 de Agosto de 1737, y Órdenes del Ministerio de Hazienda sobre Venefizios de Empleos de Indias*.
[35] AGI, Mexico, 1229, *Titulos de Corregidores y Alcaldes Mayores* (1696).

2 The Eighteenth-Century "Market" of Offices

empire. In Peru and Bolivia, it involved the forced[36] sale of merchandise – often unsold inventory – to the indigenous population at mark-up prices. Repayment was enforced by the judicial authority vested in the *corregidor* or *alcalde mayor*, who could jail those refusing to comply. As described by Juan and de Ulloa, it was "so cruelly wicked" that "a more tyrannical abuse could not be imagined" (1978 [1749]: 77).

In Peru, the desirability of *corregimientos* was thus closely linked to the ability to engage in *repartimiento* practices. For example, the province of Cercado, close to the Peruvian capital, had a low *repartimiento* quota and was therefore considered "bad." In contrast, Huarochiri – despite its lower salary (800 pesos) – had a higher quota (140,000 pesos) and was therefore considered a "first-class" province. The reason behind this discrepancy was Huarochiri's greater commercial activity, driven by the abundance of wheat, barley, and some silver mines. Finally, an intermediate case was the province of Cajatambo, which, like Huarochiri, had similar *repartimiento* quotas and some local mines, as well as textile production. However, it was deemed less desirable due to its geographic location.

Figure 2.6 illustrates the close relationship between office prices and *repartimiento* for the provinces of Peru and Bolivia at the time the data was collected (1754). The x-axis displays the log *repartimiento* quota per capita established in 1754, while the y-axis shows the log average office prices paid for that province in the prior eighty years. As the figure shows, a 10 percent increase in a province's *repartimiento* quota correlates with an 8.7 percent increase in the price paid for that post.

In Guatemala, while some commodities were forcibly sold as in the Peruvian and Bolivian cases, *repartimiento* there most commonly involved distributing cotton or maguey for women to weave cloth for colonial officials, known as the *repartimiento del algodon*. Profits came from the price differential between the finished cloth at market prices and the minimal payment to these women and for raw materials (Lovell 2005: 108). According to Solorzano Fonseca (1985), profits from *repartimientos* over a five-year period were at least double the total head taxes collected for the Crown in their respective province.

In areas of Mexico that produced valuable cochineal dye, goods were distributed to the indigenous population in exchange for monopolizing the purchase of this good. *Alcaldes* profited from the price difference

---

[36] It is disputed to what extent it was coerced, particularly in the case of cochineal producers in Mexico (Baskes 1996, 2000).

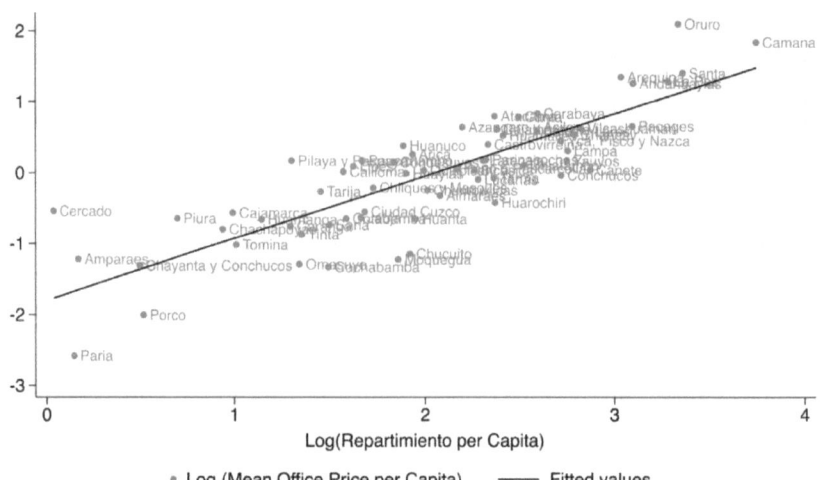

FIGURE 2.6 Office prices and *repartimiento* quotas in Peru and Bolivia

Note: Scatterplot of logged mean price per capita of Peruvian and Bolivian *corregimientos* plotted against per capita *repartimiento* quotas drawn in 1754. Variables weighted by population size of province in 1754.

between what they paid indigenous producers and what they sold to merchants reselling it in international markets. For example, although the province of Tlazazalca had good weather and opportunities for the *alcalde mayor* to benefit from cattle raising and textile production, it was deemed less profitable than the province of Apa y Tepeapulco, which produced more cochineal and traded more in cotton and textiles, thus offering greater potential benefits for the *alcalde*.

The potential for profit across the empire's provinces at this time was summarized in a unique document known as the *Yndize Comprehensibo de Todos los Goviernos, Corregimientos y Alcaldías Mayores* (Anonymous, 1777). Its purpose was to guide the choices of officials seeking a provincial governorship (*corregimiento* or *alcalde mayor*) across the empire's provinces. The alleged motivation of the author was to reveal the "true" returns to serving in these offices in lieu of the multiple (and misguiding) rumors about the different provinces in the Americas. In fact, the Peruvian viceroy count of Santisteban directly attributed the demand for these positions to the news traveling to Spain of "such and such position delivering 50, 60, 100 thousand *pesos* a year, which came at the expense of 'indigenous blood.'"[37]

---

[37] Moreno Cebrian (1977: 75, citing AGI Lima 45, Lima, May 28, 1666), own translation.

TABLE 2.3 *Rankings and prices of* alcaldías *and* corregimientos *by anonymous* Yndize

Ranking	# Sales	Avg price	Std. dev.	Min.	Max.
Best	561	6,966	6,138	500	42,952
Good	679	4,779	4,240	400	33,350
Low	323	2,337	1,840	400	18,100

Note: Means based on all *corregimientos* and *alcaldías mayores* sold in the empire between 1670 and 1751 in the current territories of Mexico, Guadalajara, Colombia, Ecuador, Chile, Bolivia, and Peru for which a ranking measure was listed. Nominal prices.

However, the viceroy's estimates were not far off. Historians calculate that an *alcalde* engaging in *repartimiento* in the province of San Antonio Suchitepéquez (Guatemala) could see a return of between 50,000 and 100,000 pesos throughout their time in office (Solorzano Fonseca 1985). Not surprisingly, San Antonio Suchitepéquez was the highest demanded province in Guatemala, in terms of the number of times sold and price fetched. Similarly, a Peruvian *corregidor* bent on profiting from office could gain around 30 to 150 times their salary during their tenure (Andrien 1982: 13). Given that wages were around 1,500 pesos, returns ranged from 45,000 to 225,000 pesos. This is consistent with other contemporaneous estimates. For instance, Juan and Ulloa (1978 [1749]: 90) estimated in the 1740s that *corregidores* must be netting profits ranging from 40,000–60,000 pesos to 150,000–200,000 pesos in the five-year term. This, after accounting for all the travel, living, and bribing expenses needed to hold these offices. With these figures in mind, it made economic sense to pay some thousands of pesos more to secure their preferred location. It also explains its allure to Spanish (and non-Spanish!) individuals, who saw in them an opportunity to raise a quick fortune in the New World before returning.

Table 2.3 shows the office prices paid and the anonymous three-category[38] ranking for a broad sample of positions across the empire. Not surprisingly, the top-ranked *alcaldías* and *corregimiento* positions across the empire were around three times more valuable (on average) than the lowest-ranked ones. Moreover, the fact that they are highly correlated with prices paid pre-1751 suggests many of these activities continued in the 1770s despite sales officially ending by then.

---

[38] There are some cases where the ranking was deemed below a "3"; however, given it is only a few cases, I included them in the lowest category.

2.3.3 Individual Characteristics

The final driver of demand were the characteristics of the individual itself. All else equal, individuals less constrained by social and reputational costs, more ambitious, and with lower risk aversion were more likely to profit from office in Spanish America. Thus, driving their higher willingness to pay. But how to distinguish these characteristics?

Naturally, it is challenging to identify traits such as risk taking, unscrupulousness, or dishonesty, even with contemporary data. However, some of these individual motivations can be at least partially captured by the extent to which these individuals were linked to the Crown through noble lineage or military careers. In late seventeenth-century Spain, social origin, ancestry, scholarship, and services rendered to the Crown were key traits to determine an individual's eligibility for office (Rosenmüller 2016).

This "traditional" notion of merit was advantageous in contexts of poor information and weak oversight. First, recruiting from certain social groups or occupations improved performance in office. When future benefits and favors depended on staying in the good graces of the Crown, individuals had lower incentives to act against its will (Allen 2005). As shown with *audiencia* members, loyalty and connections to the Spanish Crown actually improved, rather than undermined, their performance in office (Salgado 2021). Second, the fact that the nobility and connected individuals were a "known" quantity to the Crown, helped the latter select better-suited individuals. In contrast, selling positions may have led to more variation in the quality of colonial officials. With this in mind, it is not surprising the Crown preferred to select its officials from certain classes and not others.

This preference is on display when appointing (not selling) *corregidores* and *alcaldes* to provinces of what today is Mexico, Peru, and Bolivia.[39] As illustrated in Figure 2.7, the Crown clearly preferred to appoint individuals with nobility and military titles, as well as those of Spanish origin who were much less likely to purchase offices. As the figure shows, an individual with a military or nobility title saw a 25 percent increase in their likelihood of being appointed rather than purchasing their position. This probability is higher for those with military titles (27 percent) but lower for individuals of Spanish origin (8 percent) – not born in the Americas.[40]

---

[39] Former *audiencias* of Mexico, Guadalajara, Charcas, and Lima.
[40] Partial coefficients after controlling for year and province (position) fixed effects.

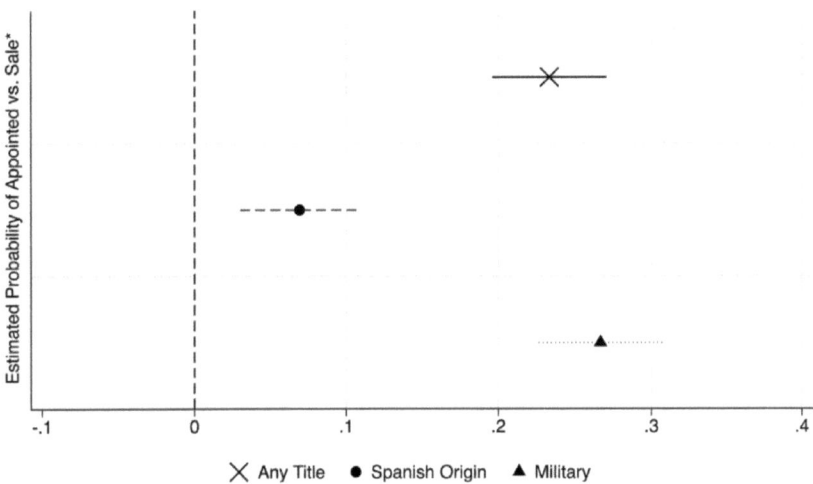

FIGURE 2.7 Probability of appointment by social status: *corregimientos* and *alcaldías*

Note: This plot corresponds to the OLS estimates of Equation (1) in Appendix to Chapter 2 (Table A.2). All estimates include province and year fixed effects.

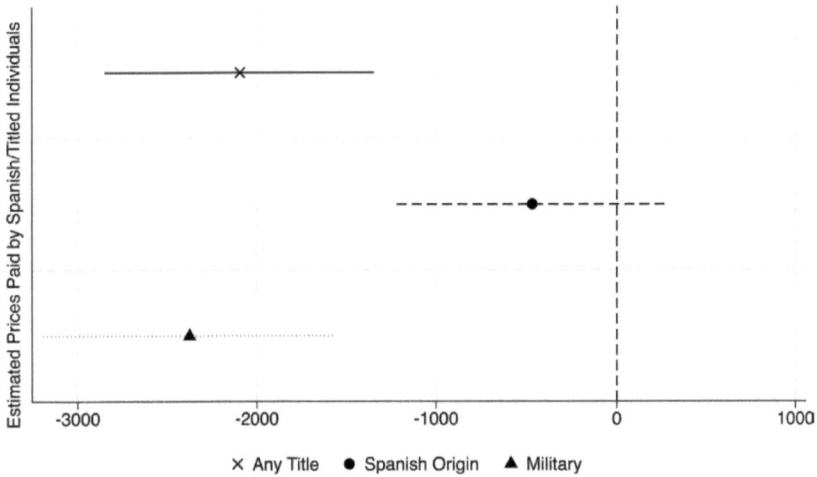

FIGURE 2.8 Prices paid by social status: *corregimientos* and *alcaldías*

Note: This plot corresponds to the OLS estimates of Equation (1) in Appendix to Chapter 2 (Table A.3). All estimates include province and year fixed effects.

By being favored for appointments in the colonial government of the Americas, these individuals effectively faced a lower cost to enter office. As shown in Figure 2.8, this "subsidy" amounted to an average of 2,000 real pesos for individuals with nobility or military titles. This reduction is mostly driven by military individuals, who paid on average 2,375 pesos less than an individual with a different career path. Finally, for Spanish buyers – vis-à-vis others – the reduction is smaller in around 500 pesos, likely because Spanish individuals were also willing to pay high prices for these positions.[41]

In sum, evidence from this section is consistent with the idea that the characteristics of an individual were also a key driver of demand and willingness to pay. Since the Crown preferred to appoint individuals with particular profiles – military, nobility, or Spanish – these groups were effectively subsidized, while everybody else had to pay the full price. The broader implications of this preference are explored in depth in Chapter 4, where I present more detailed evidence of price discrimination. Suffice to say for now that the characteristics of buyers, the rank of the position, and its profitability strongly influenced the price they ultimately paid for office.

Chapter Summary. This chapter describes the market for high-level colonial offices in eighteenth-century Spanish America. It starts by providing an overview of the territorial and institutional organization of the Spanish Empire at the time as well as the positions that constituted the "supply": their number, rank, and institutional attributes. The rest of the chapter then focuses on the determinants of demand through the analysis of office prices, buyer characteristics, and the profitability of certain positions versus others. Estimates show how, all else equal, positions with greater rank and power as well as those more profitable drew higher prices on average. It also finds that individuals of higher social status or more connected to the Crown – of military, nobility, or Spanish origin – were heavily "subsidized" to occupy office vis-à-vis those lacking those traits. Altogether, this is consistent with office prices revealing important information of the expected returns of certain positions versus others.

---

[41] Similar patterns emerge when using log prices instead of levels (see Appendix columns (4) to (6) of Table A.2).

3

Why Sell Offices?

Chapter 2 characterized the nature of the market for offices. The supply side – what was sold and how – as well as the demand – who bought offices and why. This chapter instead examines why the Crown would sell offices in the first place.

***

Traditional explanations for office-selling often center on the fiscal needs created by internal or external threats. In seventeenth-century France, Louis XIV's military ambitions in Holland revamped office-selling despite his own minister's (Colbert) opposition to sales as "one of the greatest evils of the Kingdom" (Swart 1949: 14). In Qing-China, conflict and threats inevitably spurred the sale of titles and rank – key to occupying offices in the government (Peng 2019). In the sixteenth- to seventeenth-century Ottoman Empire, the need for a professionalized army placed an even greater burden on the treasury, leading to a more venal bureaucracy (Lewis 1958: 121). At first glance, the Spanish case also appears driven by the need to finance its multiple wars in Europe.

In Charles II's own words, office-selling was necessary to meet the *urgencias presentes* (pressing needs) following his defeat in the War of Devolution (1667–68) and the prospect of a new military conflict with France. It is not a coincidence that office-selling started in earnest during the Franco–Dutch War (1672–78), intensified during the Nine Years' one (1688–97), and reached its peak during the Spanish (1700–14) and Austrian Succession (1740–48) wars. A failure to secure revenue, the Crown went, could result in military defeat and disintegration of the empire. Once the emergency passed, there would be no need to resort to these measures, it reasoned (Swart 1949). Furthermore, since these wars often involved British and other Protestant powers, office-selling also served as a defense of the catholic religion (Sanz Tapia 2011: 155). The fact that the practice spanned two different dynasties (Habsburg and Bourbon) shows this was not driven by differences in governing ideologies but other structural causes. The question is, which ones?

Beyond wartime revenue, there were three other potential benefits the Crown could derive from office-selling. First, it reduced the need for constant monitoring of its officials abroad. Selling usufruct rights of a position in exchange for a fee (the office price) could incentivize them to exert more effort in office, particularly when effort is hard to observe (Allen 2005; Johnson and Koyama 2014). Similarly, it may have also served to coopt or garner political buy-in by local elites in the Americas (*criollos*[1]), who would then be invested in the survival of the empire and not challenge the Crown (Grafe and Irigoin 2012). Finally, it could have also been a way to assert monarchic control vis-à-vis viceroys by wrestling away the appointments of certain offices (*corregidores* and *alcaldes mayores*) and displacing the nobility altogether (Rosenmüller 2016).

This chapter centers on contrasting the existing explanations for office-selling with the available evidence. Were sales a pure revenue-driven enterprise of shortsighted rulers? Could have office-selling served the Crown in other ways? If so, how? Unlike existing studies solely focused on specific time periods (e.g., during the Habsburg or Bourbon dynasties, see Sanz Tapia 2009[2]); on a specific type of position sold (e.g., only *audiencia*, or fiscal positions)[3]; or on certain emblematic cases, such as the sale of the viceroy position (Domínguez Ortiz 1965); the analysis includes the complete set of high-ranking positions sold between 1670 and 1751. Combining this dataset with the economic, geopolitical, and fiscal characteristics of the positions sold, it is possible to establish which factors better explain the timing, frequency, and type of sales, and which do not.

---

[1] Individuals born from Spanish parents in the American colonies.
[2] Albeit only focused on Habsburg Spain, Sanz Tapia (2009) provides a comprehensive view of the sale of all positions, focusing on the question of whether sales were driven by corruption or necessity.
[3] Burkholder and Chandler (1977) provide an groundbreaking study of the sale of *audiencia* positions to document a policy of centralization by the Spanish Crown in the late eighteenth century. Similarly, Andrien (1982) looks at the sale of fiscal positions in Colonial Peru in the late seventeenth and eighteenth centuries to illustrate the reasons behind the corruption and economic stagnation of this territory at the time. Sanz Tapia (2011) does an excellent analysis of the sale of fiscal positions between 1632 and 1700.

In all, the chapter shows that the Crown's wartime justification might have been incomplete and misleading in two ways. First, despite the large number of offices sold – and the havoc they wreaked in the colonial administration – the total amounts of funds obtained in a given year were only a fraction of the Spanish military expenditures at the time. In other words, while wars spurred sales, sales did not make war. Instead, anecdotal accounts show funds from office-selling likely helped smooth consumption of the royal household, not its armies. Moreover, in contrast to its urgent tone, the Crown did have other financing available, but chose not to use it.

Second, despite the characterization of office-selling as another "irresponsible," "confiscatory," and "arbitrary" act of (absolutist) fiscally pressured (North and Weingast 1989: 804) and shortsighted rulers willing to trade "valuable long-term assets for small but immediate gain" (Gailmard 2017: 677), the Crown was not completely indifferent to long-term governance and geopolitical consequences in the Americas. Analysis from the type of positions sold shows *some* restraint in selling the most sensitive positions in the Empire and in limiting the influence of local elites and unconnected officials. For example, the data shows a clear reluctance of the Crown to sell *audiencias* and military governor positions – important offices with security and defense roles – but less qualms to sell *caja* positions, *corregimientos*, and *alcaldías mayores*. Consistent with awareness of the revenue-governance trade-offs posed by sales.

The rest of the chapter is organized as follows: Section 3.2 presents the reasons why premodern monarchies recurred to office-selling. Section 3.3 then uses data from the Spanish case to adjudicate between existing explanations. Section 3.4 concludes by discussing the findings.

3.1 THE CASE FOR OFFICE-SELLING

From a contemporary (and Weberian) perspective, the practice of appointing officials in exchange for money would be considered corrupt; an affront to meritocracy; and a hallmark of dysfunctional bureaucracies. Namely, a prime example of how the Spanish Crown lacked the foresight and patience to reap the benefits of good governance and sustained economic growth.

Yet, this was not the main source of opposition at the time. Most contemporary critics did not contest the Monarch's right to sell offices per se, but the sale of positions administering justice. In fact, selling offices provided several advantages to monarchs, often outweighing its downsides.

Testament to its utility was its global prevalence, under different institutional forms, in the Vatican, France, England, the Ottoman Empire, and China (Swart 1949).[4] Its widespread nature points to systemic causes that can be grouped in four. First and foremost was the ability of office-selling to raise revenue when needed; second, it could incentivize officials to perform in office, addressing agency problems; third, it could help displace (or empower) specific classes or social groups if so desired. Finally, it could also enhance survival of the regime by creating a class with vested interests in the perpetuation of the status quo. How each of these explain the Spanish case?

3.1.1 Sales to Incentivize Officials

Beyond the official explanation of wartime needs for revenue, office-selling could have helped reduce agency problems for the monarch (principal) in an environment in which monitoring is difficult. Selling the rights to occupy a position or carry out a task is a good way to align the incentives of the monarch with that of its official (agent) without having to exert more oversight.

The best example is that of collecting taxes on behalf of the royal coffers. In this case, the monarch has a strong desire to collect all the taxes due to him or her. Yet this requires effort by the official. If the monarch cannot monitor this effort, the result may be less taxes collected. By instead allowing the tax collector to purchase its position in exchange for a fixed amount paid in advance – tax farming – the monarch can be sure that all of the taxes will be collected as the official uses them to recoup its investment and even make a profit. Selling rights to tax allowed monarchs to "outsource" certain tasks, generally tax collection, while obtaining more revenue than they would have obtained otherwise. Because purchasers become residual claimants of output (in this case taxes), office-selling provides very strong incentives to exert effort with very little monitoring costs for the Crown (Johnson and Koyama 2014; Allen 2005).

Aside from inducing effort, office-selling could also serve as a screening device, aiding selection. Since only those with the highest (marginal)

---

[4] Among these, the case of France is one of the most salient due to its influence over French society and duration (Doyle 1984: 831). In England, office-selling dated at least to the Normand kings, of which Richard I "Lion Heart" is a prominent example, using the revenue to finance the crusade (Fischer and Lundgreen 1975: 473). Yet, office-selling in Spain arguably took place at a lower rate than in England or in France (Fischer and Lundgreen 1975: 487; Swart 1949).

return to the position would be willing to pay, sales allocated positions to those who valued them most (Root 1991). Moreover, if the position was rather minor, with limited scope for corruption or overtaxing, and the ability to pay for the position correlates with the skills needed in office, this may reduce the potential for ill-suited individuals to enter office in the first place (Weaver 2021).

This ability to induce effort was one of the main attractive features of office-selling vis-à-vis its alternative: patronage or discretionary appointment. For instance, if the Spanish Crown only appointed "favorites" and not necessarily those better suited for the position, patronage would lead to a decline in the quality of bureaucratic activity as they may feel less incentivized to perform accordingly (Aghion and Tirole 1997; Prendergast and Topel 1996). This was France's Louis XIV explanation for Spain's decline of the seventeenth century: Charles' II continuous appointment of his favorites (Eissa-Barroso 2017: 135).

3.1.2 Sales to Enhance Survival

Second, in addition (or in lieu) to helping select and incentivize officials, sales might have also benefited the Crown by creating stakeholders interested in the survival of the empire. As put by Swart (1949: 13), office-selling was not necessarily a threat to an absolutist regime. To the contrary, in France, the proliferation of officeholders (*la noblesse de robe*) meant a large segment of the population became invested in the continuation of the system that held its most valuable assets (offices).

In the Spanish-American case, selling high-level appointments to local elites could have made them more interested in the survival of the regime (Grafe and Irigoin 2012). For example, by allowing a degree of representation in the colonial government and in the management of its treasure. This is particularly plausible for the case of lifetime appointments in the *audiencias* and treasuries, overwhelmingly bought by local elites (*criollos*) who had the means (wealth), local connections, and desire for social standing associated with them.

3.1.3 Sales to Displace Social Groups or Actors

Finally, besides incentivizing effort, aiding selection, and imperial survival, office-selling could have also simply reflected a shift in the notion of merit in public administration. Traditionally, "deserving" recipients of high-level offices were those associated with a specific social class (i.e., the nobility). By instead appointing officials based on money, selection followed a more instrumental (and modern) rationale based on its utility to the Crown (Rosenmüller 2016). Money in exchange for positions was more "useful" to the Crown than appointing the aristocracy, as was customary. Therefore, it comes as no surprise that in both France and Spain, the strongest opposition to office-selling came from the nobility, as they were displaced by the rising bourgeoisie who overwhelmingly purchased these posts (Swart 1949: 11).

In the specific case of Spain and Spanish America, there were two advantages to displacing the nobility. First, that office-selling disrupted the networks of power and connections existing between the aristocracy – the usual recipient of appointments – and the Council of Indies – the body usually recommending who to appoint. Instead, it allowed the King to partake in some of the monetary profits it created. Second, it also had the advantage of wrestling away the customary power of viceroys in the Americas to appoint certain officials – *corregidores* and *alcaldes* – within their jurisdiction. Therefore, reasserting the power of Madrid vis-à-vis viceroys in the Americas (Rosenmüller 2016).

In the following section I examine to what extent are these explanations supported by the empirical evidence. Does the timing and number of sales conform best to a wartime revenue-centered explanation as claimed by Charles II? Or, was office-selling instead (or also) a way to improve the Crown's ability to incentivize its colonial agents? Did it help the Spanish Crown assert control vis-à-vis viceroys? To what extent did sales make local elites more invested in the survival of the empire?

3.2 WHY SELL? EMPIRICAL EVIDENCE

The main justification of Charles II for office-selling was that it would bring much-needed revenue to the royal coffers. This was certainly a time of military conflict in Spain. A cursory look at the number of European wars[5] involving Spain reveals that of the eighty years of office-selling, fifty-one of them were spent in one conflict or another.

---

[5] A list of wars involving Spain during this period were: the Franco-Dutch War (1672–78), War of the Reunions (1683–84), Nine Years' War (1688–97), War of the Spanish Succession (1701–14), War of the Quadruple Alliance (1718–20), Anglo-Spanish War (1727–29), War of the Polish Succession (1733–38), War of Jenkins' Ear (1739–42), and the War of the Austrian Succession (1740–48).

This likely is an overestimate, as the intensity of war varied, but it still portrays a near constant shadow of war.

3.2.1 Office-Selling for Wartime Revenue?

An initial look at the data throughout the whole period shows that indeed selling *any* position was much more frequent during war times (n = 2028, 78%) than during peace times (n = 594, 22%). That is, the volume of sales during wars relative to peace times was larger by a ratio of almost 4 to 1. Moreover, if we include the year before the start of the war and the year immediately after – which could exhibit some lingering fiscal needs – then the result is even more striking: 2,364 (90 percent) are sold due to wars, whereas only 258 (10 percent) during peace. Thus, initially consistent with Charles' II claims: Years in which Spain was engaged in European Wars, sales were much more frequent.

Yet, was the intensity of sales the same across all conflicts? No. Despite the near constant state of war in these years, as illustrated by the shaded areas of Figure 3.1, the share of positions sold varied with the

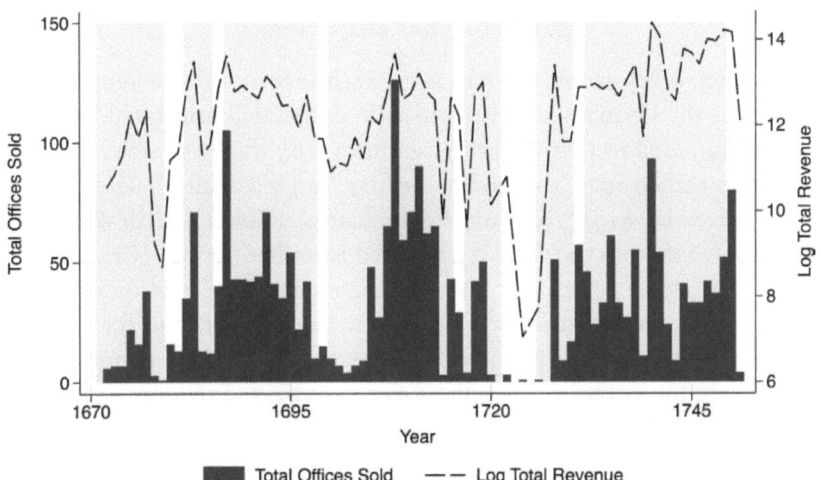

FIGURE 3.1 Total offices sold and revenue collected (1670–1751)

Note: *Audiencia* seats, *corregimientos*, *alcaldías mayores*, *caja* positions, and military governors (*gobernadores*, *capitán-general*). War years shaded.

war in question. The Nine Years' War (1688–97), the Spanish Succession (1701–14), and the Austrian Succession/Jenkins' Ear (1739–48) one, amassed the most sales. Conversely, periods of peace in Europe (non-shaded) show an almost a complete absence of sales.

In terms of the (log) revenue obtained (dashed line), Figure 3.1 shows an almost constant amount – except for peacetimes, which naturally reduced the amount of income obtained. It also illustrates the clear increase in the price of offices between 1730 and 1750, when the total number of positions drops but revenue remains almost constant.

In addition to the overall correlation between the timing of wars and sales, there also appears to be a strong relationship between the length of war and the number of positions sold. In particular, the longest and most protracted military conflicts of this eighty-year period – namely, the Spanish Succession War (1701–14) and the Anglo-Spanish War of Jenkins' Ear (1739–48) – had more sales and revenue collected in the later years of the conflict than in the earlier ones.

In all, the data described earlier documents a close relationship between the timing and length of European wars involving Spain and the positions sold. Yet, was the revenue from offices the only financial option? Was it meant to fund wars?

3.2.2 Economic Desperation?

According to key economic indicators, at the eve of office-selling, the situation of the Crown was less financially desperate than stated. At least when compared to that of earlier centuries (i.e., sixteenth century) – the ones that earned Spain the term of the first "serial defaulter" (Drelichman and Voth 2010: 813).[6] To start, the cumulative amount of debt was large, but it was far from the crisis it had faced in earlier periods (Grafe 2011; Gonzalez Enciso 2007). For instance, the interest rate paid on this debt was rather constant at around 5 percent, much lower than the peak of 10 percent it faced in 1503 (Grafe 2011: 15). In fact, the period 1678–1698 were the years in which the Crown contracted the lowest amount of short-term debt in terms of *asientos* (Gelabert 2009: 26). Rather, it appears that the Spanish Crown turned instead toward internal debt from major towns in the Peninsula (Grafe 2011: 15).[7] Despite Charles' claims to the contrary, in the late seventeenth century the Crown had

---

[6] The reign of Philip II was characterized by multiple bankruptcies.
[7] This is broadly consistent with accounts questioning the presence of a seventeenth-century crisis (Klein and Serrano 2019).

3 Why Sell Offices?

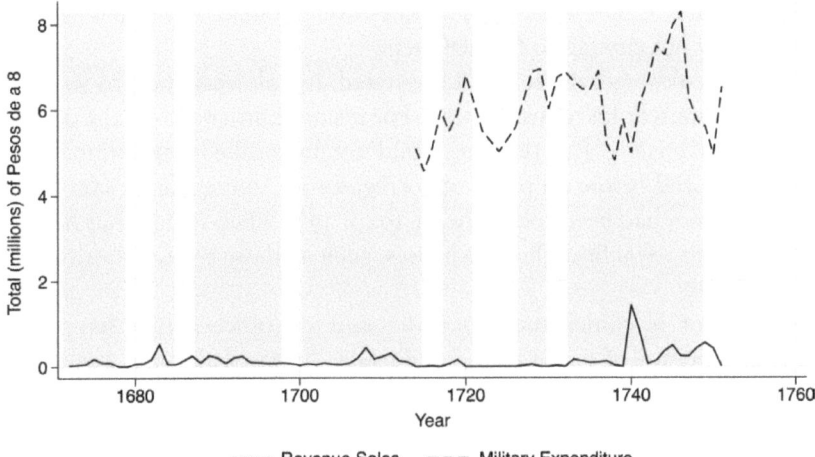

FIGURE 3.2 Total revenue and military expenditure by the Crown (1670–1751)
Note: War years shaded.

some foreign financial options but it chose not to use them, consistent with what Gonzalez Enciso (2007) calls the new "anti-debt mentality" of the period.

On the fiscal front, the Crown did face a liquidity problem partly due to a lower fiscal burden per capita in the Peninsula at the time. Data from the European State Finance Database shows that 1683 is the year with the lowest tax per capita of the seventeenth century in Spain (Ucendo and Lanza García 2008: 186). Together with less treasure arriving from the Americas, it meant that the total amount of revenue for the Crown in both nominal and real terms was overall lower than in previous years (Ucendo and Lanza García 2008: 183). This suggests that the Crown may have faced true liquidity constraints at the start of sales, which it preferred to meet with loans from towns rather than recurring to international creditors or short-term loans (*asientos*).

In terms of the use of the proceeds from sales, how much could have office-selling contributed to the war effort? The answer is: not much. As shown in Figure 3.2, relative to total expenditures of the Crown, revenue from sales constituted a very small portion of the needed income to finance expenditures even in years of numerous sales at high prices. Moreover, a sizeable share of the funds depicted were in fact deposited in the Americas (not in Madrid) and therefore of no immediate use to the Crown. Given this, it is unlikely that the income obtained from sales funded wars. While wars spurred sales and brought in revenue – they were likely not enough to finance them.

Instead, although never explicitly stated, its role was likely to smooth the royal households' consumption. For instance, in 1680 – in the depths of the fiscal crisis – "[…] the King could not undertake his traditional trip to the Escorial before an office of *corregidor* in America and two offices of *contadores* had been sold" (Swart 1949: 39). Office-selling thus helped defray other royal household expenses, such as those related to travel or funeral costs.

It is not a coincidence that the end of office-selling happened during a period of peace in the Peninsula. In particular, the years following the end of office-selling (1753–62) were years with more balanced budgets for a change (Freire Costa et al. 2021: 7). Year 1748 also marks the start of a decade of relative peace following the end of the Austrian succession and Anglo-Spanish War. Conflict would resume with the Seven Years War in 1753 but only with active Spanish involvement from 1762 onward, when the British occupied Havana and Spain lost the Florida Peninsula.

Yet, the Seven Years War also highlights the limits to a purely war-centered explanation for office-selling: Why office-selling does not restart with the Seven Years War (1762)? One possibility is that this was the first European conflict that took place in the colonial territories themselves, heightening the sense of threat among settler elites, which facilitated levying new taxes in the face of foreign enemies (Arias 2013). Years of smaller deficits could have also improved the Crown's liquidity, making it unnecessary for the Crown to recur to office-selling again. More likely, governance concerns played a greater role than in earlier periods. The fact remains that after 1751, sales have stopped.

3.2.3 Sell Offices to Solve Agency Problems?

While the evidence supports the idea that wars were an important driver of the timing and number of sales, they might not have been the only reason. In fact, office-selling could have been the preferred mode of financing precisely because it solved a perennial problem of the Crown: How to assert its will overseas given its inability to monitor its own officials. The chief manifestation of it was how to increase the amount of revenue these individuals remitted to Spain, especially at times of need.

3 Why Sell Offices?

TABLE 3.1 *Share of total contribution from Indies*

Year	% contribution from Indies
1577	0.10
1594	0.27
1599	0.21
1613	0.15
1623	0.10
1640	0.09
1655	0.03
1666	0.02
1688	0.03

Source: Ucendo and Lanza García 2008: Table 6, p. 176.

Despite perceptions to the contrary, by 1680 the Spanish American Empire brought in relatively little revenue to the Crown. As shown in Table 3.1, the share of revenue coming from the Indies was generally only a fraction of the Crown's total income. At the eve of office-selling, income from the colonies was only 3 percent of the total Crown's revenue in 1688, from a peak of 27 percent in 1594. This statistic shows the relative *unimportance*, in fiscal terms, of the overseas territories as a significant source of revenue in the late seventeenth century. Moreover, even when adding other sources,[8] for example, those obtained via extraordinary means, seigniorage, or taxing officials (*media anata*), the picture does not change. As of 1688 – when office-selling roughly starts – direct income from the Indies constituted a mere 4 percent of the Crown's total revenue (Ucendo and Lanza García 2008: 176).

Given this bleak fiscal panorama for the Crown, office-selling was a key way to seize economic surplus from the colonies – particularly from its indigenous population – to its own coffers. The implicit assumption being that buyers would (at the very least) recoup these payments by all means available. Selling the position was thus a way to partake in these

---

[8] That is, revenue not obtained via taxes, monopoly rights, customs, church contributions, and so on. For example, this is revenue obtained from the *Media Anata* (payments by public officials) and other extraordinary means.

rents without incurring the agency costs – such as monitoring or incentivizing officials – to do so.[9]

This exact sentiment is expressed by the Marquis of Villarias – chief minister of Philip V – who, in 1739, argued that in the face of the limited resources brought in by the Indies and the enormous expenses needed to protect these territories from British attacks, it was then justified to obtain resources from those kingdoms in any way possible, namely sales.[10]

Yet, by the same logic, office-selling should have started earlier or lasted longer as the Crown was perennially cash-strapped. Instead, as shown in Figure 3.1, the Crown sharply alternated between selling and not. It would also imply that the Crown should sell all and every available position, but did it?

3.2.4 Heterogeneity in Types of Positions Sold

A deeper look into the type of positions sold illustrates some of the "restraint" shown by the Crown during sales. Namely, it does not seem that all positions were sold at the same rate. Thus suggesting that there were other considerations aside from pure revenue. In particular, Figure 3.3 panels (a) and (b) disaggregate the temporal trends of Figure 3.1, distinguishing by the type of position sold – whether *audiencia* seats, treasury positions, military governor, or *corregimientos* & *alcaldías*. Across both panels, dotted lines represent the number of sales of *corregimientos* & *alcaldías*; solid lines those of *audiencia* seats; dash-dot lines the military governor positions; and dash those in the treasuries (*cajas*). Periods of European wars are again shaded.

As shown in Figure 3.3, there are large differences in the intensity at which different positions were sold. Not all positions were sold in equal numbers nor fetched the same amount of revenue. In sheer quantity (panel a), *corregimientos* and *alcaldías mayores* (dot) were by far the position most frequently sold. The second most demanded were fiscal ones (dash) followed by military governors (dash-dot). At a much lower frequency, barely visible, were the sales and revenue coming from *audiencia* seats (solid).

Similarly, when focusing only on peace times – nonshaded periods – sales for all positions are lower, particularly those of higher rank

---

[9] An alternative interpretation consistent with this empirical pattern is that due to overlapping jurisdictions, the Crown was redistributing rents from other entities extracting from the indigenous population (e.g., Church tithes, hacienda owners, and mine owners) to itself.

[10] AGI, Mexico 1970. *Marques de Villarias a Su Majestad*. Buen Retiro, Diciembre de 1739.

3 Why Sell Offices?

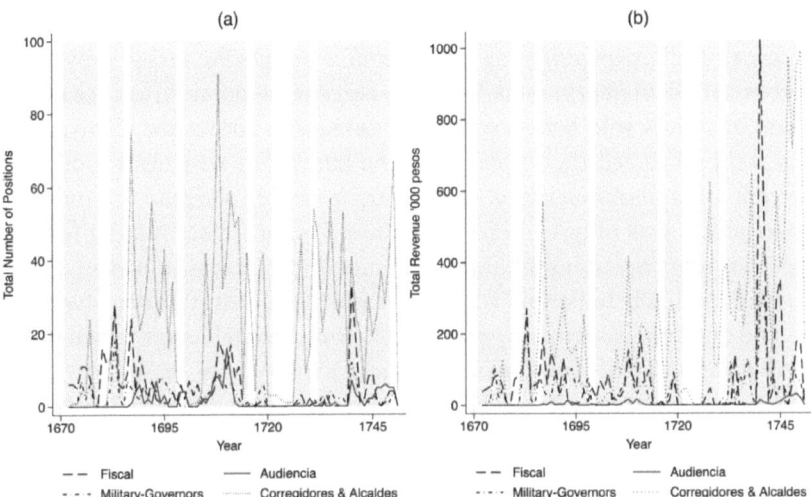

FIGURE 3.3 Total revenue collected by type of position (1670–1751)

Note: All prices and revenue calculations account for inflation in Spain and are reported in *pesos de a ocho*, following standard exchange rates at the time (see Appendix to Chapter 3).

(*audiencias* and military governors). Specifically, of the 594 positions sold during peace, 75 percent were *corregimientos* and *alcaldías*, followed by 16 percent of those from treasuries. In contrast, barely any *audiencia* seat or military governorship was sold if the Crown was not involved in war, with 3.5 percent and 4.8 percent of all transactions, respectively.

In addition to quantity, the most successful positions in bringing revenue were the *corregimientos* and *alcaldías* (panel b). The only exception was the year 1741 and some interwar periods. The success of *corregimientos* and *alcaldías* in raising revenue was not due to the fact that they were the most expensive. If anything, provincial ruling positions were the cheapest of all the high-ranking ones. On average, a *corregimiento* or *alcaldía* could fetch around 4,700 pesos, followed by fiscal positions at 8,000, military governors at 9,000, whereas *audiencia* seats fetched an average of 13,000 pesos per seat. Instead, *corregimientos*, *alcaldías*, and treasury offices were the most frequently sold office of all.

Why? The simplest explanation is that there were more of these positions than others. While they were indeed more – there were around 320 provinces and 80 *cajas* with 2–3 officials each – the same pattern emerges after weighting by the total number of positions in each category. Specifically, at times of no demonstrable need (peace), 23.9 percent of all *corregimientos* and *alcaldías* were sold versus only 15.9 percent of all *audiencia* seats.[11] This 8-percentage point difference in the share of offices sold between the two categories shows the Crown had less scruples to sell the former than the latter. For treasuries too: 23.8 percent of transactions took place during peace, whereas for military governors it was only 13 percent. In sum, even after accounting for the fact that *audiencias* and military governorships are less numerous, they are still less likely to be sold when there is no demonstrable need (war).[12]

The question is then, why was the Crown more reluctant to sell high-level positions (*gobernaciones*, *audiencias*) than lower ones (provincial governorships, treasuries)? The answer suggested by the data is that the Crown, with all its "irresponsible," "shortsighted," and "confiscatory" practices, may have had a shred of concern of the consequences of sales in the Americas. Whether due to the complaints from the Council of Indies and the nobility – displaced by purchasers – or to actual qualms about the functioning of the colonial administration, there was *some* restraint, particularly when harder to justify in revenue terms.

Another reason behind the disproportionate sales of *corregimientos* and *alcaldías mayores* was the limited impact they had on the formulation of overall policy as well as their limited territorial jurisdiction. Although provincial rulers had enormous leverage over the indigenous population in their capacity as justice administrators and tax collectors, they had little influence over broader military affairs, mining, or fiscal policy outside of their province. Even if it was well-known that *corregidores* and *alcaldes* used office to extract economic surplus from the population, the consequences would be borne primarily by the latter, largely sparing the Crown in the short term. For example, the costs of putting down rebellions was paid by the local treasuries and manned by local militias, not disbursed by the Crown.

Moreover, the main argument against selling *corregimientos*, *alcaldías mayores*, and treasury offices was that it would undermine future tax revenue for the Crown. Yet, this was too little of a treasury to make a difference to the Crown. As shown in Figure 3.4, the amount of revenue collected via head taxes (*tributo*) in the colonies – a tax exclusively paid by the indigenous population – was a small proportion of the total

---

[11] Conversely, 76.1 percent of all *corregimiento* and *alcaldías* sold took place during war, while this was 84.1 percent for *audiencia* seats.
[12] In fact, one could argue that military governors were the most restrictive of all.

3 Why Sell Offices? 61

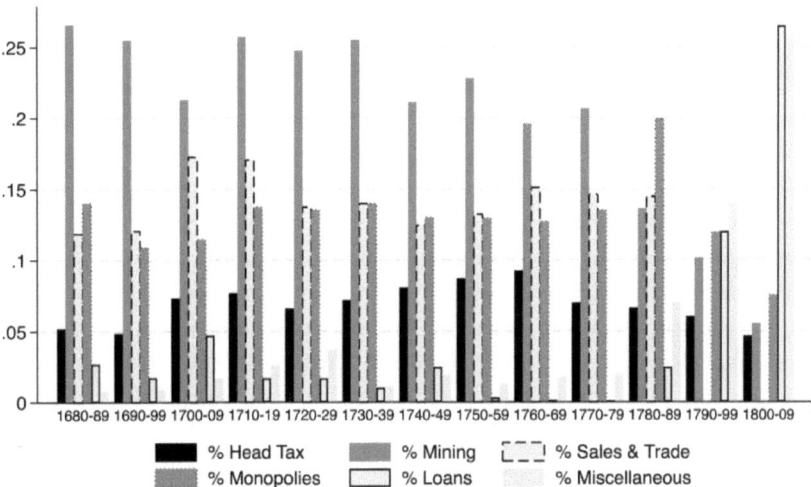

FIGURE 3.4 Share of tax income by different sources (1680–1810)
Own construction based on totals per decade across the *audiencias* of Charcas, Lima, and Mexico – roughly Bolivia, Peru, and Mexico, respectively – divided by each category. Summary of Tables 3.2–3.8; Tables 4.1–4.6; Tables 5.1–5.7 of Klein (1998).

revenue collected in the royal treasuries across the empire. Combined with the fact that not much treasure was remitted to Spain in the first place (see Table 3.1), it meant its overall fiscal importance might have been small to negligible.

Displayed in Figure 3.4 is the share of head taxes collected from the indigenous population throughout the entire eighteenth century, compiled by Klein (1998). As shown, even in the most populous territories (now Bolivia, Peru, and Mexico), it never surpassed 9 percent of the total. This is true even after office-selling stopped and attempts were made to improve collection (Bourbon Reforms). In contrast, major sources of revenue, such as those from mining or monopolies, were generally outside of the scope of *corregidores* and *alcaldes*.

Together, the fact that overall revenue from the Indies was negligible, of which head taxes was an even smaller account, helps explain why the Crown privileged the sale of *corregidores*, *alcaldías*, and treasuries.

3.2.5 Geopolitical Considerations

In addition to their low policy and fiscal impact, the sale of *corregimientos*, *alcaldías*, and treasuries also limited the geopolitical exposure that came from selling *audiencias* or military governorships. Namely, there were also strategic reasons to sell them.

Primary sources – reproduced in Table 3.2[13] – show that a set of offices was very rarely or ever put for sale by the Crown due to the geopolitical and governance concerns it created for the Empire. This includes certain military governorship positions as well as *audiencia* seats such as the position of *Presidente* (most senior member with special attributions). For instance, on May 13, 1740, in the midst of the Anglo-Spanish War, internal correspondence between the King and the *cámara de Indias*[14] shows the former authorizing the sale of some *audiencia* seats (*plazas togadas*). However, in a later document from July 18th, the King was made aware that buyers were usually not the "best suited" for the position. The King then backtracked from authorizing *audiencia* sales altogether, as those positions exposed the empire to grave military dangers.[15] Albeit a large number of *audiencia* positions ended up being sold, many more would have been authorized if not for the reluctance of the Crown.

The Crown was also particularly reluctant to sell positions in strategic regions, those prone to rebellion, or exposed to foreign attacks. For example, in the Crown's view, the *gobernaciones* of Florida and Tejas (now in the US), Santo Domingo (Dominican Republican), and Cumana (in Venezuela) ought to be properly ruled by loyal individuals of military training to defend the region from foreign enemies if necessary. Therefore, not for sale. In fact, of the few recorded instances of the Crown rejecting purchasers were the offers in 1713 by Don Pedro de Rivera, who sought to purchase the administration of the Fort of San Juan de Ulua (Veracruz, Mexico) as well as the offer by Don Antonio Gonzalez for the position of *Gobernador* of San Juan de Puerto Rico, mentioned earlier.

Threats to Spanish rule also came in the form of violent uprisings of the indigenous population (*indios levantados*), particularly in frontier regions. This concern precluded the sale of the position of President of the *Audiencia* of Guatemala and the Government of Nicaragua, considered vulnerable to these threats and to British presence in Mosquito Bay (Nicaragua). Other posts were restricted simply due to their strategic location, such as the military governor of Veracruz and Cartagena, which served as "entry" and trading points to the viceroyalty of New Spain and

---

[13] This document is also cited in Burkholder and Chandler (1972) to highlight the geographic distribution of *audiencia* sales. Here it is used to emphasize the patterns of sales and the trade-offs the Crown faced.
[14] The supreme council within the broader Council of Indies.
[15] AGI, Mexico 1970. La Cámara de Indias, a 18 de Julio de 1740.

Santa Fe and thereby in need of "good" military rulers. Interestingly, the Crown did not think these ideal subjects could be found via sales.

Table 3.2 provides the list of positions that had not been sold since 1717 due to their strategic and military importance. Given their geopolitical status in the empire, the Council of Indies deemed it of paramount importance to appoint "ideal" subjects of renowned loyalty and a military background to promptly organize its defense in case of invasions or attacks. Notably, none of the excluded positions involved a *corregimiento*, *caja*, or *alcaldia mayor*.

TABLE 3.2 *List of positions excluded from sales since 1717 and their reason*

Type	Location	Reason	Main concern
Military governor	La Florida	Frontier	England, France
Military governor	Tejas & Presidios	Frontier	France
Military governor	Veracruz	Strategic	Trade, entry New Spain
Military governor	Campeche	Strategic	Trade
President (*Audiencia*)	Guatemala	Internal	Indigenous revolts
Military governor	Nicaragua	Internal & frontier	Indigenous revolts, England
Tenencia general	Portobelo	Strategic	Trade
Military governor	Cartagena	Strategic	Trade, entry Santa Fe
Military governor	Chocó	Strategic	Trade (Darién River)
Military governor	Santa Marta	Strategic	Trade
Military governor	Maracaibo	Strategic & frontier	Trade, Dutch
Military governor	Caracas	Strategic & frontier	Trade, Dutch, England
Military governor	Cumana	Strategic & frontier	Trade, Dutch
Military governor	Isla de la Trinidad e Isla de la Margarita	Strategic	Trade, security
General Captain	Isla de Cuba	Strategic	Trade, security
Military governor	La Habana	Strategic	Trade
Military governor	Santiago de Cuba	Strategic & frontier	Trade, England (Jamaica)
President (*Audiencia*)	Santo Domingo	Frontier	France, England
Military governor	Puerto Rico	Strategic	Trade, security

(*continued*)

TABLE 3.2 (*continued*)

Type	Location	Reason	Main concern
Military governor	Tabasco y de la Isla del Carmen (Laguna de Términos)	Strategic	Trade, England
Military governor	Buenos Aires	Strategic & frontier	Trade, Portugal
President (*Audiencia*)	Chile	Strategic & internal	Security, Indigenous revolts
Military governor	Valdivia, la Concepción y Valparaíso	Strategic & internal	Security, Indigenous revolts
President (*Audiencia*)	Presidencia de Panamá	Strategic & frontier	Trade, England

Source: AGI, Mexico 1970. *Nota de los Empleos que para su provision en la America se han estimado por militares y que desde el año 1717 se han excluido del beneficio por las razones que militan para ellos.* Madrid, Buen Retiro, 1 de Junio de 1740.

The mere existence of this list suggests that the Crown thought that selling certain positions was not a good idea. In theory this could be due to reasons other than governance. Yet, the accompanying internal correspondence also suggests that the Crown knew that many purchasers were not well suited for the post and, by extension, did not deem them appropriate. Moreover, the list was not cheap talk but consistent with the data: *audiencia* seats and military governors are precisely the two positions systematically undersold in the data.

In sum, despite the need for revenue, the Crown was not ready to just sell "everything" even during times of extreme fiscal need – such as wars against Britain. Instead, it appears it actively tried to contain the damage to positions that would have limited externalities, even if at the expense of the local indigenous population as documented in the following chapters. While office-selling was certainly attractive in helping the Crown seize hidden rents, this was directed to lower ranked positions (*cajas, corregimientos*, and *alcaldías*). For higher-ranked ones, it showed greater restraint, as their performance was key to safeguarding the empire.

This governance consideration also helps explain why the Spanish Crown never properly institutionalized sales. Unlike the French or Qing-China, there was no special body overseeing the practice. Thus, suggesting they did not see it as a permanent solution to agency problems in the Americas.

3.3 WEAKENING VICEROYS & CO-OPTING LOCAL ELITES?

The final explanation for office-selling centers on whether office-selling served to (i) enhance the survival of the empire by creating vested interests and (or) to (ii) displace (empower) certain groups of actors.

3.3.1 Sales to Empower Local Elites?

By the first account, office-selling could have served the Crown by co-opting elites vested in perpetuating the system and not in overthrowing it. In this view, while the Crown loses some revenue by allowing local elites to appropriate some of the economic surplus of the territories overseas, it instead lengthened its own survival (Irigoin and Grafe 2008; Grafe and Irigoin 2012). While these were not openly stated reasons behind office-selling – at least for which there is any record – they could have served as key motivations too. The question is then, how well do they fit the data?

At first glance, there is some reason to think the Crown was – through sales – empowering local elites. Using individual-level data from officials who purchased (or were appointed) to positions in the *audiencia* from Burkholder and Chandler (1977) in the eighteenth century, it is clear that these were overwhelmingly drawn from local elites. As shown in Panel A, Table 3.3, only 10 percent of purchasers were born in Spain, with the rest (90 percent) coming from local elites. In contrast, 85 percent of appointees were Spanish, with the difference between the two statistically

TABLE 3.3 *Place of birth of purchasers versus appointees*

Individual Trait	Mean purchased	Mean appointed	Difference	P-Value
Panel A: *Audiencia* members (1687–1750)*				
Born in Spain?	0.1	0.85	−0.75	0.00
	N = 127	N = 171	(0.03)	
Panel B: *Corregimientos* and *alcaldías mayores* (1670–1750) §				
Born in Spain? Peru & Bolivia	0.81	0.85	−0.045	0.17
	N = 672	N = 162	(0.033)	
Born in Spain? Mexico	0.63	0.86	−0.23	0.00
	N = 754	N = 206	(0.035)	

* Own construction using *audiencia* data from Burkholder and Chandler (1977). § Own construction using primary collected data from colonial archives. Standard errors in parenthesis. N refers to the number of observations per category.

significant at the 95 percent level. The question is, to what extent is this reflective of a broader pattern? After all, *audiencia* purchasers represent the smallest fraction of positions sold (3.5 percent).

Therefore, Panel B of Table 3.3 instead analyzes a broader sample of individuals who purchased positions of *corregimientos* and *alcaldías* in the same period for key territories in the Empire.[16] This information comes from the approximately 2,000 sales that occurred between 1670 and 1751 collected from the colonial archives in Spain. Key for this analysis is that they contain individual information such as the name, explicit titles (e.g., military, nobility), and place of birth (e.g., from the Indies or the Peninsula) of the purchaser. Although there is less rich information for *corregidores* and *alcaldes* – likely due to their lower rank and greater number – it is possible to know their broad social status and birthplace.

The question is: Are purchasers of *corregimientos* and *alcaldías* more likely to be from Spain or from Spanish America (*criollo*)? Panel A presents the results for *corregidores* in Lima and Charcas (now Peru and Bolivia), while Panel B does so for *alcaldes mayores* in Mexico for the period 1670–1751. Overall, there is little difference in the birthplace origin of purchasers vis-à-vis appointees to provincial offices in Peru and Bolivia (81 to 85 percent) but a large one in Mexico and Guadalajara. In the latter case, appointees were much more likely to be Spanish (86 percent), while purchasers tended to be local (63 percent). The difference is a whopping 24 percentage points and statistically significant. Thus, supporting the idea that office-selling might have served to create local stakeholders in the empire in this particular period.

Yet, Figure 3.5 illustrates how these changes were only temporary, as the share of Spanish-born ministers increased exponentially after the end of sales.[17] Therefore showing that the Crown's motivation to sell positions to create buy-in among local elites might have been a short-lived one. By the mid eighteenth century, the Crown was more concerned with limiting the extent of *criollo* influence at the top of the colonial administration, rather than encouraging it. If office-selling were a tool to enhance regime survival by co-opting elites, it was a short-lived one.

---

[16] Namely, all the provinces of the *audiencia* of Lima (now Peru), Charcas (now Bolivia), Mexico (now central-southern Mexico), and Guadalajara (northern Mexico), which represent 70 percent of *corregimientos alcaldías* sold in the eighteenth century.

[17] This pattern for *audiencia* sales has been thoroughly documented by Burkholder and Chandler (1977).

3 Why Sell Offices?

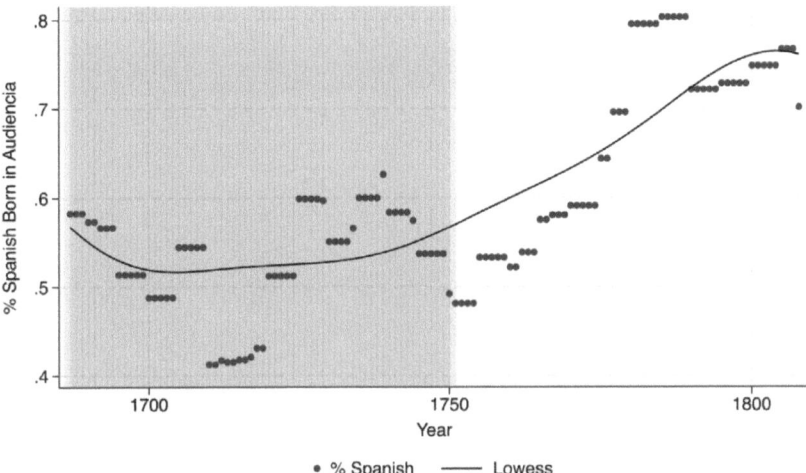

FIGURE 3.5 Type of officials: Spanish members in the *audiencia* (1687–1800)
Note: Office-selling period shaded. Source: Own construction from Burkholder and Chandler (1977).

3.3.2 Sales to Displace Traditional Recipients of Offices?

The final explanation of office-selling is that it reflected a shift in the perception of "merit" by the Crown. Instead of privileging individuals of a particular social background and connections, office-selling reflected a new utilitarian view of government. It could have also provided an opportunity for the Crown "to gain oversight, appropriate resources, and weaken the viceroys" by centralizing appointments previously in their hands (Rosenmüller 2016: 1). By wrestling away the sale of posts from viceroys, the Council of Indies and the nobility (customary recipients of these positions), it was more in control of the colonial administration.

Figure 3.6 presents the temporal trends in the social background of those ruling *corregimientos* and *alcaldías mayores* in Peru, Mexico, and Bolivia for most of the eighteenth century. Namely, whether the official holds a military title[18] or a nobility one such as that of marquis or count, or belonged to one of the main knighthood orders (*Caballero* of the *Santiago*, *Alcántara*, or *Calatrava* order).

Using this data, both panels show that the period of office-selling (shaded) exhibits the lowest share of members of the military or the

---

[18] I only consider those with a military title explicitly denoted in their *alcalde* or *corregimiento* appointment. Not whether they had military experience, as it would most clearly capture those whose career was in the military.

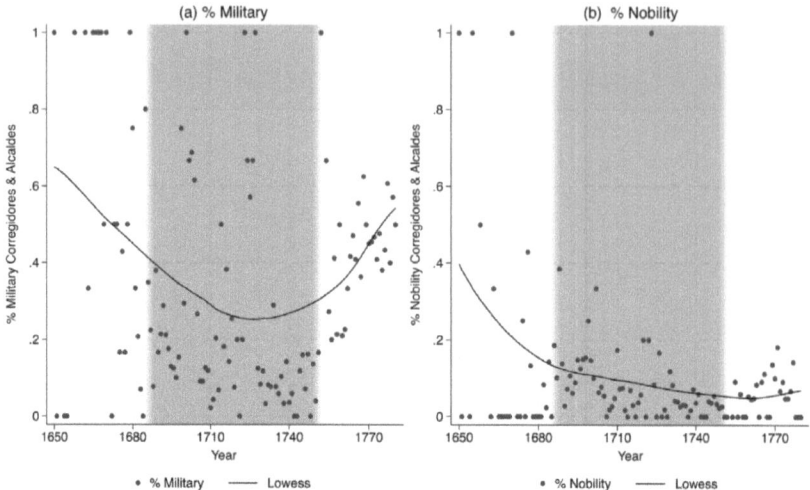

FIGURE 3.6 Military and nobility officials in *corregimientos* and *alcaldías*

Note to Figures 3.5 and 3.6. Office-selling period shaded. Figure 3.5 shows the average share of Spanish members across all the *audiencias* of the empire. Figure 3.6 plots the share of *corregidores* and *alcaldes mayores* (either bought or appointed) that are of military (a) or nobility (b) origin, between 1650 and 1780 for the provinces of what is now Mexico, Bolivia, and Peru.

nobility entering provincial positions. However, panel (a) shows the percentage of *corregidores* and *alcaldes* with military titles sharply increases with the end of sales (U-shaped pattern). In contrast, the presence of nobility *corregidores* and *alcaldes* never fully recovered, consistent with a permanent shift in the preferences and priority of the Crown as hypothesized by Rosenmüller (2016). From both panels, we can conclude that there is a *partial* undoing of the traditional notion of merit – with nobility classes permanently displaced but military individuals – already preferred prior to sales – returning and exceeding their previous levels.

The final possibility is that office-selling was instead a way to assert monarchic control vis-à-vis the viceroys. In particular, the sale of *corregimientos* and *alcaldías mayores* reduced patronage opportunities for viceroys and weaken the influence of the aristocracy and the Council of Indies, who effectively held a monopoly of the posts and assignment process.

As shown in Figure 3.6. panel b, the nobility was permanently displaced from these positions. Yet, this was likely more a *consequence* of the policy, than the *cause*. For example, the purpose of office-selling was not to intentionally limit posts to the aristocracy, if anything the Crown openly avowed to seek those "known in court" and with "appropriate qualities," namely those of high social status. The problem is that individuals lacking these traits were the ones with the highest ability and willingness to pay. Second, the fact that viceroys were sidelined was an unavoidable step in sales, still, many of the appointments required Viceregal approval, a way for the latter to extract some additional benefits from purchasers sanctioned by the Crown.

Finally, while the Crown might have gained more appointments to sell at the expense of viceroys, it often came at the cost of overall less control of its overseas administration. The difficulties in removing purchasers from office – without due compensation – and the limited ability of Madrid to actually uncover wrongdoing during these officials' tenure effectively meant a *reduction* in monarchic oversight.

In fact, a major consideration for ending sales was precisely to improve governance in the overseas administration. While sales ended at a time of peace and more balanced budgets in Madrid, it happened when the Crown was more seriously committed to improving its administration. As put by Burkholder and Chandler (1977), the end of *audiencia* sales in the mid eighteenth century was part of an empire-wide effort to "try to shift power back to Madrid" and "regain control" to improve the colonial administration.[19] A pattern supported in the data independently collected for *corregimientos* and *alcaldías* (Figure 3.6).

3.4 A REVENUE-GOVERNANCE TRADE-OFF

The chapter documented the important role of European warfare to explain the timing and number of offices sold. Yet, this explanation is limited in two ways. First, while wars spurred sales, its proceeds did not fund war. Earnings from sales were too little – relative to the military expenditures of the Spanish Crown – to shape the decision to enter or prolong wars. Instead, they were likely destined for the consumption of the royal household, or to secure favors from powerful brokers, which could help the Crown in other ways. Furthermore, despite claims to the contrary, the Crown had other sources of financing – its situation

---

[19] Along with stopping sales, there was some discussion to improve governance in the colonies by increasing wages and creating a career-based system so that "good" governors could be promoted to future posts (Moreno 1977: 604). The latter proposals never materialized.

being less dire than in previous centuries. Opting for office-selling was a policy choice.

The second limitation of war-centered explanations arises from the *composition* of the sales themselves. Some offices – *corregimientos*, *alcaldías*, and treasury positions – were disproportionately sold while others were deliberately kept off the market. Why? Despite the "urgent" need for revenue, office-selling did not take place indiscriminately enough to make revenue the overriding concern of the Crown.

Instead, it is likely that the Crown was somewhat sensitive to the protestations of the Council of Indies (and the nobility) as well as to the potential threats to the territorial integrity of the empire. Sales were concentrated in the set of offices with the lowest policy influence – those of *corregimientos*, *alcaldías mayores*, and treasuries – constituting around 90 percent of all positions sold. Due to their lower rank, it was also the set of positions that would lead to the least "trouble" for the Crown in terms of complaints from the Council of Indies or the nobility. *Corregidores* and *alcaldes* were also unlikely to endanger the survival of the empire or put a dent on the major sources of revenue from the Americas (mining, trade, and monopolies). The type of taxes collected by these officials (indigenous poll taxes) was a very small share of the Crown's revenue anyway.

The disproportionate sale of *corregimiento* and *alcaldías mayores* also shows that economic appropriation from the population – particularly indigenous – ranked low in the Crown's list of priorities. Or at least lower vis-à-vis the threats posed by foreign powers. While it knew very well that these officials would not be of the "highest quality" – to the point that they preferred not to have purchasers in key defense positions – it was clearly a lesser evil for the Crown. Albeit not for the population in the Americas.

The following chapters explore the short- and long-term consequences of this choice from the viewpoint of the colonial population.

Chapter Summary. Why did the Spanish Crown sell offices? The chapter explores the rationale behind the sale of important executive, judicial, and fiscal positions across the colonial administration. The royal justification portrays sales as a measure of last resort to meet urgent fiscal needs created by European wars. Based on the analysis of the pattern of sales and the fiscal situation of the Crown at the time, this chapter argues that this account falls short in two ways. First, proceeds from sales were unlikely to be destined to fund war directly, nor was office-selling the only financing option available. Instead, and second, the timing, frequency, and type of positions sold reveal that the Crown was more selective than commonly acknowledged. Privileging the sale of positions that allowed it to seize economic surplus from the colonial (indigenous) populations without jeopardizing the territorial integrity of the empire by selling geopolitically sensitive posts. These findings question the extent to which office-selling was the sole product of the Crown's irrationality, or to create buy-in by local elites, or as a way to chiefly weaken the power of viceroys at the time.

4

Office-Selling-Turned-Venality

Chapter 3 explored the limits to wartime-revenue explanations for office-selling. While key to understanding the timing and intensity of sales, the Crown harbored serious concerns about the suitability and motivations of some of the purchasers and their consequences for governance in the colonies. For this reason, it privileged the sale of positions with the lowest policy impact and outright avoided the sale of those most geopolitically sensitive. Was the Crown correct in doubting purchasers? This chapter and Chapter 5 further examines the revenue-governance trade-offs posed by office-selling.

***

Did office-selling worsen the quality of the colonial administration at the time? From Chapters 2 and 3, it is clear that purchasers had different social backgrounds than appointees: more likely to be *criollos* in the *audiencia* and less likely to be from the nobility and the military among *corregimientos* and *alcaldías*. But were they "worse" for the colonial population, particularly indigenous?

Opinions on the matter stood divided. On one side were those who believed that sales resulted in worse colonial governance by granting positions to those lacking "merit" (Moreno 1977: 75), "competence and probity" (Lohmann 1957: 130), or the "preparation or vocation" to serve (Sanz-Tapia 2009: 43). In other words, it would lead to "tyrants or thieves" (Moreno 1977: 71). The view was shared by the Council of Indies: Those who purchased offices would be the "worst, and most ambitious, from which we could only expect but the oppression of their subjects."[1] Other contemporaries concurred, arguing that the ideal traits for an official could not be found in those who purchased positions (Juan and Ulloa 1978 [1749]: 94). These criticisms centered on selection: Bad *types* of individuals actively seeking positions in the colonial government for self-enrichment purposes, often at the expense of the indigenous population, the royal coffers, or both.

The focus of these critiques on selection comes from the fact that it was the most realistic way for the Crown to influence the performance of colonial officials (Eissa-Barroso 2017: 135). Given the Spanish Crown was never able to fully monitor and control its officials abroad[2] – due to a combination of difficult communications, low wages, and the lack of a fully institutionalized bureaucracy – the only way it could steer policy was at the "selection stage" (Eissa-Barroso 2017). Case in point was the careful choosing of viceroys by Philip V, credited with a diminished prevalence of corruption scandals in the viceroyalties' courts at the time (Eissa-Barroso 2017: 142).

However, in principle, office-selling could have also been detrimental to the quality of the colonial administration by providing greater incentives for extraction than otherwise (not by selection). Namely, that the monetary transaction itself gave buyers a license and incentive to extract they would otherwise not have. Similarly, by selling offices, the Crown would lose the moral high-ground to punish officials for self-dealing, as it was effectively engaging in similar activities. Finally, the transactional nature of office-selling meant that buyers could not be removed from office without reimbursement, limiting the Crown's ability to punish wrongdoing. Combined, changes in the profile (selection) and in the incentives of buyers could undermine the functioning of the colonial administration.

Alternatively, office-selling may have had no impact on the colonial government whatsoever or may even have had a positive one. Despite representing a different class of officials, their performance might not have changed at all. To start, it is unclear that the quality of colonial officials was ever "good" in the Empire. Certainly not from today's standards. Moreover, from the viewpoint of the indigenous population, abuse and exploitation have always been there. First by *encomenderos* and conquistadores, and later by *corregidores* and *alcaldes*. Given that

---

[1] AGI, Mexico 1970, *Extracto de Consulta hecha por el Consejo de Indias en 21 de Agosto de 1737, y órdenes del Ministerio de Hazienda sobre Venefizios de Empleos de Indias*.

[2] This was a common problem of empires at the time. Gailmard (2017) argues that agency problems in the British empire in North America was a key reason behind the emerge of separation of powers in the latter.

the traits considered "good" or "best" suited for office at the time – noble lineage, prudence, loyalty, manners, or social capital – may not be necessarily associated with higher honesty, moderation, or a better managerial capacity, this is a serious possibility. In fact, having the wealth necessary to purchase a position may actually be more likely to reduce the marginal value of economic exploitation than that predicted by place of birth, manners, or "being known" at court (social standing). Therefore, even if sales changed the profile of colonial officials, it might have been for the better.

The chapter adjudicates these claims with the available data. Were sales detrimental to the *quality* of the colonial administration? According to its critics, sales attracted a particular *type* of profit-seeking official: "ambitious," with execrable behavior and generally "undeserving," which for the Council of Indies meant those not belonging to the nobility or military classes. Yet, are sheer differences in social background and careers enough to show that purchasers would have behaved differently in office than appointees?

This chapter examines this claim through two statistical exercises. The first exercise estimates the likelihood that times of fiscal distress caused by wars attracted a particular type of buyers. During these wars, the Crown was much less scrupulous and less likely to properly vet purchasers, with all its associated downsides. If this is when officials with "bad" traits are disproportionately entering office, it is consistent with them taking advantage of the fiscal desperation of the Crown. Empirically, we should then observe that the profile of purchasers worsens as the fiscal distress increases with the length of war.

The second exercise complements the first by testing whether purchasers with "bad traits" are disproportionately flocking to positions with higher potential profits from office. Using the profitability rankings introduced in Chapter 2, it is possible to know where *corregidores* and *alcaldes* expect to make more profits during their term. If those the Council deems "bad" are disproportionately buying these positions, then the Council's complaints have some basis. Purchasers did not just want to serve in any office – they were looking for the profits.

But what and why are some traits considered "good" or "bad" in the first place? Section 4.1 presents the philosophical and theological reasons behind the "ideal" type of official at the time. Section 4.2 turns to political economy arguments as to why office-selling undermined the selection of these "ideal" officials. Section 4.3 presents the evidence from the statistical exercises, while Section 4.4 concludes by discussing the implications of these findings.

4.1 "IDEAL" OFFICIALS IN THE SEVENTEENTH- AND EIGHTEENTH-CENTURY SPANISH EMPIRE

The late seventeenth and eighteenth centuries view of merit was one based on the idea of innate characteristics tied to social origins (Rosenmüller 2016: 2). Although there were other "general" requirements common to all those serving in office, stemming from their gender (male), age (at least twenty-six years old), being a vassal of the Crown, and not having committed crimes against religion (Lohman-Villena 1957), high(er) social status and connections to the Crown were a basic precondition for office.

In this view, "worthiness" was passed through generations in a way that privileged the nobility and those of higher standing. It is no coincidence that the titles of *corregidores* and *alcaldes* listed as merits of an individual those of his relatives – grandparents, uncles, and fathers. In the same way, one's performance in office put on the line the reputation of the whole family. This view of merit also underpins many of the formal and informal requirements to occupy office in the Spanish empire. Such as residency conditions, place of birth, social capital, and/or past employment.

For example, a key criteria for colonial officials was to be "known in Court". While this is correlated with social status – the higher the status, the higher the visibility – it also helped keep appointments within a class and relay private information to the Crown, which could be used in selecting better officials for the position. Absent this information, the Crown would be selecting officials "in the dark."

Drawing from a certain social class also worked to discourage "newcomers" and limit the pool of potential officials. That is, until office-selling came along. Indeed, as hinted in Chapter 3, in 1650, around 80 percent of the Crown's appointments (on average) were to individuals with a military or nobility title. Precisely those who fulfilled the requirements of innate merit and from which the Crown was likely to have better information. This share would steadily decline throughout the first half of the eighteenth century – while sales were in place – and only started to recover after sales ended in 1751.

These requirements were especially germane to the high-level positions studied here, such as those of *corregidor*, *alcalde*, or *audiencia* members. Figure 4.1 presents a sixteenth-century characterization of these officials in the *audiencia* of Lima (now Peru) through the eyes of Guaman Poma de Ayala, an indigenous nobleman and contemporary illustrator.

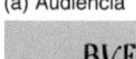

FIGURE 4.1 Depictions of *audiencia* council members and *corregidores* in sixteenth-century Peru.

Panel (a): Members of the civil chamber (*oidores*) in the *Audiencia* of Lima, XVI century. From: Guamán Poma de Ayala, Felipe, fl. 1613. Nueva crónica y buen gobierno: (codex péruvien illustré)/Felipe Guamán Poma de Ayala. Paris: Université de Paris, Institut d'ethnologie, 1936. xxviii, 1168 [i.e., 1178]. Source: www.memoriachilena.gob.cl/602/w3-article-74476.html. Panel (b): *Corregidor* of a Peruvian province in the sixteenth century with his scrivener. Nueva crónica y buen gobierno: (codex péruvien illustré)/Felipe Guamán Poma de Ayala. Paris: Université de Paris, Institut d'ethnologie, 1936. xxviii, 1168 [i.e., 1178] p. Source: www.memoriachilena.gob.cl/602/w3-article-74477.html.

In panel (a) he depicts the members of the *audiencia* in session, while panel (b) portrays a Peruvian *corregidor* with his scrivener (panel b).

Why was social status an important requirement for holding office? According to Rosenmüller (2016), deep theological reasons associated with the notion of distributive justice of Thomas Aquinas underpinned the preference for the nobility. This coincides with the view of distinguished jurists[3] as well as the arguments presented in primary documents by the Council of Indies. The latter, in voicing their displeasure with sales, argued that the administration of justice was part of the Divine

---

[3] Solórzano y Pereira. Politica Indiana VI. Xiii. 2, 3, 4; p. 1 (cited in Parry 1953, p. 5).

Mandate of the Sovereign that could not be sold away, implicitly advocating for the status quo. Yet, beyond particular conceptions of justice, merit, and sovereignty, there were also political economy reasons why selecting from a limited pool had advantages to the Spanish Crown. I explore each in detail.

4.1.1 Dependence on Royal Favor

The main advantage of limiting appointments to social classes connected to the Crown was that it could incentivize behavior that did not contravene its rulings or interests overseas. By virtue of controlling nobles' reputation[4] and officials' career path (particularly military) via shared social networks, the Crown would be in a better position to incentivize colonial officials to not commit "offenses" against their Majesty or "wrongdoings" – primarily actions that undermined the royal treasury or endangered the Empire's territories.

There were two main ways through which this took place. First, by making their future career path and social advantage dependent on royal favor, officials might have been naturally more aligned with the Crown's goals and interests and find it too costly to contravene the wishes and interests of His Majesty. For instance, when appointing viceroys to the Empire, Philip V sought individuals "personally attached to him who were selfless and zealous about royal service" (Eissa-Barroso 2017: 135). Again, the concern was less on impeccable behavior in office but on reducing the likelihood of egregious incidents against the Crown. The underlying idea was that "dependence on royal favor [is] more likely to guarantee moderation in office" (Eissa-Barroso 2017: 146). Being in the good graces of the King and the court more generally would guarantee future appointments and commissions for the current official, his descendants, and extended family.

As visible in the titles of *corregidores* and *alcaldes mayores* sold, many of these appointments were a reward for past services of fathers, uncles, or even grandparents. For example, the main merits of Don José Mudarra y de la Peña making him worthy of an *Alcaldia Mayor* in Mexico in 1698 were the "merits" of his father, grandparents, uncles, and "other ascendants" who had served for many years, sacrificed their lives in the King's service, in fulfillment of their noble obligations.[5] In fact, a concern raised

---

[4] Namely, being "in favor" or "in the graces" of His Majesty.
[5] AGI, Mexico, 1221. José Mudarra y de la Peña 1698.

by those opposing sales was that loyal servants of the Crown would be passed over by opportunists who, through monetary offers, were able to secure postings in the colonial government.[6]

To the extent that dependence on royal favor was a real consideration, it would naturally be stronger for those in the nobility and military classes, with the latter having greater career incentives and the former more social-reputational costs. In some cases a military career was crucial for positions exposed to internal rebellions (e.g., rebellious provinces in the Andean highlands) or in close contact with foreign powers.[7] For example, the appointment of *Capitán* Don Juan Francisco Cortes explicitly stated the "necessity that this post be filled by an individual with military experience for the security and defense of that land" who has served His Majesty more than twenty years in the army and the *armada*, among others. Yet, individuals with a military title were also a favored group to rule non-threatened areas, particularly in the post-sales period.

For these reasons, office-buyers were viewed with suspicion, as they owed their position and future career to their own money and not to the Crown.

4.1.2 "Good" Character

In addition to dependence on royal favor, the ideal individual would be someone of a higher social class, not from humble origins or "mechanical" occupations. Having "worked with their hands" disqualified an individual to serve in a position imparting justice (Rosenmüller 2017a: 5). The requirement was of such importance that viceroys often used the excuse of low social status to deny approving positions appointed by the King. Such is the case of Ramon Espiguel de Ávila, a Knight from the Order of Santiago, who had purchased the *corregimiento* of Mexico City in 1708 but whom the viceroy claimed "all Mexico knew" that this individual had served as a cook assistant and pastry chef.[8] Interestingly, there were no special education requirements of being a *letrado*, except for the case of *audiencia* members, who by the nature of their jobs, ought to be versed in legal matters (Burkholder and Chandler 1977).

---

[6] Céspedes del Castillo, Guillermo: Historia Social de España y América, Barcelona, 1961, tomo III, pag. 838; Lorente, Sebastian: Historia del Perú bajo los Borbones, Lima, 1871, p. 38. Cited by Moreno Cebrián 1977: 80.

[7] See Chapter 3 for the list of territories and provinces considered under foreign threat or prone to internal strife.

[8] AGI, Mexico 1970, Carta del Virrey.

The prevailing view was that the "select provenance" of high-status individuals made them "less likely to accept bribes," a hallmark of corruption at the time (Rosenmüller 2017: 6). Similarly, as previewed in the loyalty discussion, "good" traits were transmitted by one's lineage or their ascendancy: The good deeds or traits of relatives made one equally likely to possess them. In contrast, office-selling allowed "aspiring middle-class groups that had money but lacked a noble pedigree" to enter office (Rosenmüller 2017: 5). In their view, these groups' "ambition to advance beyond the social status they were born into" (Rosenmüller 2017: 5) was a great disqualifier for public office. Ambition also figures negatively in the Crown's internal correspondence, when it worried that under sales "only the worse and most ambitious individuals would seek offices in the first place."[9]

4.1.3 Social Networks

However, beyond mere classism, social status and connections could also serve other roles. In particular, it was the main way for the Crown to obtain information from office seekers. The requirement of belonging to "known" families (*de gente conocida*) – essentially a requirement of belonging to certain social groups – also guaranteed that the Crown would have some information about this official. For example, the sale of the *alcaldia mayor* of Malinalco to Don Pedro Gonzales de Mores was approved by the King on May 11, 1713 only after it was ascertained that Don Pedro was of Spanish origin, born in the villa Pozuelo del Rey in Spain, from "known people," was forty-six years old, and at the moment was a resident of Mexico City.[10] This information showed that Don Pedro had an acceptable level of social connections –no egregious crimes – thus acceptable for this rather low-level position.

"Being known" was thus one of the few mechanisms to gather an individual's information, a type of background check, at a time when information gathering was slow and difficult. Albeit this information might have been poorly correlated with performance in office at the time, it came along with other social markers (place of residence, connections)

---

[9] AGI, Mexico 1970, *Extracto de Consulta hecha por el Consejo de Indias en 21 de Agosto de 1737, y órdenes del Ministerio de Hazienda sobre Venefizios de Empleos de Indias*.

[10] AGI, Mexico 1970, *Informes de Pedro Gonzales de Mores, en que solicita la futura de la Alcaldia Mayor de Malinalco por 400 doblones*.

such that it could impose some reputational costs on the individual if it did not exert "moderation" in office.

4.1.4 Place of Birth

Another important way which kept the pool of officials small and within a social stratum was through explicit rules forbidding officials to rule the territories they were born in. This meant that those born overseas, even if from Spanish parents (known as Spanish-Americans – *Españoles Americanos*, or later called *Criollos*), were naturally disadvantaged for the highest-ranking positions (*audiencia*) as they would most likely be born in the territory they were seeking to rule (Burkholder and Chandler 1977). In the same vein, officials (particularly *audiencia* members) needed a permit to marry someone from the district they rule and needed to not have immediate family in positions they may deal with in office (Lohman-Villena 1957), further working against the aspirations of many *criollos*. The idea that local ties would prevent officials from fully performing their duties in office and being disloyal towards the Crown was one of the main ways in which the Spanish Crown limited the entry of local elites to the most important positions in the Empire's government. While some at Court might have believed that those born in the colonies were "less capable," this was not the main driver behind the *criollo* exclusion policy (Burkholder and Chandler 1977).

4.1.5 Unacceptable Behavior

Through these mechanisms – dependence on royal favor, social networks, family ascendancy, and place of birth – instances of "wrongdoing" in the administration could be lessened. Whereby wrongdoing was understood as behavior "disloyal" to the Crown or of causing "harm" to its interests, albeit what this meant changed over time. Examples of wrongdoing ranged from accepting bribes in exchange for judicial rulings at the expense of the royal treasury; the outrageous treatment of the indigenous population; or to engage in treason by aiding foreign enemies, to name a few.

Strictly speaking, wrongdoing did not mean that officeholders were not to profit from their position, for example, by accepting "some" gifts, or engage in "some" illicit commerce with foreign powers, to name a few possibilities. Everybody understood that the official was appointed to benefit economically from it. It was only profit in "excess" that was considered against his majesty's interests. For example, Juan and

Ulloa (1978 [1749]), while arguing in favor of appointing officials, stated that the expectation is not for the latter to not exploit the indigenous peoples at all, but only to do so in "moderation." For them, "[appointees] might exploit the Indians to some degree, [but] they would not be as tyrannical or unruly as the present appointees [purchasers], who, from the moment they are appointed, think only of the wealth they will accumulate during the five years they will hold office" (p. 94). Against "ambition," "moderation" was key.

Now, what constituted "moderation" versus "egregious" excesses is not clearly established (probably purposefully), with possible geographical and temporal variation. Yet, from the text in the appointment documents, the numerous inspections (*visitas*) and from the opinions of the Council of Indies, it is clear that there were standards of what the Crown and the Council considered acceptable – with departures from the latter clearly punished even if symbolically (Eagle 2017: 103). "Disloyalty" was a serious charge that even those who would have the greatest reasons to disavow the Crown – such as the Indigenous population – felt offended by such charges (Juan and Ulloa 1978 [1749]). Acts that deprived the Crown of its due revenue were considered disloyalty, for example.

What is relevant for the context of the seventeenth- and eighteenth-century Spanish Empire is that the restrictions of social status and place of birth likely served as mechanisms to align colonial officials' behavior with those of the Crown; facilitate the screening of colonial officials and transmission of private information; and police the behavior of key officials in the Spanish Empire. The visibility, notoriety, and dependence on royal favor of individuals of higher social status might have deterred egregious violations of existing rules. A similar case is that of seventeenth-century Britain, where appointing high social status individuals was optimal in a context of poor information and monitoring since it allows the monarch to "police behavior" by choosing individuals with higher reputation costs in the form of social capital (Allen 2005, 161).

The question is, to what extent did office-selling made more (or less) likely these traits among colonial officials?

4.2 CAN OFFICE-SELLING SELECT "GOOD" OFFICIALS?

There were at least three reasons why office-selling could undermine the selection of "ideal" officials. The first, given by the Council of Indies, focused on the fact that purchasers were inherently unlikely to perform well in office because credit constraints would price out good officials. The second, emphasizing characteristics of the position itself – argued that office-selling could lead to positive outcomes if the position's returns were fixed (salaried). Namely, if the officials could not profit from it. This was Jeremy Bentham's (1825) view. Finally, if purchasers could not choose positions that capitalized on their own networks and skills, office-selling might have had little impact on performance.

4.2.1 Credit Constraints

According to the Council of Indies – in a long memorial chiding the King for selling *audiencia* posts[11] – there were only three circumstances that would justify the need to sell positions of justice. First, if the purchaser had the desirable qualities (*idoneidad del sujeto*). Second, if the price was not excessive, and third, if sales were due to public necessity. For the Council – quoting Saint Thomas de Aquinas' Letter to the Duchess of Brabant – ideal officials were "poor" ones. A notion that effectively precluded any purchasers from ever being "good."

Beyond moral and theological arguments, the Council pointed to a more general fact that "good" but credit-constrained officials could be priced out of the market for offices. Namely, that office-selling would lead to individuals with "merit" but economically constrained to be displaced by those able to pay but who did not always fulfill the desired traits of "competence and probity" (Lohman Villena 1957: 130).[12] Financial constraints would be specially binding for the case of military officials, who could be incentivized to perform in office but who might lack the ability to gather the large sums needed to pay for the position. This constraint also applied to the Council's favored class (the nobility), which did not always possess the most liquid assets in the way merchants did, instead living off their rents (i.e., from properties or loans, for example). Resulting in these groups being displaced by more "liquid" buyers.

---

[11] See AGI, Mexico 1970. *Extracto de Consulta hecha por el Consejo de Indias en 21 de Agosto de 1737, y Ordenes del Ministerio de Hazienda sobre Venefizios de Empleos de Indias* (original notation).

[12] Work by Hollyer (2009) formally shows that when offices are sold, credit-constrained but high-quality officials may be left out of office due to their inability to pay.

4.2.2 Rent Availability

The second mechanism through which office-selling opened the door to "worse" officials is if the position in question was compensated via "fees"[13] and not salaries. In principle, officials in the *audiencia*, *gobernadores*, treasury officials, *corregidores*, and *alcaldes* were all entitled to a yearly fixed wage. In practice, this was heavily taxed, paid late or not at all, confiscated during emergencies, and, as shown by officials' correspondence, ultimately insufficient to cover the travel, subordinates' wages, and living expenses associated with the positions. In other words, wages were low, which, coupled with the lack of guarantees for future appointments once the term in office concluded (for *corregidores* and *alcaldes* in particular), meant that officials had either little incentives to exert effort (inefficiency) or instead tried to obtain returns via other means (exploitation). In either case, the result may be detrimental to the performance of the colonial bureaucracy.

The underlying principle is that *if* there were ways to profit from office and salaries are guaranteed, purchasers would be more likely to take "care" of them than otherwise. Yet, as documented in Chapter 2, many positions in the empire's administration allowed for sizeable side-gains from office – for example, by exploiting the indigenous population, or expecting bribes from illicit commerce. In these circumstances, purchasers are indeed expecting significant returns from exploiting their position and they are willing to bid "high enough" to get it.

4.2.3 Improved Matching

In addition to purchasers "not being poor" and earning their wage by the equivalent of "fees" in Spanish America, buyers could also select into the positions that maximize their profits. Prior to sales, appointees were less able to choose the places that matched their skills and networks – that is, self-select. Officials would be as likely to be sent to Riobamba, in Ecuador or to Conchucos, in Peru, depending on the positions soon to vacate. In contrast, office-selling allowed individuals to choose the position to bid for, even before the position vacates (*futura*). While officials could certainly lobby the Crown (or the Council of Indies) prior to sales, it was no guarantee that their desired position would be awarded, as it

---

[13] Bentham (1838–43 [1825]: 247). The argument is that if it was rewarded with fees, it would have incentivized exploitation of the position. This was also applicable to non-fee awarding positions (salaried) as there was no incentive to overexploit the position.

depended on royal whims, "who" was in favor at the time, and when the office would vacate.

An illustrative example comes from the period after office-selling ends in 1751, when the Crown restored patronage. In 1757, the *corregimiento* of Arequipa was soon to vacate and the list of individuals seeking the position (via patronage) who had sent a letter stating their interest and merits was thirty-seven.[14] If at random (which was not), there was a 1/37 chance of being appointed to that office, thus it was hard to know for certain what would happen. What many office-seekers did instead was to send files to multiple positions in the hope that one would land – whether that was the one that maximized its own abilities and connections was not guaranteed, introducing uncertainty to the appointment process.

In sum, there are at least three mechanisms through which office-selling could worsen the *type* of officials in the colonial administration. First, if individuals with the traits necessary to perform in office are credit constrained and cannot purchase the positions. Second, if the position in question is compensated via "fees," meaning they could recoup what they paid by exploiting their subjects. Third, if office-selling facilitates better matches between the officials' networks and skills and the potential profit of specific positions (sorting). For example, a purchaser with merchant connections could better capitalize on them by buying a *corregidor* office with high potential for *repartimiento* to sell leftover inventory, or contraband in coastal areas, to name some profitable matches.

4.2.4 Beyond Selection: Incentivizing Extraction

Aside from changing the type of officials, office-selling may also worsen performance, but not necessarily due to selection. Instead, office-selling may directly impact the incentives of provincial rulers to exploit their office. This could be due to three reasons: The first is that sales implicitly gave buyers a "license to extract" to recoup their investment which they did not have before. For example, in *Secret News*, Juan and Ulloa (1978 [1749]: 95) stated that appointing officials in exchange "[...] for a money payment is the same as approving or consenting to the extortions perpetrated on the Indians [...] Even if these officials have the highest character, they still become corrupt." In their view, the mere fact of selling the position legitimized extraction from the population, regardless of their individual traits.

---

[14] AGI, Lima 476. *Pretendientes a corregidor de la ciudad de Arequipa año 1757.*

The second reason is the one provided by the Council of Indies, who citing the Roman Emperor Severus Alexander, argued that office-selling would make the Crown reluctant to punish purchasers engaging in the same type of self-dealings as the Crown, with this lenience being a cause for unhappiness in Republics.[15] Office-selling would lead to poor governance, but not due to a fundamental difference in the traits of those appointed and those who bought their position.[16] Rather, it is the monetary transaction itself the source of evil. This is the same concern voiced by other historians, namely, that the monetary transaction "worsened greed" by implicitly encouraging profiting from the position (Ramos Gomez 1985: 174) given that buyers would need to recoup their investment (Lohman Villena 1957: 130).

Finally, office-selling made it challenging for the Crown to use removal from office as a deterrent for misconduct. Although all officials served under the permission and grace of His Majesty, individuals who purchased their position could not be removed without monetary compensation. This resulted in the reinstatement of corrupt officials, despite evidence of wrongdoing, due to the inability of the Crown to reimburse them (Burkholder and Chandler 1977). Buyers, aware of these limitations, believed the likelihood of removal to be low to nonexistent.

In what follows I set aside the role of incentives for a moment and focus on the consequences of office-selling for the profile of officials we observe. From the standpoint of the *local population*, were the traits of colonial officials associated with more or less appropriation of economic surplus?

4.3 UNCOVERING SELECTION IN THE DATA

Chapters 2 and 3 showed that purchasers are indeed "different" from appointees, are they necessarily *worse*? Albeit it is difficult to predict behavior (in this case, performance in office) just by looking at the traits of buyers, two statistical exercises can help us detect whether particular types are sorting into particular offices.

---

[15] AGI, Mexico 1970, *Extracto de Consulta hecha por el Consejo de Indias en 21 de Agosto de 1737, y órdenes del Ministerio de Hazienda sobre Venefizios de Empleos de Indias*.

[16] This is the stated logic for why tax farmers who purchase their position tend to overtax: the monetary payment provides an incentive for increased extraction, but it may not entail a change in the type of official.

The analysis relies on the characteristics of individuals purchasing *corregimientos* and *alcaldías* between 1670 and 1751 as well as from those doing the same across the eleven *audiencias* of the empire.[17] The difference with Chapter 3 is that instead of comparing the characteristics and social background of purchasers versus appointees, the comparison is now only among purchasers. The goal being to examine whether "bad" traits – at least according to the Council – are much more likely to be found at certain times and in certain places. Are "undeserving" purchasers sorting into positions with greater rents and at times of greater permissibility by the Crown (war)? If so, the Council might have been correct in its distrust.

Following the discussion earlier, I focus on traits associated with "ideal" officials at the time. In the case of *audiencia* members, these are three: First, purchasers' place of birth. Were they born in the *audiencia* they seek to rule (Native)? Second, did the *audiencia* member acquire a "waiver" to enter office? Namely, exemptions from rules forbidding local connections through marriage, family ties, property ownership, or age limits. Finally, was the purchaser removed from office later in his term – due to blatant evidence of corruption? In the case of *corregimientos* and *alcaldías*, I use measures of social status – nobility, knighthood, or military titles – the main indicator of "merit" for the Council of Indies.

4.3.1 Type of Purchasers in the Shadow of War

Figure 4.2 presents the estimates from an OLS regression of the length of key wars[18] and the likelihood that purchasers exhibit the most undesirable traits for the Council – ruling the *audiencia* born in (native), being eventually removed from seat, and requesting waivers. The reason to focus on war is that these are precisely times in which the Crown is more likely to overlook red flags among purchasers due to the fiscal distress these events induced.

As shown, an additional year at war increases the likelihood of the purchaser entering office being eventually removed from office due to misconduct in 0.014 or 4 percent of the mean. The same is true for waivers,

---

[17] There were 2,019 appointments to *corregimientos* and *alcaldías* between 1670 and 1751 in Mexico, Peru, and Bolivia. Of these, 1,499 were sold and 520 appointed (25.8 percent). There were 380 members entering the *audiencias* from 1687 to 1751. Of these, 160 purchased their position (42 percent).

[18] The war of the Spanish Succession (1701–14) and the war of Jenkin's Ear/Austrian Succession (1739–48).

4 Office-Selling-Turned-Venality

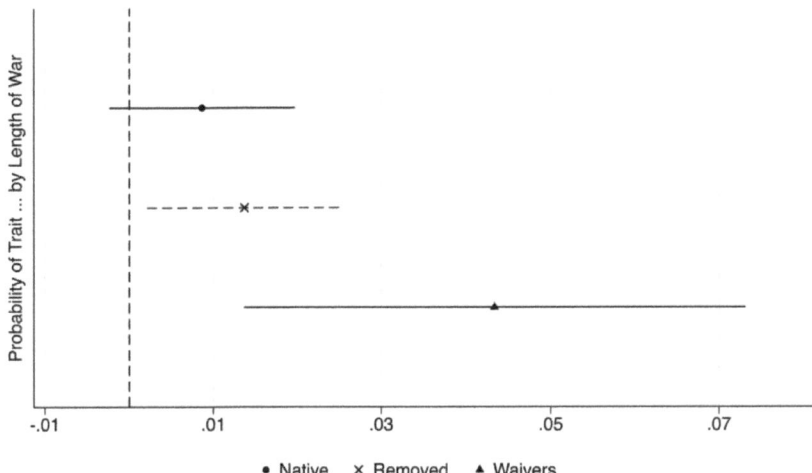

FIGURE 4.2 Key wars and characteristics of *audiencia* members (1687–1751)

Note: OLS estimates with 95 percent Confidence Intervals. See estimating Equation (2) and full results in Appendix to Chapter 4 (Table A.4). Table A.4. Includes *audiencia* fixed effects and standard errors clustered by year. Wars considered: Spanish Succession (1701–14), Austrian Succession (1739–48).

which for each passing year increase the average number in 0.043 or 4 percent of the mean. In contrast, there is little difference by place of birth of *audiencia* purchasers: They appear as likely to enter irrespectively of the year at war. In any case, evidence from the *audiencias* (a limited set of sales) can tell us only so much. The key is then to examine whether we see similar patterns in the sales of *corregimientos* and *alcaldías mayores*.

From Chapter 2 and 3 we know that appointees are more likely to have higher social status. The question here is: Are the presence of these traits higher (lower) during lengthier wars?

Consistent with results for the *audiencia*, Figure 4.3 shows that individuals with traits the Council associated with more "ambition" were more likely to enter office during long and protracted military conflicts. The longer the war dragged on (and the Crown became more fiscally strained), the more likely it was to allow "unsavory" characters who would be nonetheless willing to pay. Across all categories, the coefficients are negative and generally within conventional levels of statistical significance. In particular, an additional year at war reduced the likelihood of a titled individual to purchase this position in 0.007 or 3.2 percent of the mean. This is mostly driven by the sharp reduction of purchasers from the knighthood orders in Spain (Santiago, Calatrava, or Alcántara,

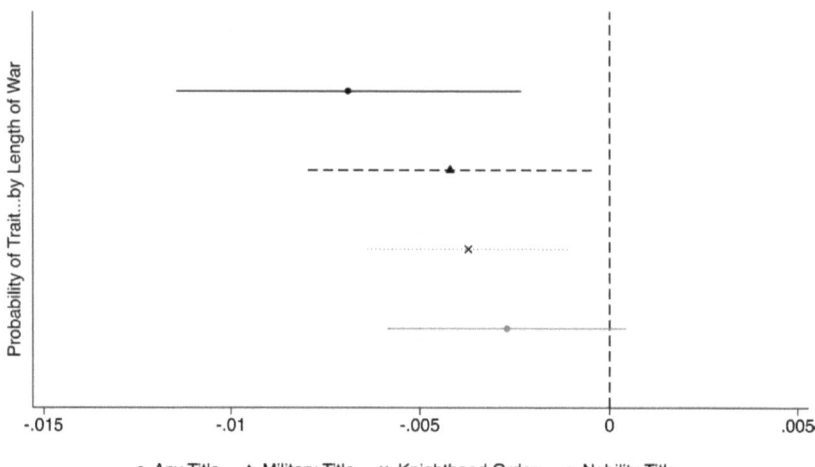

FIGURE 4.3 Key wars and social status of *corregidores* and *alcaldes* (1670–1751)

Note: OLS estimates with 95 percent Confidence Intervals. See estimating equation and full results in Appendix to Chapter 4 (Table A.5). Includes *province* fixed effects and standard errors clustered by province. Wars considered: Spanish Succession (1701–14), Austrian Succession (1739–48).

primarily), with a 0.004 reduction or 6.2 percent of its mean. However, it is visible across all categories.

In all, while purchasers were much less likely to hold a title in the first place, this was even *less* likely the longer the war and the more fiscally desperate the Crown became. Likely due to the fact that war lowered the bar they had to clear to enter office in the first place and facilitated *sorting* – buying the positions that would best match their skills.

One alternative explanation for these results is that this is instead driven by availability. As the pool of titled individuals is lower during wars – likely occupied in the war effort – they are simply appearing to be less numerous. To further distinguish whether this is the product of a more lenient Crown, or just simply less officials available, I then turn to the characteristics of the positions they bought.

4.3.2 Wars, Province Profitability, and *Types* of Colonial Officials

Building on the measures of profitability introduced in Chapter 2 – namely, the three-category anonymous ranked index – I examine whether more profitable positions attract buyers with "worse" traits as wars drag

4 Office-Selling-Turned-Venality 89

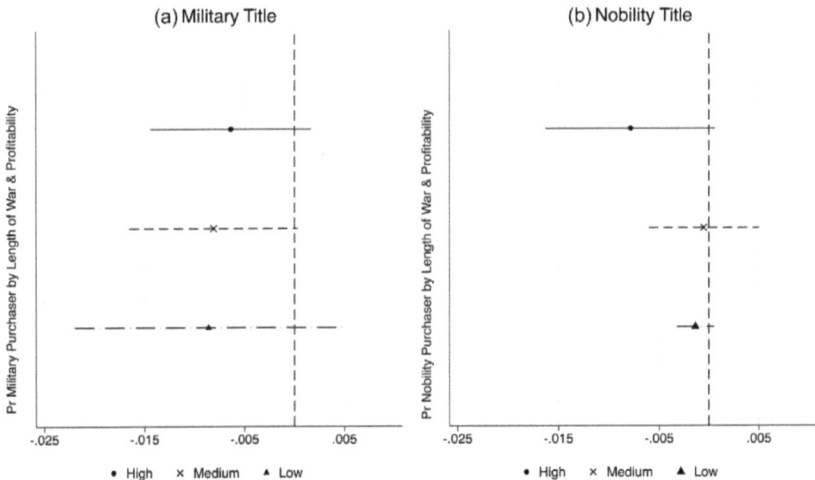

FIGURE 4.4 Key wars and social status of purchasers by office profitability

Note: OLS estimates with 95 percent Confidence Intervals. Figure 4.4 displays the coefficients of estimating Equation (2) of the Appendix to Chapter 4 in three different samples: those with high, medium, and low profitability, depending on 1770 secret rankings. *Corregimientos* and *alcaldías* of Peru, Bolivia, and Mexico (1670–1751).

on. If so, this would be consistent with sorting or selection taking place. For example, if individuals of lower social status or lacking a military career disproportionately choose offices with high profit potential and pay higher prices for them at times of war, this is not random. It is about buying the positions they are more likely to profit from.

As in the previous exercise, the analysis accounts for the possibility that certain characteristics of the province – say wages, prestige, career prospects, or geopolitical importance – may correlate with the measures of profitability and the prevalence of certain types of individuals by including provincial fixed effects. Based on the three-category ranking (high, medium, and low), it is possible to see how the effect of wars – approximating the Crown's fiscal desperation – changes the profile of colonial officials. Absent sorting or selection, there should be no statistical differences in the profile of officials for the same position by level of fiscal distress of the Crown, particularly for the same level of expected profitability.

Instead Figure 4.4(a) starts by presenting how the likelihood of a purchaser with a military title is consistently negative as wars drag on, for all levels of profitability. In terms of magnitude, each additional year of war reduces in around 0.006 the likelihood of a purchaser with a military title, or 3.8 percent of the mean. Given the average length of these wars in the sample is three years,[19] this translates into a 12 percent reduction of this mean. The overall interpretation is that military officials were generally displaced, regardless of the level of profitability of the province.

In contrast, Figure 4.4(b) shows that the displacement of the nobility is more pronounced precisely for the most profitable positions. While for medium- and low-profit provinces, the length of wars changes little the likelihood of a member of the nobility buying an office, it does significantly reduce them for the most profitable ones. In other words, purchasers were less likely to hold a nobility title, particularly for the positions where they could profit the most and during longer wars.

The fact that higher profitability goes hand in hand with "worse" profiles is consistent with the main concerns of seventeenth- and eighteenth-century jurists opposing sales. For example, Castillo de Bobadilla (1759) argued that office-selling incentivized individuals lacking the credentials but "brimming with ambition," to be the ones most likely to be selected by offering higher prices.[20] If buyers were not actively sorting, we would not expect the profile of buyers to differ much among highly profitable positions and those less so, particularly when the Crown is more fiscally desperate and less likely to vet candidates' profiles. But that is what happened, particularly for those with a nobility title: not only are they less likely to purchase offices, they are also less likely to do so for the most profitable ones and when the Crown is most desperate.

While this is of course not evidence of their behavior or performance in office – the subject of Chapters 5 and 6 – it provides evidence of sorting. Purchasers lacking the career and social status not only disproportionately bought offices but also flocked to the most profitable ones at times in which the Crown was more desperate. Displacing certain social groups along the way, particularly those from the nobility and military classes.

From the viewpoint of the population in the Americas, the prospects of being ruled by these purchasers were ominous. Not only were these individuals less attached via reputation and social constraints to the Crown, but their mode of entry, when the Crown was more fiscally desperate and for positions most profitable, suggest their motivation was never in holding office per se. Instead, the prospect of monetary gains

---

[19] Because provinces are sold at distinct points in time, the length of war between them varies.
[20] Castillo de Bobadilla: *Politica para corregidores y senores de vasallos, en tiempos de paz y de Guerra*, Madrid, 1759, tomo I, libro I, cap. II pag. 48. Cited by Moreno Cebrian p. 75.

likely shaped their decision to enter some offices vis-à-vis others. In the next chapters I examine what this entailed for colonial governance and the welfare of the indigenous population they ruled.

4.4 DISCUSSION

This chapter builds on the differences in the profile of colonial officials documented in Chapter 3 to ask: What can the changes in these profiles really tell us about the motivations of colonial officials? Surely, office-selling led to an influx of individuals *lacking* traditional markers of merit, such as social connections, military careers, or a family history of services to the Crown. But, why would this entail any significant changes in the functioning of the colonial administration? Opponents of sales could simply be defending the prevailing *status quo* and the privileged status of the noble and military classes as opposed to a sincere concern for governance in the administration.

Through the analysis of when and where do particular types of purchasers flock to, it is possible to know more of what purchasers intended the offices for. Did they seek offices simply as a way to improve their career credentials or social standing? In some cases, it could have been the case. For example, Herzog (2004) contends that purchasers in the Quito *audiencia* seats did not necessarily seek economic benefits but only greater social recognition. If that is the case, then there would be little statistical differences in the profile depending on when they enter, early during wars or not, and *where* they enter, to more profitable places or not.

However, on average, I find that certain *types* purchasers were more likely to enter office the more fiscally constrained was the Crown and the more profitable the position was. Those less socially connected and less dependent on royal favor disproportionately flocked to profitable positions, precisely when the Crown is less likely to vet them properly. Or, more likely to overlook red flags. Thus inconsistent with a general desire to serve, but rather seeking financial gains.

These findings lend support to the eighteenth-century critics of office-selling, who claimed that it allowed "worse" officials to govern in the Spanish colonies. While some historical accounts portray the practice of office-selling in a negative light (Parry 1953; Sanz Tapia 2009), it is not always on the grounds of negative selection but rather on more general "corruption" claims by the Spanish Crown. Moreover, the few historical accounts that do zero-in on selection as a negative externality from office-selling often do so for a limited set of positions, such as *audiencia* seats (Burkholder and Chandler 1977) or fiscal offices in the *audiencia* of Peru (Andrien 1982), which comprise 4 percent and 16 percent of all sales in the period, respectively. By providing a broader picture of how office-selling led to a *different*, and likely *worse*, class of officials of colonial offices, it is possible to reach more general conclusions of the impacts of this policy.

Aside from providing evidence of selection, the above results also help us understand the role of patronage at the time. In particular, the results imply that patronage, while imperfect and prone to favoritism, may have led to the selection of better individuals in Spanish America vis-à-vis office-selling. While this is not to say that patronage is ideal in general, there are certain contexts in which it may lead to better results than the alternative. Particularly when it allows the use of private information in the appointment, impedes active sorting, and credit constraints are not too severe.

Evidence from other settings seems to corroborate the potential upsides of patronage. For example, in contemporary China, the way to appoint competent officials is via private information that is only available via connections (Jia, Kudamatsu, and Seim 2015). A similar role is played by social status in premodern bureaucracies such as seventeenth-century Britain (Allen 2005), where the discretionary use of private information led to the positive selection of navy officers in the eighteenth century (Voth and Xu 2020). Directly relevant to the Spanish Empire is work by Salgado (2021), who shows that *audiencia* members with personal and social connections to members of the Council of Indies – due to patronage – performed better in office than those not connected. Because purchasers were much less likely to be connected, it is consistent with the findings of this chapter.

Finally, the fact that office-selling changed the *type* of individuals serving in the colonies suggests that the effects on governance in the Empire will outlive the end of sales. In Spanish America, the sale of *futuras* meant that many individuals who have purchased their position would still be occupying office decades after the policy had officially ended. Moreover, if the behavior of those purchasing positions departs significantly from the norm, they may also have lasting impacts on the culture and institutions of the provinces they rule. For instance, *corregidores* and *alcaldes* engaged in overtaxing the population may prompt rebellions eroding local customs and the attractiveness of serving in a particular province. In this sense, the effects of office-selling may be felt beyond the particular time period it takes place.

4 Office-Selling-Turned-Venality

In Chapter 5, I explore the impacts of office-selling on the functioning of the empire's administration in the America. Namely, how office-selling undermined the few mechanisms of hierarchical oversight existing within the administration between viceroys, *audiencia* members, and that of *corregidores* and *alcaldes mayores*.

Chapter Summary. The previous chapters reveal that purchasers have markedly lower social status and fewer connections to the Crown. For critics of office-selling, this lack of social status constituted prima facie evidence of their "undeserving" nature and the "ambitious" behavior they will exhibit in office. Yet, this is not necessarily the case: Low-status purchasers may not act differently or may be simply seeking an opportunity to advance socially. This chapter tests the validity of these claims by combining data on the individual characteristics of buyers with the timing and profitability of the position they sought. Statistical exercises reveal that, in line with its detractors, office buyers with "worse" traits flocked to positions that offered higher profit potential and at times in which the Crown was more desperate and less likely to vet them. From the point of view of the colonial populations, this was negative selection: sales abetting those with the most to gain financially and the least ability to rein in to enter the colonial administration. Namely, *venal* officials. These findings set the stage for future chapters exploring the consequences of this change in the colonial administration.

5

Captured Administration

Eighteenth-Century Audiencias and Corregidores

Qué importa que los oidores[1]
Tengáis grandes orejas
Sino percibís las quejas
Sino escucháis los clamores
Contra los corregidores[2]
           (Eighteenth-century *pasquin* quoted in Bridhikina 2007: 261)

Chapter 4 shows that purchasers most at odds with traditional notions of merit disproportionately flocked to profitable positions, particularly when the Crown was vetting less carefully (wars). Thereby confirming some of the worst fears of the detractors of office-selling. This chapter investigates how the presence of purchasers altered the institutional functioning of the colonial administration (this chapter) and undermined the welfare of the indigenous population (Chapter 6).

***

The quote mentioned earlier comes from a *pasquin*, a form of popular, political–satirical, and sometimes subversive verses circulated in La Plata (today Sucre), capital of the *audiencia* of Charcas (now Bolivia) in the late eighteenth century. Their clandestine and anonymous nature made them a perfect vehicle to criticize political authorities and shine light on uncomfortable truths (Revilla Orias 2009). In the case of the *pasquin* above,

---

[1] An *oidor* is a member of the *audiencia* of higher rank than *alcaldes del crimen* or *fiscales* and devoted to civil (as opposed to criminal) cases.
[2] Translation: *"It matters not that oidores [audiencia members] / have big ears / if you do not hear the complaints / if you do not hear the claims / against the corregidores."*

5 Captured Administration

it refers to a pervasive concern at the time: The lack of oversight from higher-up levels in the colonial administration (*audiencia*) over lower-level ones (*corregidores, alcaldes*). For the population, the situation was deemed worrisome enough to deserve its own verses.

In principle, colonial *audiencias* oversaw lower-ranked officials in its territory (such as *corregidores, alcaldes*, and *caja* officials) and in some cases, the activities of the viceroy himself. This was part of an intricate system, whereby oversight took place vertically – from higher-ranked to lower-ranked officials – but also horizontally – with different branches sharing the same function as a way to keep each in check each other through competition. The overall goal was to provide information to the Crown and reduce the divergence between its own policy goals and those of its officials. This chapter argues that office-selling undermined this system by facilitating collusion between (vertical) and across (horizontal) different layers of the colonial administration, with negative consequences for the population, primarily indigenous.

As lyrically expressed in the *pasquin* above, collusion between *audiencia* members and other subordinate officials – particularly *corregidores* and *alcaldes mayores* – was rampant. Contemporaneous observers Juan and Ulloa (1978 [1749]: 84, 88, 89) agreed. In their travels around the *audiencia* of Quito and Lima, they personally witnessed how well-founded charges of abuses by *corregidores* against the indigenous population were often buried in the *audiencia*, thanks to the personal connections between them.

In fact, this is precisely what a 1776 letter of the Bishop of Arequipa to the King argues.[3] The letter blamed the pervasiveness, ruthlessness, and disastrousness of extractive activities[4] of *corregidores* in Peru on the failure of the *audiencia* and the viceroy to halt it. In his opinion, oversight was so lax, the letter went, that not only no *corregidor* was ever punished in its posttenure assessment (*juicio de residencia*), but they ended their terms almost "canonized" with the most glowing assessments coming from these reports. Such praise seemed at odds with the rampant extraction and discontent in many provinces, the letter argued, and could only be explained by the outright collusion between *corregidores* and *audiencia* members: To profit from office, *corregidores* needed powerful allies to shield them against investigations into their dealings as well as to finance their multiple (forbidden) enterprises.

---

[3] AGI, Indiferente 1713, Carta del Obispo de Arequipa (1776).
[4] In the form of *Repartimiento*.

96   *The Venal Origins of Development in Spanish America*

Historical accounts also point to these links, particularly in the *audiencia* of Lima. For example, Carrillo Ureta (2019) documents how a faction of *audiencia* judges in Lima routinely shielded a network of *corregidores* from legal consequences due to their social, economic, and kinship ties. Historians have unearthed how *corregidores*, *alcaldes*, and *audiencia* members colluded in the extraction of rents from the local population through the practice of *repartimiento* (Stein 1981; Lynch 1992; Andrien 1982) – the forced sales of goods at markup prices – or the exploitation of local labor for textile production (*obrajes*) and agriculture. These activities were possible given the broad judicial and legislative powers of the *audiencia*, allowing it to rule "on behalf of special interests if they so desired" (Campbell 1972: 4).

This chapter provides quantitative and qualitative evidence of the role of office-selling in facilitating this type of collusion, particularly where more intensely practiced. As shown in Figure 5.1, office-selling drastically changed the composition of the royal *audiencias* at the time. For instance, in some years purchasers came to represent 100 percent of sitting members in the *audiencias* of Charcas (Bolivia), Santiago (Chile), and Panama. Albeit for other *audiencias*, the impact of sales was small to negligible. This is the case of the *audiencias* of Manila (Philippines) and Santo Domingo (Caribbean Basin), for reasons that will become apparent below.

In addition to differences across *audiencias*, Figure 5.1 also highlights how, despite sales ending in 1750, the presence of members who have purchased their seats continued well beyond this date.[5] This happened whenever a purchaser entered office very young and continued serving until his retirement or death. The question is, how did their presence impact the colonial administration as a whole?

Combining this information with the price paid for *corregimientos* and *alcaldías mayores*, I conduct two statistical exercises. In the first, I examine whether, *all else equal*,[6] the presence of more purchasers in the *audiencia* led to price increases for the positions they oversee (i.e., *corregidores, alcaldes*). If the values of *corregimientos* and *alcaldías* increase

---

[5] I consider as purchasers all those members that enter via sales to an *audiencia* position even if they were afterward promoted or reappointed to other positions without a monetary exchange. This also explains changes in the share of purchasers post-1750 (after sales ended). Namely, driven by individuals who initially bought their position and were later transferred elsewhere.

[6] Throughout the chapter, I address alternative explanations to the patterns observed, such as time trends.

5 Captured Administration

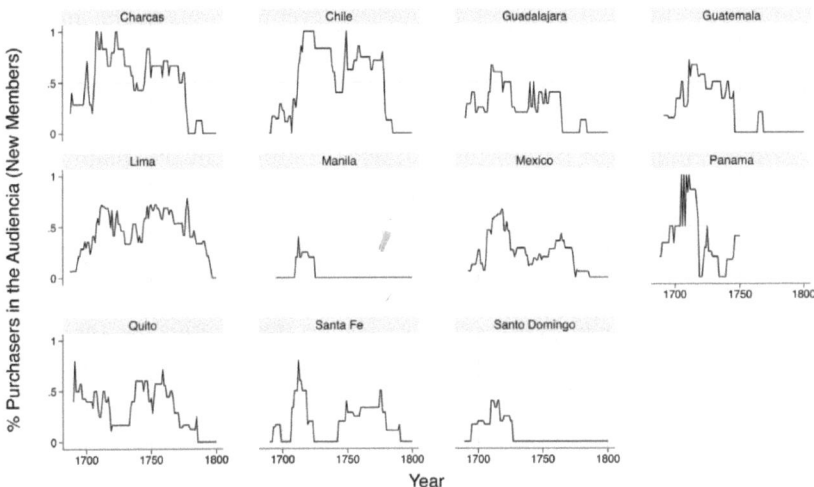

FIGURE 5.1 Share of purchasers across Spanish American *audiencias* (1687–1800)

Source: Own construction from Burkholder and Chandler (1977). Note: The figure includes "supernumerary" positions, which do not officially serve as members but receive a salary and perform some duties. The figure excludes those appointments sold as *futuras* until the individual actually occupies a position. The *audiencia* of Panama was briefly closed from 1718 to 1722 until its final abolition in 1751. Note that the figure excludes the *audiencias* of Buenos Aires, Caracas, and Cuzco, as these *audiencias* were created after the office-selling period ended (1750).

in response to the rise of purchasers in the *audiencia*, it would be consistent with a weakening grip of the latter on the former. Given prices are a meaningful measure of the expected returns from office – particularly that coming from appropriating economic surplus (Pietschmann 1972; Garfias and Sellars 2020; Guardado 2018; 2022) – their increase reflects greater opportunities to do so. If, on the contrary, prices do not change in response to the composition of the *audiencia*, this would suggest that other factors – not the composition of the *audiencia* – are more important in determining provincial office valuations.

In the second exercise, I then examine whether the effect of the composition of the *audiencia* on provincial governorship prices varies according to their geopolitical importance. Since certain *audiencias* faced serious security threats from foreign powers and were considered strategic for geopolitical reasons, they were shielded from sales as a way to guarantee that only the best qualified served in it. In these strategic territories, listed in a document by the Council of Indies, only the most competent and loyal individuals occupied the highest-level positions in the *audiencias*. If weak oversight is driving up the valuations of *corregimientos* and *alcaldías*, then the effect should be mostly driven by the *audiencias* the Crown worried *less*. That is, those less threatened by foreign powers.

Finally, in the last part of the chapter, I complement the quantitative findings with historical and contemporary accounts of actors and historians on the topic. The idea is to illustrate the numerous ways in which *oidores* who had purchased their office aided and abetted (directly and indirectly) the extractive activities of *corregidores* and *alcaldes* for the most part of the eighteenth century. The section centers on the *audiencia* of Lima (Peru), but draws evidence from the *audiencias* of Quito (Ecuador), Santiago (Chile), and Charcas (Bolivia).

In the following, I present a brief overview of the oversight role of the *audiencia* in the early eighteenth century.

5.1 AUDIENCIA OVERSIGHT IN THE SPANISH COLONIAL ADMINISTRATION

A sign of the complexity, if not necessarily efficiency, of the Spanish colonial administration ca. 1700, was its extensive reliance on vertical and horizontal checks within its organization. By vertical checks is meant higher-ranked officials overseeing the performance of lower-ranked ones. In turn, horizontal checks took the form of overlapping jurisdictions – with the same powers or functions (e.g., fiscal, judicial, and executive) given to different authorities. The goal being to induce competition and conflict that would "prevent officials from unduly building up personal prestige or to engage in corrupt or fraudulent practices" (Haring 1947: 122).[7] In this way, the Crown could be continuously informed (Phelan 1960) and serve as "the ultimate arbiter" of these conflicts (Grafe 2011: 35).

In hierarchical terms, at the top of the administration sat the King with its auxiliary bodies in matters related to the Indies – the Council and the Secretary of Indies (from 1717 onward). Together, they appointed and oversaw the viceroy and members of the *audiencias* and *gobernadores*. Viceroys were in principle of higher rank than *audiencias* and

---

[7] This system contrasts with that developed in British North America, whereby checks and balances were achieved by assigning different powers to different branches (Gailmard 2017).

gobernadores, but because they had overlapping functions, the latter effectively served as an institutional counterweight to the former. Moreover, the *audiencia* could rule in the viceroy's absence and had a direct line of communication to the King – thus able to present its own version of events in court.

Broadly speaking, *audiencias* were tasked with limiting the undue gains by *corregidores* and *alcaldes*.[8] To perform its oversight duties, the *audiencia* relied on three main mechanisms: first, a posttenure assessment (*juicio de residencia*) meant to "clear" the name of those officials after their time in office. In these evaluations, one *audiencia* member (usually the President) would designate (together with the Viceroy) a special judge to evaluate the outgoing official and establish whether he fulfilled his duties while in office (e.g., followed the Crown's rules, collected taxes, did not mistreat the local population, etc.). The length of the evaluation ought to last sixty days and another sixty if there was need for more information from the public. If *corregidores* and *alcaldes* were found guilty of fraud, malfeasance, mistreatment, or illicit commerce (*repartimiento*), the ruling was then turned to the *audiencia* for ratification. This mechanism was explicitly noted in the appointment title of *alcaldes mayores* and *corregidores*. For example, the title of *Alcalde Mayor* of Huejutla (Mexico) to Antonio García in 1747 was unambiguous in that the latter's performance would be evaluated in the *audiencia* of Mexico, following established custom.[9]

A second mechanism was to conduct investigations into the specific charges prior to the end of the *corregidor* or *alcalde's* tenure. These types of investigations, known as *comisiones*, would be prompted by serious allegations; for example, if the population (either Spanish or indigenous) was harmed by this official in such a way that the *audiencia* felt compelled to investigate in-depth.[10] Similarly, the Crown could direct the *audiencia* to look into certain matters it deemed necessary. *Audiencia* members were also tasked with "visiting" the provinces and protecting

---

[8] Codified in the *Laws of the Indies*. "Ley XLVI, Que los virreyes procuren remediar las ganancias ilícitas de los gobernadores. ... para cuyo remedio ordenamos a los virreyes, y presidentes [de las *audiencias*], que comuniquen con sus *audiencias* los medios y prevenciones más convenientes, para estorbar las ganancias ilícitas de que usan las justicias, contraviniendo a su propia obligación y juramento, y a la esperanza que deben tener, de que procediendo con pureza, y administrando justicia, como deben, serán por Nos renumerados."

[9] AGI. Mexico 1221. *Titulo de Alcalde Mayor a Antonio García*. 14 de Marzo de 1747.

[10] See Law of Indies. Libro V, Titulo 15, De las Residencias, y Jueces que las han de tomar, Ley xviiij.

the indigenous population from illegal actions by local officials, priests, and often their own indigenous authorities (Bridikhina 2007). For example, in the *audiencia* of Charcas – where the largest silver mine of Potosí was located – one member had to travel to Potosí once a year to oversee the silver tax collection and protect the interests of the indigenous population involved in mining, which were often at the mercy of local officials.

Finally, the *audiencia* also served as the last court of appeal for all cases in the Americas, except for a limited number that were decided directly by the Council of Indies in Spain (Kahle 1951: 32). This meant that many cases against *corregidores* and *alcaldes* were in the hands of the *audiencia* as a check to their rule. A system that allowed for trading favors and facilitated self-dealing.

It should also be noted that in the case of Mexico, there was a different judicial body the Indigenous population could resort to, namely, the *Juzgado General de Naturales*. This judicial body served as a first instance court for indigenous complaints (parallel to the role played by *corregidores* or *alcaldes*) whose cases could then be remitted to the viceroy for resolution and/or to the *audiencia* of Mexico (see Franco-Vivanco 2021).

Due to its importance, a pliant *audiencia* was a key ally for a profit-seeking *corregidor* or *alcalde*. *Audiencias* had the ability to overturn or simply not ratify indictments from their posttenure assessments (*residencias*), such that they could end with no final ruling (Pelayo 2009: 114). Given the threshold needed to decide cases was low, it was possible for a few *audiencia* members to steer cases and outcomes as needed. For example, minor civil and criminal disputes were decided with a simple two-member majority in large *audiencias* such as Lima and Mexico (and even less for smaller ones). Yet, this low threshold relative to the total number of members was necessary as ministers were often absent due to travel, commission work, sickness, or inspecting the provinces.[11] For major civil or criminal cases, the threshold was three votes at least for major *audiencias* (and lower for smaller ones). In this way, two to three members could coordinate and decide judicial outcomes.

Audiencias thus became a forum for litigation in which the Spanish and Indigenous population alike would raise their complaints against *corregidores* and *alcaldes* and partake in the legal system with petitions, memorials, and filing cases, especially where there were advantages to doing so. For example, the indigenous nobility and elite often sought recognition

---

[11] This chronic shortage of members also made it difficult to assign officials to inspect the provinces.

of their noble lineage, as it came with royal prerogatives (Castro Flores 2019). For the indigenous population, litigation was also a form of resistance to Spanish rule, often preceding full-blown uprisings (Stern 1990) and would even recur to the *audiencia* "opportunistically" as a way to "contest and win economic resources" (Thornton 2011: 139).

In addition to its judicial roles, the *audiencia* also represented the pinnacle of social prestige at the time, as direct representatives of the Crown. Members of these councils were held in the highest social esteem – as evidenced from the way they were addressed, their clothing, and other ceremonies associated with the position. For example, in the presence of *audiencia* members, the archbishop's page had to stop holding the latter's tunic as a sign of deference to the *oidor* (Bridikhina 2007: 258). During the public procession, the *audiencia* (together with the viceroy) was to occupy the "head" of the procession due to their higher hierarchy. During special religious ceremonies, they were also to occupy elevated seats on the right side of the shrine, representing their highest status. The event could also not start without their presence, so they were often ordered to be punctual (Bridikhina 2007: 292–294).

5.1.1 Institutional Safeguards in *Audiencias*

Given the important social, judicial, and oversight duties vested in the *audiencia*, the Crown was keen to appoint officials both capable and attuned to its own policy preferences and goals. For example, officials that would increase treasure remitted to Spain, fight illegal contraband, or even limit the extraction of the indigenous population, depending on its focus at the time. To appoint those best suited for the *audiencia*, the Crown implemented a number of selection and incentives mechanisms. First, unlike *corregidores* and *alcaldes*, a seat in the *audiencia* entailed a lifetime appointment or until a promotion came along. Second, there was a rotation rule whereby members had to move up the *audiencia* ladder after five years. Given the clear hierarchy among *audiencias*, young lawyers started their careers in a less important *audiencia* (say, Chile) and, via promotions, ended up serving in some of the most prestigious ones (say, Mexico or Lima), to later maybe retire in Madrid. The rule was meant to provide enough career incentives to keep them in line with Madrid's interests.

Another consequence of the rotation rule was that it limited potential connections of *audiencia* members with the local population. The latter was also the purpose of measures banning *audiencia* members from marrying local women; from having family ties to other government officials in the same *audiencia*; and from acquiring property or investing in economic ventures in the *audiencia* they ruled. Other social connections, such as godparenting or their presence in weddings and funerals, was also prohibited.

Third, and finally, the Crown was very reluctant to allow individuals born in the colonies (known as Spanish Americans or *criollos*) to serve in important positions of the colonial government. Albeit there was no explicit rule against it, it was driven by the belief that *criollos* were less loyal to Madrid and more likely to favor local interests instead of those of the Crown. This differential appointment policy meant that *criollos* were rarely appointed to positions of political importance, even if wealthy, connected, and highly educated. For this reason, they would be the first to take advantage of office-selling to purchase these positions instead (Burkholder and Chandler 1977). A more subtle form of discrimination.

The advent of office-selling effectively did away with these institutional safeguards as the Crown was willing to turn a blind eye to these rules – in exchange for a fee. For example, it often waived the rule forbidding marriage, family, or property ties if financially compensated. Similar waivers could be obtained for underage individuals and those without proper law degrees who were then allowed to serve as *audiencia* judges. Expectedly, the widespread use of waivers signaled a major departure from the prevailing standards at the time. Finally, the process of promotion (rotation) and the ability to remove members of the *audiencia* effectively broke down during office-selling. Because sales often entailed "jumping the queue" for seats in key *audiencias*, promotions for nonpurchasers were delayed, often indefinitely (Burkholder and Chandler 1977).

The consequences of *audiencia* sales had been thoroughly noted in previous studies. The argument explored here is the extent to which they also facilitated the extraction activities of other officials.

5.2 OVERSIGHT AND OFFICE-SELLING: EMPIRICAL EVIDENCE

As argued by the Bishop of Arequipa, a key driver of economic appropriation by *corregidores* and *alcaldes* was the lack of oversight they faced from the top. This section explores the empirical basis of these assertions by using the prices paid for *corregimientos* and *alcaldías* to estimate how responsive they are to changes in the composition of the *audiencia*. The key idea is that price dynamics can help capture the degree of collusion within colonial institutions.

The first statistical exercise is to compare whether the presence of more buyers in the *audiencia* altered its ability or willingness to oversee the activities of *corregidores* and *alcaldes*. For example, a positive statistical relationship between prices and *audiencia* composition would suggest the latter is a major consideration for the valuations of *corregimientos* and *alcaldías mayores*. Namely, that the monetary valuation of lower-level offices responds to changes in the potential for oversight from the *audiencia*.

Figure 5.2(a) and 5.2(b) reports the estimate of the growth in prices of *corregimientos* and *alcaldías* due to changes in the share of purchasers in the *audiencia*. The sample includes transactions that occur within five, ten, or twenty-one years from each other, corresponding to 50, 75, and 95 percent of all observations, respectively. Estimates show that for transactions less than five years apart, a 1 percentage point increase in the share of purchasers is associated with an average increase in prices of 27 pesos. If we include transactions within ten years of each other, the difference is of 19.8 pesos. Finally, increasing the window between sales expectedly leads to rather small and statistically insignificant effects, as there is a weaker relationship between the composition of the *audiencia* in a given year t and the prices paid for provinces twenty years or more later.[12] Further details are available in the Appendix to Chapter 5.

Figure 5.2(b) in turn further examines the robustness of these results by looking at (log) growth rates to account for scale effects. Consistent with the findings in levels, an increase in the share of purchasers in the *audiencia* of 10 percent is associated with an increase of 4 percent in the prices *corregimientos* and *alcaldías mayores*, whether they are five or ten years from each other. Again, for transactions with a significant number of years in between, the results are weaker, as expected.

5.2.1 Geopolitics and Audiencia Quality

The findings above show that prices grew disproportionately where there are more purchasers in the *audiencia*. Yet, it is important to check whether prices are responding to weaker top-down oversight from the *audiencia* and not to other reasons that may be also varying with the presence of purchasers.

---

[12] Estimates also take into account slow changing traits (fixed effects), common shocks (year fixed effects), and the tendency of certain type of data to follow the same trajectory by using first differences and controlling for the number of years between sales.

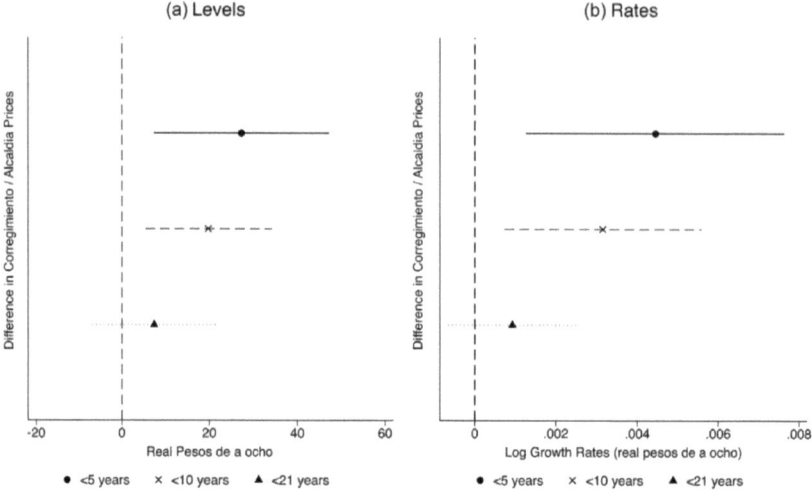

FIGURE 5.2 Price growth and purchaser presence in the *audiencia*

Note: OLS estimates with 95 percent Confidence Intervals. See estimating Equation (3) and full results in Table A.6 of the Appendix. All estimates include provincial, year, and type of position fixed effects. All standard errors clustered by province.

To distinguish between these possibilities, I use the fact that a main determinant of the Crown's decision to sell or not was whether it was geopolitically vulnerable. The latter was a key consideration in the seventeenth and eighteenth centuries, a time in which European powers – mainly Britain, France, and the Dutch – jockeyed for more territories and (or) market access in the Americas, posing a perpetual threat to the Spanish Empire. In fact, a number of territories across the Empire were in near-constant siege from foreign powers and allied smugglers and privateers, keeping local authorities and the Spanish Crown in high alert. In these *audiencias*, the Crown instead sought to appoint members following the highest selection criteria rather than to sell them. Because *audiencia* members bore direct responsibility in organizing military defense during foreign threats, the Crown was fearful that sales would allow unprepared individuals to serve in office, leading to a deficient defense of the Spanish Empire (Burkholder and Chandler 1972: 202). In contrast, in *audiencias* less exposed to attacks by foreign powers, the Crown was more comfortable with allowing sales as they did not hamper the territorial integrity of the empire. These geopolitical threats thus introduced differences in the selection and quality of members entering their *audiencias*.

Now, which *audiencias* were considered "under threat"? Based on the deliberations between the King and the Council of Indies, the

5 Captured Administration

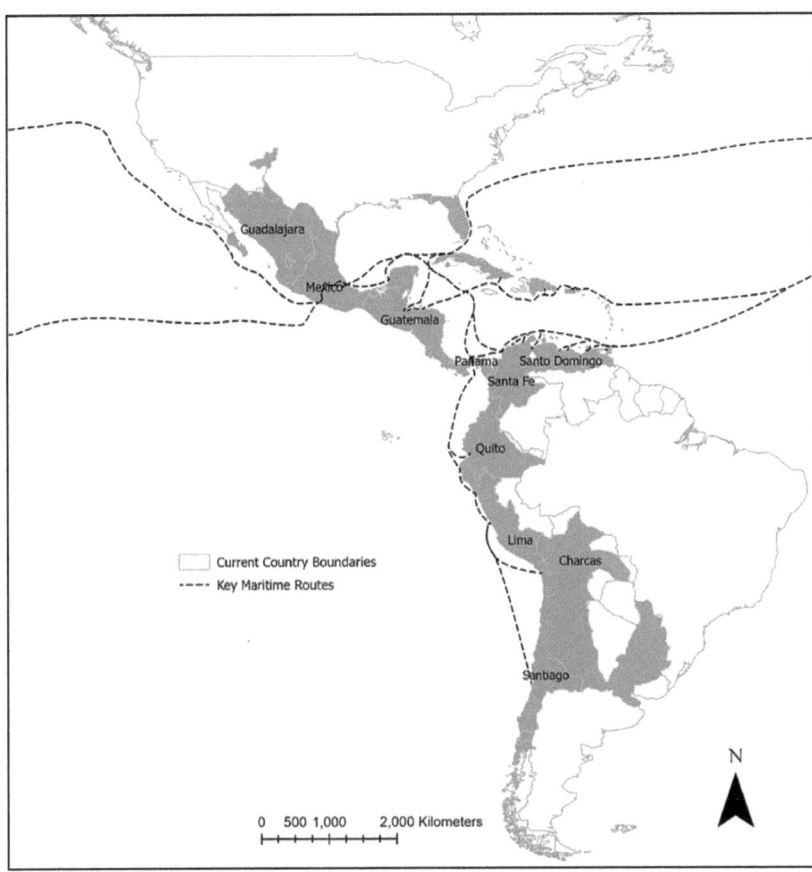

FIGURE 5.3 Geopolitical concerns based on the positions excluded from sales

Source: Own construction based on Stangl (2019a; 2019c) and territories listed by the Council of Indies/King correspondence and cross-checked with the available sales data.

Crown actively sought to limit sales in locations along maritime routes that European powers, smugglers, and pirates could follow – particularly those of British, Dutch, and French origin. Figure 5.3 presents the geographic distribution of key maritime routes at the time. As noted, the majority of strategic and vulnerable territories were located in or around the Caribbean basin, where all major European powers (French, Dutch, and Britain) also had territorial possessions. Although piracy had almost disappeared by the eighteenth century, foreign armies and the possibility of territorial invasion were still a possibility, as exemplified by the occupation of Havana during the Anglo-Spanish war of 1762–63.

Furthermore, smugglers were still a major threat to the commercial monopoly of the Crown in Spanish America and a reason why the Crown sought "better" equipped *audiencias* to battle them.

Based on the geopolitical considerations of the Council, I classify the *audiencias* into those "most" and "least" prone to sales.[13] Among those *most* prone would be that of north Mexico (Guadalajara), Peru (Lima), Ecuador (Quito), and Bolivia (Charcas), due to their "safer" location along the Pacific shore and their lack of frontier status (as of the mid eighteenth century). In contrast, those less prone to sales would be those based in the Caribbean (Santo Domingo), the Philippines (Manila), central-south Mexico, Guatemala, Panama, and Colombia (Santa Fe) due to their greater exposure to European powers and being located in frontier territories. Finally, although Chile would be considered a "safer" *audiencia* due to its location on the Pacific, it was frequently threatened by indigenous rebellions, so as a robustness I examine the results with and without including Chile in this category.

To assess visually how this difference mattered throughout the eighteenth century, Figure 5.4 plots the average share of purchasers sitting in the *audiencia*, depending on the level of geopolitical threat faced. As shown, *audiencias* threatened exhibit a systematically lower share of their members sold than those considered safer starting in 1717. This gap reaches its highest point during the mid eighteenth century wars with Britain, namely, Jenkins' Ear war (1739–48), which overlaps with the War of the Austrian Succession (1740–48). This pattern of sales across *audiencias* lends empirical support to the lists of excluded positions, particularly after 1717 (as stated). With the end of sales (1751), the share of sitting purchasers declined across the board such that by 1800 the differences between threatened and nonthreatened *audiencias* were less stark.

The question is then: How consequential were these *audiencia*-level differences for the valuations of *corregimientos* and *alcaldías mayores*? Figure 5.5 panels (a) and (b) present estimates of the effect of these differential patterns for the prices of *corregimientos* and *alcaldías* they oversaw, on average. As shown, all of the effect on price growth is driven by the territories where the Crown less carefully screened purchasers of high-level offices.

---

[13] See: AGI, Mexico 1970. *Nota de los Empleos que para su provision en la America se han estimado por militares y que desde el año 1717 se han excluido del beneficio por las razones que militan para ellos.* Madrid, Buen Retiro, 1 de Junio de 1740.

5 Captured Administration

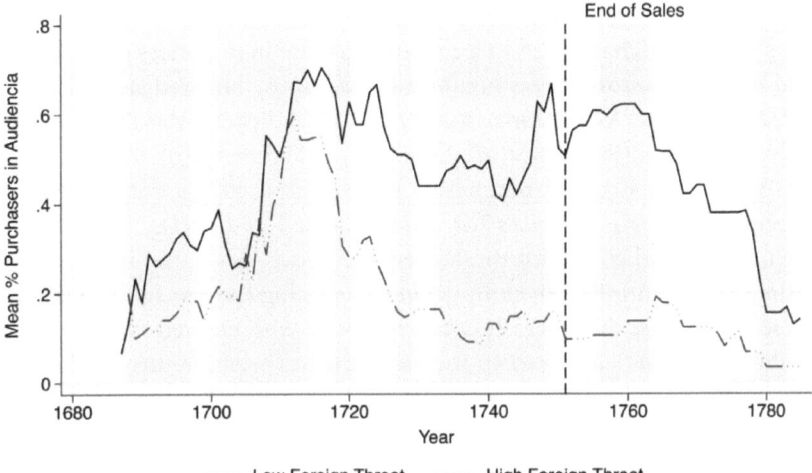

FIGURE 5.4 Mean share of purchasers in *audiencias* by foreign threat status
Note: Years during which Spain is involved in European Wars are shaded.

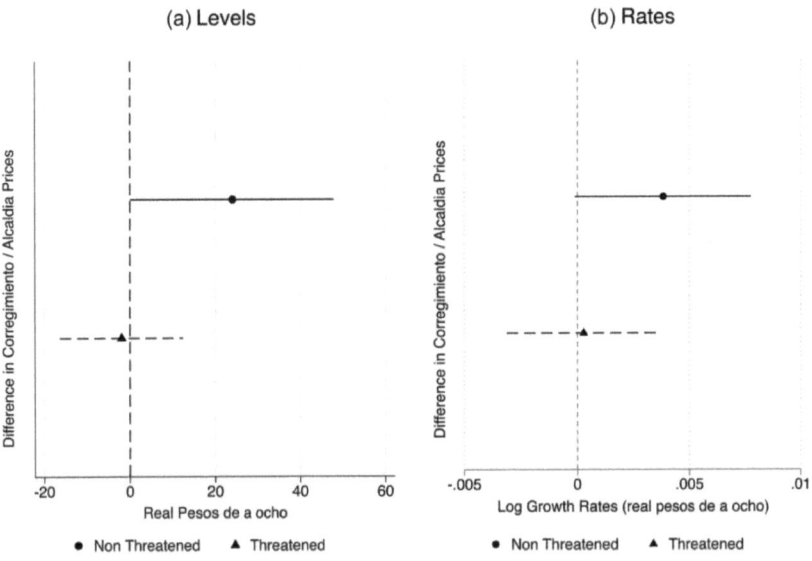

FIGURE 5.5 Price growth and purchaser presence in the *audiencia* by geopolitical threat

Note: The analysis focuses on the sample of transactions less than ten years apart from each other. OLS estimates with 95 percent Confidence Intervals. See estimating Equation (3) and full results in Table A.7 of the Appendix to Chapter 5. All estimates include provincial, year, and type of position fixed effects and standard errors clustered by province.

In terms of magnitude, Figure 5.5(a) shows that a 1 percent increase in the share of purchasers led to a 24 peso increase in the prices of *alcaldías* and *corregimientos* in nonthreatened *audiencias*, but had no effect on threatened ones. As a comparison, across all *audiencias* this difference is only 19.8 pesos (Figure 3.3(a)). Similarly, in Figure 5.5(b), a 10 percent increase in the share of purchasers is associated with a corresponding 4 percent increase in prices for nonthreatened *audiencias*, while there are no statistical effects for threatened *audiencias*. The latter implies that estimates are entirely driven by *audiencias* facing less foreign threats. In these territories, there was less worry about who entered via purchase in the *audiencia*, leading to an increase in the expected returns of lower-level officials (*corregidores*, *gobernadores*, and *alcaldes*) as reflected in office prices. The next question is: Are specific traits of *audiencia* members particularly responsible for this result?

5.2.2 Unwilling or Unable to Rein-in *Corregidores* and *Alcaldes*?

In principle, there are two main mechanisms through which *audiencia* members weakened oversight. If they are unwilling to police officials or if they are unable to. While the former most closely relates to collusion, the latter is driven by inefficiency. In the collusive explanation, purchasers might have been unwilling to fulfill their duties due to self-dealing. For example, some *audiencia* members had strong economic, social, and filial connections with the officials they were supposed to oversee. This was the case of members who owned haciendas or mines or were directly related to those who did, and relied on local *corregidores* and *alcaldes* to unduly mobilize cheap indigenous labor for agricultural production and mining, among other activities. Similarly, *audiencia* members with strong merchant connections or commercial interests could benefit from the illicit *repartimiento* activities of *corregidores* and *alcaldes* by financing and protecting the distribution of their merchandise among the indigenous population. In return, *audiencia* members provided legal cover for these activities.

Alternatively, *audiencia* members who purchased their posts may lack the appropriate law degree or qualifications. Inefficiency would lead to a backlog of cases such that the threat of punishing the transgressions of lower-level officials is no longer credible. For example, in the 1720s the Crown had to increase the number of judges in the *audiencia* of Mexico due to the backlog of cases (around 11,000) that had rendered the *audiencia* futile (Burkholder and Chandler 1977).[14] Another notorious example was that of "minors" – namely, those members (purchasers) who did not fulfill the age and therefore experience required to serve in such a high position, but whom nonetheless paid the Crown a waiver to turn a blind eye. According to this mechanism, the rise of purchasers facilitated profit-seeking activities of *corregidores* and *alcaldes* due to a lack of competence in handling policy and judicial matters.

This section compares which group of traits might have had a larger impact on the prices paid for lower-level offices. Are prices mostly responding to the inefficiency of purchasers in the *audiencia*? Or, rather, are they most responsive to the characteristics associated with economic connections? To disentangle the relative importance of these mechanisms, I rely on the historical–biographical information on individual traits of new *audiencia* members entering office between 1687 and 1751 in the Spanish American *audiencias* (and the Philippines) and examine the change in their respective provincial prices.

If we find that the change in prices is driven by differences in the education background and age profile of purchasers rather than in their local connections, then it is likely that office prices are responding to inefficiency and incompetence in the *audiencias* rather than to self-dealing. The opposite is true if we find that the traits most closely associated with potential collusion are driving the surge in prices. In order to facilitate these comparisons, I created two measures that capture each of these dimensions in the sample of *audiencia* purchasers. The idea is to test which group of traits or "dimension" plays a larger role in determining the increase of prices documented earlier. See Appendix for details of these measures.

Figure 5.6 presents the results from this exercise by comparing the importance of each group of traits on the price of lower-level offices. As shown in both cases, the most important traits driving price growth were those capturing the local connections of members with the *audiencia* they ruled – either in the form of marriage, waivers, or having relatives in other government positions. In contrast, the share of highly educated purchasers show no relationship to lower-level office prices. This lends credence to the Crowns' concern of limiting the presence of locally connected members in the colonial administration as it might lead to a more

---

[14] This was also the case in the colonial treasury, where the sale of treasury and accounting positions to unqualified individuals led to an increase in uncollected debts and poor accounting in the Peruvian treasury (Andrien 1982).

110 *The Venal Origins of Development in Spanish America*

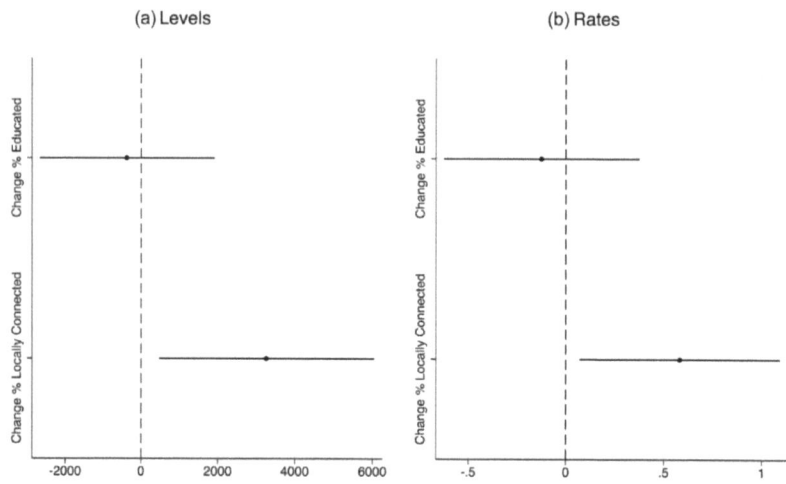

FIGURE 5.6 Price growth and purchaser presence in the *audiencia* by individual traits

Note: OLS estimates with 95 percent Confidence Intervals. See estimating Equation (3) and full results in Table A.8 of the Appendix to Chapter 5. All estimates include provincial, year, and type of position fixed effects and standard errors clustered by province.

permissive environment for collusion and self-dealing. However, this is not because *criollos* were corrupt per se – including a control for the presence of "native" members does not change the result. Thus showing that the most important driver of office valuations was the local connectedness of *oidores* and not the *criollo* origin per se.

5.3 EXTRACTIVE COMPLEMENTARITIES: *AUDIENCIAS*, *CORREGIDORES*, AND *ALCALDES MAYORES*

The quantitative analysis shows that the value of provincial governorships rose as the share of purchasers – particularly those locally connected – also increased in the *audiencia*. Implying that the two are intrinsically related, the question is "how?"

Unfortunately, large *n* analysis as the one conducted earlier would be impossible for this task. The secretive and hidden nature of individual *quid-pro-quo* transactions lend systematic records naturally missing.[15] Yet, there is an abundance of studies on particular *audiencias* and (or)

---

[15] Even in contemporary settings, this data is difficult to compile.

5 Captured Administration

members involved in collusive activities – itself a reflection of their prevalence and the attention they attracted from the Crown and contemporary observers. In what follows I rely on these case studies and link them to the statistical evidence above. The goal is less to establish a statistical relationship but to characterize the specific ways office-selling might have facilitated collusion across the Empire.

The section centers on the case of the *audiencia* of Lima (with supportive evidence from Charcas, Chile, and Quito) and the cases of notorious members who (not surprisingly) entered via sales and used their office for self-dealing. The reason to focus on these *audiencias* is that they represent the territories where the quantitative evidence suggests this type of collusion would be more likely. Therefore, presenting the most illustrative examples of this activity. In contrast, we would be less likely to find instances (or they could be less representative) in *audiencias* where members are more carefully vetted and screened (e.g., Mexico). This is not to say that collusion is inexistent in the latter, the difference is simply one of degree.[16]

The picture that emerges from these accounts is that the connections between *alcaldes*, *corregidores*, and *audiencia* members were both commonplace, mutually advantageous, and facilitated by office-selling. As we will see, the Peruvian *audiencia* presents the most abundant and flagrant exchanges of favors between *audiencia* and *corregidores*, often at the expense of the indigenous population through the practice of *repartimiento* and forced labor in mines and haciendas. In other *audiencias*, namely Charcas (Bolivia), the source of profits mostly concerned mining activities and the administration of indigenous labor. In Quito (Ecuador), access to contraband, coerced labor for *obrajes*, and profits from tribute were the key nexus linking both levels of government. Finally, the type of complementarities in Chile centered on the cooptation of all levels of government via family or marriage ties, thus able to shape policy more generally. However, contraband was also rampant among the highest level of the Chilean colonial administration.

5.3.1 *Audiencia* of Lima (Peru)

By far the most abundant source of examples of collusive behavior comes from the *audiencia* of Lima (now Peru). As the capital of the viceroyalty of Peru, ca. 1700, its jurisdiction extended over roughly all

---

[16] Information from the *audiencia* of Guadalajara is too sparse to be included.

of Spanish South America (and Panama).[17] Naturally, this granted Lima *audiencia* members with unrivaled powers, except perhaps those of the *audiencia* of Mexico, to influence policy issues ranging from taxation, land distribution, mineral and *encomienda* rights, commercial licenses, interim office appointments, among many others. This, in addition to serving as the final instance court in most criminal and civil matters in these territories.

Not surprisingly, the office-selling period attracted a large number of buyers into the *audiencia* – 67 percent of all new entrants to be exact. Consistent with the analysis above, these buyers were usually born in the *audiencia* (*criollos*): 63 percent of all new members during sales, representing 89 percent of all purchasers. They also had strong local economic, family, and social connections. For example, among purchasers, 64 percent eventually married a *criolla* from the local elite; 26 percent had a known family relationship with a *corregidor*; 32 percent of purchasers had known connections to mercantile interests through the Lima *Consulado*, or merchant guild, as well as with "newer" merchants from Cádiz. Finally, 38 percent had property and business interests (or their children) in the Lima *audiencia*, generally *haciendas* – focused on agricultural production – or *estancias* – on cattle. In addition to *haciendas*, in at least one case, a member had known mining interests in the mercury mine of Huancavelica that would also benefit from coerced labor, given their chronic labor shortage and terrible work conditions. It should be noted that these reflect only *direct* connections, while indirect ones (via marriage, friendship, or business endeavors) are vastly larger, hence more difficult to quantify. For instance, textile production (*obrajes*) and mule transportation activities – carried on by indigenous labor – were also linked to the clientelar and family network of *audiencia* members.

Given these members' extensive network of connections across all levels of government; the immense power they amassed within the *audiencia* itself; and the long-lasting impact they had on colonial policy, it is no surprise their notorious fame among contemporaries[18] and in the historiography. Of particular relevance for this chapter is the long-lasting faction led by purchaser Pedro Bravo de Rivero, known to routinely exchange

---

[17] This jurisdiction was subsequently reduced with the creation of the viceroyalty of Santa Fe (roughly Colombia, Venezuela, and Panama), albeit later reinstated. The creation of the viceroyalty of Rio de la Plata, roughly present-day Argentina extending into the *audiencia* of Charcas (now Bolivia) also meant a loss of "power" to these *oidores*.

[18] Viceroy Amat y Junyent would single out numerous members of the *audiencia* for their corrupt dealings – namely Pedro Bravo de Rivero – even if accused of corruption himself.

judicial protection for economic favors with a network of *corregidores* linked by economic, social, and family ties during their time in office.

5.3.2 The Lima Faction

Pedro Bravo de Rivero served in the *audiencia* from 1733 to 1778, an unusually long time (double the average of the period[19]), which also contributed to his outsize influence on Peruvian affairs. He was born in Lima and had paid 20,000 pesos in Madrid – a sizeable amount at the time – to enter office. As was common at the time, he married into the local Peruvian elite: His father-in-law was a previous member of the *audiencia* and was serving as treasurer at the time.[20] His own influence would outlive his tenure in office – as his son Diego would serve in the *audiencia* after his death.

During this long-lived tenure, he formed a faction of like-minded members that would dominate the Lima *audiencia* during the late second and third quarters of the eighteenth century. The other known members of this faction were Pedro Bravo de Castilla (term: 1746–56), Francisco Ortiz de Foronda (term: 1730–69), and José Tagle Bracho (term: 1740–95) (Carrillo Ureta 2019). Non-coincidentally, all the members of this faction were (1) born in Lima; (2) had purchased their position; and (3) had all requested (purchased) one or more waivers, as they did not fulfill the criteria set by the Crown to serve in the *audiencia*, particularly those outlawing local connections in the form of marriage and/or property.

For the purposes of this chapter, the most striking characteristic of this faction was the extensive economic and family links it shared with the *corregidores* serving in the Peruvian provinces. For instance, Bravo de Rivero himself was connected either through economic or friendship ties to twenty-two *corregidores*, around half of the total in Peru (Carrillo Ureta 2019). Per se, these connections needed not result in collusion or any illicit behavior. Yet, it was well documented that *audiencia* members often provided legal protection for connected *corregidores* when facing charges or even had their postterm evaluation foregone (Carrillo Ureta 2019: 110). In fact, a fellow *audiencia* member contemporaneous to the faction bitterly complained about the lack of prosecution against the well-known abuses of the *corregidor* of the Canta province, Manuel de

---

[19] Among those entering office between 1687 and 1751.
[20] In the Tribunal de la Santa Cruzada.

la Torre Quiroz, which could only be explained by his family relation to José de Tagle y Bracho (Carillo Ureta 2019: 111).

Aside from the cover-ups, Bravo de Rivero, together with three other *audiencia* members, played a key role in legalizing *repartimiento*. Prior to 1751, during the height of office-selling, the practice of forcing sales of goods and credit to the local population at inflated prices was explicitly outlawed, yet served as a key source of profits for *corregidores* and merchants. Although the stated purpose legalizing *repartimiento* was to limit its prevalence via regulation, in practice, it incentivized and expanded the possibilities to profit from it. Given their own connections with *corregidores*, the legalization of *repartimiento* was at the very least marred by conflicts of interest if not motivated by the expectation of directly profiting from it. In fact, Bravo de Rivero and Ortiz de Foronda allegedly possessed blank titles of *corregimientos* ready for sale in the secondary market upon approval of the measure (Carrillo Ureta 2019: 35).[21] Other types of illicit activities involving the faction include their participation in contraband and illegal commerce – an accusation wielded by the viceroy Amat y Junyent – as well as fraud accusations against José de Tagle Bracho of embezzling funds from the soldiers of the Callao fort (Quiroz 2013: 107).

While this faction was one of the most notorious ones, other *audiencia* members were also involved in illicit activities. Such is the case of Antonio Hermenejildo de Querejazu (purchaser, term: 1744–91) – son of a prominent Lima merchant – as well as Alvaro Bernardo de Quiros (nonpurchaser, term: 1713–34) (Quiroz 2013: 98), both accused of contraband. Similarly, member Pablo de Olavide (purchaser, term 1744–50) was charged with fraud and removed from office (Quiroz 2013: 109).

In sum, blatant cover-ups and the implementation of policies for their own advantage are just a few examples of the type of behavior facilitated by office-selling. Although some of these accounts are based on Bravo de Rivero's enemies, especially those from Viceroy Manuel de Amat y Juniet, the accounts are also supported by other Peruvian viceroys with less conflicts of interest (e.g., Viceroy Castelfuerte) and by the statistical analysis above. It is no coincidence that all of these *audiencia* members

---

[21] Bravo de Rivero would also participate in the secondary market of sales of *corregimientos* appointments. For example, *corregidores* appointed by the Crown could declare themselves sick in Lima, not travel to their assigned positions, and instead "sell" the rights (to extract) to a third party with the authorization of the Bravo de Rivero (Carrillo Ureta 2019: 35).

had purchased their post, were locally born, had family connections to other branches of government, and bought numerous waivers. These characteristics are associated with strong motivations and ability to reap the most social, economic, and political gain from their post. This is not to say that Crown appointees were not involved in illicit activities as well, they were just not as profitable or blatant. In the following, I examine the patterns of *audiencia-corregidor* dealings in Charcas (roughly present-day Bolivia), Quito (Ecuador), and Santiago (Chile).

5.3.3 Beyond Lima

The cases of Charcas, Quito, and Santiago are closely intertwined with that of Lima, as they shared strong economic, political, and even social ties with the capital of the viceroyalty. Politically, these were *audiencias* subordinate to that of Lima, such that most of their key decisions were to be reviewed by the latter, conferring them a "lesser" status. Yet, they were often used by officials as a springboard to obtain a coveted position in the Lima *audiencia*. For example, if there were no openings in Lima, purchasers would seek those in Charcas for the geographic "proximity" and the possibility of being eventually promoted to Lima (Burkholder and Chandler 1977). In this way, a position in the Charcas *audiencia* "[...] not only helped to secure and extend their economic power, but to confer the highest prestige and status they could aspire, especially if they were later promoted to Lima or the Council of Indies [in Spain]" (Bridikhina 2007: 2151).

5.3.3.1 *Audiencia of* Charcas *(Bolivia)*

This was the case of at least thirteen members who, originally from Lima, bought a seat in the Charcas *audiencia* (today Bolivia) during the office-selling period (1687 to 1751). These sales represented three-fourths of all seats sold in that *audiencia*, which was also smaller in size. Similarly, the four presidents[22] ruling Charcas from the first half of the eighteenth century – were all purchasers born in Lima. Purchasing seats in nearby *audiencias* was thus a way for Peruvian elites to secure their dominance in the Bolivia region as well – with the Concha, Tagle, Villalta, and Bravo de Rivero families in power in both Lima and Charcas in this period (Carrillo Ureta 2019). In fact, at one point, ministers Nuñez de Sanabria

---

[22] Presidents of the *audiencia* had additional prerogatives and power above that of regular members.

and Nuñez de Rojas, father and son, would be serving in Lima and Charcas, respectively (Jiménez 2016: 270). The latter were also related, by marriage, to the Concha and Villalta families.

Economically, the *audiencia* of Charcas (Bolivia) was particularly attractive for individuals with connections and commercial interests in southern Peru, mainly the Cuzco area. Since Cuzco was a key distribution site for both imported goods from Spain and the export of silver, it played a key role for *repartimiento* – supplying the goods *corregidores* distributed in southern Peru – but also for mining, the main economic activity in Charcas. This meant that connections between *corregidores*, ministers in the *audiencia*, and mining interests in Potosí naturally complemented each other.

Specific cases of *corregidor-audiencia* family ties include that of Nicolás Jiménez Lobatón, who purchased the presidency[23] of the Charcas *audiencia* in 1746 for 22,000 pesos and was himself married to a Cuzco native.[24] His son, in turn, purchased the *corregimiento* of Chilques and Masques – where he possessed an hacienda (Carrillo Ureta 2019) – which was also located in the Cuzco bishopric.[25] Similarly, Tomás Vázquez de Velasco, son of former *audiencia* President Pedro Vázquez de Velasco (1663–70) would be named to rule Vilcashuamán (in southern Peru). Furthermore, two of the President's brothers (Andrés and Tomás) would also be named to rule the *corregimientos* of Canta and Tinta in Southern Peru, respectively. Finally, Tomás Martín de Poveda, nephew of the former president of Charcas, Bartolomé González de Poveda (1673–85), was also appointed *corregidor* of Chayanta, this time in the Charcas territory itself (Jiménez 2016: 117).

As in the case of Lima, accusations against *corregidores* in the Charcas *audiencia* could be easily dismissed or lightly penalized, depending on their connections. Such is the case of *corregidor* Manuel Fernández de Valdivieso, accused by peasants from Atacama of excessive *repartimiento*; forced sales of their leather, wool, and livestock at below market rates; forced labor; excessive fines; and appropriation of an indigenous gold mine (Hidalgo Lehuede 1982: 200–201).[26] Despite a first instance official

---

[23] Senior member of the *audiencia* with additional prerogatives.
[24] Doña Constanza de Costilla Valverde y Cartagena, daughter of the treasury official of the Holy Crusade in Cuzco.
[25] Furthermore, the Jiménez' Lobatón were also related to Lima *oidor* Pedro Bravo de Rivero by marriage and involved in numerous joint businesses.
[26] Fernández de Valdivieso is also famous for documenting alleged witchcraft among the population (see Hidalgo Lehuede 1982).

finding the charges credible, the *Audiencia* favored a settlement, which greatly undermined the potential punishments for the *corregidor*.

In mining topics – the most important policy area under the Bolivian *audiencia's* portfolio – the *audiencia* was considered more attuned to the needs of miners in the region and often interceded in their favor to thwart reformist attempts from the Crown (Gonzalez Casasnovas 2000: 427–428)[27]. For example, the *corregidores* of Potosí supported the idea of cash payments to make up for missing *mita* workers (forced laborers) and hire free laborers – a policy the Crown considered abolishing (Cole 1983: 310), but which was supported in the *audiencia* (Cole 1983: 315).

5.3.3.2 Audiencia *of Quito (Ecuador)*

In the *audiencia* of Quito there was also an influx of Peruvian-born ministers (*limeños*) during the office-selling period (nine out of thirty-one), of which a majority (six) have purchased their position. In Quito, *Limeños* constituted the largest minority after that of Spanish-born officials. However, the presence of *Limeños* was complemented with locally born *Quiteños* (three, all purchasers) as well as those from Santa Fe (three, all purchasers) and a *Panameño* (purchaser). Altogether, the "Americans" bloc easily outnumbered the "Spanish".

As in the cases described earlier, the influx of these purchasers makes one wonder whether these were motivated by self-enrichment. For example, Herzog (2004) makes the argument that access to the *audiencia* of Quito was primarily for social prestige and status purposes and not for self-dealing ones. While this may be true, they were also, as their Lima counterparts, involved in numerous corruption scandals. Such is the case of ministers Cristobal de Ceballos Morales and Lorenzo Lastero de Salazar (purchasers) and Tomás Fernández Pérez (appointed), accused by the viceroy of Peru of trafficking with justice by accepting bribes (Burkholder and Chandler 1982: 84–85). Similarly, purchaser Pedro Gomez de Andrade faced charges of illegal commerce in his prior appointment in Panama, and there were still suspicions about his conduct.

In Quito, one of the main sources of income was that of the *obraje* – namely, a textile factory – which thrived with the abundance of indigenous labor and the trade policy of the Crown to restrict imported textiles.[28] Owners of *obrajes* were thus socially connected to colonial

---

[27] Such is the case of Pedro Vázquez de Velasco – a purchaser – known to advocate for mining interests.
[28] Conversely, this sector would enter a crisis in the eighteenth century with French contraband flooding the market and sinking prices.

authorities; for example, the Presidents of the *Audiencia* of Quito – (a) Zozaya, (b) Araújo y Río, and (c) Montúfar as well as minister, (d) Lastero de Salazar – all have married into families of *obrajeros* (Ortiz de la Tabla Ducasse 1982: 20).[29]

In addition to *obrajes*, lucrative contraband through Ecuadorian ports was a major source of rents. One of the main accusations against the President of the *Audiencia* Juan de Zozaya (a purchaser also involved in the *obrajes* business) was the flourishing of contraband in the *audiencia* at the expense of the Royal Treasury, aided by two *audiencia* ministers, Lastero de Salazar and Ceballos Morales (Herzog 2000: 89).[30] Contraband was also the main accusation against President José de Araújo y Río, an accusation made by opposed merchant groups (Herzog 2000). Not surprisingly, both of the accused were purchasers, native to the *audiencia*, and with strong local connections. Even ministers in charge of combating contraband would be involved in it. Such is the case of José de Llorente, accused by a merchant from Cartagena of confiscating his goods and asking for a payment in return (Herzog 2000: 102). While one could question the veracity of the accusations as driven by enmity, it is telling that no other *type* of official faced the same accusations.

Another set of colonial officials deeply involved in contraband was that of the *corregidor* of Guayaquil, who oversaw the only port in the *audiencia*. According to Clayton (1975: 16), this was a generalized occurrence among *corregidores* of Guayaquil and other officials who "permitted this trade to exist." Given ministers of the *audiencia* were in charge of overseeing their performance, it is hard to believe they were unaware of it. Rather, it is likely they would either willfully ignore it or even cooperate with these activities. For instance, while visiting the provinces, *audiencia* member Antonio de Torres Pizarro was accused of actively colluding in mutually profitable ventures with the officials from the mining Loja province, which he was supposed to be supervising (Orellana Sánchez 2019: 82).

A direct connection between *audiencia* and *corregidores* was that of minister Juan Dioniso Larrea Zurbano of Quito. A member of the Larrea family, with strong links to the economic and political elite in Quito, he also had strong local connections by marriage. His own son, Francisco Javier, would serve as *corregidor* of Riobamba. More extensive

---

[29] Some see a continuity between former *encomienda* owners in the sixteenth century and the eighteenth-century hacienda owners and *obrajeros* (Ortiz de la Tabla Ducasse 1982).
[30] There is also some debate as to whether the abettors were Lastero and Ceballos or Ricuarte (purchaser) and Sierra Osorio (appointee) (see fn. 245, Herzog 2000: 89).

are the links of *oidor* Juan Sánchez de Orellana y Espinosa, whose own father Antonio would serve as *corregidor* of Zaruma and whose half-brothers would serve as President of Quito (Fernando Félix), *corregidor* of Latacunga (Pedro Javier), Otavalo and Quijos y Macas (Juan José), and even of Tarma, in Peru (Nicolás). Albeit his tenure would be short due to his lack of qualifications, he nonetheless exemplified the sprawling networks of family connections and the economic interests, for example, in *obrajes*[31] that often accompanied purchasers.

Relationships between officials often extended beyond the geographic confines of the *audiencia*. Such is the case of the president of the *audiencia* of Quito, José de Araujo y Río, himself a close friend of Pedro Bravo de Rivero (in Lima), and whose brother-in-law, Victorino Montero del Águila became *corregidor* of the coastal province of Piura y Paita (in Lima) – an important port bordering the Quito *audiencia*. Among the three, they organized a profitable contraband business (Hill 2005; Carrillo Ureta 2019) involving the import of non-Spanish goods, avoiding taxes, and reselling the goods at markup prices or even using them for *repartimiento* purposes among the indigenous population.

As in Charcas, officials from the Lima *audiencia* would also end up serving in Quito, particularly if these represented a promotion. For example, former *corregidor* of Huancavelica Antonio Fernández de Heredia went on to occupy the Presidency of Quito, despite failing to provide key documentation clearing his performance at the mine (Jiménez 2016: 490). Altogether, the links between *corregidores*, *oidores*, and key social and economic sectors of the colonial apparatus resemble those of other *audiencias*. While mining was not a major activity in Ecuador as in Bolivia or Peru, illicit contraband and labor from indigenous populations for *obrajes* in Quito were key sources of profits there.

5.3.3.3 Audiencia *of Santiago de Chile*

Finally, the case of Santiago (Chile) exhibits similar patterns to those above: 56 percent of those entering during the sales period did so by purchase. Given its role as "subordinate" *audiencia*, it was a necessary step for those seeking promotion to Lima and Charcas – although it should be noted that only 28 percent of those entering the *audiencia* during sales were ever promoted. Instead, belonging to the *audiencia* of Santiago offered unique economic opportunities for those connected to

---

[31] According to Ortiz de la Tabla Ducasse (1982: 20), the Larrea Zurbano family was one of the main *obrajero* families in the *audiencia*.

the economies of Cuzco and Puno in Southern Peru or to certain regions of Charcas (Bolivia). In fact, of those ministers entering office between 1687 and 1751, only 8 percent were Chileans (all purchasers), while 16 percent were from Charcas (all purchasers), 36 percent were from Lima (2/3 of them purchasers), 4 percent were from Santo Domingo (all purchasers), and the rest, 32 percent, were from Spain (all appointed).

Such a large presence of *criollos* was certainly a reflection of the economic opportunities available in the *audiencia*, albeit arguably lower than in the other two cases due to the early depopulation of the indigenous population. Chief among them were the ample possibilities for smuggling along the vast Chilean coastline. As in the ports of Guayaquil (Ecuador) and Piura y Paita (Peru), contraband in the port of Concepción – one of the main ports in the *audiencia* – was also rampant. For this reason, the Crown ordered that a member of the *audiencia* had to rotate and serve as *corregidor* of the province. Yet, the measure turned out to be ineffective as *audiencia* members themselves quickly became involved in the activity. Minister Juan Corral Calvo de la Torre, a purchaser of the *audiencia*, was known to be actively colluding with French smugglers (Villalobos 1961: 57–58). Similarly, the governor of Valparaíso – another Chilean port – was openly friendly to smugglers and asked for 5 percent of their sales, an amount justifiable given the large amount he had to pay to access his position in the first place (Villalobos 1961: 58). The involvement in contraband extended to the highest spheres of government, namely, the governor of Chile, Juan Andres Ustariz, who relied on the governor of Valparaíso and *corregidor* of Quillota to charge his own 6 percent to French smugglers (Villalobos 1961: 59).

In addition to smuggling, there is also evidence that *audiencia* positions were useful for social advancement, which in itself brought other economic opportunities. The excellent portrayal by Barbier (1972) shows the social links established by royal officials essentially undermined eighteenth-century Bourbon attempts to insulate colonial officials from local influence (Barbier 1972: 429). These social connections translated into economic advantages due to their ability to influence colonial policy, for example, by exerting their "maximum opposition" to policies that could have been "[...] advantageous to royal finances"[32] but at the expense of the colonial population. For example, Schiaffino (1999: 137) mentions the collusion between members of the *audiencia*

---

[32] Silvestre García to Minister of the Indies Julian de Arriaga January 31, 1774, in SM, vol. 195, pp. 312–313, cited by Barbier (1972: 430).

5 Captured Administration

and the *corregidor* to auction tithes at below market prices by artificially restricting other bids, in detriment of the Royal Treasury. Moreover, as in Lima, Quito, and Charcas, *corregidores* were also involved in profitable commercial activities, for example, by limiting competition from other merchants in areas under his jurisdiction, effectively monopolizing trade and selling goods at markup prices (*repartimiento*). The latter practice would continue even under the *subdelegados*, after the introduction of the *Intendencia* system in the 1780s (Schiaffino 1999).

While not as prolific in the literature as the other three, the Chilean case still illustrates why office-selling might have facilitated the complementarities between *audiencia* members and *corregidores* and *alcaldes mayores*. These networks were not limited to a single *audiencia* but expanded beyond jurisdictions to create cross-*audiencia* networks.

5.4 AN EARLY "AMERICAN" GOVERNMENT?

This chapter combines statistical evidence and historical case studies to document the complementarities between higher-level officials (*audiencia* members) and lower-level ones (*corregidores* and *alcaldes*), as enabled by office-selling. *Audiencias* in which purchasers became a majority were highly attractive places to rule by *corregidores* and *alcaldes* seeking a quick fortune. As documented in the cases of Lima, Quito, Santiago, and Charcas, office-selling facilitated the emergence of a network of business, family, and clientelar relationships which enabled all sorts of profit-seeking practices – particularly those at the expense of the royal coffers and the indigenous population.

Prior to office-selling, these networks certainly existed, but outside of the colonial administration. The key role of sales was to place these networks at the center of the colonial administration. By facilitating sorting, it enabled collusion and networks between levels of the colonial administration (*corregidor-audiencias*). In a parallel world, in which the Spanish Crown would have only sold one level of the colonial administration, say *corregimientos* and *alcaldías*, these officials would have faced *some* oversight from the Spanish appointees in the *audiencia*. The sale of both levels of the administration rendered vertical checks futile.

Yet, the concurrent sale of both high-level and low-level officials was a key way to maximize the revenue the Crown could collect from sales. Loosening oversight from high-level offices inevitably increased the profitability of lower-level positions, resulting in higher prices – a fact documented here. However, consistent with the revenue – governance trade-off outlined in Chapter 3, looser oversight did not happen everywhere but was concentrated in the *audiencias* facing fewer foreign threats. The better screening of buyers for seats in the *audiencia* of Mexico, Guatemala, Panama, Santo Domingo (Caribbean basin), and Santa Fe (Colombia) translated into *oidores* more aligned with the Crown and naturally less connected with lower-level *corregidores* and *alcaldes*. The result is an exponential increase in prices in some *audiencias* but not in others.

It is also noteworthy that the revenue obtained by the Crown likely did not come at the expense of local or *criollo* elites – who paid for these positions but were able to recoup their investment in different ways. Rather, it came at the expense of the economic surplus of the indigenous population and the Crown's own revenue. As put by Lynch (1992: 74–75): "[...] while the Americanisation of the bureaucracy [via sales] may have been a victory for the creole elites, it was a further setback for the ethnic communities and those who had to supply tribute, taxes, and labour, groups who found themselves without allies under the new alignment." The arrival of purchasers shrunk the economic surplus of the indigenous population via extractive activities such as repartimiento, an important reason behind the many rebellions documented in Chapter 6.

Finally, beyond the immediate effect of sales on weakening oversight mechanisms, the entry of these *criollo* elites into high-ranking positions may have also planted the seed of the future disintegration of the Empire. As also put by Lynch (1992: 77): "[Criollo Elites] began to regard their own *audiencia* district as *patrias* and to claim that in addition to their intellectual, academic, and economic qualifications they had a legal right to hold all offices within their boundaries." In this sense, "the sale of offices came to form a kind of American representation in government" (Lynch 1992: 77).

But what kind of government would this be? If anything, the episode of office-selling casts doubt on the idea that the colonial administration could have been better in the hands of the *criollo* elites – at least from the viewpoint of indigenous population. While we do not know what would have happened if *criollos* were able to enter office by appointment as opposed to being sold, the fact remains that the rise of purchasers in the *audiencia* (mostly native *criollos*) facilitated the profit-seeking activities of *corregidores* at the expense of the indigenous population and sometimes the royal coffers. Maybe, in a parallel world in which the Crown decided to appoint local elites to the colonial administration free of charge, the outcome might have been different.

5 *Captured Administration* 123

In all, what this chapter shows are the negative institutional consequences created by office-selling in the Americas. Even if the Crown sought to limit the negative externalities by restraining itself from selling geopolitically sensitive locations – the influx of purchasers at all levels undermined the system of vertical and horizontal checks of the Spanish Empire.

Chapter summary. The first consequence of sales was to facilitate the capture of the colonial administration by local elites, enabling self-dealing across its ranks. By examining the composition of *audiencia* councils, the chapter shows that the value of offices under their watch (*corregimientos*, *alcaldías*) exponentially increased with the share of purchasers in the *audiencia*, consistent with laxer oversight. The effect is driven by the *audiencias*, where the Crown was less concerned about the quality of its members as they faced lower geopolitical threats. It is also driven by the influx of members with strong local connections that would particularly benefit from colluding with lower-level officials. This statistical evidence helps substantiate the many historical accounts of profitable complementarities between *audiencia* members and *corregidores* and *alcaldes* in the territories (now countries) of Peru, Bolivia, Ecuador, and Chile. These networks and connections would prove difficult to eradicate, even after the end of sales.

6

To Flee or to Fight

Indigenous Responses to Venality

> [L]os infelices sufren castigos, y vilipendios, sin poderse remediar, por no llegar a oídos de quien los consolaría, y como único medio eligen el de ausentarse, o levantarse contra el corregidor que les gobierna, para desahogarse en parte de sus aflicciones; en cuyos tumultos se causan las muertes, y desordenes que son consiguientes, por no haber quien les contenga, y aun en este caso siempre quedan los espíritus dispuestos a nuevas sublevaciones [...][1]
>
> Viceroy Manuel de Guirior to the King of Spain (1777)

The previous chapter shows how office-selling facilitates profitable complementarities between high-level officials (*audiencias*) and lower levels ones (*corregidores*, *alcaldes*). Capitalizing on credit constraints, high rent availability, and the ability to self-select into positions, buyers flocked to positions *where* and *when* they would face less oversight. The direct consequence was increased appropriation of economic surplus from the (indigenous) population by officials through any means available – what I call *venality*. This chapter examines two consequences of greater exploitation: The rise in violent uprisings and the geographic displacement of the indigenous population.

***

---

[1] AGI. Indiferente 1713, Legajo 196, *Carta de Manuel de Guirior al Rey*. Lima 20 de Agosto de 1777. Translation: "The unfortunate (indigenous people) suffer punishments and slanders without remedy because their plight does not reach the ears of those who would remedy them. As their only means, they choose to either leave or rise up against the *corregidor* who governs them, in order to partially relieve their afflictions. These riots lead to deaths and disorder, with no one to contain them, and even in that case, spirits remain disposed to new uprisings."

6 To Flee or to Fight

The longevity of the Spanish Empire in the Americas – roughly 300 years[2] – masks the extent to which its rule, particularly as exerted by its officials, was actively contested and resisted at the local level. This chapter links these resistance activities – in particular, the violent opposition to colonial officials via riots, uprisings, and out-migration – to changes in the colonial administration driven by office-selling.

Clearly, uprisings and migration are not the only or even the most prevalent form of indigenous resistance. In fact, from the Spanish viewpoint at the time, there were a myriad of other examples of indigenous defiance to their rule. Their appearance, customs, and "failure to adhere to the sacraments, idolatry [...]" (Schroeder 1998: xiv) were all seen as means to challenge the institutional, cultural, and most importantly, economic demands brought about by colonizers.

The indigenous population also assiduously relied on the legal system as a nonviolent way to voice their grievances and concerns. In Mexico, the use of litigation was widespread through the cases submitted to a specialized court – the *Tribunal General de Indios* – devoted to Indigenous claims which often ruled in favor of indigenous claimants vis-à-vis local officials and landowners (Franco Vivanco 2021). In Bolivia, the indigenous nobility often sought legal recognition of their lineage in the colonial *audiencia*, as it carried special rights (Castro Flores 2019). In Ecuador, some of the early discontent against *corregidores* was voiced in the *audiencia* as a way to legally contest abuses (Albornoz 1976). As put by Stern (1987), legal battles were part of a repertoire that included physical distance (migration), lack of cultural assimilation, local uprisings, and even full insurrection.

Despite the numerous examples of indigenous resistance, in this chapter I exclusively focus on uprisings and migration for two reasons. The first is that these actions were very costly to those involved: Once undertaken, they could not be easily "undone." Individuals who left their community forfeited their right to the community's land, turning instead into wage laborers, tenants, or sharecroppers elsewhere. Their costliness can thus tell us something about the prevailing conditions they faced: that it was extreme enough as to warrant these measures. Moreover, as starkly put by the Peruvian Viceroy's introductory quote, migration (*ausentarse*) and/or rebellion (*levantarse*) against royal

---

[2] Longer for territories which did not gain independence in the first quarter of the nineteenth century (i.e., the Philippines, Cuba, and Puerto Rico).

representatives was also a constant worry of colonial officials – both for the loss in property and life involved as for the costs of mobilizing rural militias to combat them.³

The second reason, and key for this chapter, is that due to the undercover nature of the extractive activities of *corregidores* and *alcaldes*, it is often impossible to know their true extent and egregiousness. After all, there are very few incentives for *corregidores* and *alcaldes* to record their activities and unduly obtained profits. Yet, under very plausible assumptions – namely, that revolts serve as a mechanism to voice deep discontent – the presence of uprisings and (or) systematic migration can serve as a reflection of the severity, grievousness, and widespread nature of *corregidor'* and *alcaldes'* activities.⁴ In particular, if we observe that the areas most affected by office-selling also exhibit a large number of uprisings and indigenous resettlement, these would suggest some connection between them.

At first glance, the onset of office-selling in 1670 and the changes it brought to the colonial administration *do* coincide with the end of the so-called *Pax Hispannica* – the period with a relative absence of violent uprisings against colonial rule. After the first expeditions of conquest and pacification, historians⁵ noted the lack of major overt challenges to colonial rule under the Habsburgs – sixteenth to seventeenth centuries. Yet, the start of Bourbon rule in 1700 brought with it an increase in the number of rebellions, some of them the largest and most concerted efforts in Spanish America, particularly in the second half of the eighteenth century (McFarlane 1995; Coatsworth 1988). Notable examples include the Tzetzal rebellion in the *audiencia* of Guatemala (1712), the Túpac Amaru one in Peruvian and Bolivian territories (1780), the *comunero's* rebellion in the Viceroyalty of New Granada (Colombia) in 1781, as well as the Quito rebellion of 1764.

These events have inspired a large literature analyzing their causes, consequences, and the creation of typologies based on the movement's

---

³ There were no standing armies to combat these types of insurrections across most of Spanish America at this time.
⁴ One concern is that areas prone to uprisings were disproportionately sold and at higher prices. However, one would expect that "rebellious" provinces to negatively affect demand such that any positive relationship between prices and uprisings has already "priced-in" these traits.
⁵ See McFarlane (2021). For a challenge to this notion, see Murdo J. Mcleod's (1998) who instead highlights the continuous low-level conflict within Spanish America.

leaders, social base, and (or) the precipitating factors.[6] The most common explanation for these rebellions was the introduction of Empire-wide fiscal innovations and tax increases as well as changes in long-established jurisdictions. Examples include increases in the *alcabala* tax rate, changes to the way in which it was collected, and the expulsion of the Jesuits from the colonial territories, all Bourbon reforms launched in the second half of the eighteenth century.[7] Other accounts point to demographic factors, such as the explosive population growth in the second half of the eighteenth century, which put pressure on land and led to a decline in real wages and living standards (Arroyo Abad et al. 2012) – an important cause behind rebellions (Tutino 1986).

The main contribution of this chapter is to show that royal administrative policies of the early eighteenth century are a key contextual background to understand the breakdown of the *Pax Hispannica* in Spanish America. While empire-wide fiscal innovations indeed precipitated uprisings, these were not implemented in a vacuum. Rather, in contexts long exposed to the venality of *corregidores* and *alcaldes*. By appropriating "too much" economic surplus, these officials might have lowered the opportunity costs of uprisings as well as changed the culture or "predisposition" of the indigenous population to rise up in arms. Moreover, because the end of sales in Madrid did not put an end to venal practices in the Americas,[8] these activities persisted well beyond 1751. Likely exacerbating the effect other macro reforms would have.

In fact, this was the "official" explanation for the increase in uprisings held by high-level authorities – Viceroys, Bishops, and Royal Envoys – at the time. As shown in the introductory quote and in the letters explored in Section 6.2, there was a strong belief among high-level circles that *corregidores* and *alcaldes* were directly and indirectly responsible for the rise in uprisings at the time. Restoration of the *Pax Hispannica*, they argued, started with the removal of the figure of *corregidor* and *alcalde* altogether – the basis for the future administrative reforms in the empire. But, were these officials right?

This chapter provides statistical evidence of the role of office-selling in bringing about the end of the *Pax Hispannica*. Namely, it explores to what extent provinces in greater demand during sales (1670–1750)

---

[6] See Coatsworth (1988) for a comparative view of these rebellions across the main territories of Spanish America and their classification in different types.
[7] A long literature tends to attribute to global or regional shifts in economic conditions, as well as to other more short-term fluctuations (Coatsworth 1988).
[8] Certain officials were appointed for life or had yet to enter office via *futuras*.

exhibit a greater likelihood of uprisings and displaced populations. Is this probability greater in the office-selling period or afterwards? Did office-selling exacerbate subsistence crises leading to rebellion? Answers in the affirmative would help us understand the role of administrative and personnel policy – not just fiscal measures – to understand the geography and timing of rebellion in eighteenth-century Spanish America.

This analysis also helps reconcile the gap between macro-level explanations for rebellions, such as those centered on Empire-wide (Bourbon) reforms and the discontent they created, with the fact that many uprisings were driven by inherently local reasons. For example, Van Young (2001) argues that in eighteenth-century Mexico, more than 50 percent of the rebellions studied involved the contestation of local authorities and local grievances. Similarly, Taylor (1979) shows how many indigenous uprisings can be traced to single "arbitrary acts of public officials" and not necessarily to some broad change in colonial policy. The target of attacks in these cases was typically "[…] a colonial official or a building identified with outside authority, usually the *casas reales* (government offices) or the jail" (Taylor 1979: 119).

This chapter makes the case that the particular type of local governance is a key condition to understand how the empire-wide reforms of the Crown spelled the end of the *Pax Hispannica*. Areas of the empire with greater exposure to office-selling-turned-venality had a lower threshold for rebellion in the presence of these macro-reforms. Venality made the fuses "shorter," flare-ups "quicker," and grievances "deeper." To the best of my knowledge, this is the first empirical evidence tying the policies of sales with the intensity of uprisings across key territories in Spanish America.[9]

6.1 THE "OFFICIAL VIEW" OF UPRISINGS

According to the views of prominent colonial officials at the time, the blame for the surge in uprisings fell squarely on the activities of *corregidores* and *alcaldes mayores*. At least in the most populous territories in the empire: that of Mexico, Peru, and Bolivia. Their abuse of the *repartimiento* system, the excessive tax rates (above those authorized by the Crown), and the cruel treatment of the Crown's indigenous subjects' figure prominently in these accounts.

---

[9] Earlier work by Guardado (2018, 2022) focused only on the case of Peru.

Although the views of the higher echelons of the colonial government should be taken with caution, they provide a snapshot of the prevailing sentiment in these circles. For instance, the accusations against *corregidores* and *alcaldes* could be a ploy to distract from the true effect of other empire-wide measures implemented. Or, they could simply reflect their ignorance of the motives of uprisings, or serve as a way to strategically blame actors they aim to discredit, among other possibilities.

On the other hand, discerning the true causes of uprisings was also in the best interest of the Crown and its officials. Uprisings were costly for the local coffers – which officials sought to minimize when possible: Revolts were expensive to put down, as it required mobilizing troops and replacing destroyed infrastructure, and so on. Revolts also disrupted trade, made it difficult to control the indigenous population, and undermined the supply of certain types of indigenous labor – a key factor of production – as well as the reliability and size of the taxable base. Maintaining a minimum level of welfare could go a long way in preserving the integrity and longevity of the empire as well as fulfilling the Crown's Christian role.

6.1.1 Visitadores, Viceroys, and the Church: Uprisings in Official Correspondence

Among the most illustrative accounts are three letters from the Viceroy of Peru, royal inspectors (*visitadores*) José Antonio Areche and José de Gálvez, as well as the Bishop of Arequipa. Although written after the end of sales, they help highlight how many of the practices popularized during the 1670–1750 period still remained in place. If anything, they may have only worsened over time. These letters also suggest that toward the third quarter of the eighteenth century, the Crown was well aware of the role of *corregidores* and *alcaldes* in driving the surge of uprisings in Mexico, Peru, and Bolivia, explaining its later reformist impulse.

The first document is a letter from the royal envoy (*visitador*) to the *audiencia* of Lima (now Peru), José Antonio Areche, dated May 16, 1780. In it, he points to the numerous transgressions of the *corregidores* against the indigenous population as the major driver of the uptick in uprisings. The letter singles out the practice of *repartimiento* as well as (in his view) the incorrect implementation of the reforms to the *alcabala* (sales) tax as the main policies that local officials exploited for their own gain. The document ends with a stark warning to the Crown, stating there would be no peace among Peruvian provinces unless the *repartimiento* activities of *corregidores* are completely banned.[10]

Areche's letter, written on May 16, 1780, was sent just six months before what was considered the largest rebellion against colonial rule across the empire: that of José Gabriel Condorcanqui – Túpac Amaru. Starting in the province of Canas y Canchis, the rebellion would spread to fifteen other provinces spanning the territories of Peru and Bolivia, and last for the next two years (roughly). Non-coincidentally, the precipitating factor of the uprising was the anger against the excessive exactions of the *corregidor* of Canas y Canchis, which led to his imprisonment and later execution by the rebels. Anger was also directed to the forced labor drafts to the mines (mit'a) and to the odious *repartimiento*.[11] Although the May 1780 letter of *visitador* Areche appears chillingly prescient, it was actually informed by the numerous uprisings that had occurred *prior* to Túpac Amaru and the prevailing sense of discontent against the activities of *corregidores* in the territory. By the time of his letter, there had been at least ninety-five recorded uprisings since 1700.[12]

Areche's view was also supported by the Viceroy of Peru, Manuel de Guirior, who explicitly links the frequent uprisings in the territory to the "excessive" *repartimiento* of the *corregidores*, as noted in the introductory quote.[13] The letter goes on to say that even though there was an established quota for *repartimiento* in each province set by the *audiencia* since 1751, the *corregidores* often exceeded it. Although the rest of the letter is concerned with the conflict between *corregidores* appointed by the King and those on an interim basis, it sheds light on the perceived drivers of uprisings in the viceroyalty of Peru.

From a different quarter, that of ecclesiastical authorities, the 1777 letter from the Bishop of Arequipa also decried the practice of *repartimiento* as a source of misery among the population, not only indigenous but also mestizo and Spanish. Exploitation from *repartimientos* was such that many indigenous towns could not pay their yearly tithe obligations to the Church – as they feared for their life if they did not repay

---

[10] AGI, Indiferente 1713, No. 195. *Visitador general del Peru Jose Antonio de Areche al Rey*. The main argument of the letter is that revenue would be higher if *repartimientos* were abolished.

[11] See Chapter 2 for a detailed description of the practice and its relationship to office prices.

[12] Data from O'Phelan (1988) and Gölte (1980).

[13] AGI, Indiferente 1713, No. 196, Lima 20 de Agosto de 1777. *Manuel de Guirior al Rey*.

6 To Flee or to Fight

the *corregidor* the goods they were forced to purchase. More ominously, but ultimately accurate, the Bishop raised the specter of a "general uprising" not only among the indigenous population but also one that would include mestizos and even Spaniards, as they suffered from the unbearable yoke imposed by the *corregidores*.[14]

These warnings were not limited to the Viceroyalty of Peru, as around the same time (1768), the royal envoy to New Spain (now Mexico), José de Gálvez, would complain about the "tyrannical" *repartimiento* activities of the *alcaldes mayores* there, which not only affected the indigenous population but also undermined the royal coffers by reducing the proceeds from sales taxes (*alcabala* tax).[15] More importantly, the royal envoy directly linked the *repartimiento* activities of these officials to the recent destruction of the cochineal plants (a source of red dye) by indigenous communities, a form of sabotage against the excessive exploitation of the crop proceeds.[16]

The underlying theme of all of these letters was the decline of indigenous welfare due to the activities of *corregidores* and *alcaldes*. Yet, these views were not new. Accounts from the office-selling period (1670-ca. 1760), for example, from the Secret News report, show that *corregidores* were already undermining the welfare of the indigenous population and the Crown was well aware of it.

In fact, already by the first round of sales (late seventeenth century), the plight of indigenous groups in Madrid reached such a level that it prompted the Council of Indies and the King to change the text of the appointment titles of *corregidores* and *alcaldes mayores* – which had remained very similar for almost a century – as a way to warn incoming officials against abuses. In the new wording, there were explicit references to the type of exploitation officials should *not* commit while in office.[17] Yet, the inherent inability to monitor officials meant these warnings were largely ineffective.

---

[14] Indiferente 1713, *Carta del Obispo de Arequipa (1776)*. Arequipa 10 de Abril de 1776. "... es temible un general levantamiento, no solo de los indios, sino también de mestizos, y españoles, porque todos gimen bajo de tan insoportable yugo."

[15] Because most of the commercial dealings of the *corregidor* were illicit, they did not pay the appropriate sales tax.

[16] Indiferente 1713, *Informe y Plan de Intendencias Que Conviene Establecer En Las Provincias de Este Reyno de Nueva Espana*. Mexico 15 Enero 1768. José de Gálvez.

[17] The text approved in 1530 of the appointment swear-in does not include any of these provisions. See *Recopilacion de Leyes de los Reinos de las Indias* (1841). Libro Quinto: Titulo Segundo "De los Gobernadores, Corregidores, Alcaldes Mayores, y Sus Tenientes y Alguaciles," Ley VII.

An illustrative example is the 1698 title of Francisco Lienzo Pontelos, as *Alcalde Mayor* of Huautla (in the *audiencia* of Mexico), which explicitly states how *corregidores* and *alcaldes* in the Indies (and he personally) are forbidden from using indigenous communal savings (*cajas de la comunidad*) for their own purposes. They were also barred from relying on the indigenous population for any kind of personal service.[18] Especially when travelling around the province, they ought to not coerce the Indians into providing supplies and lodging. Similar warnings were included after the practice of *repartimiento* became legal in 1751: The swearing-in text starting of 1757 now included an explicit warning to incoming officials *not* to exceed the amount and goods and the prices established in each *audiencia*. Failure to observe these rules would be "vigorously and severely punished."[19] Clearly, the Crown had already received notice of actual or potential abuses in the practice of *repartimiento*.

The fact that these admonitions and complaints against *corregidores* and *alcaldes* are a recurrent theme in the eighteenth century showed their lack of success. The question is, were these complaints *lower* prior to the office-selling period? While we do not have complete evidence, there are scattered accounts that suggest that complaints against *corregidores* prior to office-selling were different in nature and focused on locations that would not see higher valuations and uprisings throughout the eighteenth century.

For instance, a collection of letters from the parishes of the bishopric of Cuzco in Peru described the state of affairs of different provinces toward 1689 (Villanueva Urteaga 1982). The view portrayed is far from rosy, but these letters contain less complaints about *corregidores* at the time, than what would emerge eighty years later. Instead, most of the complaints centered on the depopulation caused by the mining *mita*, also enacted by *corregidores*. While by itself this does not constitute *prima facie* evidence[20] of lower exactions at the early stages of office-selling, it suggests that at least the geographic scope and the nature of the *corregidor* activity were different at the time. In fact, there is a very weak correlation between where *corregidores* had documented abuses in the 1680s, when most positions had not

---

[18] AGI. Mexico 1219. *Titulo de Francisco Lienzo Pontelos, 8 de Marzo de 1698*.
[19] AGI. Mexico 1229.
[20] There are also reasons to suspect the denunciations by priests, as they may have their own incentives to report (or not) the activities of *corregidores*, as sometimes they served as allies and others as competitors in the appropriation of indigenous surplus.

been intensely sold, and the price levels those provinces would have (on average) in the next sixty years. Thus suggesting that office-selling brought a new and distinctive burden to the locations where it was most intensely practiced. But how closely do the geographic patterns of rebellion follow that of office-selling?

6.2 EIGHTEENTH-CENTURY UPRISINGS & OFFICE-SELLING IN SPANISH AMERICA

A vast literature has dealt with the topic of uprisings and rebellions in eighteenth-century Spanish America. Yet, by and large, these studies have focused either on major rebellions as stand-alone events or those of a particular territory. Examples of major rebellions are those of Túpac Amaru, the *Comuneros* rebellion in Nueva Granada, or the Quito Rebellion.[21] Another approach has been to focus on a particular territory and the prevalence of uprisings there.

However, studies compiling all known instances of rebellion across all or at least a number of *audiencias* of the Spanish Empire are scarce – the notable exception being Coatsworth (1988). Part of this gap is driven by definitional problems (what counts as an uprising?), comparability, researchers' interests, and sheer data availability. The result is a somewhat geographical and event-skewed view of eighteenth-century rebellion with more studies from Peru, Bolivia, and Mexico and greater interest in major events: Tzetzal rebellion, Quito uprising, Santa Fe's *comuneros*, or Túpac Amaru.

Keeping these constraints in mind, in this chapter I collected all the available data[22] on uprisings from different areas of the Empire to test whether the geographic distribution and intensity of these uprisings are linked to higher demand for office both during the sales period and afterwards. Guided by the approach and complementing the sources used in Coatsworth (1988), I collected all "village riots" or rural uprisings for

---

[21] An exception to this trend is the work by Tutino, examining a unique rebellion in the Tehuantepec isthmus (1980).
[22] The data on rebellions documents better the cases of Peru, Bolivia, and Mexico vis-à-vis other areas of the empire. For instance, O'Phelan 1988 and Gölte 1980 provide excellent compilations for the case of Peru and Bolivia, while Taylor (1979) and Tutino (1980) do the same for Mexico. Similarly, I rely on data collected by Macfarlane (1984) for Nueva Granada (now roughly Colombia); Navarrete (1982), and Martinez Pelaez (2021 [1985]) for Guatemala; and Segundo Moreno Yánez (1985), Albornoz Peralta (1976), and Becker (2008) for Ecuador.

eighteenth century Peru, Bolivia, Mexico, Ecuador, Guatemala, and Colombia.[23] Namely, violent episodes that reflect discontent against colonial officials or colonial policy either because they are directly against the latter or cite a particular policy as their motivation. Uprisings against private individuals in their role as *hacendados*, *encomenderos*, or plantation owners are not included in the analysis. In line with the literature, I also do not call them revolutions, as they do not aim to bring about independence but rather express discontent at the prevailing situation.

With this information I created a province-year dataset where each year in rebellion is coded as a 1 and years in peace are coded as 0. The data runs from 1700 until 1808 in all cases except that of Peru and Bolivia, where I stopped in 1780 – thus excluding the Túpac Amaru rebellion (1780–1782) and its aftermath.[24] The reason to stop at 1808 is the Napoleonic invasion of the Iberian Peninsula, which changed the nature of uprisings by introducing other dimensions as causes of conflict. The reason to exclude major rebellions is that due to their magnitude and complex dynamics – involving numerous social actors and geographic territories – they reflect all manners of discontent (and opportunism) often unrelated to the actions of particular colonial officials and policies.

6.2.1 Descriptive Patterns

Figure 6.1 provides a visual representation of the yearly distribution of these rebellions across the territories of Peru, Bolivia, Mexico, Ecuador, Guatemala, and Colombia, throughout the eighteenth century. As noted, the data replicates some of the patterns identified in the literature: First, the greater intensity of rebellions across the Spanish Empire in the late colonial period, say, post-1760 relative to the period prior to it. Second, the relatively higher prevalence of uprisings in the *audiencias* of Peru and Bolivia, in absolute terms.[25]

---

[23] Roughly the former *audiencias* of Lima, Charcas, Mexico, Quito, Guatemala, and Santa Fe, respectively.
[24] The analysis excludes major uprisings in each case: Túpac Amaru in Peru-Bolivia; Tzetzal in Guatemala; *comuneros* in Nueva Granada; the post-1808 revolts in Mexico; and the *Rebelión de los Barrios* in Quito.
[25] Even after including the spike in revolts in the *audiencia* of Mexico in the early nineteenth century, the number of revolts in the Lima and Charcas *audiencias* is still higher in absolute terms.

6 To Flee or to Fight   135

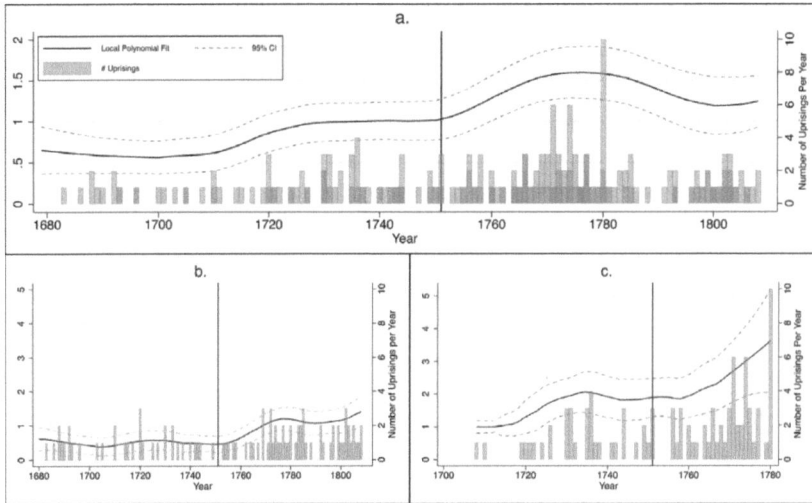

FIGURE 6.1 Uprisings and the end of the *Pax Hispannica* (1680–1808)

Notes: a. All territories; b. Only Mexico; c. Peru and Bolivia. Local polynomial fit line with corresponding 95 percent Confidence Intervals. DV: Uprisings in a given year. Vertical line: year 1751. Sources: Own construction based on data from O'Phelan (1988) and Gölte (1980) for Lima and Charcas; Taylor (1979) and Garfias and Sellars (2022) for Mexico; McFarlane (1984) for Santa Fe; Navarrete (1982) for Guatemala; and Moreno Yánez (1985), Albornoz Peralta (1976), and Becker (2008) for Quito. Lima and Charcas end in 1780 due to the Túpac Amaru rebellion and aftermath.

Consistent with the existing literature, it is clear from Figure 6.1 that the majority of rebellions took place post-1760. Because these rebellions coincide temporally with the intensification of the Bourbon Reforms at the hands of Charles III, the literature has generally associated the rise in uprisings with the implementation of the reforms. In particular, the updating of tax-collection records, redrafting workers for labor in the mines, or reducing tax exemptions (*alcabalas*), to name a few (O'Phelan 1988).

In light of these accounts, it might appear that post-1760 uprisings have nothing to do with the earlier office-selling policy. After all, by then, Crown appointees have already replaced *corregidores*. Yet, this might be inaccurate for two reasons: First, the effect of *corregidores* who have purchased their post could have been felt well beyond their time in office. This would be the case if the appropriation activities of *corregidores* pushed the population to the verge of subsistence or if it fostered a culture or predisposition for rebellion. In these cases, future rebellions would be more likely precisely where the activities of venal *corregidores* were more extractive.

136   *The Venal Origins of Development in Spanish America*

Second, some of the most extractive practices by colonial officials became institutionalized, ensuring their persistence. For example, the empire-wide legalization of *repartimiento* due to the active lobbying of *audiencia* members who have purchased their post was a major driver of rebellions. Finally, the weaker oversight from the *audiencia* and regional treasuries – who remained in office even after the end of sales – continue to facilitate abuses by *corregidores* and *alcaldes*, even if the latter were appointed. As a result, the consequences of office-selling would still be felt due to the numerous *audiencia* and treasury holdovers.

6.2.1.1 Uprisings Across Audiencias
Given the different ways in which office-selling impacted colonial governance, it is likely that in *audiencias* where sales were more intense, there is also a higher prevalence of rebellion in absolute terms. Figure 6.2 examines whether this is the case. As shown, across all six *audiencias* for which data is available, the years in which more purchasers sat in the *audiencia* are associated with a greater number of rebellions on average, even after accounting for particular year shocks (year fixed effects) in panel b.

While these patterns are consistent with the idea that office-selling had some influence over the intensity and distribution of uprisings, they are also drawn from a limited number of independent observations – namely, from those *audiencias* with uprising data available (six). Other accounts could explain this difference, for example, the greater geopolitical risk in the *audiencias* of Mexico, Santa Fe, and Guatemala meant that officials might have been less lenient or more repressive in these areas, leading to fewer rebellions. Or they would have become more attuned to local conditions, to name some possibilities.

6.2.2 Uprisings in *Corregimientos* and *Alcaldías*

To account for these alternative possibilities, the rest of the chapter is instead devoted to examining whether provinces with more sales also exhibit more uprisings both during and after the period of sales. By looking *within* each *audiencia*, it is possible to isolate *audiencia*-level explanations.

Anecdotally, some of the rebellions against authorities documented in Mexico (Taylor 1979) took place in provinces that had been heavily sold in the years immediately before the uprising. For example, the population's refusal to pay head taxes to the *alcalde mayor* in Xochimilco in 1720 was

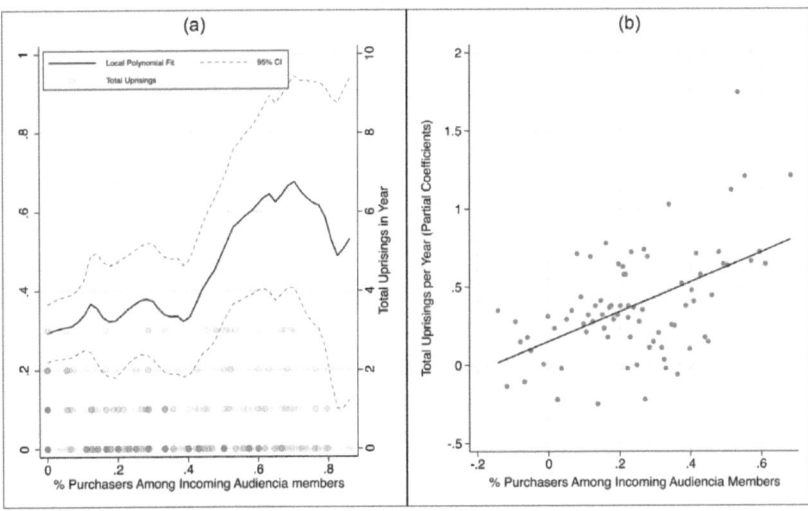

FIGURE 6.2 Yearly uprisings and *audiencia* composition (1680–1780)

Notes: Panel (a) Local polynomial fit line with corresponding 95 percent Confidence Intervals. Panel (b) binned scatterplot including year fixed effects. DV: Total uprisings in a given year. Sources for uprisings: See note Fig. 1. Sources for *audiencia* purchasers: Burkholder and Chandler (1977).

preceded by the sale of this position eight times since 1687. Similarly, the 1730 revolts (*excesos e intento de asonada*) in Ixtlahuaca were also preceded by frequent sales of the *alcalde* position since 1675. The "mutiny" by locals in 1766 in Huichapan also took place in a province frequently sold, with prices well above the average for the *audiencia* of Mexico.

In the case of Lima and Charcas, the links are more explicit – thanks to the greater level of detail of the available sources (O'Phelan 1988; Golte 1980). For example, the 1708 indigenous uprising in Huanuco (Viceroyalty of Peru) was directed against the *corregidor* Francisco Fernandez De Sandoval, who had bought his appointment in Madrid in 1694 for around 3,200 pesos – a quantity he was probably interested in recouping. Similarly, the 1731 uprising in Cotabambas targeted *corregidor* Juan Bautista Fandino for increasing the *mita* requirements. Fandino had bought this position in 1712 for 2,000 pesos. In many other cases, the identity of the *corregidor* is unknown or does not match those sold by the Crown, likely due to the reliance on interim appointments[26] and the

---

[26] After the end of the term of a *corregidor* appointed by the King, the Viceroy could appoint an interim one who would serve in office until the new official arrived.

fact that these were often transferred to a third party. Was the fact that these individuals bought their position (and how much they paid) leading them to take actions angering the local population?

6.2.2.1 Price Spreads to Measure Venality

One concern with comparing the intensity of rebellions with office-selling measures (prices or quantity) is that of omitted variable bias. Namely, that a third factor might be driving both, higher prices and a greater likelihood of rebellion. Such is the case of provinces with a large indigenous population, which would both facilitate rebellion and attract higher bids. To address this possibility and isolate the role of venality, I focus not on average prices, but on their differences or spread.

Specifically, the analysis is based on the gap in the price paid for a province at times of war in Spain minus that paid during peace. The idea is to capture price differences driven by more or less vetting from the Crown and not by factors such as the size of the indigenous population, location, or other time-invariant characteristics. As shown in Chapter 4, individuals that enter at these times and locations have particular motivations and are very different in visible traits than those normally appointed. It also limits comparisons to provinces sold and to variation in demand driven by wartime periods exogenously driven in Europe. Further details in the Appendix explain the construction of this variable.

Table 6.1 presents the average number of uprisings per capita in Mexico, Peru, and Bolivia, divided by the degree of spread in prices and the time period. For the sales cut-off I use the year 1760 as a date by which most purchasers would have exited their position of *corregidor* or *alcaldes* (even if many *audiencia* purchasers would still be in place).

The top panel shows how in Peru and Bolivia, the average number of uprisings is greater in provinces with a larger price spread during the period of sales than for those with a smaller one (0.738 versus 0.382). The pattern is less stark for the *audiencia* of Mexico, where the number of uprisings per capita is practically the same in provinces with both high and low venality. This could be because the effects of venality will only become visible at certain critical junctures, as we will see. In absolute terms, there are more uprisings per capita in Peru and Bolivia, with 0.738 rebellions per capita – well above those of Mexico (0.192).

More relevant for this chapter is the bottom panel, which clearly portrays how the end of the *Pax Hispannica* in the second half of the

TABLE 6.1 *Mean differences in uprisings before and after sales: Mexico, Peru, and Bolivia*

	Peru & Bolivia	Mexico
	Number of Rebellions Per Capita*	
	During Sales: 1680–1760	
High price spread	0.738	0.192
N	34	48
Low price spread	0.382	0.235
N	33	48
	After Sales: 1760–1808 §	
High price spread	1.355	0.574
N	34	48
Low price spread	0.625	0.243
N	33	48

Notes: § Dates post-sales are 1760–1780 for Peru and Bolivia, and 1760–1808 for Mexico. The case of Mexico includes provinces from the *audiencia* of Mexico (excluding Yucatán peninsula, Chiapas, Guadalajara *audiencia*, and northern territories). Sources: See notes Figure 6.1. High price spread = above median. Low price spread = below median.

eighteenth century is primarily led by high-price-spread provinces. As shown, across all types of provinces, there is a visible increase in the number of uprisings vis-à-vis the first half of the century. But this increase is disproportionately concentrated in provinces with a higher rate of venality. In Peru and Bolivia, high-spread provinces roughly doubled their per capita rate. In Mexico, high-venality areas also double their rate of uprisings, creating a large gap vis-a-vis areas less affected by sales.

6.2.3 The Intensification of Uprisings Postsales: Mexico, Bolivia, and Peru

These patterns are consistent with the idea that the effects of office-selling become much more salient in the second half of the century. However, it is important to account for factors varying across provinces (i.e., population) and time (i.e., economic shocks) that may also be driving these uprisings. Therefore, to further isolate the role of office-selling from other explanations, Figure 6.3 presents the regression coefficients for

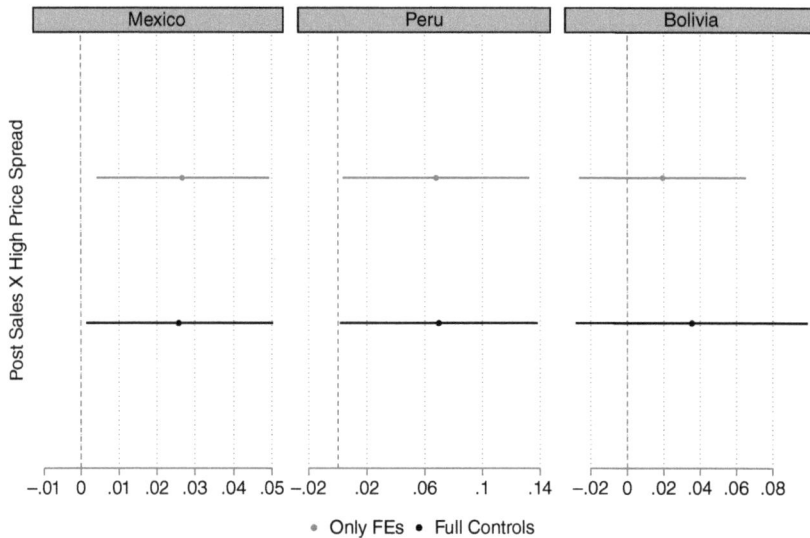

FIGURE 6.3 Venality and postsales uprisings: Mexico, Peru, and Bolivia

OLS Estimates with 95 percent Confidence Interval in lines. All estimates include year and province fixed effects. Controls for Mexico from Sellars and Garfias (2022): year dummies interacted with average maize suitability, elevation, area of province, malarial presence, distance to Mexico city and log (indigenous population in 1700), own construction. Controls for Peru and Bolivia: year dummies interacted with elevation, area, distance to Lima and log (indigenous population in 1754). Clustered robust standard errors in parentheses. Sources: See note Fig. 1. See estimating Equation (4) and Table A.9 in Appendix to Chapter 6 for full results.

the same relationship but within a regression framework. Namely, does the geographic prevalence of uprisings change in the second half of the eighteenth century? Due to data availability, this analysis is concentrated in the territories of Mexico, Peru and Bolivia. However, Section 6.3 explores qualitatively how uprisings may be also changing in other areas of the Empire (in Ecuador, Colombia, and Guatemala).[27]

As shown in the estimates of Figure 6.3, in both Mexico and Peru, there is a visible increase in the average number of uprisings after 1760[28]

---

[27] Not included due to data limitations are the *audiencias* of Guadalajara, Manila, Panama, Chile, and Santo Domingo. In the case of Santo Domingo, data exists but involves mostly uprising in plantations. (Coatsworth 1988).

[28] For the case of Mexico, I take the year of 1760 as the cut-off year when all purchasers are no longer in office. For the cases of Peru and Bolivia, I have the date of the first post-sales appointment, thus reflecting the year when purchasers stop being in power.

6 To Flee or to Fight

vis-à-vis the earlier period, driven by provinces with the highest price spread in the period of sales (1670–1750). The increase is more muted for Bolivia, where the average number of uprisings is about half that of Mexico and Lima. The latter does not mean that venality did not exacerbate uprisings in Bolivia, just that the difference between the two periods is smaller and more imprecise, as noted in the coefficients and standard errors. By limiting comparisons to their own provincial mean, it takes into account cross-provincial differences that may be driving uprisings, such as their location, geography, agricultural suitability, among others.[29] For example, capturing the fact that provinces in southern Peru might be more rebellious than others, or more populous, or have a geography more amenable to uprisings, to name a few possibilities. Similarly, estimates account for policies in a particular year that may heighten anticolonial sentiment.

In all, results show that part of the increase in the late eighteenth-century uprisings was spearheaded by areas blighted by earlier venality. In this context, the prospect of higher taxes from an increase in the *alcabalas*, establishment of *aduanas*, or of updating tax rolls (*revisitas*) – common Bourbon reforms – would be more violently resisted than elsewhere. For example, the leading explanation for the eighteenth-century spike in uprisings has to do with the increase in the fiscal demands by the Crown (O'Phelan 1988), which deprived regional elites of rent-seeking opportunities (Garfias and Sellars 2022) and translated into more revenue from indigenous head taxes and *donativos* (Chiovelli et al. 2024). If these pressures had a higher impact in more vulnerable locations due to a history of surplus appropriation, there is a heightened probability of a violent outcome (rebellion). Estimates of Figure 6.3 show that the geography of uprisings in the late eighteenth century correlates well with the presence of earlier venality.

Another way to test whether places with a history of venality led to underlying "grievances" that translate to rebellion, is to examine subsistence crises. Namely, instances in which the population was pushed to the verge of subsistence due to weather events – such as droughts and floods. While declines in agricultural income are commonly associated with more violence, do they lead to more uprisings in places where they tap into preexisting discontent due to venality?

---

[29] Albeit this approach does not fully control for population – as it is a variable that changes over time – I include the earliest measure interacted with time, to account for these differences.

6.2.4 Subsistence Crisis, Venality, and Uprisings in Mexico and Bolivia

The subsistence shock studied is drought or flooding, which I measure using the Palmer Drought Severity Index (PDSI). For the case of Mexico, this measure is provided by Cook and Krusic (2003) and made available by Garfias and Sellars (2022), albeit only focused on Central Mexico. For the cases of Peru and Bolivia, I use the self-calibrated PDSI[30] (scPDSI) provided by the South American Drought Atlas (SADA) from Morales et al. (2020), which covers most of South America from 1400 to 2000. One constraint with the South American atlas for Peru is that its measurements are limited to the central and southernmost part of the current Peruvian territory,[31] meaning that the analysis in this section is limited to these areas.

Using this data, Figure 6.4 starts by showing the temporal distribution of "weather anomalies" in Mexico, (southern) Peru, and Bolivia throughout the eighteenth century, as measured by their respective drought index. The red lines are meant to highlight key values in the index, such as the "normal" range (−0.5, 0.5), as well as "abnormal" values. Namely, those outside of the −2 and 2 range. For example, a value of −2 is considered a moderately dry year, while that of 2 is a moderately wet one. It should be noted that extreme values do not necessarily predict disasters on their own. In fact, whether a single year leads to crop loss or devastating floods depends on the preexisting humidity/dryness of the soil. Yet, some of these abnormal values do coincide with known historical episodes of drought, as can be seen in the graph.

In the case of Mexico, the well-known drought of 1785–1786 called "the year of hunger" exhibited an average PDSI of −0.064 in 1785, just barely below normal, but −1.34 and −1.066 in 1786 and 1787, respectively. It would only recover positive values in 1788. Thus showing that while there is not a one-to-one correspondence between extreme PDSI measurements and crop failure, on average, the data is able to capture some of these phenomena. Panel (a) also captures the drought spell in the early 1800s, an important factor behind the wars of independence in Mexico (Tutino 1986). Although conflicts for independence are not analyzed here, due to their national character and motivation,[32] Figure 6.4(a) finds support for the role of subsistence crises.

---

[30] The use of self-calibration PDSI indexes is meant to address spatial comparability issues of PDSI values.

[31] See www.cr2.cl/datos-dendro-sada/ for a map of the areas covered.

[32] Garfias and Sellars (2022) provide an excellent account of how "local" rebellions convert into national ones.

6 To Flee or to Fight

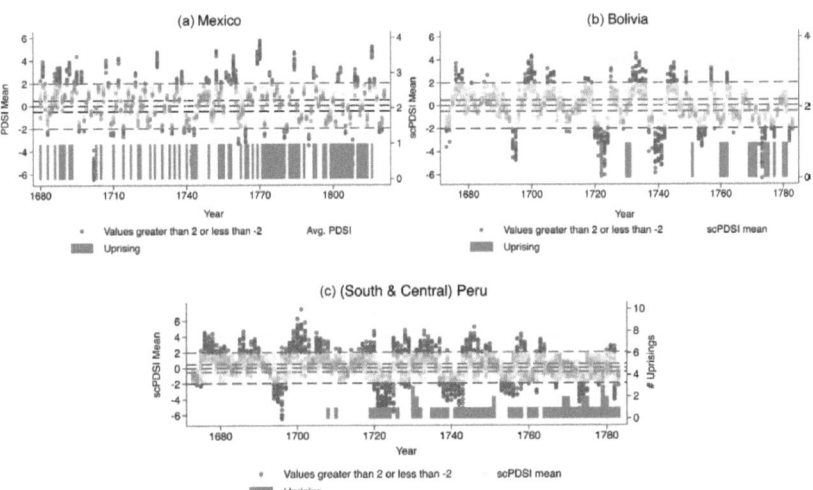

FIGURE 6.4 Weather anomalies and uprisings in Mexico, Bolivia, and Peru

Sources: Conflict data see note Fig. 1. Source of scPDSI data for Peru and Bolivia Morales et al. (2020). Source of PDSI data for Mexico Garfias and Sellars (2022).

In the case of Bolivia (panel b), the lack of abnormal weather events in the mid 1750s to mid 1770s coincide with the stability and even decline of agriculture and livestock prices observed in Potosí in the same years (Tandeter and Wachtel 1983). Similarly, the drought of the late 1770s and 1780s – in some cases reaching extreme values of –6 – not only coincided with a cluster of uprisings, as shown in Figure 6.4(b) but also could potentially explain the swell of support in the region for the Túpac Amaru/Túpac Katari rebellion that would take place in its midst (1780–82). Given this background of drought, it is less surprising that the extractive activities of the *corregidor* of Canas y Canchis, Antonio Arriaga, and the introduction of the *aduana* – internal custom houses – serve as catalyst to the largest armed threat to colonial rule prior to the wars of independence. In fact, this drought will continue past 1780 (although our analysis ends in that year), and lead to well-documented spike in prices in Potosí and Charcas in 1784–1785 (Tandeter and Wachtel 1983).

Finally, for the case of Central to Southern Peru – areas for which the scPDSI measures are available – variability in the index is correlated with historical instances of El Niño (and La Niña) Southern Oscillation (ENSO). For example, historical instances of ENSO identified by paleoclimatologists Gergis and Fowler (2009) identify at least 8 events in the period 1687–1785. The latest one, from 1775 to 1785, coinciding with

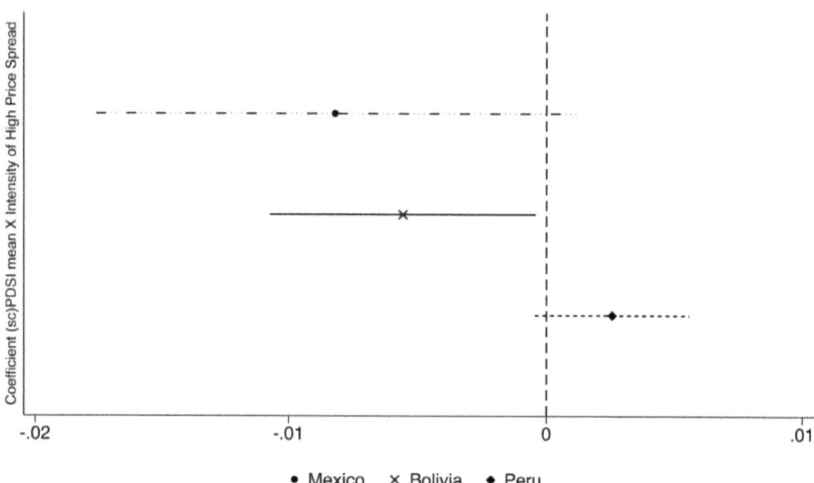

FIGURE 6.5 Subsistence crises, uprisings, and venality: Mexico, Bolivia, and Peru

OLS Estimates with 95 percent CI in lines. Year and Province fixed effects included in every specification. For a description of additional controls, see note of Fig. 3. For sources of uprisings, see notes of Figure 6.1. See estimating Equation (5) and Table A.10 in Appendix to Chapter 6 for full estimation results and equation.

the Túpac Amaru rebellion and associated with drought for the Bolivian Altiplano. However, ENSO events in Peru wreak agricultural havoc by alternating between intense rains and droughts, thus leading to crop loss, pests, and landslides, depending on the area. For example, in southern Peru, the average value of scPDSI values is 0.688 but 0.180 for non-Niño years, suggesting greater prevalence of floods or "wet" years during El Niño, which also lead to subsistence crisis.

Indeed, Figures 6.4(b) and (c) appear to reflect longer spells of drought (negative values) followed by extremely wet years (positive values) in Bolivia and Peru, but less so in Central Mexico.[33] Yet, in both cases – Bolivia and Mexico – clusters of uprisings appear visually correlated with climatic conditions, but how strong is this relationship?

Figure 6.5 presents estimates of the extent to which the onset of subsistence crises led to greater discontent and whether, in turn, this relationship is stronger in places with larger price spreads. As shown for Mexico and Bolivia, more negative values in the drought indices (less wet) are correlated with a greater probability of uprisings in the period

[33] This could be reflecting differences in measurement of the drought indices or instead real differences in climate variability in both territories.

prior to 1808 in Mexico, and 1780 in Bolivia, particularly where venality had been more intense. In contrast, for the case of Central and Southern Peru, for which the scPDSI measure is available, I find that it is instances of floods – or wet periods – the ones more associated with uprisings (positive values). Likely due to the way drought and floods relate to El Niño/ La Niña patterns in Peru. All estimates control for an array of provincial characteristics interacted with year indicators. Although future research could further establish these patterns, for example, examine the role of variability – as opposed to just the contemporaneous levels of drought – these estimates are a starting point to understand the historical relationship between climate and violent uprisings.

6.2.5 From *Corregidores* and *Alcaldes* to *Subdelegados*: Uprisings in the Late Colonial Period

So far, the analysis has focused on the distribution of eighteenth-century uprisings, and whether it depends (or not) on earlier experiences with venality. The underlying argument is that even if not physically in power, many of the practices, interests, and cultural predispositions created and/ or consolidated during the office-selling years (1670–1750) outlived them.

For example, the Viceroy of Peru, Manuel de Guirior, feared that the experience of uprisings may change a communities' disposition for future ones (*queda el espiritu dispuesto*). That is, that the experience of resisting official authority would remain in the collective memory and easily activate when the occasion merits. Or, the repressive response by colonial officials might have soured the population even more against colonial authorities. In either of these scenarios, the changes brought about by office-selling facilitated the occurrence of future uprisings, even if the policy has officially ended.

Yet, one key reform in the eighteenth century – the introduction of the *Intendencia* system – was explicitly implemented to improve the colonial administration and forever dislodge the practices of *corregidores* and *alcaldes mayores*. The idea of *intendentes* was to create an additional administrative level between that of *corregidores* and *alcaldes* and the *audiencia*. By replacing the former with *subdelegados* – in principle better selected and paid – there would be lower appropriation of economic surplus of the population, more fiscal revenue for the Crown, and less rebellions throughout the empire, the thinking went.

Yet, its implementation would be uneven, as shown in Figure 6.6 panel (a). Between 1783 and 1787 it had been only implemented in the

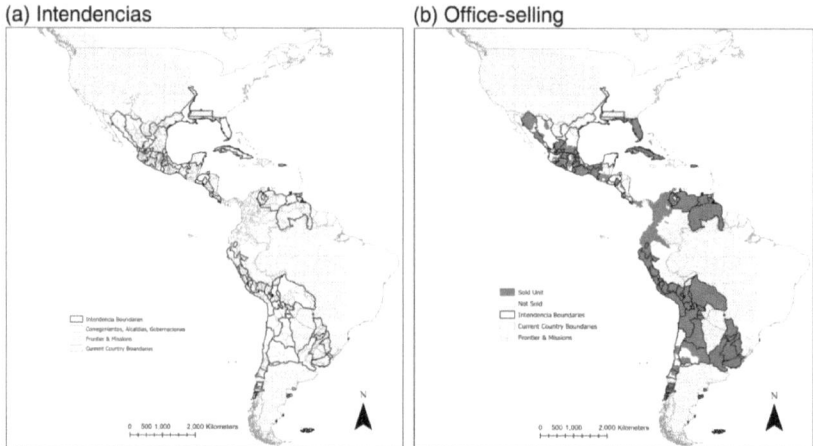

FIGURE 6.6 Late eighteenth-century *intendencias* and *subdelegados* reform and office-selling.

Note: Sources of Panel (a) HGIS Indias from Stangl (2019c). Panel (b) own construction using sales data.

viceroyalty of New Spain, Peru, and Rio de la Plata, as seen by the administrative units created – *intendencias*. These new units, roughly the size of five provinces, would keep the existing *corregimientos* and *alcaldías* jurisdictions in place and rename them *subdelegaciones*. This reform also saw the creation of the Viceroyalty of La Plata and that of two new *audiencias*, one in Cuzco in Peru and another in Caracas, roughly today's Venezuela and formerly part of the *audiencia* of Santa Fe (Colombia).

Despite these high-level changes, there are questions of the extent to which these reforms improved *local* governance, that is, at the level of *corregimiento* and *alcaldia mayores*, now *subdelegaciones*. For example, even after the introduction of the *intendencias* in 1786, there are good local accounts of how the new *subdelegado* would simply continue the practices of the now-extinct *corregidores* and *alcaldes*.[34] This was the case of *subdelegados* still engaging in the (explicitly prohibited) practice of *repartimiento* in Bolivia (Gavira Márquez 2021), in central Mexico and Oaxaca (Cuesta Alonso and Moreno 2021), as well as Peru (Navarro and Ruigome 1993). Sometimes even in complicity with the Intendente, as in the case of Fresnillo, Mexico (Cuesta and Medina 2021). Thus, showing the difficulty in eradicating this source of profits.

---

[34] See Solórzano Fonseca [This citation is only Solórzano Fonseca (1985)] (1985) for Guatemala. Langer (2016: 353) for the case of *subdelegados* in today's Bolivia.

As shown in Panel (b) in gray, the new *intendencias* oversaw territories with a strong history of venality at all levels. Moreover, while uprisings did fall in Peru and Bolivia after the major Túpac Amaru rebellion in 1780–1782, likely due to the brutal fate they encountered, this is not the case of Mexico, where the overall trend continued up to 1808, see Figure 6.1(b). As described in the following section, uprisings in Santa Fe, Guatemala, and Ecuador remained either constant or were even greater in the period 1785–1808.

In all, the statistical analysis supports the claim in official correspondence blaming the uprisings on the activities of the *corregidor* or *alcalde* mayor. While these positions were no longer sold, they continued the practices from earlier times, thus explaining why price spreads from before 1760 keep explaining the intensity of rebellion after it.

6.3 UPRISINGS IN THE "PERIPHERY": GUATEMALA, QUITO, AND SANTA FE

Beyond the two most important viceroyalties – Peru, Bolivia, and Mexico – evidence of uprisings in the *audiencias* of Guatemala, Ecuador, and Colombia is scarcer but still informative. The main constraint to conduct a large-n analysis as before is the small number of provinces in each *audiencia*. For example, Guatemala had ten *alcaldías mayores y corregimientos*, of which only eight were sold. In Ecuador, only ten provinces were sold systematically, while this is eight for the case of Colombia. Therefore, I use more descriptive evidence focusing on changes in the motivations for uprisings and their geographic distribution in each case.

Despite the limitations of the data, similar patterns emerge to those observed in the larger *audiencias*. First, consistent with the end of the *Pax Hispannica*, there is an increase in the intensity of rebellions, especially in the post-1760 period. Second, and partly as a result of its greater intensity, uprisings cover a broader set of geographic provinces. Yet, the vast majority in all cases have to do with fiscal policies of the Crown and the way they were implemented by particular colonial officials. Table A.11 in the Appendix to Chapter 6 shows the places, number, and stated reasons for the uprisings in Guatemala, Ecuador, and Colombia.

6.3.1 Guatemala

Despite being a place highly exposed to venality, its low number of *corregimientos* (ten, of which only eight where intensely sold in the

1670–1750 period) complicates the analysis of cross-sectional variation in uprisings and that of office-selling. Nonetheless, thanks to the excellent sources enumerating all events according to a common criterion as in Martínez Peláez (2021 [1985]) and Navarrete (1982), it is possible to examine the geography of rebellions in eighteenth-century Guatemala.

In descriptive terms, Guatemala saw the number of attempted uprisings in the pre-1760 period (ten) double its rate in the post-1760 one (twenty). While Guatemala's population likely did not double between 1760 and 1808, it did increase over this period, adding to the fiscal pressure created by the Bourbon Reforms and providing fertile ground for uprisings and conflict over land. These uprisings, called *motines*, were characterized by a lack of premeditation and the reliance on rudimentary weapons (Martínez Peláez 2021 [1985]: 167–168). These explosions of discontent were often due to "ruptures" with established custom caused by colonial officials and, for some, a necessary "escape valve" key to the duration of the empire, as they do not necessarily aim for independence but restoration to a prior equilibrium (Martínez Peláez 2021[1985]).

In this context, what role did venality play? The main stated cause behind uprisings in this period was the collection of head taxes (*tributo*), cotton *repartimiento* activities – whereby the *alcalde* distributed cotton to be weaved by indigenous women – and the use of indigenous forced labor for public (or private) works. However, these exactions were not personally enforced by colonial officials themselves but through the indigenous representatives in the communities – the *gobernador indio* – as described in the archival sources. These indigenous leaders were instead the frequent target of riots, and their elections a source of discontent.[35]

Evidence from the Guatemalan archives show that colonial officials were more likely to be mentioned in the office-selling period than afterwards. Prior to 1760, the uprising in Chiapas (1693) killed the *alcalde mayor*, while that of Santa Catarina Ixtahuacan (1743) expressed discontent for the *alcaldes' repartimiento* and exactions in Viejo (1759) and in Santa Lucia Utatlan (1760). In this first period there are also uprisings targeting the indigenous tax collectors (Chiquimulilla, 1742;

---

[35] This is also a side consequence of the limited number of provincial jurisdictions whereby indigenous intermediaries – community leaders in charge of collecting the taxes on behalf of the *corregidor* and *alcalde* – become a common target of uprisings.

Guazacapan, 1752; and Comalapa, 1755), a form of indirect discontent against colonial officials. These uprisings also freed those unjustly imprisoned for abuses in the cotton *repartimiento* (1679, Totonicapan and Viejo, 1759).

In line with previous cases, *motines* after 1760 until 1808 – before the Napoleonic invasion – are clearly more diverse geographically and much more frequent. First, in terms of uprisings directly targeting royal officials due to exactions, there are only three (Escuintla, 1775; Coban, 1803; and Ciudad de Guatemala, 1766). Although the discovery that communities were hiding tribute payers caused a separate uprising in Macholoa (1801). Instead, and second, the most numerous set of uprisings were those targeted against indigenous authorities. These were leaders who collected exactions on behalf of royal officials – but likely obtained some side benefits from doing so.[36] While not directly against the *corregidor* and *alcalde*, their discontent against these representatives was also discontent against the former.

A difference with the earlier period though was the number of uprisings against priests, who became a frequent target of popular rage (Comalapa, 1774; Patzun, 1796; Soloma, 1803). Finally, this period also reveals new causes such as problems with the distribution of meat (Retalhuleu, 1783), general drunkenness, and disorder (Jilotepeque, 1791; Momostenango, 1785), opposition to sanitary measures to control an epidemic (Nebaj, 1798) and land conflict with an hacendado (Villa de la Gomera, 1794). The takeaway from this period is that while the causes may not have changed dramatically, the population did exhibit a "shorter fuse" with more visible outbursts in the immediate period before the wars of independence.

6.3.2 Quito

Economically and jurisdictionally, the *audiencia* of Quito served as an entrepôt in the eighteenth century: linked to the *audiencias* of Lima and Charcas by trade, but jurisdictionally part of Santa Fe, depending on the exact year. As in the case of Guatemala, the *audiencia* of Quito is one with few *corregimientos* (fourteen) but with a large indigenous presence. This limited number of jurisdictions presents a challenge when

---

[36] This is the case of the *motines* of Patzun 1801, Santiago Atitlan 1800, Nebaj 1793, Santa Barbara Totonicapan 1790, Chiquimula 1802–1804, Dolores Izalco 1794, Jalteva 1769, and San Martin Perulapan 1767. See Martínez Peláez (2021 [1985]).

comparing across provinces, but through accounts of Moreno Yánez (1985), Albornoz Peralta (1976), and the data collection made by Becker (2008), it is possible to reconstruct the patterns observed.

In total, between 1670 and 1808, the *corregimientos*[37] of the *audiencia* of Quito recorded 27 uprisings or attempted ones, according to Becker's (2008) accounts. A more conservative number based on Moreno Yánez (1985)[38] and complemented with other sources totals eighteen. Nonetheless, both of these datasets exhibit patterns consistent with that of other cases. First, it is clear the increase in the number of rebellions in the post-1760 period[39] as well as the broader geographical distribution of these events. Both accounts coincide in the role of key colonial actors: first, *encomiendas*, which are still prevalent in Quito in the eighteenth century. Second, the *corregidor*, who is in charge of the collection of head taxes and the use of debts to extract forced labor, as well as, third, church authorities. Landowners, albeit mentioned, figure less prominently in the description of these uprisings.

However, unlike the case of Guatemala, where the post-1760 sees a diversification in the motives of rebellion, in Quito almost all uprisings up to 1808 are invariably about taxation. Notoriously salient are, first, head taxes (*tributo*), second, attempts to prevent taxation in the form of impeding the census, as well as, third, protests against the forced labor drafts known as the *mita*. In the case of Quito, *mita* labor was not used to work in the mines but for public works such as roads and sometimes in *obrajes* (textile factories). While not particularly common, uprisings against religious taxes, tithes (*diezmos*), and directly against priests also took place. One particularity of the *corregidores* in Quito is that they did not profit as much from the forced sales of goods (*repartimiento*), but instead used their taxation authority to extract labor from the indigenous population, which they could then monetize.

In terms of frequency, data from Becker's (2008) recopilation shows that *corregimientos* with mid levels of price spreads are the ones exhibiting the most uprisings per capita throughout the period 1680–1808. This is the case of the *corregimientos* of Riobamba, Otavalo, Ibarra, and La Tacunga. In contrast, three *corregimientos* frequently sold but

---

[37] Other uprisings took place outside the boundaries of the *corregimiento* and are not counted here.

[38] Moreno Yanez (1985) considers some of Albornoz' accounts duplicates, for example.

[39] Becker (2008) records seven pre 1760 and twenty post-1760. Moreno Yanez records three pre 1760 and fifteen post-1760.

that saw a lower frequency of indigenous uprisings per capita were those of Quito, Guayaquil, and Cuenca. This is not because there was no discontent – after all, the major rebellion "de los Barrios" took place in Quito in 1764. Instead, the higher administrative status of Quito or Cuenca made it more socially desirable – driving up prices. Similarly, and second, the main source of gains from holding positions in Guayaquil came mainly from contraband (and not extraction of the indigenous population). In these cases, venality was present but it was of the type less likely to spur immediate riots.

Prior to 1670, there is little mention of the role of the *corregidor* as a cause behind uprisings. The conquest of the province of Guayaquil (1540s) and the Esmeraldas frontier (1560–1620) are the most prominent of indigenous uprisings, as well as the early resistance to the *encomienda* and to the fulfillment of *mita* obligations (i.e., in 1623 in Latacunga). However, Albornoz (1976) does mention the instructions of the *audiencia* to the *corregidor* to not exceed its collections of the *tributo* in Otavalo in 1615, an early indication of its future role.

It is not until 1677, when indigenous authorities travel to the *audiencia* to report the activities of *corregidores* and tax collectors exceeding themselves in the collection of the *tributo*, that this official is more frequently mentioned. Particularly after 1760, there is an exponential increase in *corregidor*-related revolts, such as in the 1761 tax uprising in La Tacunga. Another string of uprisings took place in 1764, when several towns of Riobamba rebelled against a new census. Resistance to a new census continued in 1771 in Latacunga, 1778 in Guano, and 1781 in Alausi. The 1766 uprising in Ambato was also related to the collection of head taxes, which would happen again in 1780 in Pelileo (same region). In the latter case, the collection of *tributo* will be cancelled for the year. A 1768 uprising in a textile *obraje* (previously owned by the jesuits) attests to the brutality of this institution, which relied on labor drafts from taxes owed to the Crown.

In terms of non-*tributo* taxation, uprisings become more salient in the last quarter of the eighteenth century, in the context of the intensification of the Bourbon Reforms. An example is the 1777 rebellion against the royal monopoly on salt, tobacco, and alcohol, which was not exclusively indigenous as it also included mestizos. The same year saw an uprising in Otavalo against the establishment of a custom house (*aduana*), which would have taxed those transporting goods between provinces. The *aduana* is also mentioned as a cause behind the 1803 major uprising in Guamote, together with the collection of tithes. Finally, opposition to

152   *The Venal Origins of Development in Spanish America*

the *mita* continues to motivate uprisings, as in 1784 in Calpi and 1791 in Cayambe. Reforms to the *alcabala*, which would now incorporate transactions involving indigenous producers, led to a riot in Riobamba in 1794.

In all, the frequency of taxation-related uprisings in these areas points to a region whereby economic demands are met with strong resistance. Although it is not possible to ascertain statistically whether venality is behind the increase in the mentions of "corregidor," "tributo," and "census," they were anecdotally more frequent in areas exposed to venality in the earlier half of the century. In what follows, I examine eighteenth-century uprisings in the *audiencia* of Santa Fe, now Colombia, an *audiencia* with a very different ethnic composition and with coastal areas of high geopolitical importance for the Crown.

6.3.3 Santa Fe (Colombia)

Beyond the well-known *comunero* rebellion of 1781,[40] the *audiencia* of Santa Fe – now roughly Colombia – does not figure prominently in its overt challenges to Spanish colonial authority. For example, it is not included in Coatsworth's (1988) comparative account of Latin American uprisings. Yet, as argued in McFarlane (1984), there was no lack of popular opposition to the colonial government, as seen in the number of judicial files stored in the *audiencia*. While indigenous uprisings are fewer, they can still inform us of the role the *corregidor* played and how this may have changed during and after the end of office-selling within the broader context of the Bourbon Reforms.

Unlike other cases, the *audiencia* of Santa Fe had a much lower indigenous presence due to the large toll epidemics and the explicit policies of extermination of the early colonization period. Santa Fe also had much less territory organized in the form of *corregimientos*, essentially nine, of which only three saw a consistent number of rebellions (Coyaima y Natagaima, Sogamoso, and Tunja).[41] Not surprisingly, *corregimientos* with rebellions also had the highest frequency of sales during the period and exhibit particularly large price spreads.

---

[40] A large-scale conflict over the taxation jurisdiction and administrative reform in the *audiencia* of Santa Fe, but with roots in deep social discontent (Phelan 1978).

[41] These are: Chita, Coyaima y Natagaima, Guatavita, Los Panches, Mompox, Sachica, Sogamoso, Tunja, and Zipaquira. Other parts of the *audiencia*, namely the *Gobernaciones* of Antioquía, Cartagena, Chocó, Mariquita, and Popayán saw a larger number of events.

6 To Flee or to Fight

Unlike previous cases, these *corregimiento* uprisings are concentrated in the pre-1760 (7) rather than in the post-1760s (2). However, this fact masks the large increase of "civil disturbances" observed in other areas, as in the case of the *Gobernaciones* of Popayán, Chocó, Los Llanos, and Cartagena, but that were not ruled by a *corregidor* or *alcalde mayor*. McFarlane (1984) associates these uprisings with various fiscal measures in the context of the Bourbon Reforms and opposition to the introduction of a royal monopoly on alcohol (*aguardiente*). The only major Indigenous uprising was in 1781 in Los Llanos *gobernación*, a territory bordering the *audiencia* of Quito (Ecuador).

Focusing exclusively on *corregimientos*, most rebellions happened in the Tunja and Sogamoso provinces, homeland to the indigenous Muisca and Chibchas groups, as well as in Coyaima and Natagaina, home to the indigenous Pijao, Dujos, and Babadujos tribes, which concentrated most of the indigenous population by the mid eighteenth century. What can be concluded from the descriptions, is that these uprisings were not related to the royal tobacco or alcohol monopoly. Instead, they were directed against royal officials seeking to increase their exactions (1740 in Tunja, 1731 in Coyaima, and 1752 in Sogamoso) or arrest their indigenous representative (1705 in Tunja). Enforcement of the royal monopoly on *aguardiente* (liquor) and the destruction of illegal stills provoked a riot in 1756 in Coyaima (Ibagué). Opposition to colonial officials also took place in Tunja, during an attempt to influence the selection of *alcaldes* in 1802, or in the context of broader conflicts with private citizens (1727 and 1809 in Tunja, 1743 in Cali).

From the partial view these descriptions provide, there is still a sense of the commonalities with the other cases studied. As elsewhere, uprisings are a form of discontent for disruptive or abnormal exactions and not about questioning the legitimacy of the Crown. They were more frequent in those *corregimientos* sold, but the low number of provinces per *audiencia* does not lend itself to fully analyze the role of price spreads. Finally, from what we can infer of the uprisings that did take place, there appears to be more variation in the targets of these uprisings in the second half of the eighteenth century, as in Guatemala.

6.4 "FLEEING": AN ALTERNATIVE?

The alternative strategy to violent uprisings was that of "escaping." As put by the Peruvian Viceroy in the introductory quote, aggrieved individuals would leave (*ausentarse*) as a way to escape abuses from *corregidores* and *alcaldes*.⁴² However, this measure was almost as costly as the uprising itself. Abandoning one's community and the right to land that came with it meant a lifetime of wage laboring or sharecropping on other people's land or of servitude in the cities. Not a decision to be taken lightly. Yet, this was a route frequent enough to be singled out by authorities. In fact, it was sufficiently common as to change the ethnic composition of certain areas throughout the eighteenth century.

Prior to office-selling, there were well-known cases of large population movements during the sixteenth and early seventeenth centuries in Peru and Bolivia. Mainly driven by the introduction of forced labor for mining activities (*mit'a*). However, these had subsided by the mid seventeenth century due to the decline of silver production and the rise of "free" wage labor around the mines. By the eighteenth century, the *mit'a* became less associated with out-migration and more with corruption and appropriation of economic surplus.

In Mexico, indigenous migration was also common (Zevallos 1999; Robinson 1988; Lecoin 1988) with deep roots in the pre-Hispanic era (Michelet 1988). These migrations were also often motivated by forced labor drafts (*repartimientos de indios*) for mining and agriculture (Gibson 1964) and the need to find work to fulfill the payments of royal taxes or for mere survival (Zevallos 1999). For example, in both Mexico and Peru, indigenous populations found in major cities plentiful work opportunities. It is not coincidental that 47 percent of the population of the city of Cuzco in 1754 was *forastero* or migrant – a reflection of a population on the move.

The question of this section is: To what extent does the nature of colonial governance led to indigenous displacement away from the eighteenth-century provincial capitals (*cabecera*) where authorities resided? For example, excessive appropriation of economic surplus could prompt a form of "fleeing" as a way to systematically reduce their exposure to colonial officials. The more scattered and distant from authorities, the less exposed they were, and the more difficult it was to monitor and collect their taxes. Movements away from officials would thus limit extraction and enhance survival (Zevallos 1999; Aguirre Beltran 1991), explaining the current presence of indigenous enclaves away from these officials.

---

⁴² These taxes were tied to a particular community, such that by abandoning it, they relinquish both rights and obligations.

Some of these decisions to move were done on an individual basis, but others were done by entire towns, often with the consent of higher-up authorities. Data from judicial claims in Mexico show some *pueblos* actively sought permission to found new towns, leave old lands, claim empty lots, or fought to preserve existing ones. These legal battles also show that these population movements were not meant to represent a total rupture with the state such as those of runaway slaves' communities (maroons) established in *palenques* (McFarlane 1990). Instead, these were migrations meant to carve their own space, retaining the rights and privileges of *pueblo* status albeit in a new setting.[43] For example, cases brought to the *Tribunal de Indios*, a special court devoted to indigenous litigation in Mexico, exemplify some of these movements.[44]

In 1675, the court conceded permission to indigenous populations (*naturales*) to found a new town (*pueblo*) subordinate to the existing one of San Pedro Purugatio,[45] a town 39 kilometers from the provincial capital (Valladolid, now Morelia). In 1685 it conceded permission to found another town in a valley near Atotonilco and explicitly ordered the *alcalde mayor* to inspect and measure the land and establish their jurisdiction.[46] A different form of migration was to lay claim to unused lands and then seek royal recognition. Such is the case of San Juan Aixtengo in Tlaxcala, who sought ownership over empty land at the bottom of some hills.[47] Or those of Sichu and Escamela in Veracruz, which requested land for the indigenous communities already established in other places.[48] Movements of entire communities, while rare, did take place, such as those seeking permission to leave their current town to return to their original one. More frequently, indigenous communities kept "inching" away to limit their exposure to colonial officials.

To illustrate, panels (a) to (f) of Figure 6.7 show how, ca. 1770, most of the indigenous population was already settling farther from the colonial

---

[43] See Franco-Vivanco and Guardado (2024) for the jurisdictional considerations behind these population movements.
[44] For an overview of its role and importance for the indigenous population, see Borah (1982) and Franco-Vivanco (2021).
[45] Septiembre 7, 1675. Archivo General de la Nación Instituciones Coloniales, Real Audiencia, Indios (058), Contenedor 15, Volumen 25. Expediente 91, Fojas: 74 vta.-76r.
[46] Febrero 1 1685. Archivo General de la Nación Instituciones Coloniales, Real Audiencia, Indios (058), Contenedor 16, Volumen 28. Expediente 175, Fojas: 149v.
[47] Junio 22, 1680. Archivo General de la Nación Instituciones Coloniales, Real Audiencia, Indios (058), Contenedor 15, Volumen 26. Expediente 59, Fojas: 59.
[48] 1695. Archivo General de la Nación Instituciones Coloniales, Real Audiencia, Indios (058), Contenedor 18, Volumen 32. Expediente 324, Fojas: 288v-289r.

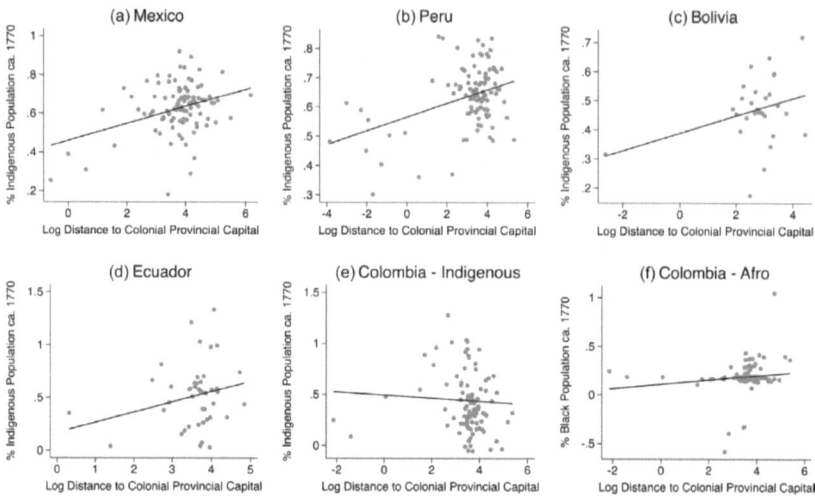

FIGURE 6.7 Ethnic composition of parishes ca. 1770 and distance to provincial *cabecera*

Note: Binned scatter plots of residualized means after accounting for latitude, longitude, and altitude and provincial fixed effects. Sources of parish data: Stangl (2019a).

authorities in capitals (*cabeceras*) relative to other ethnic groups (mestizos and whites). Using parish data from Stangl (2019a), it is clear there is a higher density of dots farther from the headquarters of the *corregidor* or *alcalde* (upper-right quadrant). This pattern is present for *audiencias* of various sizes and economic importance, such as the main viceroyalties (Mexico, Peru, and Bolivia) as well as those in the "periphery" (Ecuador). However, the case of Colombia presents an interesting contrast, with displacement mostly taking place among afro-Colombians and less so for the indigenous population. Further research could ascertain the extent to which colonial officials of Santa Fe relied more on the appropriation of the economic surplus of this population vis-à-vis that of indigenous communities. Finally, since the data is in shares, all nonindigenous populations (white, mestizo) exhibit the opposite pattern, located closer to *cabeceras*.

While informative, these patterns could not be necessarily driven by exposure to venality in the earlier eighteenth century. Therefore, using the cases with greater number of parish data available (Mexico and Peru), Figure 6.8 examines whether indigenous segregation is much stronger in places where the price spreads indicate more venality in the first half of the eighteenth century. That is, if we take two parishes with the same share of indigenous population, is the one in the province with greater venality further away from the *cabecera* (capital)?

6 To Flee or to Fight

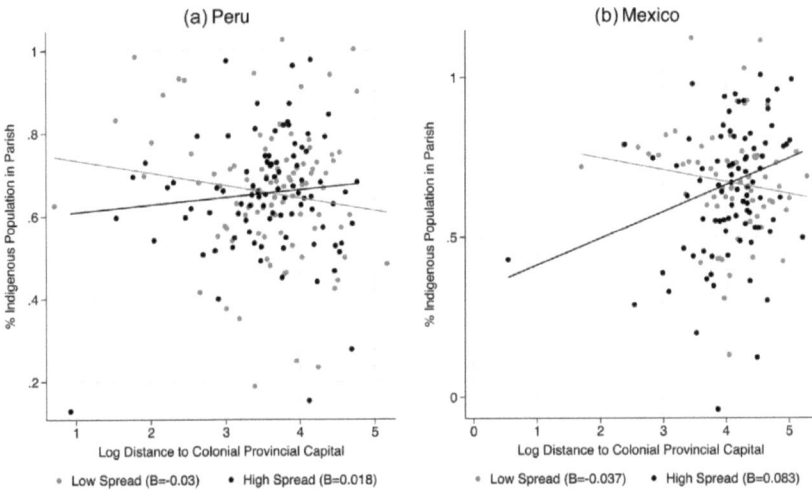

FIGURE 6.8 Indigenous segregation ca. 1770 and histories of venality: Mexico and Peru

Note: Binned scatter plots of residualized means after accounting for latitude, longitude, and altitude and provincial fixed effects. Sources of parish data: Stangl (2019a).

As shown in Figure 6.8, the answer is yes. Higher price spreads were generally associated with an increase in the share of indigenous parishioners in both Mexico and Peru. However, the effect is larger in Mexico (as shown by the steeper slopes), but still present in both cases. In contrast, provinces less exposed (low price spread) exhibit a negative and weaker slope.

Altogether, these findings support the idea that differences induced by the history of local governance might have led to processes of geographic segregation that characterize the region today. More directly pointing to the legacies of venality is the fact that this pattern differs from that observed at the start of the colonial period, when indigenous communities, as shown by early data from Peru (1572) and Mexico (1549), were instead in close proximity to *cabeceras*. See Figure A.1 of the Appendix.

Now, is this pattern reflecting "fleeing" or "displacement"? It is impossible to know from the data the extent to which this was a voluntary movement by the indigenous population, or instead reflects displacement or explicit segregation policies. Were indigenous populations looking for a new town due to encroachments from mestizos and Spanish peoples? Was migration instead an opportunity to put some space between their communities and venal officials? There are likely elements of both: mestizos and Spaniards emboldened by venal officials seeking to dispossess and segregate indigenous communities. While these communities are observing the increase in extraction and trying to put more distance with the Spanish-mestizo world. For the purposes of this chapter, what matters is that this process was much stronger in places where colonial officials had the incentives to engage in greater economic appropriation, even for the same levels of indigenous population.

These patterns will also persist throughout the end of the colonial period and into the independent era, albeit with some variation across countries. In the long-run, this source of ethnic segregation will prove highly distortionary: creating pockets of indigenous communities outside of the reach of markets and public goods funded by the state. Thus leading to an array of regional inequalities that will shape the politics and state-building paths of the nascent Spanish American states.

6.5 FLEEING AND FIGHTING

This chapter shows that eighteenth-century indigenous displacement and uprisings in Spanish America were not randomly distributed, but shaped by their local histories of colonial governance. Provinces with a history of venality saw a greater number of uprisings per capita, with stronger differences in the post-1760 period. Evidence from weather patterns documents how the presence of drought (Mexico, Bolivia) and wet years (Peru) made uprisings much more likely, particularly in provinces with more intense venality. These provinces also saw a much more pronounced process of geographic segregation of the indigenous population vis-à-vis provinces where venality was more muted.

What do these findings saw about office-selling and its consequences for indigenous welfare? At the very least, it shows that it contributed to the crescendo of uprisings observed throughout the eighteenth century as well as to the general patterns of segregation observed among the indigenous population. Around 1670, prior to office-selling, historians tended to paint a bleak picture for the reign of Charles II and the economic state of the Spanish Empire. Fiscally "bankrupt," demographic "nadir," and profound economic "depression" are common themes in these descriptions.[49] Yet, this was also a period which lacked systematic (recorded) violent challenges to royal officials and the Crown's fiscal policies. Accounts from the Cuzco parishes highlight the qualitatively

---

[49] There are some challenges to this view (see Klein and Serrano and 2019).

different exactions colonial officials were engaging in the period, particularly from what the late eighteenth-century accounts show.

This would change in the eighteenth century due to a number of reasons: demographic, Empire-wide policies, and geopolitical, to name a few. Among these, this chapter argues, the worsening governance by colonial officials also played a role. The institutionalized appropriation of economic surplus that they brought about outlived their time in office and became even more consequential at critical junctures, such as the period of reform starting in the 1760s. These experiences will be key for the process of independence and postcolonial developments as seen in the next chapter.

Chapter Summary: Aside from elite collusion and administrative capture, the arrival of venal officials spelled the end of the *Pax Hispannica* – primarily in the key Viceroyalties of Peru and Mexico but also in its other territories. Through the collection of eighteenth-century local-level uprising data across six countries, the chapter shows that provinces in high demand during sales exhibited a disproportionate number of uprisings per capita vis-à-vis those less demanded. Administrative venality also exacerbated subsistence crises created by eighteenth-century weather events such as drought in Mexico or El Niño(a) in Peru and Bolivia. In addition to more uprisings, provinces ruled by more venal officials also saw greater geographic segregation of the indigenous population. By the 1770s, provinces more exposed to venality show stronger signs of displacement of indigenous populations away from their original sixteenth-century locations. Together, these findings show that as the colonial era approached its end, different areas of the empire already had different "baggage" depending on their earlier exposure to venality: with those more exposed experiencing more uprisings and more displacement than those less so.

7

Colonial Venality and Nineteenth-Century State-Building

Chapter 6 showed how greater exposure to office-selling led to more uprisings and indigenous displacement in Spanish America throughout the eighteenth century. This chapter discusses how earlier legacies from venality continue to impact the nature of political representation, violent conflict, and ethnic segregation in the aftermath of independence in the nineteenth century.

***

Just short of the 300-year mark, the different kingdoms comprising the Spanish Empire were unwittingly thrown into a protracted independence process they had not foreseen. Prompted by the Napoleonic invasion of the Iberian Peninsula in 1808 and the imprisonment of the Spanish King Ferdinand VII, colonial societies throughout the Western Hemisphere had to reckon with questions of sovereignty, legitimacy, and the source of power absent royal authorities in Spain. In the Iberian Peninsula, the Cortes of Cádiz, embodying the Spanish government in exile, drafted a liberal constitution recognizing the sovereignty of the Spanish American kingdoms in 1812. Such recognition marked a point of no return for the Empire, with the pursuit (or not) of independence tied to the fate of this document.[1]

7.1 THE CHALLENGES OF INDEPENDENCE

In some parts of the empire, the fight for independence was disruptive, lengthy, and costly, particularly where Spanish interests were the strongest,

---

[1] For example, in Spain, the reinstated Ferdinand VII first disavowed the Cádiz Constitution but was later forced to recognize it, which made independence more attractive to elites in Mexico and Peru.

such as in Peru and Mexico. In others – namely Argentina, Paraguay, Chile, and Colombia – independence came as a quicker and relatively costless affair. For yet another group of countries, Cuba and the Philippines among them, independence would not arrive until much later. Nonetheless, it is safe to say that by 1825, most territories in continental Spanish America found themselves having to organize, consolidate, and administer their nascent states.

The challenges for the newly "decolonized" Spanish American countries were huge. Governments soon realized that in the short run, removing Spanish fiscal and trade restrictions or expelling its highest-ranking officials did not translate into visible economic gains (Coatsworth 1993, 1978; Prados de la Escosura 2008). In fact, the benefits of independence did not outweigh the immediate costs these countries had to assume in terms of international defense (Coatsworth 1993). Domestically, civil conflict over the organization of the new republics further undermined government finances and the functioning of the economy. Not surprisingly, the fifty years after independence have been named the "Lost Decades" (Coatsworth 2008; Bates et al. 2007; Curvale and Przeworski 2008).[2]

7.1.1 Continuity and Transformation in Local Governance Postindependence

Yet, the economic and conflict turmoil of the postindependence period often overshadows the continuity in governance at the local level. For all the national-level changes, local institutions represented in the colonial *cabildos* – or city councils – the basis of future municipalities – not only continued but also strengthened in the vacuum of power created by high-level conflict. The same is true of indigenous communities and *pueblos* – who often took no sides on these wars and enjoyed a period of unprecedented autonomy until the 1870s.

There are three general reasons behind this local-level continuity. First, the turmoil itself revolved around conservative attempts to restore aspects of colonial rule – such as the status of the indigenous population and church privileges – versus adopting a liberal vision based on individual citizenship rights and ownership, leading policies to see-saw and favoring the status-quo. Second, even with the liberal faction prevailing in the 1870s, governments could or would not always implement their agenda, particularly at the local level. Finally, as hinted

---

[2] See Prados de la Escosura (2009) for a challenge to this view.

in the introduction, despite all the high-level conflict, the population itself was rarely partitioned, thus retaining many old (colonial) regional allegiances and hierarchies.[3] For all the territorial fragmentation and conflicting stances, at the end of the day, the "pull" of the colonial administrative organization was highly influential for the configuration of states we see today.

Combined – high-level turmoil, autonomous local governance, and continuity in regional hierarchies – facilitated the persistence of administrative aspects of the colonial organization. Specifically, the chapter outlines three significant legacies: First, the limited political representation and the continuation of specific colonial policies related to taxation and labor coercion. Second, the geographic persistence of violent uprisings, and third, the segregation of the indigenous population away from major urban centers and capitals.

For the first legacy, the data shows that many areas of the Spanish Empire never really abolished highly extractive colonial policies – particularly those related to taxation and labor coercion. For example, in Ecuador, debt peonage practices (*concertaje*) from colonial times remained in place in the Republican era (Rivadeneira 2019). In other cases, policies initially abolished, were later reinstated. This is the case of Guatemala, where labor drafts (*repartimientos*) that had fallen into disuse immediately after independence were revived with the late nineteenth-century coffee boom (McCreery 1994). Similarly, in Bolivia, the colonial *tributo* – a vassal tax owed by indigenous communities to the Spanish Crown – continued both nominally and practically until the 1920s. These were not just "conservative" policies as many took place under "liberal" governments, in principle opposed to such practices.

A key factor sustaining these vestiges of Spanish rule was the political malapportionment and delay in the formation of local representative bodies in rural Spanish America. Despite the fragmentation of political power across the empire in the aftermath of independence, the control over local government fell in the hands of local elites, represented in the *cabildos*. Using the date of creation of *municipios* in Peru and Mexico, this chapter shows that the *corregimientos* and *alcaldías mayores* with a longer history of venality in the eighteenth century were less likely to recognize the incorporation of new local governments in the form of

---

[3] In fact, in no case did these states establish a capital different from what had been a viceregal or *audiencia* capital in the past.

ayuntamientos immediately following independence. This phenomenon was not driven by differences in population size but rather correlated with local venal legacies.

In terms of violent uprisings in the nineteenth and early twentieth centuries, I find strong geographical continuity in the presence of nineteenth-century conflicts in the areas more exposed to venality in Peru and Mexico. The claim is not that colonial venality directly caused these conflicts but that they lowered the threshold of rebellion making them more likely, particularly in certain junctures, such as the wars of independence (1810–20) and revolution (1910–20) in Mexico. Or during state-centralization measures that increased labor and tax contributions from indigenous communities to national projects such as the creation of a network of roads (Elizalde et al. 2021; Carter 2023). Or, throughout the gradual but relentless process of land dispossession observed in Peru in the late nineteenth century and twentieth century. Despite the changes in regime type and prevailing ideology, violent flares were more frequent in the former *corregimientos* and *alcaldías mayores* more exposed to venality in the eighteenth century.

Finally, the third legacy involves the segregation of the indigenous population away from key capitals and urban areas. While a common and natural response to venal officials in colonial times, it had the effect of limiting the integration and access of these communities to markets (of labor or goods), exacerbating inter- and intra-regional inequalities. As will be shown, this pattern will worsen in the nineteenth century in some places and take different forms in others. This displacement was largely driven by the breakdown of the implicit pact between the Crown and indigenous communities, which gave free rein to land grabbing and dispossession by landowners during the export boom in the last quarter of the nineteenth century (Saffon-Sanin 2015).

Together, these three legacies will lead to greater regional heterogeneity and undermine – to a greater or lesser degree – the consolidation of the nascent Spanish American states of the nineteenth century.

7.1.2 Bridging Colonial and Postindependence States

By tracing the venality legacies of the colonial era, this chapter relates to the literature on nineteenth-century state-building and state formation in Latin America. The common theme of this literature is the focus on the actions, events, and policies undertaken in the nineteenth century (postindependence) as central drivers of the states' capacity (or lack thereof) in the region. Key accounts focus on the decisions of local elites to support (or oppose) centralizing efforts by the state (Soifer 2015; Kurtz 2013); the choice of national actors to incorporate (or not) peripheral regions (Mazzuca 2021); the inclusion (or not) of export elites into ruling coalitions (Saylor 2014); and the prevalence (Centeno 2002; López-Alves 2000), type (Thies 2005), or outcome (Schenoni 2021) of violent conflicts, to name a few.

While all of these accounts have explanatory power, this chapter instead shows that key intervening factors and mechanisms in this literature – such as elite preferences, regional heterogeneity, economic geography, and the nature of conflicts in Spanish America – may have deep colonial roots. These legacies thus shaping the paths available (and unavailable) that these countries could have taken. For example, "elites" did not spring into life in the 1820s, particularly at the local level, their status and capital often came from practices and activities from colonial times. Regional economic heterogeneity – a key barrier to stronger state capacity in federal countries (Mazzuca 2021) – did not originate with independence. Similarly, the lack of transformative effects of two critical junctures – that of the nineteenth-century global commodity boom and the massive European immigration to the region – in countries with high exposure to Spanish administrative venality is not coincidental. Finally, the lack of inter-state wars – a feature of the region (Centeno 2002; López-Alves 2000) – may also be a by-product of the more or less clear demarcated jurisdictions left by the Spanish. And the list goes on. While the colonial era does not explain everything, it is important to recognize its influence, especially as postindependence actors and regimes not only substantially "borrow" from the colonial playbook but also, in some cases, seem unwilling or unable to stray from it.

One reason the colonial period is often overlooked is the apparent lack of correlation between key state features (i.e., fiscal, military capacity) in colonial times and those in the postindependence era. In particular, scholars note how tax collection or the size and strength of royal armies just before independence – to name two of the most common indicators of state strength – are poor predictors of subsequent fiscal capacity and the monopolization of violence circa 1900 (Soifer 2015) and even today (Chiovelli et al. 2024). The best example is Chile, a net recipient of fiscal transfers (*situado*) that lacked a standing army in colonial times. Yet, by

1900, it was already one of the strongest states by almost any indicator. In contrast, Mexico, the main generator of royal revenue in 1800 and where most troops were stationed, did not translate into a strong state by Weberian standards around 1900 (or 2000 for that matter). Thus suggesting that the strength of the colonial administration is a poor predictor of its postindependent success.

Yet, this dimension might not be the most telling indicator. As highlighted in the previous studies, key determinants of the state-building and state formation process lie in the nature of local elites, regional economic and ethnic heterogeneity, and the prevalence of conflict. Therefore, the question is, to what extent did the colonial period shape these key drivers – and with it – the state capacity of Spanish American countries?

In the rest of this chapter, I show how the legacies from colonial venality – limited representation and onerous labor and taxation policies, violent conflict, and ethnic segregation – continued to reverberate in the postindependence period.

The main obstacle to empirically examining the nineteenth century in Spanish (and Latin) America more generally is the paucity of systematic records vis-à-vis that from other periods.[4] Nonetheless, leveraging evidence from multiple sources – nineteenth-century subnational conflict records, indigenous settlement patterns, administrative censuses, date of creation of local municipalities, among many others – it is possible to piece together the consequences of venality after independence (roughly from the 1820s to the beginning of the twentieth century).

7.1.2.1 *Continuity in Fiscal and Labor Policies*

The promise of independence was that of freedom from the yoke of colonial taxation and the arbitrariness of its officials. Yet, after the dust settled and the Spanish were gone, some areas saw a remarkable continuity in taxation and labor coercive practices. In some cases, they were "never abolished," while in others they were initially removed but later reinstated ("resurrected") when need arose. Sometimes, the latter coincided with the arrival of *conservadores* (conservatives) to power who restored certain aspects of colonial rule in new legislation. Yet,

---

[4] Administrative records required the presence of consolidated states and peaceful times, which do not fully characterize Spanish American countries in the early nineteenth century.

liberal governments were also known to implement colonial practices in the face of economic necessity.

As argued in earlier work, most notably Kurtz (2013),[5] the prevalence of different forms of labor coercion in the nineteenth century had the potential to undermine state-building projects, particularly if the latter were premised on the modernization of labor markets. After independence, very few places in Spanish America had labor markets that would qualify as "free". The sole exception was somewhat that of Argentina (and Uruguay), which are not included in this analysis due to their light colonial imprint. The ubiquity of labor coercion thus challenged modernization projects across the region, albeit to different degrees.

Alongside labor coercion, independence was premised on dismantling the colonial fiscal apparatus, particularly taxes based on ethnicity or collective membership. Examples include the *mit'a* – the forced labor contributions to mining by Peruvian and Bolivian indigenous communities – abolished in 1821, and the *tributo* (vassal tax), which saw a more staggered end. Yet, the dismantling the colonial fiscal system left the nascent governments with few sources of income, as it reduced the per capita tax take of independent governments in the region (Irigoin 2016: 190). Consequently, these governments became increasingly reliant on indirect taxation such as sales taxes, monopolies on key products (salt, tobacco, and alcohol), tariffs, and customs (Centeno 2002). Facing bankruptcy, the new republics also resorted to two main instruments: international debt (see Queralt 2022) and – as shown later – the slowing down of the removal of colonial taxes or even their reintroduction.

Illustrative cases of this continuity are those of Guatemala, Ecuador, and Bolivia, where practices common in the eighteenth century reinvented themselves – sometimes under different names but with the same purpose of providing labor and revenue, albeit now in the "national interest."

7.1.3 Coerced Labor in Guatemala

In Guatemala, the initial turmoil and the weakness of the state after independence meant that indigenous communities enjoyed unprecedented autonomy until at least the 1870s (McCreery 1994), when the introduction of coffee cultivation for export began to curtail this

---

[5] Kurtz (2013) also argues that other factors, namely the timing of the masses' incorporation into politics, were detrimental for Argentina's state consolidation.

newfound freedom. The shift to coffee production occurred as cochineal, previously the main export, fell in international value with the invention of artificial dyes. Yet, instead of fulfilling the liberal view of capitalist and individual property development, the turn towards coffee "generalized, strengthened, and perpetuated non-capitalist modes of exploitation" such as the (re)introduction of labor drafts and the official sanctioning of debt peonage contracts (McCreery 1994).

In practice, these forms of "noncapitalist" labor entailed the central government mandating departmental governors (*jefes*) to supply laborers to coffee producers as a matter of national interest, effectively instituting agricultural labor drafts. Popularly known as *mandamientos*, the 1876 decree by liberal President Rufino Barrios (1873–85) outlined the rules by which local politicians could "recruit" workers for coffee production, who would then be sent to work on a coffee *finca* (farm) for a prespecified amount of time and wages.

A key provision in these rules was the exclusion of individuals who were already in debt to coffee producers to serve in the *mandamientos*. Under this provision, indigenous peoples would be able to remain in their communities and avoid recruitment into the drafts if they were indebted to a nearby *finca*. Because *mandamientos* quickly became known for their hazardous and difficult work, debt peonage in the coffee *fincas* – in the form of contracts with advance payments – was the preferred form of wage labor for these communities (McCreery 1994)[6] and became fully legalized in 1894 (Dessaint 1962). This preference only strengthened when President Rufino Barrios replaced *mandamientos* with *zapadores*, whereby labor drafts were redirected to public works, such as road construction. Faced with the option of debt peonage in a *finca* close to their community or government-mandated labor drafts, many communities sought the former.

Whether in the form of *mandamientos* or *zapadores*, both policies were directly molded from colonial *repartimientos*, albeit wrapped in the language of nineteenth-century liberalism. Labor drafts had existed in Guatemala since the seventeenth century. In the 1760s, it was the colonial *audiencia*, the one in charge of allocating workers for the export of highly valuable cochineal and wheat.[7] Although the impact

---

[6] In Peru, a similar form of coerced labor known as *enganche* committed workers, generally highland indigenous populations working for the coastal sugar plantations.
[7] Before this date, the issuance of *repartimientos* were in the hands of local officials and landowners, which the *audiencia* attempted to centralize in the 1760s (McCreery 1994).

of the *repartimientos* was uneven at the time, with some areas (particularly around the capital) significantly more affected, it provided a blueprint for subsequent governments to follow at a time of high labor demand, this time for coffee.

Administrative data on indigenous presence, coffee cultivation, and wage-laboring information from the municipal census of 1881 and 1893 support this narrative. In 1881, only 8 percent of the Guatemalan population in coffee areas was classified as wage laborers (*jornaleros*). By 1893, the proportion of wage laborers in coffee areas had quadrupled, reaching 31 percent on average – indicating that nearly a third of the Guatemalan population was employed in wage labor in these municipalities. Although the 1881 population count excludes key departments, even after limiting the analysis to municipalities counted in both 1881 and 1893, there is a steep increase in wage laboring in coffee areas by the latter year.

In turn, Figure 7.1 plots the relationship between indigenous presence and wage laboring in coffee municipalities and how it varies with eighteenth-century venality in Guatemala. Panel (a) shows that at the beginning of the coffee boom (1881), the relationship between indigenous presence and wage laboring in coffee municipalities is very similar regardless of their previous exposure to venality. However, this relationship had changed by 1893. Panel (b) shows that by 1893, at the height of the coffee boom in the region – the role of these colonial legacies becomes clear: There is a disproportionate increase in wage laboring in areas previously exposed to colonial venality. In fact, panel (c) corroborates that the positive relationship between wage laborers and indigenous presence is driven by areas cultivating coffee and not by other crops, as there is no difference outside of the coffee-producing ones. Panels (a) to (c) thus show that provinces with greater venal exposure in the past performed differently as the demand for wage laborers in coffee plantations increases.

The differences do not simply reflect indigenous presence, as the average is very similar in both sets of provinces: 70 percent of the population is indigenous in provinces with high colonial venality and 68 percent among those of low venality. They also do not reflect preexisting predispositions to agricultural work, as the 1881 data on agricultural laborers (*labradores*) does not show a difference by colonial venality.[8]

---

[8] In particular, the share of the indigenous population, which is positively related to the share of agricultural workers, does not vary significantly with the legacies from colonial venality as of 1881.

7 Colonial Venality and State-Building

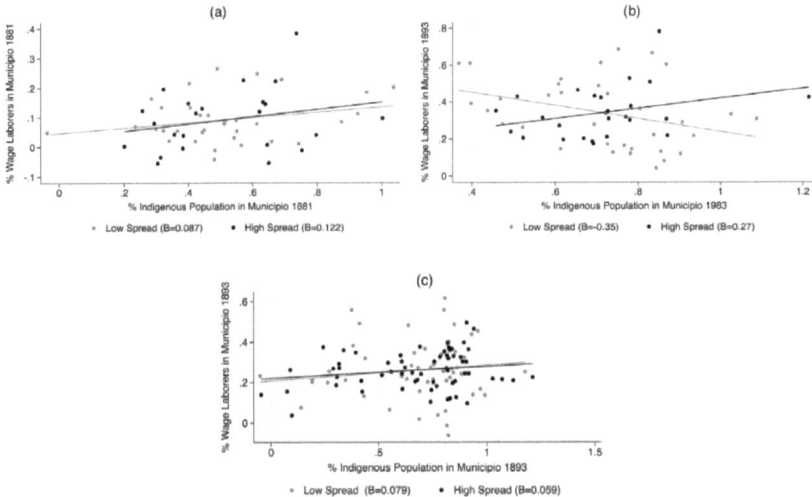

FIGURE 7.1 Venality and coffee wage laborers in Guatemala (1881 and 1893)

Note: Panel (a) 1881 wage laborers in coffee municipalities. Panel (b) 1893 wage laborers in coffee municipalities. Panel (c) 1893 wage laborers in non-coffee municipalities. Source: panel (a) 1881 municipal census. Excludes Departments of Peten, Huehuetenango, Totonicapán, and Quiché due to the lack of wage laborer data. Panels (b) and (c) 1893 municipal Census. Contemporary coffee cultivation information provided by INE. Note: Binned scatter plot of the mean of the residuals of the y-variable after accounting for municipal elevation, latitude, longitude, and colonial province fixed effects, against the mean value of x within equal-sized bins. All figures divide the sample in provinces with high (dark) and low price spreads (gray) in colonial times. Solid lines show the best linear fit using OLS.

Importantly, the patterns of Figure 7.1 do not imply that coffee cultivation areas are disproportionately located in areas of poor colonial governance. If anything, 33 percent of the municipalities in low-venality provinces currently report coffee cultivation, compared to 26 percent of those in high-venality provinces. Instead, the evidence here supports the notion of a faster transition from self-subsistence farmers to wage laborers in export-oriented landholdings.

But why was this labor legislation and coercion so successful in mobilizing indigenous communities? While this data cannot provide conclusive answers, it does allow us to rule out some possibilities. One explanation is that this policy might have been easier to implement in organizationally stronger communities. Yet, this feature could have also facilitated opposition to it. Another possibility is that landowners

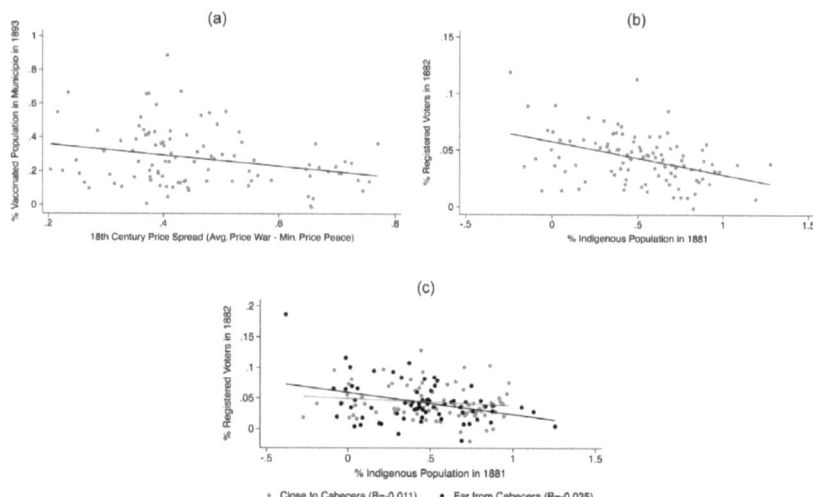

FIGURE 7.2 Colonial venality, public good provision, and voter registration

Note: Panel (a). Municipal vaccination rates (1893). Panels (b) and (c). Registered voters in 1882. Source: Panel (a) 1893 Census. Panel (b) and (c) 1882 municipal voter rolls. Notes: Binned scatter plots (see note Fig. 1 for construction details). Controls: Latitude, longitude, elevation, and province fixed effects. Panel (c) divides the sample in provinces with high (dark) and low price spreads (gray) in colonial times. Solid lines show the best linear fit using OLS.

found it easier to coerce these communities by expropriating their landholdings or by force. The results from Figure 7.1 also support a third reason: Labor coercion was greater in places with a history of venality, due to stronger elites bent on extraction and weaker political opposition.

As shown in Figure 7.2 (a), municipalities with higher price spreads are also those where vaccination rates – a common measure of state capacity and public goods – are lower in the nineteenth century, even after accounting for sheer distance to capitals, population size, and share of the indigenous population. One mechanism to explain this result is that of greater *political* disenfranchisement of the indigenous population. As shown in panel (b), the share of registered voters (registered over eligible) declines as the share of indigenous population in the municipality increases, consistent with disenfranchisement. Albeit this degree of disenfranchisement varies little by higher or lower price spread with this limited data, colonial venality did lead to the geographical segregation of the indigenous population, likely facilitating political exclusion. As shown in panel (c), political disenfranchisement is stronger precisely as the indigenous presence concentrates farther from the colonial *cabeceras*, in turn a product of earlier colonial policies. In other words, although the ability to participate in elections in Guatemala was generally limited, it was even more so in municipalities where the indigenous population had been earlier displaced. Because these estimates control for indigenous population size, this discrepancy is not simply capturing farther or depopulated areas. Instead, it suggests that political power was more diluted where indigenous segregation is higher.

In all, the evidence from late nineteenth-century Guatemala documents how practices not only served as a blueprint for labor coercive policies but also shaped the way they were implemented on the ground. In areas where these legacies had been stronger, the effect on wage laborers, political disenfranchisement, and the underprovision of public goods was also stronger. Even after accounting for the size of the population and distance to key population centers, among other controls.

In fact, the dynamics of forced labor documented earlier would not undergo significant changes until the early twentieth century. Only the decline in commodity prices at this time would ease forced labor drafts in the form of *mandamientos*. Yet, this period also brought a renewed reliance on vagrancy laws to compel those "without useful occupations" into wage labor in the 1920s and 1930s. By then, many indigenous communities were already working as debt peons at nearby *fincas* as wage laborers to supplement their income, easing the need for labor in that sector.

7.1.4 *Concertaje* in Ecuador

A different form of coerced labor was the practice of *concertaje* in Ecuador, whereby peasants' fiscal debts to the Crown were to be repaid not in kind but in exchange for work in *haciendas* or textile factories. *Indios conciertos* describes the population that fell into this category, a label not officially abolished until 1918 and which saw its apogee in the early nineteenth century (Botero Villegas 2008, cited by Rivadeneira 2019).

On its surface, *concertaje* could appear unrelated to colonial venality, as its main beneficiaries were private landowners (*hacendados*) and textile factory owners (*obrajeros*). Yet, its roots can be directly traced to the "debt" element central to the relationship between colonial officials – the *corregidores* – and the indigenous population in Ecuador. In Ecuador, unlike the other Andean cases of Peru and Bolivia,[9] the colonial *corregidor*'s profits mainly came through the collection of head taxes (*tributo*) and not *repartimientos de mercancías* per se. The *corregidor* would tax those exempted or double the tax rate as a way for the population to rake up their debt to the Crown (i.e., himself), which had to be repaid in labor. In other words, the *corregidor* used the debts from poll taxes to coerce indigenous people into working not only in different types of *haciendas* and *obrajes* (textile factories) but also in public works, livestock care, and other agricultural tasks (Juan and Ulloa 1978 [1749]: 75). Compensation for this labor going directly to the *corregidores* and to the royal coffers.

In principle, once the debt was paid, workers were "free" to return to their own activities. In practice, workers kept accumulating debts such that they lengthened the amount of time needed to work and their debts were passed from one generation to another (Juan and Ulloa 1978 [1749]; Oberem 1981). In the face of labor scarcity, this mechanism of labor indebtedness became a popular way for *hacienda* and textile factory owners to retain indigenous labor in their service. By assuming the responsibility to pay head taxes to the *corregidor* while increasing the debt of workers in their service, they could "keep" workers for longer. From the perspective of the indigenous population, this debt mechanism in *haciendas* was often preferable to the direct indebtedness to *corregidores* (Juan and Ulloa 1978 [1749]; Botero Villegas 2008) as it allowed greater locational choice and the work was often less onerous than that assigned by colonial officials.

Through direct payments or indebted labor, *corregidores* clearly benefited from this mechanism. As shown in panels (a) and (b) of Figure 7.3, the willingness to pay for this position in the eighteenth century is positively associated with the size of the tributary population (panel a) and the total taxes collected (panel b). Because the price data precedes the tributary data, it is consistent with these relationships being present in 1750 and persisting until 1780, particularly since many purchasers were still in office. More relevant for this chapter is Panel (c), namely the relationship between the size of the tributary population and that subject to *concertaje*, available from Rivadeneira (2019). As shown, for areas with higher price spreads, the relationship is positive, but for those with lower price spreads, there is no discernible relationship. This is

---

[9] Which appear to have benefited more from the practice of *repartimiento*.

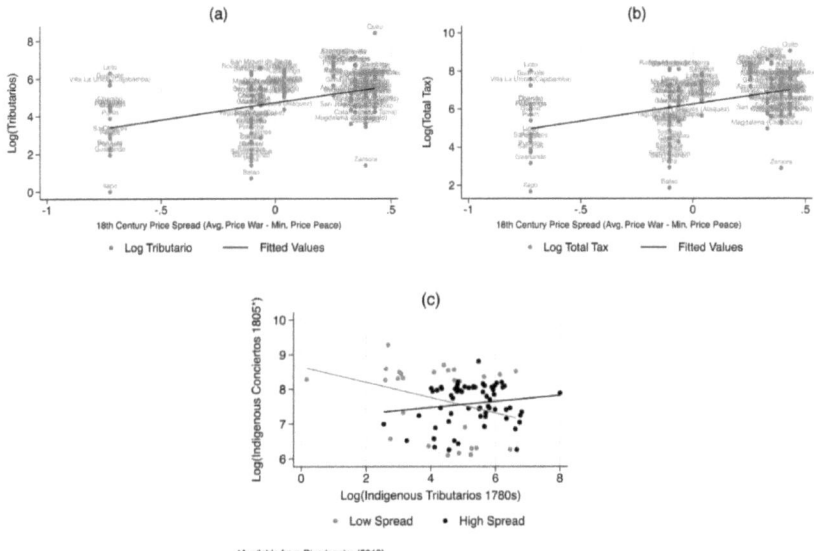

FIGURE 7.3 Eighteenth-century price spread poll tax payers and *concertaje* in Ecuador

Sources: Panel (a) and (b) 1780's Tributary data come from corregidor accounting records from the Colonial Archives (AGI). All rates are equivalent to dos tercios or 2/3 of the total payment of the years. Panel (c) uses province level data of 1805 indigenous population under concertaje, from Rivadeneira (2019). Notes: Panel (a) and panel (b) are scatterplots while panel (c) is a binned scatter plot (see notes Fig. 1) controlling for latitude, longitude, and elevation of the district and dividing the sample in provinces with high (dark) and low-price spreads (gray) in colonial times. In all figures, solid lines show the best linear fit using OLS.

consistent with a larger tributary population being more likely to become a *concierto*, but mostly in areas with greater venality. However, the relationship should be viewed as indicative only, given Ecuador had a low number of *corregimientos* in colonial times (14). Still, the case exhibits similar patterns to those of other settings (Peru, Mexico, and Bolivia), where more data is available.

More importantly, the advent of independence did not alter the continuation of *concertaje*: The share of the indigenous population under *concertaje* changed very little from 1785 to 1830. Moreover, liberal legislation passed in 1833 to abolish the intergenerational transmission of debt did not apply to *concertaje*, underscoring its enduring importance for the Ecuadorian highland economy (Rivadeneira 2019: 9; Oberem 1981: 315). Its formal abolition only took place in 1918, but was immediately followed by its twentieth-century version in the form of *huasipungo*, whereby *hacienda* owners gave workers a plot of land in exchange for labor – another form of debt peonage (Oberem 1981) that is strongly correlated with the earlier practice of *concertaje* (Rivadeneira 2019: 13). According to these authors, this correlation only began to weaken with extensive land reform in the second half of the twentieth century.

7.1.5 *Tributo* in Bolivia

The final example of policy persistence is the *tributo* tax in Bolivia. *Tributo* was the head tax owed to the Crown by all indigenous males between eighteen and fifty-four years old, reflecting their status as vassals. Despite being a relic from colonial times, and contrary to the main tenets of liberalism at the time – as it was an ethnicity-based tax – its abolition was uneven over time and space after independence. In Colombia and Mexico, it was abolished early on, in 1821 and 1832, respectively; in Peru only in 1854, with an earlier unsuccessful attempt; and in Ecuador in 1857 after an earlier attempt in 1823 (Sánchez-Albornoz 1978: 201). Moreover, even after its official disappearance, other exactions would take its place. For example, Mexico reintroduced a special tax targeting indigenous communities – the *contribución territorial indígena* – in the 1830s. Similarly, at the local level, states and regions continued to collect it.

In the case of Bolivia, the continuities between the colonial and postcolonial policies are stark. The colonial *tributo* persisted in both name[10] and form well into the Republican era (Langer 2009). In fact, it would have a greater fiscal role after independence than it did during colonial times (Sánchez-Albornoz 1978: 217). As shown in Table 7.1, throughout most of the nineteenth century, *tributo* remained as a tax applied to every individual of indigenous origin residing in a community. Those without land (*forasteros*) would be largely exempt,[11] and only those landed would continue to pay the *contribución territorial indígena* but at a higher rate (Sánchez-Albornoz 1978). *Tributo* would remain in place until at least 1927, though certain states or departments continued its use beyond that date, as it was an important source of local revenue.

---

[10] It was also known as the *contribución indígena* (indigenous contribution) after independence.
[11] Technically, they were encouraged to pay a personal tax, which was nonetheless difficult to collect (Sánchez-Albornoz 1978: 214).

TABLE 7.1 *Postindependence shares of indigenous taxation to total revenue: Bolivia*

	Indigenous Taxes Collected (pesos)	% Indigenous Contribution from Total
1831	716,543	42.75
1841	670,115	31.14
1852	664,156	28
1862	699,636	25.17
1871	424,723	13.75
1880	764,152	22.7

Source: Sánchez-Albornoz 1978: 198.

The consequences of the persistence of this collective tax were twofold. First, it contributed to the preservation of indigenous communities in Bolivia, as states had a fiscal interest in preserving the foundation of their tax base: organized indigenous communities (Grieshaber 1977; Langer 2009). This arrangement thus enabled indigenous autonomy in exchange for a "modicum" fee, a second-best outcome for these communities (Langer 2009; 2016). Second, many of the fiscal practices of *corregidores*, such as the enumeration criteria and collection procedures, remained unchanged throughout the nineteenth century. As in colonial times, local officials personally benefited from this system, with salaries and other in-kind payments depending on the amount of *tributo* collected (Grieshaber 1977; 110).[12]

The enduring influence of colonial fiscal policies is evident in the available data from tax counts. This data shows how the provincial quotas for *repartimiento* in the eighteenth century – regulating the commercial dealings of *corregidores* in 1751 – are still highly correlated with the size of the tax-paying indigenous population over time, as depicted in Figure 7.4, panels (a)–(e). Well into the nineteenth century, the levels of eighteenth-century *repartimiento* – a proxy for the rents to be obtained by provincial officials – continued to correlate with the size of the population paying *tributo* in 1770, 1838, and 1877. This correlation likely results from the persistence of the same enumeration practices; in fact, even the title of local officials remained

---

[12] In fact, Grieshaber (1977: 263–264) documents how postindependence local officials, also called *corregidores*, actively helped the indigenous population resist the sale of communal land in the early 1880s. The reasons were likely self-interested, as they would lose labor and personal services that indigenous communities provided to them.

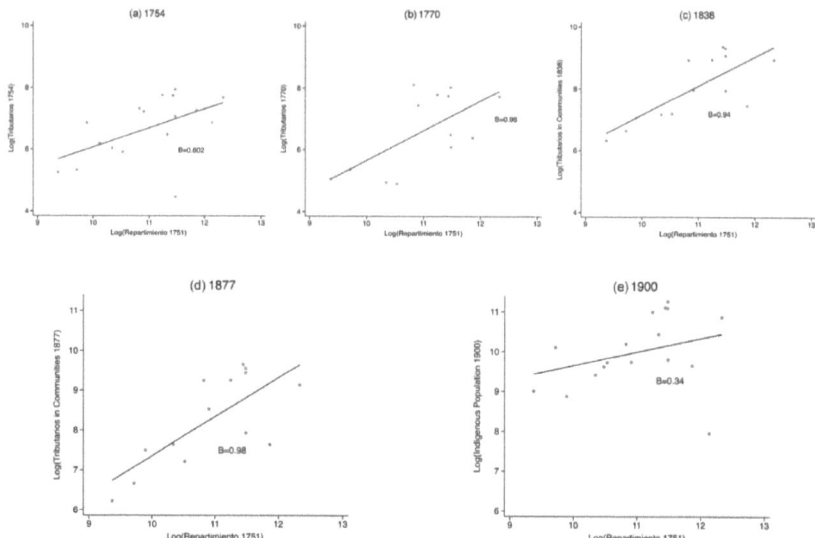

FIGURE 7.4 Colonial *repartimiento* and size of population paying *tributo* in Bolivia

Source: Tributary data for 1770, 1838, 1858, 1877, and 1900 comes from Grieshaber (1977 and 1980). Notes: All figures are binned scatter plots (see notes Fig. 1 for description). Solid lines show the best linear fit using OLS.

that of *corregidores* despite massive changes in political regimes. The relationship only starts to weaken but not disappear as of 1900, when new sources of taxation become available to the state. Although the data is limited to only sixteen provinces within the current territory of Bolivia, the findings highlight the remarkable continuity in the fiscal importance of these communities from colonial times through the early twentieth century.

7.1.6 Continuity and Local Political Representation: The Case of Municipio Incorporation in Peru and Mexico

A different mechanism explaining the local persistence of colonial practices comes from the extent to which political power fragmented and diluted in some areas vis-à-vis others. As already previewed in the case of Guatemala, opportunities for political participation after independence varied with the type of colonial legacy the region had experienced in the eighteenth century. This section explores a different measure of political representation, that of the creation of new bodies for local government in the aftermath of independence.

In colonial times, the Spanish population of cities and *villas* was represented by an elected body, that of the *cabildo* (or city council). In contrast, *corregidores* and *alcaldes mayores* were not elected and instead were a source of patronage for the viceroy or king. In the case of the indigenous population, they enjoyed sufficient autonomy that allowed them to select their own authorities or to follow custom and rely on the indigenous nobility from precolonial times, known as *kurakas*, *caciques*, or *gobernadores indios*, depending on the location. This was part of the implicit contract between indigenous and the Crown: autonomy in exchange for revenue.

These *cabildos* thus became the seat of power for local elites, themselves residents of villas and cities and dominated by local notables, generally of Spanish American origin (*criollos* or *Españoles Americanos*). *Cabildos* dealt with matters of municipal governance in provincial capitals and were headed by the *corregidor* or *alcalde mayor* as the King's representative. In fact, these councils played a prominent role during the sovereignty crises unleashed by Napoleon in 1808: They became the bodies from which provincial representatives (*diputados*) would be selected from and sent to the Cortes of Cádiz in Spain.

Due to their unique representational role as local governing councils, *cabildos* were one of the few colonial institutions with legitimate claims to sovereignty and self-government after independence. *Cabildos* would become the basis for the formation of the local *ayuntamientos* (government) and *municipios* (territorial) – and the smallest unit of self-government in the postindependence era. Their proliferation is often seen as the hallmark of the process of "balkanization" of political power after independence (Mazzuca 2021). The question is, to what extent was the claim to sovereignty extended beyond the existing *cabildo* and to the confines of the *villa* or provincial capital? How were indigenous communities – formerly governed by a parallel indigenous authority – to be incorporated in the independent era?

Analysis from municipal creation data shows shows that despite the general decentralization of political power immediately after independence, the process was slower or less intense in areas where the legacies from venality were strongest. Three reasons may explain this pattern: First, since colonial venality led to greater geographic segregation, indigenous communities, accustomed to self-rule, likely viewed *municipios* and *ayuntamientos* as extraneous and against their traditions or interest.

TABLE 7.2 *Number of* municipios *by date of creation in Peru (1525–2010)*

	Peru
Colonial (pre-1822)	458
1822–1850	16
1850–1900	301
1900–1950	489
1950–2000	563
2000–2010	48

Source: INEI.

Second, in provinces where venality was more pronounced, office holders enjoyed greater returns – in the form of taxes, labor, or social prestige – discouraging the formation of parallel bodies that could undermine these gains. Finally, the venality of the early eighteenth century provided a key way for provincial elites (non-Spanish) to access power typically reserved to Spanish-born officials. These roles often helped consolidate economic networks and enhance social status, further entrenching existing structures (see Chapter 5 for some examples).

Table 7.2 shows the number of *municipios* incorporated or legally recognized in Peru during each fifty-year period. Immediately after independence, only a few new *municipios* were created. The number of municipalities increased somewhat in the second half of the nineteenth century and surged alongside Peru's population in the twentieth century.

However, this national trend masks substantial regional heterogeneity. Figure 7.5 instead presents statistical estimates showing that *corregimientos* and *alcaldías* with higher price spreads actually had a lower likelihood of establishing new municipalities postindependence. Specifically, there was about an eight-year delay in incorporation per each unit increase in the price spread (panel a).[13] This suggests that new centers of local power were much less likely to form in areas where the economic value of office in colonial times was much higher. This result is not driven by *corregimientos* already having a large number of *municipios* (self-governing units), as the dependent variable in panels (b) and (c) is expressed in shares. Moreover, the analysis controls for indigenous population size in all cases, suggesting that these

---

[13] See the Appendix to Chapter 7 for details.

7 *Colonial Venality and State-Building* 179

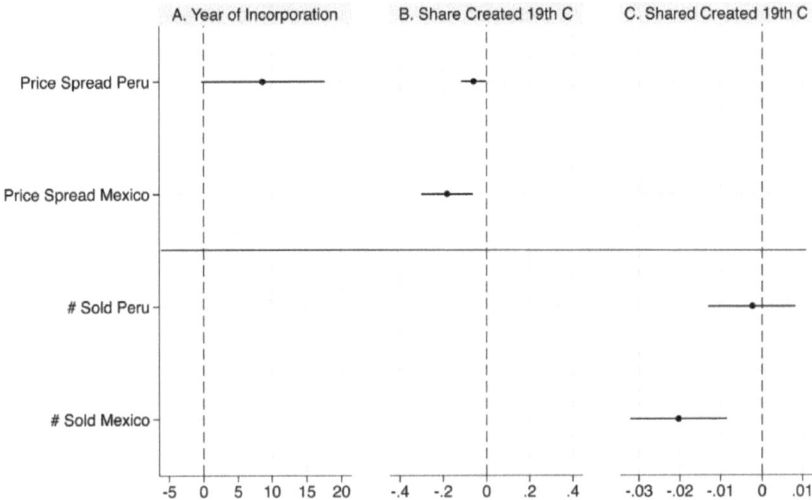

FIGURE 7.5 Timing of *municipio* creation and colonial venality in Peru and Mexico

Note: 95 percent Confidence Intervals using clustered standard errors at the province level. All specifications control for district latitude, longitude, elevation, and size of the indigenous population. Panel (a) excludes municipalities already created in colonial times. See Equation (6) in Appendix to Chapter 7 for details.

differences are visible even among areas with similar levels of preexisting indigenous population. Instead, these results reflect a form of representational delay – where, despite comparable population sizes, provinces with highly valued offices exhibit fewer representative institutions in the form of *Ayuntamientos*.[14]

This phenomenon is not limited to Peru. In Mexico, despite the early recognition of *municipios* as a political and territorial unit for every 200 inhabitants, their geographic distribution after independence mirrors that of Peru. Although there is no data equivalent to that of Peru, information from the National Institute of Statistics and Geography (INEGI)[15]

---

[14] However, this would not mean that indigenous populations lacked their own forms of self-government.
[15] While the INEGI compiles the evolution of the territorial organization of Mexico, it lacks detail in the foundational dates of *municipios* as opposed to when state constitutions recognized them. For example, in 1837 it marks almost all municipios in Puebla to have been created then, as it is the date they were recognized as relevant territorial units in the states' constitutions. However, this is not the date when they were founded.

provides the subset of *municipios* recognized before independence in 1821, which I complement with the set of *municipios* in 1900 from Sellars and Alix-García (2018).

Combining these two sources, the second row of panel (b) shows there is a lower likelihood that new *municipios* are created among provinces more valuable in colonial times. The effect in Mexico is evident both in the price spreads (panel b) and the number of times a position is sold (panel c). Across both panels, more intense office-selling delayed the formation of new local governments despite the province having similar population and geographic characteristics as others.

In all, estimates from Figure 7.5 support the idea of (intended?) limits to political representation, precisely where colonial venality was stronger. This could reflect the purposeful disenfranchisement of the indigenous population, the unwillingness of indigenous communities to participate in what was perceived as a foreign institution, or, more likely, a combination of the two. This situation meant that existing representative institutions (such as that of *cabildos*) in more venal *corregimientos* faced less competition and greater opportunities to exert their power in the surrounding territory and population. Not surprisingly, areas where local political representation was delayed are those that continue to have higher indigenous segregation and weaker state capacity in the long run, as will be discussed in Chapter 8.

7.1.6.1 *Venality and the Subnational Persistence of Conflict*

As noted in Chapter 6, the introduction of office-selling was a key contextual factor in ending the *Pax Hispannica* that had prevailed until the eighteenth century. With the arrival of venal officers, uprisings became a persistent fixture of certain locations,[16] marking an era of political violence that challenged colonial practices and officials at the local level. Unlike the fight for independence, these uprisings were generally self-contained events that did not seek to overthrow Spanish rule but were generally directed to specific aspects of its rule: *corregidores* and *alcaldes mayores*, excessive or new taxes, and, occasionally, complaints against church officials. For some, these were "monarchist" rebellions, with participants expecting the Spanish Crown to actually intercede in their favor against petty and arbitrary officials, as well as against unjust taxes and mistreatment. Even in the case of the Túpac Amaru

---

[16] On a similar vein, Fearon and Laitin (2014) show how certain locations exhibit recurrent conflict even if the causes and context have changed dramatically.

rebellion in Peru – *a posteriori* viewed as the single most important "threat" to Spanish rule – the stated goal of Túpac Amaru himself was not independence.[17]

These eighteenth-century uprisings inaugurated a cycle of violence and repression with lasting economic and cultural roots in the region. First, popular uprisings instilled a sense of threat among local elites, who responded with militarization and repression. Second, in the collective consciousness, previous experiences with uprisings created a culture of resistance, further justifying the elites' investment in a repressive apparatus. In these areas, violence and repression became the standard response to (legitimate) societal demands and a reason why rule via military means, or *caudillismo*, became the way to deal with violent threats from the population. Finally, recurrent violence led to public and private *dis*investment in health, human capital, and infrastructure, which suffered in the presence (or the mere threat) of violence. Conditions that in turn further violence, and so on.

In this section, I present statistical evidence linking the geographic distribution of eighteenth-century venality with instances of conflict in nineteenth-century Mexico and Peru. Using subnational data on violent uprisings, the analysis shows that the likelihood and intensity of these events can be explained by their history of venality. While these conflict episodes are always driven by an array of more immediate causes – such as responding to land dispossession and exploitation, national junctures of conflict, or weather-related shocks – they were much more likely in areas with a venal past.

Tracing the persistence of conflict contributes to a small but growing literature on the factors that make certain areas more prone to conflict. For example, certain regions in Asia, Africa, and the Middle East that experienced pre-1945 conflict are more likely to exhibit civil wars (Fearon and Laitin 2014: 3). In Pakistan, institutional legacies from colonialism help explain why the same provinces have been disproportionately involved in anticolonial warfare as well as in recent militant violence against the state (Naseemullah 2014). In India, areas ruled through princely states (indirectly) have become fertile ground for Maoist violence in recent times through a combination of both economic and cultural mechanisms (Mukherjee 2018; 2021). In sub-Saharan Africa, sons of the soil movements can also be linked to this

---

[17] This can be said even for the case of other major rebellions at the time: the *Comunero* Rebellion in Colombia and the Quito Rebellion.

colonial distinction (Boone 2017). What follows shows how this phenomenon is not limited to these cases but is also present in postindependent Mexico and Peru.

7.1.7 Mexico: National Conflict Junctures

The case of Mexico illustrates how the geographic distribution and intensity of conflict patterns after and during the wars of independence track the patterns of venality in colonial times. Again, the argument is not that office-selling directly caused instances of conflict postindependence. Rather, that a history of exposure to venality might have made it easier to resort to violence in the presence of other factors. For example, a history of appropriation of economic surplus may lower the threshold for rebellion due to material (lower opportunity costs) and cultural (underlying grievances) mechanisms.

Figure 7.6 panel (a) starts by showing the role of colonial venality in the immediate postcolonial period: During the wars of independence themselves, starting in 1810. Using data from the distribution of insurgent activity between 1810 and 1820 from Garfias and Sellars (2022) collected from (2014), I find continuity in the earlier conflict patterns. Namely, areas with greater venality in the previous century exhibit more insurgent activity even after accounting for an array of provincial characteristics.[18] In particular, former *corregimientos* and *alcaldías*[19] with the higher price spreads in the eighteenth century saw between 1.8 more insurgent events during the conflict, on average. Given the average number of insurgent rebellions in this sample is 2.83, this increase is equivalent to 64 percent of the mean. While the immediate cause was the elite discontent caused by the Bourbon reforms in the midst of major drought affecting peasants (Tutino 1986; Garfias and Sellars 2022), these found more fertile ground in areas blighted by earlier venality.

After independence, conflict would devolve into an on-and-off fifty-year civil war between ideologically opposed factions (liberals and conservatives), which provided a juncture for local tensions to arise. This absent state facilitated land dispossession by private landowners, fueling

---

[18] Estimates weight by district population size at the end of the colonial period (1770–1800), latitude, longitude, elevation, district area, distance to Mexico, maize suitability, and malaria propensity. The estimates report clustered standard errors at the level of the former *corregimiento* and *alcaldia mayor*, above that of the *municipio*.

[19] Recall that by the end of the colonial period these had been renamed *subdelegaciones*, but maintained their territorial extensions.

7 Colonial Venality and State-Building 183

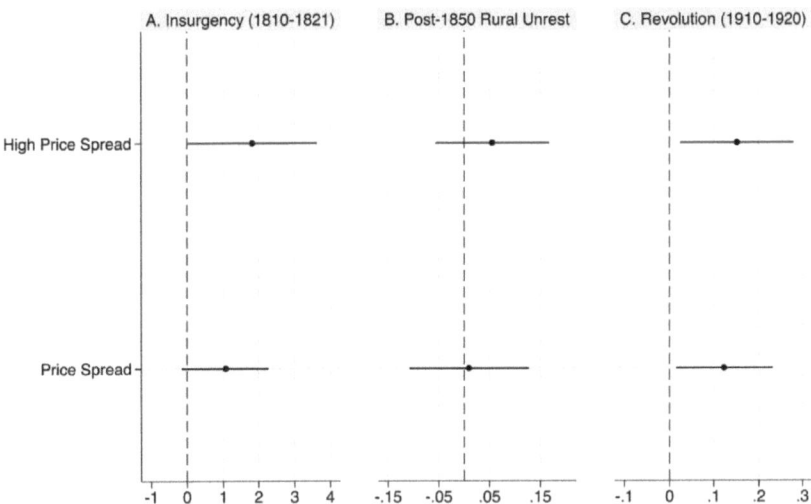

FIGURE 7.6 Insurgency, rural unrest, and revolution in rural Mexico (1810–1920)

Sources: Panel (a) Insurgency rebellions from Ortiz Escamilla (2014) and Garfias and Sellars (2022); panel (b) nineteenth-century rural unrest coded Reina (1983); panel (c) insurgent events from Dell (2012) and the *Enciclopedia de los Municipios de México*. All estimates are weighted by population either at the colonial district level (panel a) or at the municipal level (panels b and c) and control for latitude, longitude, altitude, as well as land quality from Fergusson, Larreguy & Riaño (2022) and share of sedimentary basis from Acemoglu, Fergusson, and Robinson (2020). Panel (a) in addition controls for maize suitability and malaria propensity from Garfias and Sellars (2021). See estimating Equation (7) in Appendix to Chapter 7 for details.

local tensions. Codifying the uprisings listed in Reina (1983) for the period 1850–1910 and focusing on those involving peasant and indigenous actors, I find a broad array of motivations for conflict. For example, taxation by civil and religious authorities was a major cause of a number of peasant and indigenous unrest.[20] Opposition to forceful military drafts (1853's *Ley del Sorteo*) to face foreign invasions was also a cause of riots and violent resistance, as in several municipalities of Veracruz. Demand for local autonomy was also prevalent among communities in this period. However, panel (b) shows that office-selling had a small effect on these peasant and indigenous uprisings for this period. Suggesting that the relationship is not deterministic – not every instance of unrest falls along the schisms created by colonial governance.

---

[20] This is the case of an 1868 uprising in San Cristóbal de las Casas, Chiapas, documented in Reina (1983).

Instead, in panel (c), the legacies of venality again become relevant within a broader juncture of discontent, that created by the Mexican Revolution (1910–1920). Albeit it started as an intra-elite conflict, the movement ballooned by successfully capitalizing on peasant discontent caused by drought (Dell 2012) and other underlying grievances. As shown, municipalities in former colonial districts with higher price spreads saw 0.15 more revolutionary activity than those below the median. Because the mean is 0.12, this is a sizeable effect. While these are very few episodes (three) to draw a definite conclusion, one reason why there is no effect for the late nineteenth-century unrest but a large one for the wars of independence and the Mexican Revolution might have to do with the magnitude of the disputes. Venality mattered more in "national" conflicts, albeit this is not necessarily the case in Peru, seen next.

7.1.8 Peru: Perennial Conflict

As in the Mexican case, the findings from Peru show that the spatial patterns initiated by office-selling persisted even after the nation gained its independence in 1827. Using data from Kammann (1982), I examine the degree of persistence in local conflict as explained by different levels of venality. Again, the claim here is not of a direct effect of colonial venality but that in the presence of other detonators, it made conflict more likely. For example, the limited degree of political representation in former *corregimientos* and *alcaldia mayores* shown before leaves violence as the only way to process political conflict (Curvale and Przeworski 2008).

The results of the analysis presented in Figure 7.7 illustrate how the legacies of venality continued to influence the local distribution of conflict from the mid nineteenth century to the late 1960s. This is a period marked by peasant movements to protest work conditions, wages, and tax obligations, among other issues. Specifically, panels (a) to (c) of Figure 7.7 show the relationship between the geography of colonial venality and the intensity of rural conflict. As in the Mexican analysis, all estimates include geographic and population controls.[21] A unit increase in the price spread – roughly two standard deviations – is associated with 0.27 more uprisings from 1824 to the late 1960s in panel (a). Given that the average district experiences 0.17 uprisings, these

---

[21] For Figure 7.4, panel (a), I use either population from 1754, 1972, or none, with little difference in the coefficients (0.249, 0.248, or 0.276, respectively).

7 Colonial Venality and State-Building 185

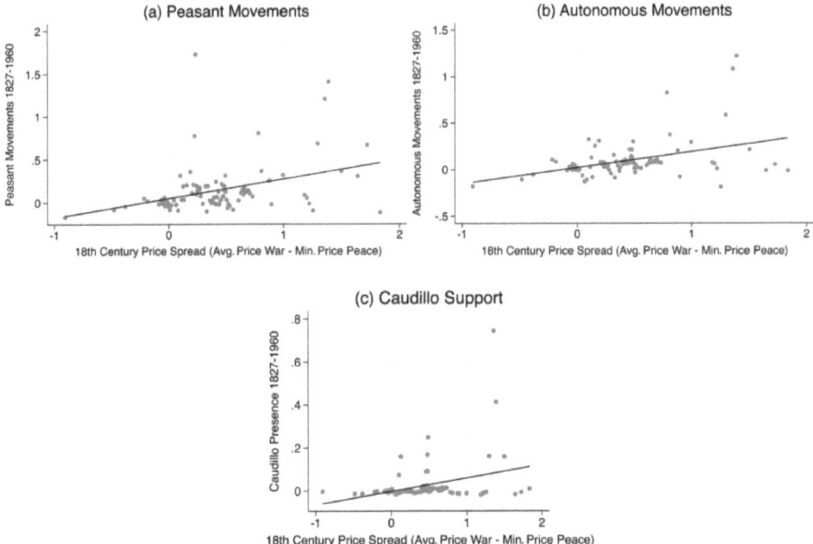

FIGURE 7.7 Nineteenth-century and early twentieth-century historical conflicts in Peru

Source of conflict data: Albertus (2020) and Kammann (1982). Note: Binned scatter plots (see notes Fig. 1) controlling for latitude, longitude, altitude, and population measures in colonial times (1754). In all figures, solid lines show the best linear fit using OLS.

estimates are 1.5 times its mean, again a sizable effect. The effect is similar in panel (b) for peasant movements related to autonomy (coefficient of 0.21) and weaker, yet still statistically significant, for the presence of *caudillos* in panel (c), a hallmark of the cycle of uprising and repression that characterizes the region.

Moreover, thanks to the detailed qualitative accounts in Kammann (1982), it is possible to understand how the past "looms large" in the nineteenth- and early twentieth-century Peruvian uprisings. Among the main reasons cited for uprisings is a reduction in tax payments, ending land dispossession, improving rural wages and working conditions, improving communal rights and autonomy for peasant and indigenous communities, and securing greater educational opportunities. Not surprisingly, many of these demands overlap with those of the Mexican Revolution (1910–1920), which were also positively associated with higher price spreads in that context.

For example, in the 1830s, Kammann (1982: 26) documents how in Huanta (department of Ayacucho), a number of peasant rebellions were sparked by the "loss of privileges" and the introduction of higher taxation in the Republican era, with indigenous demands for the restoration of the colonial system and the autonomy they previously enjoyed. The increased tax rates in Urubamba and Parinacochas also explain the support for the *caudillo* efforts of President Ramón Castilla as a way to reduce the taxes they faced (Kamman 1982: 27). Another cause of discontent was the enactment of conscription laws for the construction of national roads in 1920 (Ley Vial), which were exploited by landowners to coerce labor for their own benefit.

Over time, these conflict dynamics have had both direct and indirect costs on other political events. Recurrent conflicts over land and community autonomy explain why these areas had a higher probability of land redistribution during 1969–1980, a period when the demands of peasants aligned with national elites' objectives to dismantle traditional large landholdings (Albertus 2020).[22]

In sum, through the cases of nineteenth-century Mexico and Peru, it is possible to trace the continuities (and change) between earlier exposure to venality and subnational conflict. While not exhaustive of all Spanish American countries due to data availability, it introduces a pattern to be further explored.

7.1.8.1 *Ethnic Segregation*

The third and perhaps most consequential colonial legacy – as it underpins both the local distribution of political power and conflict – relates to the geographic patterns of indigenous settlements. Did postcolonial States exacerbate the segregation of indigenous communities in Spanish America? Or did they instead alleviate it? As shown in Chapter 6, by the 1770s, there was already a noticeable displacement of indigenous communities away from major seats of power and economic activity – the provincial capitals (*cabeceras*). This, despite the fact that the Spanish purposefully founded capital cities in close proximity to relocated indigenous settlements (*reducciones, congregaciones*) in the sixteenth century.[23] Yet, two centuries later (late eighteenth century), their distribution would be the exact opposite, particularly in more venal territories. Did the end of the colonial era slow down or even reverse the geographic segregation of indigenous communities? Or did it instead accelerate it?

---

[22] See also Albertus et al. (2016) for the Mexican case.
[23] The purpose was to facilitate access to taxes and labor (Rojas 2016: 24).

One view is that most of the geographic segregation of indigenous communities we observe today is the direct result of key postindependence policies and events. The first was the disappearance of the mediating figure of the Crown and the lack of recognition of indigenous autonomy by liberal governments, which led to an incessant assault on their land. Particularly in the last decades of the nineteenth century, when the global boom for agricultural commodities increased the value of land vis-à-vis labor (see Saffon-Sanin 2015). In addition to fueling displacement, the commodity boom also made it easier to import food and increased job opportunities in cities and urban areas, particularly in the service sectors. Thus resulting in massive migration to urban areas, a characteristic of the first half of the twentieth century. If this depopulation particularly affected indigenous communities, it could reverse earlier patterns of displacement away from urban centers. Or, exacerbate them.

An alternative view is that it was often not in the self-interest of private actors and the newly independent states to displace or dissolve indigenous communities, given their labor and revenue roles. For example, in Guatemala, Ecuador, and Bolivia, where indigenous revenue contribution was a sizeable share of the government (and officials') income. Therefore, it was in the interest of the state to preserve the integrity of these communities by limiting land grabbing. In Mexico, private actors – such as *haciendas* and *fincas* – also soon discovered the benefits of maintaining the integrity of these communities as a source of seasonal labor (Tutino 2017). For example, *haciendas* often leased land to "local big men" who in turn hired landless peasants, which helped preserve the physical integrity of the community and served haciendas well (Tutino 2017: 265–266). Although communities were often devoid of actual property rights, the community survived by strengthening its ethnic bonds and organization to "[...] fight against landowners, political authorities, and the church" (Reina 1983: 29).[24]

Similar patterns arose in Peru, where land distribution throughout the nineteenth century became one of the most unequal in Latin America (Albertus 2015). In the immediate postindependence period, indigenous communities in the highlands were able to remain in their communities due to the concentration of the cash crop and export

---

[24] "... [la comunidad] se convirtió en una forma natural de resistencia, de organización y de lucha contra los hacendados, contra las autoridades, y contra el clero" (Reina 1983: 29).

economic activity along the coast and away from areas of major indigenous settlements. Their engagement in a low-capital activity (wool production) for their basic subsistence needs meant they faced little competition from major landowners (Grieshaber 1977). Instead, as in the Mexican case, landowners found these communities a useful and reliable source of labor, either for seasonal needs, or in the form of sharecroppers and tenants. Moreover, the reliance on foreign labor (mostly Chinese) for the export of guano in the mid-nineteenth century helped the state wean itself from *tributo* (head taxes) in 1854 (Sánchez-Albornoz 1978), limiting exactions.

Finally, in both cases, indigenous communities were also protected by the inherent weakness of the states that emerged after independence. In the case of Mexico, liberal governments decreed the abolition of head taxes, the disappearance of "Indios" as a collective legal category and the privatization of communal land with the Ley Lerdo of 1857. However, the implementation of these laws was uneven and delayed until the end of the nineteenth century. At the eve of the Mexican Revolution (1910), around 50 percent of the rural population of Mexico was still living in indigenous *pueblos* (Tannenbaum 1929). In fact, by the 1930s ambitious land reforms had already restored communal lands to many of these communities, albeit they did not reinstate the indigenous *pueblo* as a legal actor per se.[25]

Whether land dispossession displaced indigenous communities away from major urban centers or they scattered due to their landless status is thus an open empirical question. Figure 7.8 plots the relationship between the distance from former colonial *cabeceras* or other key urban centers (i.e., state capitals[26]) and indigenous presence in nineteenth century Peru, Bolivia, Guatemala, and Mexico. All plots distinguish between provinces with a higher presence of venality (black) vis-à-vis those where venality was less intense (gray). As shown, these paint a variety of patterns with signs of indigenous segregation in Mexico, Bolivia, and Guatemala but less so in Peru.

In the case of Mexico, panels (a) to (c) show that already in 1800, a larger number of indigenous *pueblos* were farther from colonial *cabeceras* (panel a), particularly in provinces with greater venality.

---

[25] I thank John Tutino for this observation.
[26] This is the case of Mexico in 1895, where I instead use the distance to 1895 *Departamento* (State) capital. The reason is that due to limited availability, the data comes from 1895 districts (not municipalities), thus greatly overlapping with that of former colonial cabeceras, constraining the variation of the Log Distance variable.

7 Colonial Venality and State-Building 189

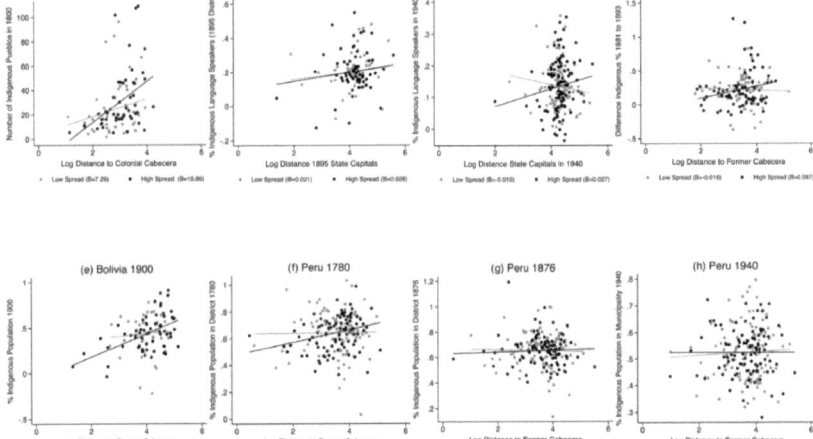

FIGURE 7.8 Indigenous presence by distance to former colonial capitals
Sources: Mexico – 1800 pueblos in Mexico from Tanck (2005); 1895 Census from INEGI; and 1940 Census from Fergusson, Larreguy and Riaño (2022). Guatemala: 1881–2 Census and 1893 Census. Peru: 1780 population from Vollmer (1967); 1876 Census; 1940 Census. Bolivia: 1900 Census (partial). Note: All figures are binned scatter plots (see Fig. 1 for construction details). Panel (a) controls for latitude, longitude, elevation, and size of *pueblo* population. Panels (b) to (h) control for latitude, longitude, elevation, and colonial province fixed effects. All figures divide the sample in provinces with high (dark) and low price-spreads (gray) in colonial times. Solid lines show the best linear fit using OLS.

Again, this is not merely capturing indigenous presence (as both types of provinces have *pueblos*), but how they have relocated over time. Fast-forward ninety years and the location of the indigenous communities – now measured as population shares of 1895 districts – is much more prevalent away from state capitals (many of which are former colonial *cabeceras*) regardless of their colonial governance.[27] Displacement away from urban centers again reappears in 1940, when indigenous presence in venal provinces concentrated further away from these capitals than in less venal ones. The differences between provinces are best appreciated by comparing the slopes of the fitted lines. For example, in panel (c), a one log point increase in distance from the *cabecera* increases the share of the indigenous population in 0.027 in venal provinces, while it decreases it in 0.019 in less venal ones. All these are consistent with

---

[27] Throughout the nineteenth century, Mexico saw a large number of territorial and administrative reorganizations.

the long-nineteenth century exacerbating the segregation of indigenous communities observed in the 1770s, particularly in former *alcaldías* and *corregimientos* with high venality.

The next case is that of Guatemala (panel d), which also exhibits signs of displacement, but where, due to the availability of two measures – the statistical yearbook of 1881 and the census of 1893 – it was possible to examine how the share of indigenous population changed during a key juncture: that of the export coffee boom. As shown, the difference is positive – showing an increase of indigenous presence away from *cabeceras* – driven by provinces with more venal governance than those less so. In fact, a comparison of the magnitude of the slopes shows that the effect is larger than that of Mexico, particularly as it is expressed in differences. The earlier findings also help understand why this displacement is concentrated in venal areas: political disenfranchisement of the indigenous population, under provision of public goods (i.e., low vaccination rates), and remnants of colonial labor coercion policies, for example.

Panel (e) in turn uses the 1900 census in Bolivia to examine the spatial segregation of indigenous communities. Although the census is incomplete – it was never finished and excluded the key department of La Paz – the municipalities for which there is data available show clear signs of segregation. As demonstrated by the positive slopes of both types of provinces, the effect is four times stronger in the more venal provinces of the former *audiencia* of Charcas – now Bolivia – than in those less venal. Put another way, the indigenous population is concentrated much farther from the capital in provinces with higher price spreads in colonial times, such as Larecaja, Oruro, or Sicasica, vis-à-vis communities in Carangas, Lipes o Tomina.

Finally, the case of Peru in panels (f) to (h) shows that if anything, there is a more uniform distribution of indigenous communities in the nineteenth century. While in 1780 the results corroborate those of Chapter 6 – the greater displacement of the indigenous population in more venal provinces – this gap is smaller in 1876 and practically inexistent in 1940. Thus pointing to two possibilities. The first, as mentioned, was the period of relative autonomy the indigenous population enjoyed in the immediate postindependence period. Largely spared from the labor requirements of the guano and sugar commodity boom as well as from the abolishment of head taxes, it is possible that their settlement pattern was "all over the place," as seen in the graphs. This does not rule out rampant land dispossession – which did take place – only that its consequence was not to silo indigenous communities into locations farther from key capitals. The second possibility is that indigenous migration to the cities took place everywhere and at similar rates, explaining the uniform distribution seen in 1876 and 1940. The question is, in the wake of the Peruvian land reforms of the 1960s and the later legal recognition of indigenous claims to land, will these communities again be displaced from key urban centers?

The following chapter examines the extent to which these patterns persisted until today. Suffice to say for now that up to the end of the nineteenth century, the pattern of indigenous segregation in areas with earlier venality was alive and well in some countries. While in others, the postindependence period and the lifting of residency restrictions in colonial times meant that indigenous populations moved back to urban areas and *cabeceras*. Generally speaking, indigenous communities that continued to provide revenue and labor to postindependence governments in ways akin to those from colonial times (i.e., Bolivia, Ecuador, and Guatemala) were better able to ensure the survival of their community. Moreover, the weakness of the emerging states, neglect of indigenous issues and the self-interest of private actors such as *finca* and *hacienda* owners at times paradoxically may have helped keep communities alive. How do these factors play out in the twenty-first century?

7.1.8.2 How Colonial Venality Shaped Postcolonial State-Building

This chapter documented the long-run relationship between the subnational distribution of eighteenth-century colonial venality and regional patterns of political representation and disenfranchisement; of persistent coercive fiscal and labor policies; spatial segregation of indigenous populations; as well as the recurrent presence of violent conflict in some regions versus others. How did these shape the process of state-building in nineteenth-century Spanish, and Latin America more generally?

This section shows how the subnational variation in colonial venality underpins and complements many of the prevailing explanations for state-building in the region. Through political, economic, and demographic channels documented earlier, legacies of venality help understand (a) the origins and motivations of different types of local elites; (b) the *loci* of internal conflict in Spanish America; and (c) the origins of regional heterogeneity – a barrier to state formation (Mazzuca 2021) and the development of strong fiscal states (Beramendi and Rogers 2022). I discuss each in turn.

LOCAL ELITES Elites feature prominently in accounts of state-building in Spanish America (Kurtz 2013; Soifer 2015; Mazzuca 2021; Saylor 2014, to name a few), as key actors that can support or undermine the centralization efforts of the new state. For example, if the central government delegated state-building tasks to them, efforts were generally less successful (Soifer 2015). Or, if elites presided over societies with a coerced or servile labor, they were likely to oppose state-building efforts that threatened their *modus-vivendi* (Kurtz 2013).

Yet, elites did not spring to life in the 1820s, in fact in many cases, their elite status was owed to the privileges accrued during the colonial period itself. The institutional continuity in local government through the *cabildos* provided a constant forum to influence the political process, at least locally. Evidence from this chapter illustrates some of the ways these local elites shaped the state-building process. In particular, the fact that provinces with a more venal history were much more likely to oppose efforts to broaden local political representation (i.e., Mexico, Peru, and Guatemala) and (or) abolish coercive labor and taxation policies (i.e., Bolivia, Guatemala, and Ecuador) in the nineteenth century is consistent with elites seeking to maintain or broaden their *modus vivendi* at the expense of state centralization and modernization efforts. Further analysis could focus on the micro-mechanisms of how they carried these throughout, what this chapter shows is that the aggregate (reduced form) relationship is there.

NEW STATES, OLD POPULATIONS As hinted at the beginning of the chapter and in the introduction, the colonial administration was fundamental to determine the distribution of the population and their regional identities. After the dust of nineteenth-century conflicts settled, three-fourths of the population and *cabildos* that existed in 1808 were still ruled by the same capital they had in colonial times. In other words, no new state emerged in which less than 75 percent of its population was ruled by a different capital than that from colonial times. This strong continuity in *populations* also meant continuity in social structures, customs, cultures, and tradition.

Moreover, one key moment of the nineteenth century that could have changed the composition of entire populations – the massive influx of European migration – largely bypassed the core of Spanish America. Although it is estimated that more than 13 million Europeans migrated to the region during this period (Sánchez Alonso 2019: 3), none of their main destinations in Spanish America (Argentina, Cuba, and Uruguay) were at the adminsitrative core of the Spanish Empire – the areas with the highest bureaucratic complexity and depth as of 1700 analyzed here.

EXTERNAL AND INTERNAL CONFLICT A second explanation for the weak capacity of Latin American states – and Spanish America by extension – is the relative lack of major international wars in its independent history (Centeno 2002; López-Alves 2000). Moreover, of the few wars that did occur, their outcomes – victories or defeats – are key to understanding subsequent state consolidation efforts (Schenoni 2021). But, why were there so few wars? Existing accounts point to cultural similarities and land abundance, for example. However, this chapter also highlights the role of well-defined administrative authorities – not in terms of borders as understood today – but in terms of jurisdictional belonging. In colonial times, jurisdictions were not territorial, but based on population centers: If settlements expanded or moved, so did the jurisdictional border. One legacy of the Spanish administrative apparatus was thus to define these units such that at the time of independence there was less conflict as to which political unit did these belong to. Testament of its success is that only one-fourth of the population actually changed jurisdictions.

In contrast to the paucity of inter-state wars, this chapter instead emphasizes the prevalence of intra-state conflict. Data on subnational conflict from Peru and Mexico shows that these are more likely where venality likely lowered opportunity costs and heightened grievances. Because these areas also exhibit lower state capacity, more limited political representation, more extractive labor and fiscal policies, and greater ethnic segregation, they are likely not contributing to strengthen the state, but undermining it, consistent with Thies (2005). Yet, given that these violent uprisings have been going on since the end of the *Pax Hispannica* in the eighteenth century, its weakening effect on state capacity likely precedes the nineteenth century.

ECONOMIC GEOGRAPHY The third explanation for weak state capacity is the degree of *within*-country regional heterogeneity that underpinned many of the new states. Large (federal) states with backward peripheries found it harder to project power beyond the center. In contrast, smaller and more homogenous states are therefore less likely to face this problem (Mazzuca 2021). For example, in large countries spatial inequalities can "poison" the politics of redistribution, undermining state capacity (Beramendi and Rogers 2022). But where do these differences come from?

This chapter shows a source of regional heterogeneity that did not disappear with independence: former *corregimientos* and *alcaldías* that started independent life with a certain baggage – such as recurrent conflict, a spatially segregated indigenous population, poor public good provision, and local elites limiting the extent of political representation. Their presence limiting their integration to national markets, lowering output and the demand for new technologies and innovation (Acemoglu and Dell 2010).

Beyond the academic literature, the normative and economic consequences of these legacies cannot be overstated. First, the delayed formation of representative institutions resulted in fewer avenues for peaceful conflict resolution, particularly for indigenous populations. By either purposefully maintaining colonial policies or failing to eliminate them, many regions in Spanish America entered the twentieth century with more colonial relics than others. Second, the geographic and cultural segregation of the indigenous population hindered their integration into the market and the construction of a national identity. Their exclusion also increased the state's operational costs, weakening its capacity to deliver public goods, further undermining its legitimacy, limiting economic opportunities, and exacerbating inter- and intra-region inequalities. Chapter 8 turns to exploring these consequences.

Chapter Summary. Did the period immediately after independence erase or reverse the legacies of the colonial era? While much changed in Spanish America throughout the nineteenth century, this chapter challenges the idea that the consequences of venality, particularly at the local level, disappeared with independence. Through a detailed examination of archival and administrative sources, the analysis unveils the continuation or revitalization of labor and fiscal policies from the colonial era; limits to the formation of new representative governments in provinces more exposed to venality; the persistence of grievances devolving into conflict; and in some countries, the continued segregation of the indigenous population. Part of this continuity lies in the strong influence of the colonial administration for the configuration of states that emerged: While much changed in terms of territory, much less changed in terms of population. Overall, these findings make the case that the legacies from earlier venality constrained the state-building paths these countries could follow in the nineteenth century.

8

Conclusion

Corregimientos *and* Alcaldías *in Spanish America Today*

The previous chapters have traced the consequences of a policy to supplement the royal household income in Madrid for the quality of the Spanish colonial administration in the Americas. By changing the type and the incentives of individuals entering office as well as their ability to sort into positions that maximized their rents, office-selling led to *venality*. The direct consequence of which was the increase in uprisings against colonial policies and its officials. It also exacerbated the geographic segregation of indigenous communities: by the 1770s, they had been systematically displaced from the provincial cabeceras they were previously close by. After independence, post-colonial governments – particularly those burdened by local legacies of venality – failed to reverse segregation, address underlying drivers of conflict, and proved slow to remove vexing fiscal and labor policies. The result is that by the early twentieth century, many spatial differences remained alive and well. What is the state of these legacies today?

***

The end of the long-nineteenth century[1] and the start of the twentieth one brought new and unprecedented challenges to Spanish America: two World Wars and a major economic depression made governments rethink their economic model twice. Politically, the nineteenth-century oligarchic republics began to crumble, to be followed by a period of military coups and one-party rule. Socially, major cities of Latin America experienced a wave of rural migration searching for better opportunities or simply

---

[1] Considered the period between 1789 and 1914.

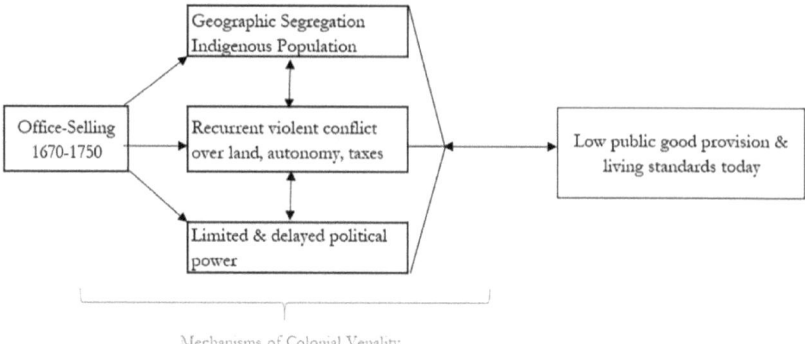

FIGURE 8.1 Summary of argument: the contemporary legacies of colonial venality

displaced by commodity-fueled land grabbing.[2] At the same time, the epidemiological transition spurred rapid population growth and, with it, social conflict across the globe (Acemoglu, Fergusson, and Johnson 2020).

Notwithstanding the seismic demographic, political, social, and economic changes the region experienced throughout the twentieth century, *vestiges* of the practices unleashed by venality can still be found locally. This chapter documents at least three ways through which deep-seated differences in governance continue to reverberate today. First, for all the recent progress for visibility and political inclusion (Yashar 2005), indigenous communities remain highly segregated (Thorp and Paredes 2011). Second, challenges to local political representation in the form of subnational authoritarianism, even as the region transitioned to democracy, have remained. Finally, as a consequence of the other two factors, the spatial disparities in the provision of public goods and living standards of the population are a regional constant. Figure 8.1 condenses the main argument of this chapter.

8.1 INDIGENOUS SEGREGATION

Once the sole inhabitants of the Americas, indigenous communities today[3] constitute a minority[4] in most Spanish American countries, often

---

[2] In fact, 70 percent of the urban growth in Latin America from 1945 to 1970 was driven by these movements (Browning 1967: 95).
[3] Defined by language use. These percentages are higher if considering self-identification and not only language.
[4] Bolivia stands as an exception; as half of the population (53 percent) speaks an indigenous language in 2012.

8 Conclusion

concentrated in enclaves far from urban centers and administrative capitals (Guardado and Franco-Vivanco 2024). Whereas in 1940, 25 percent of the Mexican population spoke an indigenous language, this percentage had declined to 15 percent in the 2010 census. In Peru, the 1940 census shows that 51.2 percent of the population identified as indigenous, which had declined to 32 percent by 2017. In Guatemala, the reduction was even more dramatic, with close to 67 percent of the population classified as indigenous in 1893 but only 32 percent speaking Mayan today. Only in Bolivia do we see a reversal of this trend, with 53 percent of the population in 2012 speaking an indigenous language compared to the 45 percent counted in 1900, though the latter number should be taken with caution given that the census was never fully completed.

The most straightforward explanation of this decline is the process of assimilation set in motion by the twentieth-century massive rural-to-urban migration, which uprooted many communities. This was further spurred by the rapid urbanization and city growth that "caught" many of these *pueblos* and communities in their midst. Yet, against these odds, some indigenous communities were able to retain their identity due to their location – historically away from fast-growing centers – or by purposefully moving further away from these centers.[5] The question is: Was this more easily achieved in provinces with a history of venality? Namely, are indigenous communities more likely to remain in enclaves in these provinces versus others? Circa 1900 in Mexico, Bolivia, and Guatemala (but not Peru), the answer was yes. But how did this change 100 years later?

Figure 8.2 explores the distribution of indigenous populations, defined by language, across key Spanish American countries, distinguishing between areas more or less affected by venality. The plots explore the extent to which similar levels of indigenous presence are more likely to be farther (closer) from current municipal or district capitals. As shown, across all countries, indigenous populations are more likely to be found living farther from these capitals, as shown by the dot density.[6] This type of displacement is the exact opposite to that observed in the 1600s, when proximity to indigenous communities was

---

[5] While the preservation of indigenous identity may be normatively desirable in and of itself, this chapter shows that when driven by geographic distance it comes at the expense of public good provision, political inclusion, and overall living standards.

[6] Note that this distance varies by country depending on the size and number of municipalities.

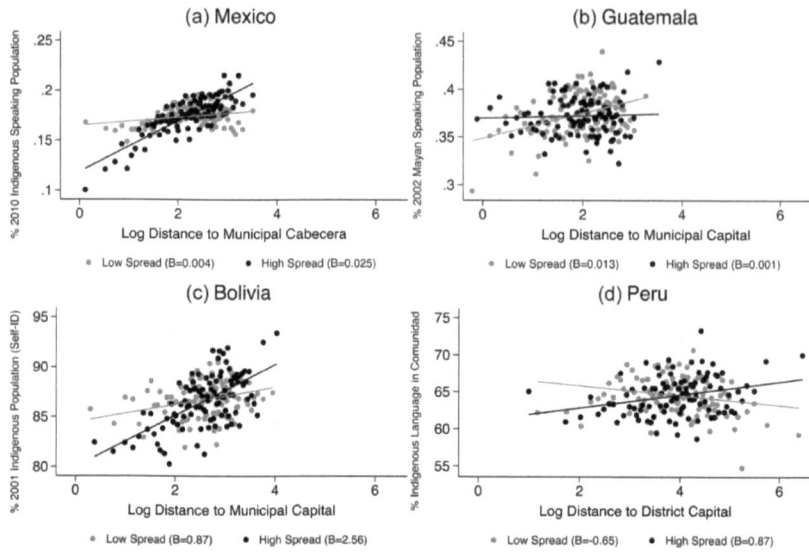

FIGURE 8.2 Indigenous segregation by venality status today

Note: Binned scatter plots. Figure 8.2 plots the mean of the residuals of the share of indigenous population at the municipal level after accounting for municipal elevation, latitude, longitude, and colonial province fixed effects against the mean value of x – in this case, the distance to key capitals – within equal-sized bins. All figures divide the sample in provinces with high (dark) and low price spreads (gray) in colonial times. Solid lines show the best linear fit using OLS. Sources: see Table A.12 in the Appendix to Chapter 8.

the basis for founding cities and relocating populations, but in line with the pattern observed two centuries later (1770s).[7]

Specifically, panels (a) to (d) depict the persistence of geographic segregation of indigenous communities today across these four countries. More relevant for this book is the fact that this segregation remains stronger in areas with higher price spreads (i.e., venal past) compared to areas where demand was more muted in the eighteenth century, except for Guatemala. In the latter case, it appears that segregation has instead become a generalized phenomenon, with lower price spread provinces now exhibiting steeper displacement than previous ones. For all other countries, as shown in 1770 and nineteenth-century data, geographic segregation is still driven by more venal areas, even in Peru.

---

[7] See Chapter 6.

Furthermore, the geographic gap between venal and less-venal areas does not appear to be narrowing today compared to earlier periods. That is, despite the sustained reduction in the share of indigenous populations throughout the twentieth century, the gap is still present. In the case of Peru, it actually reappeared after its nineteenth-century hiatus.[8] Even in Bolivia, where the indigenous population did not decline rapidly, geographic segregation is still driven by the areas where colonial governance was worse.

The costs of the indigenous population's geographic segregation are wide-ranging. Economically, segregation hindered integration into the regional and national economies, reducing overall productivity. Politically, it fueled contentious local politics, with elites fearing ethnically based conflict and even seeking to limit the political participation of indigenous populations (disenfranchisement), resulting in clientelism, electoral fraud, or outright violent repression. Finally, normatively, this spatial segregation bodes ill with the democratic principles of equality and inclusion. In fact, Section 8.2 presents evidence of subnational authoritarian enclaves, partly fueled by this type of exclusion, but now in the democratic era.

8.2 LIMITED POLITICAL REPRESENTATION

Throughout most of the twentieth century, the extent of subnational political representation and competition in Spanish America was generally restricted in two ways. The first restriction was on its ability to represent different political views, which depended on the government or military *junta*'s tolerance for competition and pluralism (or lack thereof). Most of the time, officials were appointed from the center with limited local input, even in nominally federal countries. Or, even if responsive to local interests, these were often those of aligned elites (Soifer 2015). Second, representation was also limited by the institutional authority of subnational governments to enact major policies. It was only toward the end of the twentieth century that there are serious efforts at decentralizing and devolving power to local governments.

In this context of limited political representation, the third wave of democratization of the late twentieth century had varied degrees of success, depending on the area's history of colonial governance. In regions less burdened by these legacies, democratic practices spread

---

[8] An alternative possibility is that the 1876 and 1940 census data in Peru was not of good quality – a very plausible explanation.

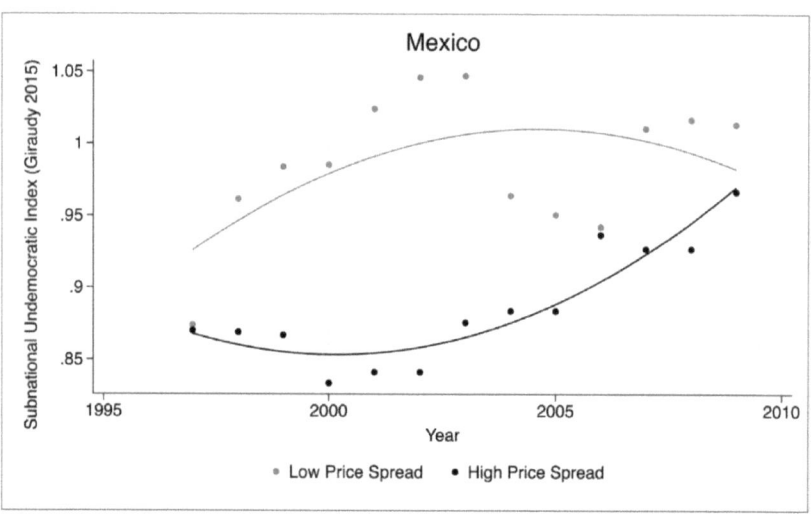

FIGURE 8.3 Subnational undemocratic regimes index by colonial venality status

Sources: State-level SUR Index – subnational undemocratic regimes – from Giraudy (2015). Available at: https://agustinagiraudy.com/data. Average price spread per state using eighteenth-century province prices. High = above median of states average. Low = below median of states average. Note: Binned scatter plot – mean values of the SUR index within equal-sized bins across years. Higher values in SUR index denote more democratic traits (closer to 0, undemocratic). Figure 8.3 divides the sample in states with high (dark) and low-price spreads (gray) in colonial times. Solid lines show the best quadratic fit using OLS.

quicker and consolidated faster. Conversely, in other areas, the process was slower and, even as of 2008, some gaps remained.[9] Figure 8.3, depicting local variation in the pace of democratization across Mexico, supports this observation. In particular, Mexican states with more venal baggage are not only less democratic on average but also show a slower adoption rate compared to others. While several different mechanisms are in place (see Giraudy 2013 for in-depth accounts) – such as the benefits to national-level politicians or barriers preventing national parties from entering local politics – the histories of colonial governance provides key background into where to expect this uneven pace of democratization.

An important consequence of this delayed and limited local political representation is the uneven quality of local governance. As noted by

---

[9] See Fox (1994) for some of these challenges in the context of Mexico.

the extensive literature on public goods, the supply of roads, schools, health clinics, and basic services (water, sewage, and electricity) is closely tied to the type of governance prevailing. For example, they reflect local demands from citizens, their political importance to national coalitions, or even the strength of developmental elites demanding these goods for their own interest (e.g., roads). If political power and representation are diluted in certain regions and populations are physically isolated, these areas become more prone to conflict or to exclusion. Consequently, the provision of public goods and their subsequent living standards are likely to be lower, fueling the spatial inequalities we observe in Spanish America today.

8.3 LEGACIES OF VENALITY AND LIVING STANDARDS TODAY

Reflecting these disparities, results from Demographic and Health Surveys (DHS)[10] data reveal widespread stunting among children under five in countries such as Bolivia, Colombia, Guatemala, and Peru. A sign of poor access to nutrition, but also to health services and economic resources. Specifically, the average child in Bolivia and Peru is between -1.42 and -1.39 standard deviations below the median of height expected for their age, respectively.[11] In Colombia, children are, on average, only -0.88 standard deviations below this global median, but an alarming -1.92 for the case of Guatemala. These simple statistics show these countries varying living standards, but may also mask important regional disparities *within* those countries.

These regional disparities are on stark display in the case of Guatemala. While children in the country sample as a whole are -1.92 standard deviations below the expected median, this number is -2.48 for those in the former *corregimiento* of Totonicapán but only -1.51 for that of Escuintla and -1.62 for that of El Valle (where Guatemala City is located). Similar patterns emerge in Colombia, where the former *corregimiento* of Chita is -1.38 below the expected median but that of Zipaquira is, on average, higher at -0.81. In other words, these unequal living standards largely depend on where these individuals live.

---

[10] For this metric, I use the USAID DHS. Available at: https://dhsprogram.com/data/.
[11] A child perfectly at the median recommended height would receive a score of 0, where 1 represents one standard deviation above this metric and -1 represents one standard deviation below.

One potential consideration is that these regional estimates could simply be capturing the geographic distribution of the indigenous population, known to suffer from chronic malnutrition. Yet, even when limiting the analysis to indigenous children, the regional differences are still salient. For example, the average degree of stunting of indigenous children in Totonicapán, Guatemala, is −2.6 but only −1.70 in Escuintla or −2.1 in El Valle. While both numbers reveal more stunting than that observed for nonindigenous children, it still varies across regions, suggesting that the disparities may be driven by differences in policy or governance and not by particular ethnic configurations.

The presence of these spatial differences is in itself a puzzle. Economic theory suggests that individuals would mitigate these through internal migration: moving to areas of greater economic opportunity, thus equalizing human capital and technology across locations. Instead, it appears that subnational disparities in Latin America are due to local productivity barriers (Acemoglu and Dell 2010: 178–179). The critical questions are, what are these barriers? What traits cause identical individuals or households to experience very different living standards based on where they live? And, key for this book, why are these disparities more salient in certain Spanish American countries?

8.3.1 Descriptive Patterns

In the following exercises, I map eighteenth-century colonial jurisdictions (*corregimientos* and *alcaldías mayores*) to their contemporary territories to examine how variation in colonial governance driven by earlier office-selling translated into differences in subnational living standards within seven key former Spanish American countries – Bolivia, Ecuador, Mexico, Chile, Peru, Guatemala, and Colombia.[12] The claim is that through the mechanisms outlined in Figure 8.1 (segregation, conflicts/grievances, and limited representation), the eighteenth-century practice of venality underpins some of the spatial inequalities observed today.

As in previous chapters, I focus on the price difference (price spreads) paid to the Crown at times in which it was embroiled in European wars

---

[12] These territories accounted for 95 percent of the Crown's sales of *corregimientos* and *alcaldías* in the empire and for about a similar percentage of the total population ca. 1700. The Caribbean territories had little-to-no *corregimientos* and *alcaldías* for sale, as well as the territory of what is now Panama and Argentina (the only exceptions are the provinces of Tucumán, Salta, and Mendoza).

and when it was in peace. As elaborated earlier,[13] the advantage of focusing on this measure is twofold. First, it is a geographically disaggregated measure of the expected returns by venal office-holders – capturing the difference in the price of a position when Spain was at war minus the price paid during peace times. Because purchasers during wartime represent a particular type of officials with a very different set of incentives – how much more they were willing to pay vis-à-vis others proxies how much more were these areas extracted than usual in this period. This is a more nuanced measure of extraction than that arising from geographic characteristics or the size of the indigenous population alone. In fact, and second, because these are price differences, it accounts for fixed provincial characteristics that do not vary between war and peace times, addressing important confounders in long-run studies. Finally, price spreads also limit comparisons to areas sold, reducing concern that unsold areas might uniquely confound the analysis.[14]

In terms of outcomes, studying subnational development differences presents measurement challenges in terms of comparability and reliability. For this reason, when pooling data, I focus on standardized measures of stunting, malnutrition in children, and low weight at birth – variables consistently collected across countries.[15] These measures constitute a "poverty rate" in settings where it is not possible to establish a monetary measure (Salvatore, Challu, and Coatsworth 2010: 6) or where "poverty lines" may be susceptible to political manipulation. Moreover, given that biological well-being does not solely depend on the availability of public services but on their use, these measures also help cross-validate the poverty and public good measures that will be used in the *within*-country analysis exercise presented toward the end of this chapter.

As an initial descriptive analysis, Figure 8.4 uses DHS data to illustrate the overall relationship between historical exposure to venality and contemporary stunting as well as some of the inter-regional differences highlighted earlier. As expected, the overall relationship between colonial venality and current living standards is negative: Higher price spreads are correlated with more stunting in children. This is not driven by the distribution of indigenous populations, as the patterns are similar

---

[13] Mainly in Chapter 6, and its Appendix.
[14] The disadvantage of focusing on the intensive margin is that the sample is reduced.
[15] Other studies examining cross-regional development in Latin America (Bruhn and Gallego 2012) focus on data from higher administrative units, namely, states.

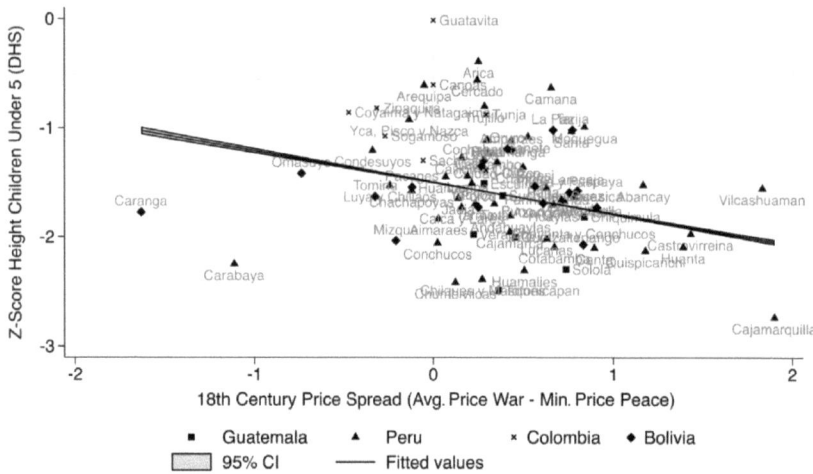

FIGURE 8.4 Provincial stunting in children by colonial venality status

Sources: Geolocated DHS surveys from Bolivia (2008), Guatemala (2014/15), Colombia (2010), and Peru (2009). Note: Dependent variable is the z-score average of height at the colonial province level. Scatter plot with 95 percent CI. Solid line shows the best linear fit using OLS.

if limiting the analysis to only these survey respondents (Appendix Figure A.2). Figure 8.4 also illustrates the subnational heterogeneity in these countries (Colombia, Peru, Bolivia, and Guatemala). For example, two different provinces of Peru, such as Arica or Cajamarquilla, exhibit markedly different degrees of childhood stunting, mirroring differences in their price spreads.

More systematically, Table 8.1 presents the estimates of the effect of price spreads – the proxy for colonial governance – on contemporary living standards across the region. Higher price spreads paid for a *corregimiento* or *alcaldia mayor* in the eighteenth century are associated with reduced living standards in Spanish America across all columns. The results are consistent regardless of the measure used: Standardized height measures from DHS surveys (Column 1), the percentage of children with stunted growth (*retraso en talla*) as reported in school-level census (Column 2) or among individual children (Column 3), and the share of those with low birth weight due to prematurity (Column 4). In other words, individuals who currently live in these areas appear to have less access to public goods, resulting in poorer biological living standards.

In terms of magnitude, Column 1 shows that a 10 percent increase in the price spread correlates with a reduction of 0.016 standard deviations in the standardized height measure of children under five. The effect is

TABLE 8.1 *Price spreads and living standards in Spanish America: pooled results*

VARIABLES	(1) Standardized Height	(2) % Stunting	(3) Standardized Height	(4) Pr Low Weight at Birth
Price spread	−0.16**	0.079***	−0.23**	0.004***
	(0.07)	(0.03)	(0.1)	(0.00)
Observations	20,064	113,389	1,834,072	2,655,119
R-squared	0.21	0.31	0.21	0.35
Data	Individual	School %	Individual	Individual
Countries	Bolivia, Guatemala, Colombia, and Peru	Chile, Mexico, Peru, and Guatemala	Peru and Guatemala	Ecuador, Mexico, and Peru

Robust standard errors clustered at the level of *corregimiento* and *alcaldia mayor* in parentheses. *** $p < 0.01$, ** $p < 0.05$, * $p < 0.1$. All specifications include country fixed effects and control for latitude, latitude square, longitude, longitude square, elevation, and elevation square of the *municipio*/district, or survey cluster they belong to. Column 1 includes survey weights. In columns 2 and 4, I also include year fixed effects to account for the multiple years included. Column 3 also controls for year of birth and sex. Column 4, in addition, controls for total births in the municipality, gestational week, and sex. See Appendix to Chapter 8 Table A.13 for sources.

more pronounced in Guatemala and Peru (Column 3), where the same price increase is associated with a 0.023 reduction in the standardized height of school-age children (not limited to those under five). Note that the latter source relies on millions of individual observations.

When examining outcomes at the school level, the results for stunting are still present. Specifically, in a sample of schools across Chile, Peru, Guatemala, and Mexico, the prevalence of stunting for age increases by 0.0079 percentage points for every 10 percent increase in price spreads. Although this increase may seem small, when evaluated against the average stunting rate of 0.26, it represents a 3 percent increase. Additionally, in Column 4, the incidence of low birth weights due to prematurity slightly increases by 0.004 for each 10 percent increase in price spreads. However, because low birth weights are relatively rare (an average of 4 percent in Ecuador and Mexico and 4.5 percent in Peru), this increase corresponds to around a 10 percent increase in their average occurrence.

In all, these estimates indicate that individuals in areas formerly governed by more venal colonial administrations experience lower living standards than those in areas where the intensity of venality was lower.

8.4 COLONIAL JURISDICTIONS OR OTHER FACTORS?

While the results so far support the idea of lasting consequences of colonial governance for current subnational disparities, it could also be driven by other factors. For example, geography or factor endowments (e.g., indigenous labor) or the overarching institutional design. To further isolate the role of the colonial past, I use fine-grained data at the locality, or *centro poblado*, level to examine how the availability of public services, measures of household wealth, and educational attainment change along the borders of former *corregimientos* and *alcaldías mayores*, using a geographic regression discontinuity design (GRDD).

The intuition behind this exercise is that localities or villages in close proximity share many traits – such as culture, environment, overarching governments, and overall history – but were governed under different *corregimientos* or *alcaldías mayores* in the eighteenth century (and *subdelegados* until the early 19th century). The goal, then, is to estimate the impact of these historical differences on their current development performance. If the jurisdiction's level of colonial venality (low or high) has no effect, then we would expect no variation in outcomes on either side of this colonial border, on average. Conversely, if outcomes vary significantly across the border, it suggests that these jurisdictions might have induced long-run differences that persist even though the colonial administrations themselves are no longer in place.

The main advantage of this design is that when the underlying assumptions are met,[16] it allows us to hold constant alternative explanations for development, such as geography, factor endowments, overarching institutional design, and culture. Moreover, because in many cases these localities were far from the province capital (*cabecera*), or did not even exist in the eighteenth century, they are likely to play a marginal role

---

[16] The main assumptions are that there is no sorting before the treatment and other factors other than changes in colonial jurisdictions vary smoothly along the border. In fact, Appendix Table A.15 shows that the sample of localities across the border exhibits similar geographic covariates in terms of elevation, distance to major bodies of water/ river, or forest (tree) cover. Importantly, these do not vary by whether the price spread in colonial times is higher/lower than the median.

8 Conclusion

in determining the desirability of the positions of *corregidor* or *alcalde mayor*, yet still be affected by the past colonial governance of the province. For the cases of Peru and Mexico, it is possible to know the jurisdiction of eighteenth-century *pueblos* and districts respectively, but for the cases of Bolivia and Guatemala, results are based on a combination of longstanding and newer settlements.

For example, the presence of mines, large indigenous populations, and land suitability would greatly impact the desirability, type of rulers, and price paid for office positions in the eighteen century. However, the long-term developmental effect of such factors would not vary discontinuously at borders unless they led to different types of local governance that affected the whole province at the time. Therefore, discontinuities observed in current outcomes are more likely to be driven by factors that change abruptly at the border, such as colonial governance.

For this exercise, I collected data from the countries that were most likely to observe subnational differences due to intense office-selling, such as Mexico, Peru, Bolivia, and Guatemala.[17] Unlike the measures of biological living standards used earlier – which are not available at very low disaggregated levels – I use measures of public service availability, household wealth, and educational attainment for settlements along the borders of former *corregimientos* and *alcaldías mayores* (see Appendix to Chapter 8 Table A.14). I use these measures because they are generally correlated with living standards, predictive of local governance, and available at very low levels of aggregation. However, because they may not be comparable across countries, I examine each country and outcome separately.

Figure 8.5 exemplifies the essence of this research design, focusing specifically on Bolivia to illustrate the methodology applied. Figure 8.5 presents a sample of current *centros poblados* within a narrow band (20 kilometers) of former *corregimiento* borders in Bolivia. Specifically, those along the border of Pacages, Sicasica, and Omasuyos, all in the province of La Paz. The key source of variation comes from the different prices paid in these three provinces: while the province of Pacages drew an average of 3,000 pesos[18] during wartime, Omasuyos drew 2,500 and Sicasica a whopping 11,000. The expectation is that localities in Sicasica are relatively poorer today vis-à-vis those in Pacages

---

[17] I also focus on these cases due to data availability. Ecuador, another potential case, does not have this type of data available as of 2021.
[18] *Pesos de ocho.*

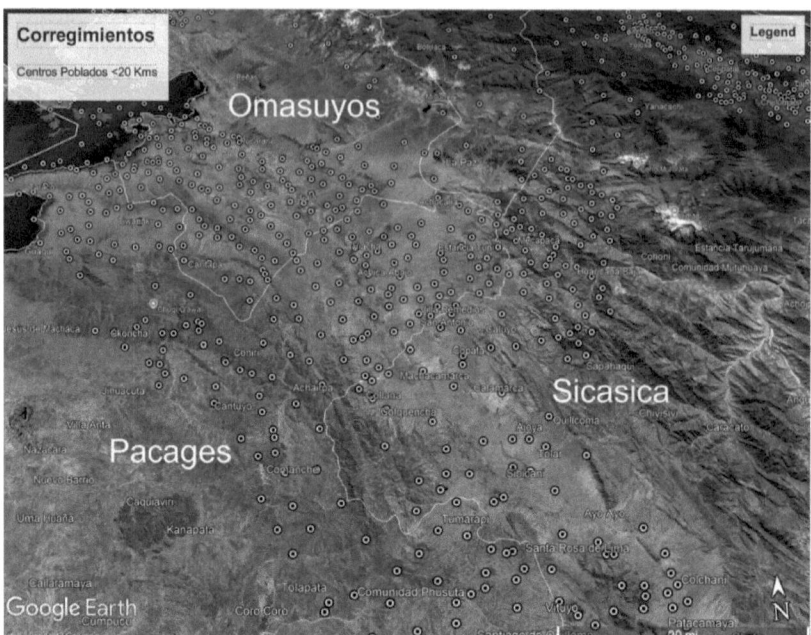

FIGURE 8.5 Bordering *centros poblados* in Pacages, Sicasica, and Omasuyos (Bolivia)

Source: Own construction using HGIS 2019 and Google Earth. Figure 8.5 depicts borders of *corregimientos* in white and *centros poblados* in dots.

or Omasuyos despite their relative closeness and similar geographic environment.[19]

Figures 8.6 and 8.7 presents the estimates of this design for Mexico, Peru, and Guatemala by depicting how the provision of key public goods exhibits discontinuities in the 20-kilometer area around long-gone colonial jurisdictions. For Mexico, I limit the analysis to the indigenous *pueblos* known to exist in 1800 from Tanck de Estrada (2005), and for Peru I limit it to settlements existing in 1780, identified by Cosme Bueno (1951 [1789]). This approach focuses on the most disaggregated data possible to show whether localities on the side of the border with the largest price spread generally exhibits worse development outcomes.

[19] In fact, when conducting the analysis only among localities straddling the Pacages and Sicasica border, it is clear that the higher price paid on the Sicasica side is associated today with a higher share of border population in extreme poverty.

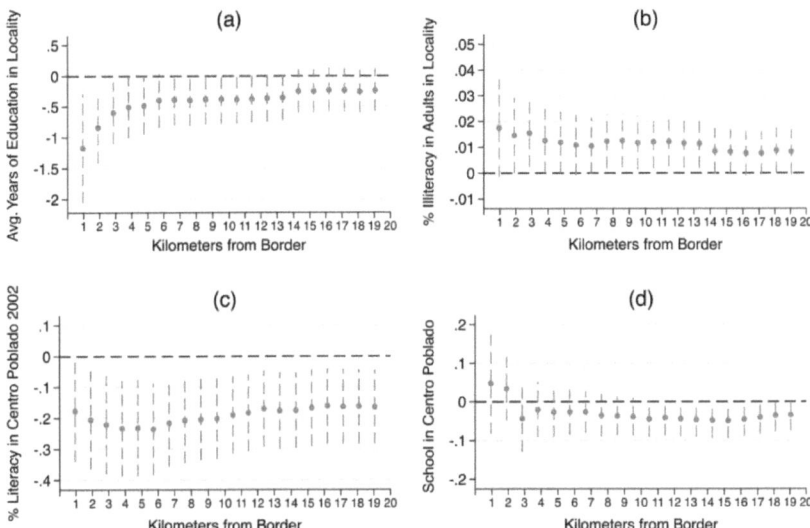

FIGURE 8.6 Price spread and educational outcomes among bordering settlements

Sources: Panel (a) mean years of education in Mexico (2010). Panel (b) % adult illiteracy in Mexico (2010). Panel (c) % literacy in centro poblado in Guatemala (2002). Panel (d) likelihood of school in 2005 centro poblado (Peru). Notes: Each dot represents the estimated difference between localities/*centro poblados* on the side of the border with higher price spreads (and their intensity) vis-à-vis those localities/*centros poblados* on the lower spread side. 95 percent CI in dashed lines. All estimates control for latitude, longitude, latitude sq, longitude sq, elevation, distance to the colonial border, distance to the border interacted with the treatment variable, and border segment fixed effects. Standard errors clustered at the border segment level. See Appendix for estimating Equation (8), details, and Table A.14 for sources.

Figure 8.6 illustrates the availability of key public goods (education) on the border side with the higher price spread,[20] namely the side ruled by officials most likely to sort themselves into office (selection) and have greater incentives to use all means necessary to recoup their investment. Panels (a) and (b) examine education and literacy in Mexico, panel (c) examines literacy in Guatemala, and panel (d) examines the likelihood of a school in *centros poblados* of Peru.

Despite their geographical proximity, localities generally experience poorer education provision today if they were part of colonial jurisdictions with relatively higher price spreads. This pattern holds for

---

[20] The price-spread variable equals 0 on the border side with lower values, while it reflects the actual price spread on the side with higher values to capture the degree of intensity.

localities that already existed in 1800 in Mexico, for *centros poblados* in districts in place as of 1780 in Peru, and for localities along the estimated colonial borders in Bolivia and Guatemala. The magnitude of the "jump" at the border also varies by country: It is largest in Guatemala, followed by that of Mexico, with Peru showing the smallest differences. These comparisons are made within border segments – localities near each other but historically belonging to different colonial jurisdictions – ensuring that the observed differences are not influenced by wider geographical or provincial disparities.

In terms of magnitude, the side of the border with the highest price spread sees a reduction in literacy of 0.09 percentage points per unit increase, or 2.3 percent of the mean, on average, in Guatemala. In Mexico, the province with the highest price spread experiences a reduction in the average schooling years of 0.38 years, which is around 5.6 percent of the mean (6.7 years in this sample). Although these two measures are not directly comparable, the estimates imply that the effect is higher in Guatemala, with provinces having the highest price spread showing a 23 percent drop in the mean levels of literacy in the country. In Mexico, the equivalent magnitude of the impact is a 13 percent difference, potentially due to more intensive treatment in Guatemala than in Mexico. Finally, the effects are weaker in Peru, where areas with the highest price spreads have, at most, a 7.7 percent lower probability of having a school in a given *centro poblado*.

While schools and schooling are important public goods, the results must be cross-validated among a wider array of services and examined in relation to broader economic conditions (i.e., poverty). Therefore, Figure 8.7 explores whether these differences extend to the availability of basic services: potable water, sewage, and electricity in Mexico (panel (a)) and public lighting in Guatemala (panel (b)). In terms of market conditions, the figure also includes data on extreme poverty in Bolivia (panel (c)), as well as the extent of unmet basic necessities in Mexico (panel (d)).

The results in panels (a) and (b) clearly show that other public goods, beyond those related to education, are also underprovided in areas with greater colonial venality. This underprovision suggests it is driven by generalized poor governance and disinvestment rather than difficulties in accessing border areas, as this would likely be similar on both sides of the colonial jurisdiction. Moreover, the underprovision of public goods coincides with poor market prospects, as shown in panels (c) and (d), where poverty is higher on sides of the border experiencing more venality. This similarity in very close localities – that in the cases of Peru and

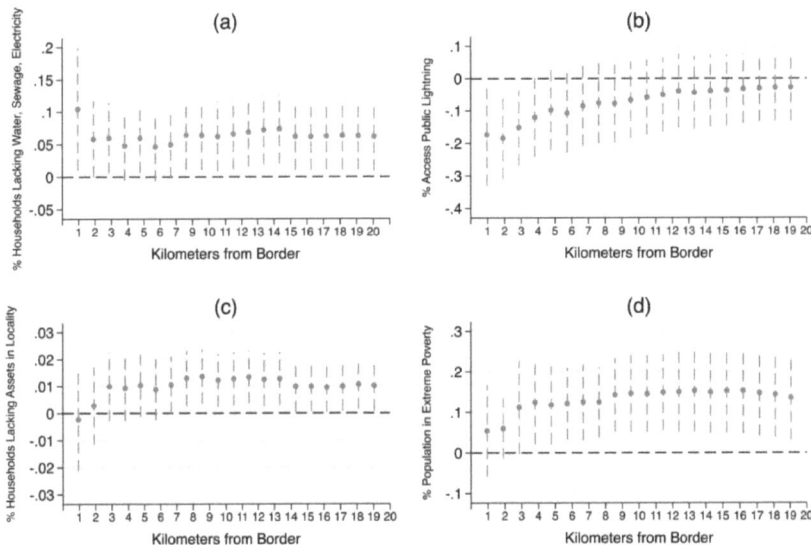

FIGURE 8.7 Price spread, public goods, and poverty rates across bordering settlements

Panel (a), share of households lacking basic services, Mexico (2010). Panel (b), share of households with access to public lightning, Guatemala (2002). Panel (c), share of households lacking basic assets, Mexico (2010). Panel (d), share of population in extreme poverty, Bolivia (2001). Notes: See note Figure 8.6.

Mexico have been in place since colonial times – likely reflects differences in historical governance rather than other factors.

Another alternative explanation is that these results reflect differences in the population's ethnic composition. While the sample in Mexico is limited to former indigenous *pueblos* on either side of the border, this is not the case for Bolivia and Guatemala, where both eighteenth-century settlements and newer ones are included. As shown in Appendix Figure A.3, areas with higher price spreads had a greater share of indigenous populations in Mexico and Guatemala, but not in Bolivia and Peru. This discrepancy could be attributed to both sides of the colonial provinces already having a sizable indigenous presence. For example, around 50 percent of the country's population identifies as indigenous in Bolivia.

In all, these results capture some of the differences induced by colonial administrative jurisdictions that no longer exist but contribute to subnational inequities today. This is not to say that factors such as the size of the indigenous population, the presence of mines, or other geographic traits did not impact long-run development. Rather, they did so by shaping the incentives and types of colonial and postcolonial officials that ruled the province, which discreetly changed at the border.[21] Moreover, because many of these localities did not exist in colonial times, the differences observed today are likely driven by the legacies of institutionalized extraction, violent conflict, and ethnic segregation as explored in Chapter 7.

In all, the historical drivers of local public good provision reveal the deep administrative roots of spatial inequalities. Existing studies document the variation in the subnational provision of public goods (i.e., Harbers 2015) through several mechanisms: The level of subnational political competition (Alves 2015; Chibber and Nooruddin 2004), level of social heterogeneity (Alesina, Baqir, and Easterly 1999) and civic engagement (Cleary 2007), or national-level technocratic autonomy (Otero-Bahamón 2016), to name a few. While these all play a role, this chapter, as in Soifer (2016), goes back to the role of colonial-driven regional heterogeneity and the particular role of the administrative apparatus in understanding the subnational provision of public goods and why it may vary by location (Otero-Bahamon 2016) or political context (Niedzwiecki 2016).

8.5 CONCLUDING THOUGHTS

What do these results entail for our understanding of economic development among former Spanish American countries? While standard economic theories suggest that the economic conditions of cross-border localities are likely to converge to arbitrage these differences – particularly over 200 years – this chapter provides historical administrative and governance reasons for why this is not the case. Regional heterogeneity is not just the product of geographic characteristics or the population that resided there. Throughout the chapters, I've shown that certain Spanish administrative policies have managed to change endowments – for example, by displacing particular groups – and to entrench poor governance in certain places vis-à-vis others.

These results have three implications for the region. First, they identify common eighteenth-century administrative drivers of subnational

---

[21] The implicit assumption is that the local development effect of initial conditions (mines or precolonial indigenous settlements), to name a few, would not "stop" or "jump" at the border. Instead, estimates from border regions uniquely capture jurisdictional and governance changes associated with these rulers.

disparities in diverse contexts in Spanish America. Second, they illustrate the conditions under which corruption, specifically venality, can have long-term costs. Finally, these findings have implications for the long-run development of other regions where venality was widely practiced, such as in Europe (France) and Asia (Iran, China), but have not yet been studied in this manner.

8.5.1 Common Administrative Roots

One common trope among Latin American(ist)s is the belief in common historical factors that allow generalizations from one country to the entire region. Best summarized by Curvale and Przeworski (2005) with the phrase "En mi pais, como en el resto de America Latina…" meaning "in my country, as in the rest of Latin America…". Yet, for all the cross-country differences across Spanish America, this book has shown how, beyond the surface, a common history does exist. Namely, the depth, complexity, and type of administrative governance the Spanish Empire bequeathed throughout. The fact that venality has similar consequences across diverse contexts highlights a latent cohesion that closely binds the region.

The different degrees of venality also serve as an alternative measure of the traditional "core" and "periphery" distinction used to characterize the Spanish Empire. Earlier typologies divided the empire between core, periphery, and semiperipheral regions (Mahoney 2010), based on the presence of minerals and indigenous populations, for example. Instead, the presence (or absence) of venality and its intensity provides a unique look into the priorities of the Crown and the way it ranked different areas of the empire by provinces, today *subnationally*. This classification also serves as a guide to where the legacies of colonialism are likely to be more pronounced.

In terms of the Crown's priorities, it is clear in Chapter 5 that it considered some locations very geopolitically important, as they were never or rarely sold at all. For example, there is only one record of sales for the position of governor of Cartagena, Colombia. Although these areas generally lacked minerals and indigenous populations, their governance (in this case military defense) was deemed sufficiently crucial as to induce self-restraint by the Crown. They also became net recipients of transfers (*situado*) testament to their importance. Their reprieve from sales also signals the Crown's distrust of purchasers and how the danger posed by venality to the preservation of the Empire was sometimes not worth the revenue.

Variations in venality can also indicate the key areas of the Empire the Crown and its officials could actually make money from. While on paper large indigenous populations or minerals could be highly profitable, they need not always translate into more income in their pockets. For example, on economic fundamentals alone, the provinces of Lampa or Azángaro in southern Peru were both similar, yet the bellicoseness of the Azángaro people made the latter relatively less attractive to purchase. In this sense, office prices better account for the process of converting factors into rents. Under this alternative characterization, the economic "core" of the empire – not the geopolitical "core" – would consist of provinces at the top of sales and price spreads, while the remaining areas would represent varying degrees of "periphery." For example, the complete absence of *corregimientos* and *alcaldías* in Uruguay, Paraguay, Argentina, and most of Venezuela would classify these as "economic periphery." This approach also shifts the focus from country-level characterizations to recognizing the jurisdictional and administrative divisions of the Spanish Empire.

In terms of the region's history, the findings presented throughout this book help revalorize the Spanish eighteenth century in the Americas. While the late Habsburg and early Bourbon (1670–1750) period has been generally portrayed in the historiography as one of stagnation and few institutional innovations,[22] this book instead portrays it as a period during which the Crown consolidated its institutional power throughout the continent, or at least consolidated it enough to make it attractive for thousands of buyers to purchase offices. Thus filling a gap in the literature, which has generally focused on the beginning (conquest, colonization) and the end (Bourbon Reforms and Independence). The significance of this intermediate period is such that its effects still resonate today.

8.5.2 The Cost of Venality

Ultimately, this book shows how, and when, certain administrative practices can lead to costly distortions and misallocation in productive factors. The act of selling positions itself was not considered corruption at the time. Beyond the warnings of the Council of Indies, disagreements primarily centered on the appropriate profile for office holders (whether paid or not) and whether sales should include positions that administer justice, not on the royal right to sell them in the first place.

---

[22] See Klein (2024), Klein and Serrano Hernandez (2019) and Peace (1998) for exceptions.

For the overseas territories, office-selling was thus akin to a huge tax increase levied from the colonial population, particularly indigenous.[23] Yet, its most enduring legacy lay in the array of distortionary behaviors it inspired in the population and in the colonial administration. As violent uprisings, population displacement, officials' collusion, and the underprovision of public goods were all exacerbated in places with greater venality. The fact that these patterns have only slowly begun to subside (if at all) suggests that while the economic surplus appropriation of *corregidores*, *alcaldes*, and countless other colonial officials was sizable, in the long run, the most damaging consequences came from the behaviors they induced in the population.

The case of office-selling in Spanish America also helps illustrate some of the challenges and dilemmas in combating corruption. The introduction of sales not only changed the type and incentives of officials in the colonial government but also further decentralized the appropriation of economic surplus. Before office-selling, officials appointed by the Crown were somewhat concerned about their careers and reputations and not always able to sort into the position they wanted. In contrast, purchasers were less constrained by precedent and motivated to maximize their profits as they fit. This shift increased both the scale of appropriation and the uncertainty around it, representing a much more damaging form of corruption, as contemporary research shows (Olken and Barron 2009; Shleifer and Vishny 1993; Fisman and Golden 2017).[24]

8.5.3 Spanish America in Comparative Perspective

Finally, how did venality fare in other contexts? Given that Spanish America was not the only empire that practiced venality, what were its long-run consequences elsewhere? As discussed earlier, the Spanish case was much less institutionalized – at least for the high-level posts studied here – than in other settings. In France and Qing-China, specialized bodies were created to specifically handle the transactions associated with purchasing positions. In Spain, despite their large number, these

---

[23] Even conceptualized as a pure revenue transfer, venality could have permanently altered the productive relationships in colonial society by leading to a generalized underinvestment in public goods, with a lower share of the population devoted to productive activities in equilibrium (Nunn 2007).

[24] This has in turn cast a shadow on decentralization, which could lead to greater corruption absent political competition (Albornoz and Cabrales 2013).

were negotiated on a case-by-case basis in the *Cámara de Indias* and authorized by the King. Beyond France and China, venality was also prevalent in the Ottoman Empire, England, and the Papal States, to name a few. Did venality also shape the economic trajectory of their modern versions?

In France, while long-run studies like this one are lacking, historians do provide clues about its consequences. For Doyle (1996), the eminent historian of venality in France, there are traces of this practice in the current class of accredited public officials – such as litigating attorneys (*avoués*) and notaries – still in place today. He also sees a broader consequence of venality in the desire for secure employment in French society, a trait remaining until today (Doyle 1984: 831). Beyond culture, venality could have also shaped its long-run development paths. For instance, at some point during the seventeenth century, one-third of the population consisted of the *noblesse de robe* and its dependents (1949: 14). To the extent that these features have "stunted the growth of commerce and industry," as noted by Swart (1949: 14), it could have had a detrimental effect on France's long-run economic performance.

In the case of China, Zhang (2022: 266–265) notes that venality[25] alienated the existing class of office-holders and intellectuals, "discrediting the imperial government's professed commitment to [merit]" and contributing to the fall of the Qing dynasty (Zhang 2022: 266). For Kaske (2008), nineteenth-century office-selling in China also prevented the introduction of necessary fiscal and financial reforms and created a class of officials employed in the bureaucracy instead of devoted to "regular employment." Did the absence of reform contribute to the Great Divergence between East and West (Pomeranz 2009)? Finally, unlike Spanish America, where the practice officially ended in the eighteenth century, office-selling in China has persisted until today (Zhu 2008), with its governance and management consequences remaining to be studied.

In nineteenth-century Qajar-Iran, the sale of positions exhibits more parallels to those of Spanish America. Provincial governorates were generally sold to members of the Shah's household, leading to similar consequences to that observed in the Americas, namely greater "affliction of the peasantry" driven by officials' need to recoup their investment and the subsequent onset of rebellions

---

[25] In China, purchasers did not directly buy offices per se but titles and degrees, which were requisites for promotion and occupying offices.

(Sheikholeslami 1971: 109–110). However, it differed primarily in the extent to which it allowed a new class of officials to access the bureaucracy, instead becoming highly exclusionary. While in Spanish America it became an opportunity for *criollos* and wealthy settlers to access power, in Iran it led to the perpetuation of the same class in power (Sheikholeslami 1971: 112), suggesting nefarious consequences for inequality and the processing of social conflict there.

While these brief characterizations provide insights into some of the consequences of venality, future studies could systematically trace its impacts on the bureaucracies of France and China, or the Iranian governorates, as done here for Spanish America.

Chapter Summary: The final chapter brings the findings to the current context of Spanish American countries. Two centuries after independence, rural conflict is a rarer occurrence than in the 1800s; yet, the spatial segregation of indigenous minorities and the limits to political representation remain. Relying on contemporary data from Bolivia, Chile, Colombia, Ecuador, Guatemala, Mexico, and Peru, the chapter shows that subnational territories with more intense office-selling in the past exhibit greater childhood malnutrition and stunting as well as low weight at birth. This is unlikely to be driven by alternative factors – such as the mere presence of indigenous populations or postcolonial developments – as the differences are visible with fine-level data only when comparing localities straddling the borders of former colonial jurisdictions. Sides of the border with greater venality have today lower public good and economic well-being vis-a-vis neighboring ones, consistent with effects running through local governance. The chapter closes with a discussion of the implications of these findings for the study of corruption, the Spanish Empire, as well as to understand other context where office-selling also took place (China, France, and Iran).

Epilogue

In 1696, the newly minted marquis of Villahermosa[1] purchased the position of provincial ruler, or *corregidor*,[2] of Huamalíes, a province in the central Andes of Peru. In exchange for the five-year appointment, he paid to the Spanish Crown 1,000 doblones (or 4,000 pesos). Such a sizable quantity was hard to justify from a career standpoint: The purchase did not guarantee future appointments, and wages were often delayed and did not cover travel and living expenses associated with position. For example, purchasers of *corregidor* position were rarely appointed to serve in higher-up positions. Socially, the province of Huamalíes was not a major population center or with a large Spanish presence. It was also not a major administrative center or seat of the bishop, and was far from where the marquis normally resided, the city of Arequipa.

Instead, according to eighteenth-century documentation, Huamalíes was a province where *corregidores* such as the marquis could profit from office by appropriating economic surplus from the population, mostly indigenous. The presence of sizeable agricultural production and the "docility" of the local indigenous population[3] meant that the commercial activities of *corregidores* – such as (forced) sales of key inputs of production (mules, tools) and consumption items (textiles) at high markup prices – were highly lucrative. Because these officials were also in charge of collecting taxes, enforcing colonial laws, and drafting labor for public works, opportunities for self-dealing abounded. Moreover, it was also likely that the marquis

---

[1] It is still a nobility title in Peru.
[2] They are also known as provincial or local magistrates in the literature.
[3] According to contemporary documentation.

never set foot in the province and instead delegated the tax collection and governing tasks to a lieutenant (*teniente*), with whom he could split the profits. Or, instead, could have resold the position in the secondary market for a profit, a common (but banned) practice at the time.

Given these returns, it is no surprise then that in addition to the marquis, Huamalíes was sold eleven more times to different buyers between 1688 and 1750, with the last purchaser leaving office around 1759. Although sales stopped in 1750, and the Crown once again appointed officials to the province via patronage, many of the practices from venal times lived on. For example, the fiscal success of *repartimiento* during the office-selling period was key to its subsequent legalization in 1751. Late eighteenth-century reports continue to describe Huamalíes as a "good" province to rule due to its potential profits from office. Yet, already by the last quarter of the eighteenth century, Huamalíes exhibited signs of discontent. In 1774 or 1776 – the exact date is unknown – there was an uprising against Domingo de la Cajiga, the *corregidor* at the time. Two additional uprisings, in 1777 and 1778, reflect the prevailing sentiment was visibly turning against these officials (Gölte 1980; O'Phelan 1988) even in a relatively peaceful corner of Peru.[4]

In addition to violent discontent, the geographic segregation of the indigenous population in the province also intensified during this period, likely due to the abuses of colonial officials. Albeit difficult to track,[5] a comparison of the share of indigenous population in 1780 and 2017 shows these were nearly identical (56 percent). However, by 2017 the standard deviation (27.5 percentage points) was much larger than that in 1780 (18). Thereby consistent with a gradual process of resettlement such that a few districts have a disproportionate share of indigenous minorities.

By the start of its independent era, Huamalíes' estimated GDP per capita in 2001 Geary-Khamis dollars was 488 – already lower than the national average (542) – and ranked 36 out of 57 provinces in 1827. This estimate also coincides with other postindependence metrics. The 1876 census puts Huamalíes in the "below average" category: The province's illiteracy rate in 1876 was 92 percent on average, with 34 percent of individuals working in agriculture, above the 87 percent national illiteracy rate and the share of individuals working in agriculture (22 percent). In terms of political representation, the number of *municipios* created in the nineteenth century was lower on average than those of other provinces, even after

---

[4] Huamalíes would not join the major Túpac Amaru rebellion of 1780–1782, for example.
[5] Huamalíes is not part of the 1572 Toledo Census.

accounting for population size. Fast forward until today, Huamalíes may not be the most impoverished province in Peru, yet, it still exhibits heightened levels of poverty and inequality. In 2009 it had a poverty rate of 38 percent (above the 26 percent nationally) and an income Gini coefficient of 0.29 – slightly higher than the average national one (0.27).

Altogether, it appears that the qualities that made Huamalies more attractive to purchase in the eighteenth century – abundant agriculture and the peaceful nature of their population – did not translate into economic success in the 21st one. One important reason, this book has argued, had to do with distortions induced by the segregation of the indigenous population, violent conflict, and delayed political representation. While most of the public's discussion around Spanish colonialism focuses on the exorbitant amounts of gold and silver extracted in colonial times; or the idea of a fiscal system involving large amount of transfers to Spain;[6] or the monopolization of public offices for Spanish natives versus locals, this focus has been misplaced. All of these policies have long ended, yet, their enduring legacy has remained: The devil is in the *local* factors, that have kept these legacies alive.

---

[6] For example, claim has been long refuted by economic historians (see Grafe and Irigoin 2012; Irigoin 2016).

Appendices

A.1 APPENDIX TO CHAPTER 2

TABLE A.1 *Mean real price and quantity of sales by office type (1670–1751)*

Type	Total Sold	Avg. Price	Std. Dev.	Min.	Max.
Audiencia seats	106	25,051.4	18,853.7	2,937.6	96,530.0
Military-Governors	218	16,180.2	18,925.7	777.15	122,290.8
Treasury official	415	13,890.4	18,917.6	550.8	158,295.3
Alcaldes & Corregidores	1,856	8,920.1	9,858.2	221.3	89,115.2

Note: Real[1] prices in *pesos de a ocho* using inflation indices in Spain.

A.1.1 Estimating the Effect of War on Type of Officials and Prices

The regression specification used in Figures 2.7 and 2.8 of the main text comes from estimating the following:

$$Y_{ijt} = a_j + \gamma_t + \beta_1 SocialStatus_{ijt} + e_{ijt} \quad (A.1)$$

Where the dependent variable Y_{ijt} takes a value of one if the individual was appointed (or if he instead had to purchase it, in which case the value is zero) for the case of Figure 2.7 of the main text and columns (1) to (3) of Table A.2. For Figure 2.8 and Table A.3, Y_{it} represents the real price in pesos paid by purchasers for a given province i in year t. The independent variable of interest is the social status of individuals, $SocialStatus_{ijt}$. Namely, whether the purchasing contract has a nobility

---

[1] Based on Spain's inflation rates.

TABLE A.2 *Probability of appointment by social status:* corregimientos *and* alcaldías

	(1)	(2)	(3)	(4)	(5)	(6)
VARIABLES	Appointed?			Log (Real Price)		
Audiencia:	Lima, Charcas, Mexico, & Guadalajara					
Any title	0.23***			-2.00***		
	(0.019)			(0.167)		
Spanish origin		0.07***			-0.57***	
		(0.020)			(0.175)	
Military			0.27***			-2.32***
			(0.021)			(0.180)
Observations	1,821	1,794	1,816	1,445	1,421	1,441
R-squared	0.522	0.478	0.528	0.894	0.896	0.894

Note: Year and province fixed effects included. *** $p < 0.01$, ** $p < 0.05$, * $p < 0.1$.
Coefficients in columns (1) to (3) represented in Figure 2.7 of Chapter 2.

TABLE A.3 *Prices paid by social status:* Corregimientos *and* Alcaldías

	(1)	(2)	(3)
VARIABLES	Real price (in pesos)		
Audiencia:	Lima, Charcas, Mexico, & Guadalajara		
Any title	-2,096.62***		
	(383.424)		
Spanish origin		-467.21	
		(383.386)	
Military			-2,375.96***
			(416.429)
Observations	1,816	1,789	1,811
R-squared	0.658	0.653	0.660

Note: Year and province fixed effects included. *** $p < 0.01$, ** $p < 0.05$, * $p < 0.1$.
Coefficients in columns (1) to (3) represented in Figure 2.8 of Chapter 2.

title (marquis, count, etc.), a knighthood title (*caballero de la orden de Santiago, Calatrava or Alcántara*), or a military title (captain, sergeant, *maestre de campo*). a_j is a province fixed effect, γ_t is a year fixed effect, and e_{ijt} represents the error term.

A.2 APPENDIX TO CHAPTER 3

A.2.1 Exchange Rates

1 *ducado* = 375 *maravedís*
1 *real de vellón* = 34 *maravedís*
1 peso de a 10 *reales* = 340 *maravedís*
1 peso de a 8 *reales* = 272 *maravedís*
1 peso *escudo* = 272 *maravedís*
1 *doblón* = 1088 *maravedís*
1 peso de a 15 reales = 510 *maravedís*
1 peso de a 20 reales = 680 *maravedís*
1 peso de oro = 850 *maravedís*

Source: John J. TePaske and Herbert S. Klein. The Royal Treasuries of the Spanish Empire in America. 3 volumes. Durham, N.C.: Duke University Press, 1982.

A.3 APPENDIX TO CHAPTER 4

A.3.1 Estimating the Effect of War Length on Officials' Type

The regression specification represented in Figures 4.2 and 4.3 of Chapter 4 is the following:

$$Y_{ijt} = a_j + \beta_1 Length\,War_t + e_{it} \quad (A.2)$$

Where the dependent variable Y_{it} takes a value of one if the individual purchasing a position has a nobility title (marquis, count, etc.), a knighthood title (caballero de la orden de Santiago, Calatrava, or Alcántara), or has a military title (captain, sergeant, maestre de campo). The independent variable of interest is $Length\,War_t$ which captures the number of years Spain is in war in Europe for two key events: the Spanish Succession War and Austrian Succession War. a_j is an *audiencia* fixed effect in Figure 4.2 of the main text (Table A.4 of Appendix) and a province fixed effect in Figure 4.3 of the main text (Table A.5 of Appendix).

For the case of Figure 4.4, estimates are also based on Equation (A.2) but samples vary by profitability levels, as specified. All estimates use Ordinary Least Squares (OLS).

TABLE A.4 *Key wars and official's characteristics in the audiencia (1687–1751)*

VARIABLES	(1) Native?	(2) Removed	(3) Waivers
Key Wars (Length)	0.009	0.014**	0.043***
	(0.005)	(0.006)	(0.015)
Observations	156	150	160
Mean DV	0.41	0.32	1.006
R-squared	0.384	0.071	0.241

Note: Sample includes all *audiencia* purchasers (156) across empire. All estimates include an *audiencia* fixed effect. Robust standard errors clustered by year in parentheses. *** $p < 0.01$, ** $p < 0.05$, * $p < 0.1$

TABLE A.5 *Key wars and social status of* corregidores *and* alcaldes *(1670–1751)*

VARIABLES	(1) Any title?	(2) Military?	(3) Knight?	(4) Noble?
Key wars (length)	−0.007***	−0.004**	−0.004***	−0.003*
	(0.002)	(0.002)	(0.001)	(0.002)
Observations	1,445	1,441	1,441	1,445
R-squared	0.216	0.193	0.167	0.179
Clusters	212	212	212	212
Mean DV	0.216	0.141	0.0625	0.083

Note: Sample includes all purchasers to provincial positions in the *audiencias* of Mexico, Guadalajara, Lima, and Charcas. All estimates include a province fixed effect. Robust standard errors clustered by province in parentheses. *** $p < 0.01$, ** $p < 0.05$, * $p < 0.1$

A.4 APPENDIX TO CHAPTER 5

A.4.1 Estimating the Effect of *Audiencia* Composition on Lower-Level Prices

Estimates presented in Figure 5.2 of the main text come from the specification represented by Equation (A.3):

$$Price_{ia,t} - Price_{ia,t-ni} = \alpha_{ia} + \gamma_t + \beta_1 \left(\%Sold_{a,t} - \%Sold_{a,t-ni} \right)$$
$$+ w_{i,t} + \pi_{a,t} + \varepsilon_{i,a,t} \tag{A.3}$$

Where $Price_{ia,t} - Price_{ia,t-ni}$ represents the difference in the prices paid for province i in *audiencia* a and year t relative to the price it had when province i was last sold in year $t - n_i$. Conversely, $\%Sold_{a,t} - \%Sold_{a,t-ni}$ is the difference in the share of individuals t who have purchased their seat in year t relative to year $t-n_i$, which is the year when province i was last sold. α_{ia} is an indicator variable that accounts for fixed differences across provinces i (fixed effect) and γ_t is an indicator variable capturing common shocks during each of the years included in the sample. $w_{i,t}$ accounts for provincial time-varying traits, such as the length of time between sales, and $\pi_{a,t}$ captures *audiencia*-specific time trends. β_1 is our estimate of interest and, if positive, would suggest that prices tended to increase with the greater presence of purchasers sitting in the *audiencia*.

A.4.2 Construction of Education (Human Capital) and Collusion (Local Connections) Variables

Human Capital. The first group of variables serves as a measure of human capital as captured by their education background and age at entry. Specifically, it captures the share of purchasers who hold a doctorate degree (the highest possible) and were above the legal limit (twenty-five years old) at the time of entry into the *audiencia*. Individuals below twenty-five were considered at the time inexperienced to serve in the highest court. If incompetence and inefficiency made *corregidores* and *alcaldes* offices more attractive, we should see that more education (e.g., higher degrees) and experience at the age of entry are associated with lower prices.

Local Connections. The second variable captures the share of purchasers with "local connections." These connections were measured based on three traits: first, whether the purchaser had known relatives in other government positions for the *audiencia* they rule. For example, *Oidor* Pedro Bravo de Rivero's father-in-law was a treasurer in the colonial administration. The second trait is whether the member is related by marriage to the *audiencia* they ruled, namely, whether the spouse was born in that *audiencia*. Marrying a "local" was very common among *audiencia* members (purchasers or not) but was frowned upon by the Crown who had to provide explicit permission to do so (*licencia*), often in exchange for a fee. Failure to secure permission often resulted in demotion and transfers to a different *audiencia*. The third component is whether the purchaser had to obtain a "waiver"

TABLE A.6 *Price growth and purchaser presence in the audiencia*

VARIABLES	(1) $\Delta\, Price_{t-k_i}$	(2) $\Delta\, Price_{t-k_i}$	(3) $\Delta\%\, Price_{t-k_i}$	(4) $\Delta\%\, Log\, Price_{t-k_i}$	(5) $\Delta\%\, Log\, Price_{t-k_i}$	(6) $\Delta\%\, Log\, Price_{t-k_i}$
$\Delta\%\, Sold_{t-k_i}$	27.217***	19.784***	7.368	0.004***	0.003**	0.001
	(10.142)	(7.328)	(6.387)	(0.002)	(0.001)	(0.001)
Observations	698	1,047	1,370	698	1,047	1,370
R-squared	0.356	0.300	0.313	0.427	0.342	0.312
Number of clusters	216	237	249	216	237	249

Robust standard errors clustered at the province level in parentheses. All specifications include a control for the time between sales, fixed effects for province, type of position, and year. Columns (1) to (3) are represented in Figure 5.3a of Chapter 5, while columns (4) to (6) are represented in Figure 5.3b. *** $p < 0.01$, ** $p < 0.05$, * $p < 0.1$

TABLE A.7 *Price growth and purchaser presence in the* audiencia *by geopolitical threat*

VARIABLES	(1) No threat $\Delta\, Price_{t-k_i}$	(2) Threat $\Delta\, Price_{t-k_i}$	(3) No threat $\Delta\%\, Log\, Price_{t-k_i}$	(4) Threat $\Delta\%\, Log\, Price_{t-k_i}$
$\Delta\%\, Sold_{t-k_i}$	23.980**	−1.903	0.004*	0.000
	(12.056)	(7.291)	(0.002)	(0.002)
Observations	554	493	554	493
R-squared	0.329	0.354	0.32	0.519
Number of provinces	105	132	105	132

Robust standard errors clustered at the province level in parentheses. All specifications include a control for the time between sales and fixed effects for province, type of position, and year. Note: The analysis focuses on the sample of transactions less than ten years apart from each other. Columns (1) and (2) are depicted in Figure 5.5(a), while columns (3) and (4) in Figure 5.5(b). *** $p < 0.01$, ** $p < 0.05$, * $p < 0.1$

TABLE A.8 *Price growth and purchaser presence in the* audiencia *by individual traits*

VARIABLES	(1) $\Delta\, Price_{t-k_i}$	(2) $\Delta\, Log\, Price_{t-k_i}$	(3) $\Delta\, Price_{t-k_i}$	(4) $\Delta\, Log\, Price_{t-k_i}$
$\Delta\%\, American\, Educ_{t-k_i}$	−384.232	−0.125	−380.612	−0.120
	(1,168.335)	(0.254)	(1,166.270)	(0.256)
$\Delta\%\, Born\, in\, Audiencia_{t-k_i}$			−183.389	−0.230
			(1,870.862)	(0.271)
$\Delta\%\, Local\, Connections_{t-k_i}$	3,266.643**	0.581**	3,352.682**	0.689**
	(1,410.818)	(0.259)	(1,574.816)	(0.292)
Observations	1,047	1,047	1,047	1,047
R-squared	0.296	0.336	0.296	0.337
Number of Clusters	237	237	237	237

Robust standard errors clustered at the province level in parentheses. All specifications include a control for the time passed between sales and fixed effects for type of position, year, and specific province. *** $p < 0.01$, ** $p < 0.05$, * $p < 0.1$

for failing to fulfill certain standards, such as being born in the district, having a local wife, or holding property in the district they sought to rule, among others. Because these rules intend to prevent close connections between the Crown's bureaucracy and the subjects they ruled, waivers provide a good proxy for the extent of local connectedness of a given purchaser.

A.5 APPENDIX TO CHAPTER 6

A.5.1 Construction of Price Differential or Price Spreads

To isolate the variation in office prices that might be indicative of worse types of officials ruling in these places due to office-selling, I center not on average prices but on *price spreads*. Namely, the difference in the average price paid for the same position at times of war while subtracting for the minimum price paid during peace. The price spread of province *j* between war and peace times can be represented by the following:

$$\text{Price Spread} = \text{MeanPrice}_{jwar} - \text{MinPrice}_{jpeace}$$

The key idea is that by differencing out the two prices, it is possible to account for position and province-specific factors that do not vary between war and peace and instead capture issues of *selection*. Why? As more fully explained in Chapter 4, the reason to focus on war versus peace is that war times bring a fiscal need or urgency not present in peace times, which would lead the Crown to overlook certain traits in buyers. As shown in Chapters 3 and 4, the Crown clearly preferred a certain profile of official, yet, it was willing to overlook these profiles at times of need. Price spreads are thus a way to capture these differences in screening and official's traits, which would impact provincial governance, across the empire while holding constant alternative factors.

The key reason is that many key determinants of prices, such as wages or their location and prestige, did not vary at all between war and peace times. In this way, price spreads are able to capture variation in prices paid for the same position that is *not* driven by these fixed traits. Instead, it will mainly capture changes in prices driven by the influx of buyers with different characteristics.

If price spreads are close to zero, it means that: first, most of the determinants in prices are driven by fixed position and provincial characteristics (wages, profitability, location, prestige, etc.), explaining the lack of differences over time. If, on the contrary, price spreads are positive, these are likely indicating that war prices are much higher on average than the minimum paid for sales, signaling the desperation of the Crown and therefore the likelihood that "worse" buyers are entering office. Finally, negative price spreads are indicative that peace prices are higher than wartime ones, thus likely to be more thoroughly vetted buyers or purchased without taking advantage of the Crown's desperation.

$$Price_{jwar} - Price_{jpeace} \begin{cases} \pm \text{ Temporal Differences} \\ = \text{ No Difference} \end{cases}$$

A.5.2 Uprisings Pre- versus Post-Office-Selling Estimation

To examine whether the patterns of uprisings change after sales, I estimate a linear regression using OLS of the form:

$$Uprising_{it} = \alpha_i + \beta_1 HighPriceSpread_i \times Postsales_t + y_t + X_{it} + e_{it} \quad (A.4)$$

Where $Uprising_{it}$ captures the presence of uprisings in province i and year t, $HighPriceSpread$ is an indicator for above the median differences in prices for province i during the period 1670–1751 interacted with an indicator for the years after 1760 ($Postsales_t$). X_{it} is a vector of controls interacting year indicators with key provincial traits, depending on the sample. α_i is a province fixed effect and y_t is a year fixed effect.

TABLE A.9 *Venality and postsales uprisings: Mexico, Peru, and Bolivia*

	(1)	(2)	(3)	(4)	(5)	(6)
	Mexico‡		Peru§		Bolivia*	
DV:			Pr (Uprising = 1)			
High price spread X postsales	0.03** (0.01)	0.03** (0.01)	0.07** (0.03)	0.07** (0.03)	0.02 (0.02)	0.04 (0.03)
Time & year FE	Y	Y	Y	Y	Y	Y
Controls	N	Y	N	Y	N	Y
Observations	3,200	3,072	5,400	5,243	2,052	1,944
R-squared	0.06	0.32	0.08	0.15	0.09	0.26
Clusters	25	24	50	49	19	18
Mean DV	0.0256	0.0247	0.0222	0.0214	0.00926	0.00977

‡ Main source of conflic data Garfias and Sellars (2022). §, * Main Source of conflict data Guardado (2018). Year and Province fixed effects included in every specification. Controls for Mexico from Sellars and Garfias (2022): year dummies interacted with average maize suitability, elevation, area of province, malarial presence, distance to Mexico city, and log (indigenous population in 1700), own construction. Controls for Bolivia and Peru: year dummies interacted with elevation, area, distance to Lima, and log (indigenous population in 1754). Clustered Robust standard errors in parentheses. *** $p < 0.01$, ** $p < 0.05$, * $p < 0.1$

A.5.3 Estimation of Weather Patterns and Uprisings

To examine whether histories of venality may exacerbate subsistence crises, I estimate a linear regression using OLS of the form:

$$Uprising_{it} = \alpha_i + \beta_1 HighPriceSpread_i \times PDSI_{it} + PDSI_{it} + T_t + X_{it} + e_{it} \quad (A.5)$$

Where $Uprising_{it}$ captures the presence of uprisings in province i and year t, $HighPricespread$ is an indicator for above the median differences in prices for province i during the period 1670–1751, $PDSI_{it}$ is the average value of the Palmer Drought Severity Index (−10, 10) for a given province and year in the Mexico sample. Or the self-calibrated Palmer Drought Severity Index (−10, 10) for the case of southern Peru and Bolivia. X_{it} is a vector of controls interacting year indicators with key provincial traits, depending on the sample. α_i is a province fixed effect and y_t a year fixed effect.

TABLE A.10 *Subsistence crises, uprisings, and venality: Mexico, Bolivia, and Peru*

	(1)	(2)	(3)
	Mexico‡	Bolivia*	Peru*
DV:	Pr (Uprising = 1)		
(sc)PDSImean X Intensity of High price spread	−0.008*	−0.005**	0.002*
	(0.004)	(0.002)	(0.001)
Time & Year FE	Y	Y	Y
Controls	Y	Y	Y
Observations	3,096	1,836	3,240
R-squared	0.325	0.269	0.181
Clusters	24	17	30
Mean DV	0.0251	0.001	0.018

‡ Main source of PDSI data Garfias and Sellars (2022). * Source of scPDSI data Morales et al. 2020. Year and Province fixed effects included in every specification. Controls for Mexico from Sellars and Garfias (2022): year dummies interacted with average maize suitability, elevation, area of province, malarial presence, distance to Mexico City, and log (indigenous population in 1700). Controls for Bolivia and Peru year dummies interacted with elevation, area, distance to Lima, and log (indigenous population in 1754). Clustered robust standard errors at the province level in parentheses.
*** $p < 0.01$, ** $p < 0.05$, * $p < 0.1$

TABLE A.11 *Uprisings in Guatemala, Ecuador, and Colombia (1680–1808)*

Corregimiento/Alcaldía	Timing	Description
(a) Guatemala		
Presales		
Totonicapán and/or Huehuetenango	1679, 1696, 1736, 1744	Repartimiento, indigenous authorities, *tributos* (head tax)
Quetzaltenango	1711	Indigenous uprising
Sololá	1743	Indigenous uprising
Chiquimula	1749	Attempted uprising
Baja Verapaz	1751	Uprising against priest
Comalapa	1755	Uprising against indigenous authorities & others
San Francisco Tecpan	1759	Uprising against indigenous authorities
Postsales		
Totonicapán and/or Huehuetenango	1785, 1793, 1798, 1799, 1802, 1803, 1805	Indigenous uprising against priest & authorities
Quetzaltenango	1711	Indigenous uprising
Sololá	1800	Indigenous uprising
Chiquimula	1749	Attempted uprising
Quetzaltenango	1785, 1802, 1806	Uprising against priest, attempts
Escuintla	1774	Indigenous uprisings
El Valle	1799	Indigenous uprising
Chiquimula	1804	Against local authorities
Chimaltenango	1791, 1796, 1801	Indigenous uprising
Alta Verapaz	1803	Against priest
(b) Ecuador		
Presales		
Quito	1677, 1695	Against Corregidor, Spanish expulsion
Ambato	1700, 1730	Against land appropriation, mining mitas
Ibarra	1679	Indigenous uprising
Cuenca	1706, 1730	Against land appropriation, reducciones

(*continued*)

TABLE A.11 (*continued*)

Corregimiento/Alcaldía	Timing	Description
\multicolumn{3}{c}{Postsales}		
Otavalo	1777, 1791	Against landowners, mining mitas
Ambato	1770, 1780, 1799	Against taxes, Spanish exploitation, defend land
La Tacunga	1761, 1766	Against taxes, and tributo (head tax)
Cuenca	1781	Against census
Riobamba	1785, 1802, 1806	Against census, taxes, tributo, mitas, tithes, forced labor, defense of land, and general exploitation

(c) Colombia

Presales

Corregimiento/Alcaldía	Timing	Description
Tunja	1705, 1724, 1727, 1740	Against tax collections, arrest of Indian authorities, priest abuses, opposition against particular judges, officials
Coyaima y Natagaima	1731, 1756	Against repartimiento, destruction illegal stills
Popayán	1743	Oppositions against particular officials
Sogamoso	1750	Against tax collectors
Santa Marta	1755, 1756, 1760	Opposition to fiscal demands and royal treasury officials

Postsales

Corregimiento/Alcaldía	Timing	Description
Popayán	1765, 1766	Opposition to alcohol monopoly
Chocó	1766	Holy week uprising, attack government
Antioquia	1793	Mob against extractive official
Cartagena	1798	Resistance to local works (forced)
Los Pastos	1800	Indigenous murder of corregidor
Tunja	1802	Opposition against particular officials
Mompox	1803	Opposition against particular judges

TABLE A.11 (*continued*)

Corregimiento/Alcaldía	Timing	Description
Sogamoso	1772	Against Spanish intruder of Indian village
Mariquita	1776	Opposition against particular judges
Los Llanos	1781	Major Indigenous insurrection

Sources: Navarrete (2013); Martínez Peláez (2021); Becker (2008); Moreno Yánez (1985); Albornoz Peralta (1976); McFarlane (1984).

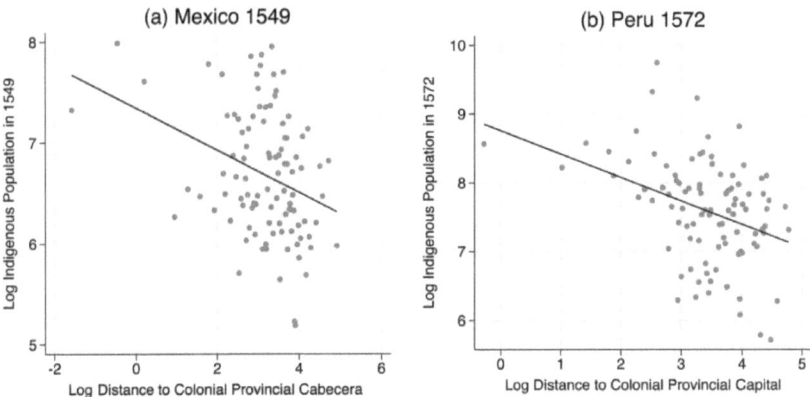

FIGURE A.1 Distance to the colonial *cabecera* prior to office-selling

Note: Binned scatter plots. Figure A.1 plots the residualized mean of the log of the indigenous population in Mexico in 1549 (panel a) and Peru in 1572 (panel b) after accounting for latitude, longitude, and provincial fixed effects, against the mean value of x – in this case the log distance to the 1700s colonial cabecera – within equal-sized bins. The solid line shows the best linear fit using OLS. Sources for Mexico: Cook and Simpson (1948), Cook and Borah (1971) from Guardado and Franco-Vivanco (2024). Sources for Peru: Cook et. al. (1975).

A.6 APPENDIX TO CHAPTER 7

A.6.1 Estimation of Municipio Creation and Venality

To examine whether histories of venality shape the degree of local political representation, I estimate a linear regression using OLS of the form:

$$Y_{i,p} = \alpha + \beta_1 VenalityMeasures_p + \mu_{i,p} + \varepsilon_{i,p} \qquad (A.6)$$

Where $Y_{i,p}$ is either (a) the year of incorporation or (b) an indicator for whether *municipio i* was created between 1822 and 1900, belonging to colonial province p. $VenalityMeasures_p$ is either the difference in the average log price paid for province p during war times minus the minimum log price paid during peace or the number of times that province was sold. $\mu_{i,p}$ is a vector of controls of municipality characteristics that always includes latitude, longitude, altitude, size of the population, and the number of existing *municipios* per *corregimientos* in colonial times. The hypothesis is that $\beta_1 > 0$, or that the higher spread in the prices paid during war and peace (venality) delayed local political representation in former colonial provinces.

A.6.2 Estimation of Nineteenth-Century Uprisings and Venality

To examine the reduced form effect of colonial venality and subsequent conflict, I estimate a linear regression using OLS of the form:

$$Y_{i,p} = \alpha + \beta_1 PriceSpread_p + \mu_{i,p} + \varepsilon_{i,p} \tag{A.7}$$

Where $Y_{i,p}$ is *municipio i*, belonging to colonial province p captures measures of conflict intensity. $PriceSpread_p$ is the difference in the average log price paid for province p during war times minus the minimum log price paid during peace. $\mu_{i,p}$ is a vector of controls of municipality characteristics that always includes latitude, longitude, and altitude as well as additional controls such as population, depending on the availability (see text). Standard errors are clustered at the province level. The hypothesis is that $\beta_1 > 0$, or that the higher spread in the prices paid during war and peace (venality) made conflict much more likely or intense, depending on the specification.

A.7 APPENDIX TO CHAPTER 8

TABLE A.12 *Data sources and variables of indigenous presence by locality*

Country	Source	Variable
Mexico	2010 *Censo de Localidades*	% population speaking Indigenous language
Guatemala	2002 *Censo de Centros Poblados*	% population speaking Mayan language
Bolivia	2001 Mapa de autoidentificación étnica por comunidades	% population 15+ by self-ID based on 2001 national census
Peru	2018 Base de Datos de Comunidades Indígenas	% population in a community speaking Indigenous language

TABLE A.13 *List of data sources for biological living standards at the individual level*

Country or *Audiencia**	<5 y/o DHS Height Data	Children's Height/ Weight Census	Birth Prematurity
Colombia	Yes	.	.
Ecuador	.	.	Yes
Guadalajara*	.	Yes	Yes
Mexico*	.	Yes	Yes
Chile	.	Yes	.
Bolivia	Yes	.	.
Peru	Yes	Yes	Yes
Guatemala	Yes	Yes	.

Sources: DHS surveys are available at: https://dhsprogram.com/. Micro-level data for height census data for Mexico and Guadalajara available at the Registro Nacional de Talla 2016 and 2017: http://rnpt.sivne.org.mx/pagina_/. 2015 National height census data for Guatemala available at: www.siinsan.gob.gt/siinsan/censo-talla 2005 Height Census for Peru available from Dell (2010) at the micro level and http://escale.minedu.gob.pe/censo-talla for school-level data. For Chile, the Mapa Nutricional 2011–2016 data is available at: www.junaeb.cl/mapa-nutricional. Micro-level data of births for Ecuador 2012–2019 is available at: https://anda.inec.gob.ec/anda/. For Mexico and Guadalajara here: www.dgis.salud.gob.mx/contenidos/basesdedatos/da_nacimientos_gobmx.html. For Peru 1999 and 2002: http://iinei.inei.gob.pe/microdatos/ *Data for births in Guatemala are available but not the gestational age of newborns which does not allow us to determine prematurity.

A.7.1 Estimation of Geographic Regression Discontinuity Results

To capture the average effect of the discrete border "jump," I estimate the following equation using OLS:

$$Y_{i,s,b,p} = \alpha_{b,p} + \beta_1 \left(PriceSpreadIntensity_{s,b,p}\right) + \beta_2 \left(bordist_{i,s,b,p}\right) + \beta_3 \left(bordist_{i,s,b,p} \times HighSpreadSide_{s,b,p}\right) + X_{i,s,b,p} + \varepsilon_{i,s,b,p} \quad (A.8)$$

Where $Y_{i,s,b,p}$ is the development outcome of interest across localities, settlements, or communities i, which are on side s of border segment b of former colonial province p. $PriceSpreadIntensity_{s,b,p}$ takes the value of 0 on the side of the border segment with the lowest price spread and the value of the average price spread on the high side. $bordist_{i,s,b,p}$ is the distance to the jurisdictional border of settlement, locality, or community i. $bordist_{i,s,b,p} \times HighSpreadSide_{s,b,p}$ takes a value of 0 on the lower spread side of the border while that of distance to the border interacted with $PriceSpreadIntensity_{s,b,p}$ on the side with the higher price spreads. $X_{i,s,b,p}$ is a vector of controls that always includes latitude, latitude squared, longitude, longitude squared, and logged elevation. α_c is a vector of border-segment fixed effects that account for differences across provinces. $\varepsilon_{i,s,b,p}$ is the error term. Standard errors are clustered at the border segment level.

TABLE A.14 *Variables and sources for* centro poblado/*locality outcomes*

Mexico

HH Assets	INEGI 2010	Share of households lacking radio, television, refrigerator, washing machine, car, computer, telephone, or internet.
HH Public Goods	INEGI 2010	Share of households lacking electicity, water access within or outside the household but inside the lot, as well as sewage.
Education Levels	INEGI 2010	Education degree completed for individuals above 15 over the number of people per age groups

Bolivia

HH Poverty	INE/UDAPE 2001	Share of households in extreme poverty

Guatemala

HH Literacy	INE Censo 2002	Share of literate population
HH Water	INE Censo 2002	Share of population with access to water
HH Electricity	INE Censo 2002	Share of population with access to electricity, solar panels, or gas
HH Sewage	INE Censo 2002	Share of population with no toilet

Peru

School	MINEDU Censo Escolar 2005	Locality with school

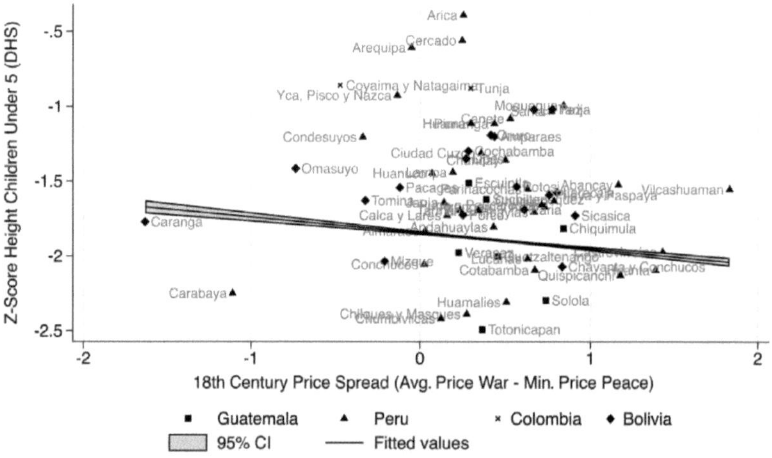

FIGURE A.2 Stunting among indigenous children by colonial venality status

Sources: Geolocated DHS surveys from Bolivia (2008), Guatemala (2014/15), Colombia (2010), and Peru (2009). Note: Sample limited to self-reported indigenous respondents. Dependent variable is the z-score average of height at the colonial province level. Scatter plot with 95 percent CI. Solid line shows the best linear fit using OLS.

TABLE A.15 Geographic differences along jurisdictional borders

(a) Mexico

Sample Kms	Log (Elevation)				Precipitation Code			
	<1	<5	<10	<15	<20	<5	<10	<15	<20
High X Price Spread	−0.007	0.035	0.057*	0.064*	0.068*	−0.021	−0.020	0.006	0.001
	(0.057)	(0.036)	(0.034)	(0.036)	(0.038)	(0.087)	(0.083)	(0.092)	(0.093)
Observations	1,433	5,936	8,827	9,977	10,721	5,935	8,826	9,976	10,720
R-squared	0.780	0.682	0.657	0.653	0.664	0.791	0.768	0.749	0.741
	Humidity Code				Distance to River			
	<1								
High X Price Spread	−0.010	−0.005	−0.121	−0.142	−0.123	0.007	0.001	−0.001	−0.001	−0.002
	(0.114)	(0.090)	(0.088)	(0.094)	(0.095)	(0.007)	(0.004)	(0.003)	(0.003)	(0.003)
Observations	1,432	5,935	8,826	9,976	10,720	1,433	5,936	8,827	9,977	10,721
R-squared	0.832	0.753	0.720	0.700	0.689	0.450	0.326	0.295	0.293	0.281
	Temperature Code				Distance to Coast			
High X Price Spread	0.056	−0.014	−0.063	−0.065	−0.057	−0.020	−0.020	−0.019	−0.022	−0.020
	(0.078)	(0.060)	(0.057)	(0.056)	(0.055)	(0.029)	(0.018)	(0.019)	(0.021)	(0.021)
Observations	1,432	5,935	8,826	9,976	10,720	1,375	5,839	8,666	9,776	10,485
R-squared	0.668	0.619	0.615	0.608	0.606	0.943	0.901	0.894	0.894	0.893

(continued)

TABLE A.15 (continued)

(b) Guatemala

	Log (Elevation)					Tree Cover				
Sample Kms:	<1	<5	<10	<15	<20	<1	<5	<10	<15	<20
High X Price Spread	0.232	0.481	0.365	0.393	0.458	−0.239	0.014	0.108	0.121	0.122
	(0.494)	(0.384)	(0.319)	(0.295)	(0.290)	(0.205)	(0.152)	(0.148)	(0.146)	(0.141)
Observations	769	3,461	6,311	7,877	8,477	838	3,760	7,001	8,730	9,364
R-squared	0.580	0.575	0.601	0.616	0.621	0.179	0.213	0.251	0.259	0.251

	Distance to Water Body					Distance to River				
High X Price Spread	−0.003	−0.017	−0.080	−0.102*	−0.087	0.027***	0.021***	0.011	0.007	0.005
	(0.068)	(0.059)	(0.058)	(0.059)	(0.057)	(0.008)	(0.007)	(0.007)	(0.007)	(0.007)
Observations	838	3,760	7,001	8,730	9,364	838	3,760	7,001	8,730	9,364
R-squared	0.556	0.545	0.574	0.588	0.603	0.199	0.127	0.087	0.074	0.077

(c) Bolivia

	Log (Elevation)					Forest Cover				
Sample Kms:	<1	<5	<10	<15	<20	<1	<5	<10	<15	<20
High X Price Spread	0.042	0.042	0.036	0.033	0.021	0.044	0.009	0.006	0.001	−0.002
	(0.032)	(0.031)	(0.031)	(0.033)	(0.035)	(0.055)	(0.010)	(0.004)	(0.006)	(0.007)
Observations	74,227	342,586	576,358	711,793	779,972	74,227	342,586	576,358	711,793	779,972
R-squared	0.748	0.702	0.689	0.686	0.688	0.322	0.378	0.326	0.306	0.260

	Distance to Water Body					Distance to River				
High X Price Spread	0.043**	0.038*	0.034	0.036	0.037	-0.003	-0.002	-0.004	-0.003	-0.003
	(0.018)	(0.020)	(0.025)	(0.026)	(0.026)	(0.006)	(0.004)	(0.006)	(0.007)	(0.006)
Observations	74,227	342,586	576,358	711,793	779,972	74,227	342,586	576,358	711,793	779,972
R-squared	0.840	0.844	0.843	0.835	0.825	0.385	0.353	0.337	0.308	0.287

Robust standard errors in parentheses clustered at the border segment level. All specifications include border segment fixed effects, distance to the border, and distance to the border interacted with the price spread.
*** $p < 0.01$, ** $p < 0.05$, * $p < 0.1$

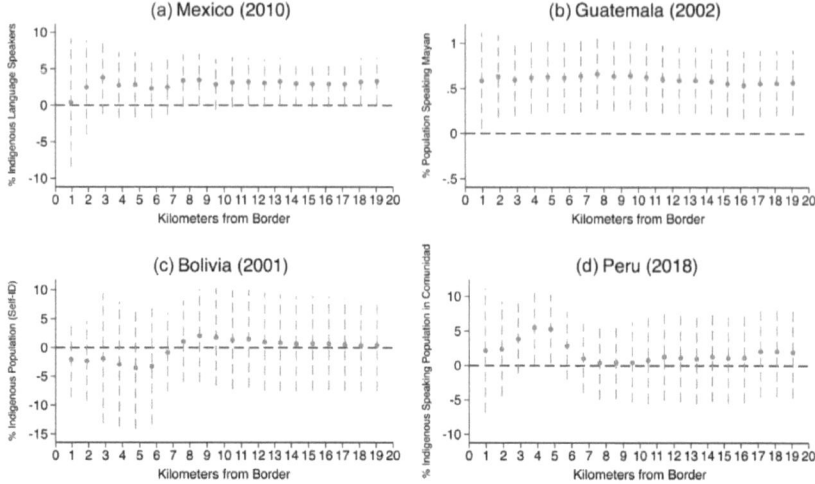

FIGURE A.3 Contemporaneous indigenous presence along colonial jurisdictional borders

Note: Each dot represents the estimated difference between localities/*centro poblados* on the side of the border with higher price spreads (and their intensity) vis-à-vis those localities/*centros poblados* on the lower spread side. Dependent variable values in panel (a) are 0–100, elsewhere 0–1. 95 percent CI in dashed lines. All estimates control for latitude, longitude, latitude sq, longitude sq, elevation, distance to the colonial border, distance to the border interacted with the treatment variable, and border segment fixed effects. Standard errors clustered at the border segment level. See estimating Equation (A.8) and Table A.12 for sources.

Bibliography

Acemoglu, Daron, and Melissa Dell. "Productivity differences between and within countries." *American Economic Journal: Macroeconomics* 2, no. 1 (2010): 169–188.

Acemoglu, Daron, Camilo García-Jimeno, and James A. Robinson. "Finding El Dorado: Slavery and long-run development in Colombia." *Journal of Comparative Economics* 40, no. 4 (2012): 534–564.

Acemoglu, Daron, Leopoldo Fergusson, and Simon Johnson. "Population and conflict." *The Review of Economic Studies* 87, no. 4 (2020): 1565–1604.

Acemoglu, Daron, Simon Johnson, and James A. Robinson. "Reversal of fortune: Geography and institutions in the making of the modern world income distribution." *The Quarterly journal of Economics* 117, no. 4 (2002): 1231–1294.

Acemoglu, Daron, Simon Johnson, and James A. Robinson. "The colonial origins of comparative development: An empirical investigation." *American Economic Review* 91, no. 5 (2001): 1369–1401.

Aghion, Philippe and Jean Tirole. "Formal and real authority in organizations." *Journal of Political Economy* 105, no. 1 (1997): 1–29.

Aguirre Beltrán, Gonzalo. *Zonas de refugio*. Fondo de Cultura Económica, 1991.

Albertus, Michael. *Autocracy and Redistribution*. Cambridge University Press, 2015.

Albertus, Michael. "Land reform and civil conflict: Theory and evidence from Peru." *American Journal of Political Science* 64, no. 2 (2020): 256–274.

Albertus, Michael, Alberto Díaz-Cayeros, Beatriz Magaloni, and Barry R. Weingast. "Authoritarian survival and poverty traps: Land reform in Mexico." *World Development* 77 (2016): 154–170.

Albornoz, Facundo, and Antonio Cabrales. "Decentralization, political competition and corruption." *Journal of Development Economics* 105 (2013): 103–111.

Albornoz Peralta, Oswaldo. *Las luchas indígenas en el Ecuador*. Guayaquil: Claridad, 1976.

Alesina, Alberto, Reza Baqir, and William Easterly. "Public goods and ethnic divisions." *The Quarterly Journal of Economics* 114, no. 4 (1999): 1243–1284.

Alix-García, Jennifer, and Emily A. Sellers. "Locational fundamentals, trade, and the changing urban landscape of Mexico." *Journal of Urban Economics* 116 (2020): 103–213.

Allen, D. W. "Purchase, patronage, and professions: Incentives and the evolution of public office in pre-modern Britain." *Journal of Institutional and Theoretical Economics (JITE)* 161, no. 1 (2005): 57–79.

Álvarez-Villa, Daphne and Jenny Guardado. "The long-run influence of institutions governing trade: Evidence from smuggling ports in colonial Mexico." *Journal of Development Economics* 144 (2020): 102–453.

Alves, Jorge Antonio. "(Un?) healthy politics: The political determinants of subnational health systems in Brazil." *Latin American Politics and Society* 57, no. 4 (2015): 119–142.

Andrien, Kenneth J. "Corruption, inefficiency, and imperial decline in the seventeenth-century viceroyalty of Peru." *The Americas* 41, no. 1 (1984): 1–20.

Andrien, Kenneth J. "Economic crisis, taxes and the Quito Insurrection of 1765." *Past & Present* 129 (1990): 104–131.

Andrien, Kenneth J. "El Corregidor de indios, la corrupción y el estado virreinal en Peru (1580–1630)." *Revista de Historia Economica-Journal of Iberian and Latin American Economic History* 4, no. 3 (1986): 493–520.

Andrien, Kenneth J. "The politics of reform in Spain's Atlantic Empire during the late Bourbon period: The visita of José García de León y Pizarro in Quito." *Journal of Latin American Studies* 41, no. 4 (2009): 637–662.

Andrien, Kenneth J. "The sale of fiscal offices and the decline of royal authority in the Viceroyalty of Peru, 1633–1700." *Hispanic America Historical Review* 62 (1982): 70–100.

Arias, L. M. "Building fiscal capacity in colonial Mexico: From fragmentation to centralization." *The Journal of Economic History* 73, no. 3 (2013): 662–693.

Arroyo Abad, Leticia, Elwyn Davies, and Jan Luiten Van Zanden. "Between conquest and independence: Real wages and demographic change in Spanish America, 1530–1820." *Explorations in Economic History* 49, no. 2 (2012): 149–166.

Arroyo Abad, Leticia, and Jan Luiten Van Zanden. "Growth under extractive institutions? Latin American per capita GDP in colonial times." *Journal of Economic History* 76, no. 4 (2016): 1182–1215.

Associated Press (2022, December 16). "Mexico president insists relations with Spain still 'paused.'" Yahoo News, December 16, 2022. www.yahoo.com/news/mexico-president-insists-relations-spain-003357226.html

Bai, Ying, and Ruixie Jia. "The economic consequences of political hierarchy: Evidence from regime changes in China, 1000–2000 CE." *The Review of Economics and Statistics* 105, no. 3 (2023): 626–645.

Baker, Andy and David Cupery. "Animosity, amnesia, or admiration? Mass opinion around the world toward the former colonizer." *British Journal of Political Science* 53, no. 4 (2023): 1132–1149.

Bakewell, Peter J. *Miners of the Red Mountain: Indian Labor in Potosí, 1545–1650.* University of New Mexico Press, 1984.

Banerjee, Abhijit, and Lakshmi Iyer. "History, institutions, and economic performance: The legacy of colonial land tenure systems in India." *American Economic Review* 95, no. 4 (2005): 1190–1213.

Banerjee, Abhijit, Rema Hanna, and Sendhil Mullainathan. "Corruption." Chap. 27 in *The Handbook of Organizational Economics*, edited by Robert Gibbons and J. Roberts. Princeton University Press, 2013.
Barbier, Jacques A. "Elite and cadres in Bourbon Chile." *Hispanic American Historical Review* 52, no. 3 (1972): 416–435.
Barro, R. J., and J. F. Ursua. "Macroeconomic crises since 1870." *Brookings Papers on Economic Activity, Economic Studies Program, the Brookings Institution* 39, no. 1 (2008): 255–350.
Baskes, Jeremy. "Coerced or voluntary? The repartimiento and market participation of peasants in late colonial Oaxaca." *Journal of Latin American Studies* 28, no. 1 (1996): 1–28.
Baskes, Jeremy. *Indians, Merchants, and Markets: A Reinterpretation of the Repartimiento and Spanish-Indian Economic Relations in Colonial Oaxaca, 1750–1821*. Stanford University Press, 2000.
Bates, Robert H., John H. Coatsworth, and Jeffrey G. Williamson. "Lost decades: Postindependence performance in Latin America and Africa." *The Journal of Economic History* 67, no. 4 (2007): 917–943.
Becker, Marc. *Indians and Leftists in the Making of Ecuador's Modern Indigenous Movements*. Duke University Press, 2008.
Bentham, Jeremy. *Rationale of Reward*. John and H.L. Hunt, 1838–43 [1825]. Reprinted in J. Bowring (ed.), *The Works of Jeremy Bentham* 2: 189–266.
Beramendi, Pablo, and Melissa Rogers. "Disparate geography and the origins of tax capacity." *The Review of International Organizations* 16 (2021): 213–237.
Beramendi, Pablo, and Melissa Rogers. *Geography, Capacity, and Inequality: Spatial Inequality*. Cambridge University Press, 2022.
Bértola, L. "El PIB per cápita de Uruguay 1870–2016: Una reconstrucción." *PHES Documento de Trabajo* 48 (2016).
Bértola, L., and J. A. Ocampo. *The Economic Development of Latin America since Independence*. Oxford University Press, 2012.
Besley, Timothy, and Marta Reynal-Querol. "The legacy of historical conflict: Evidence from Africa." *American Political Science Review* 108, no. 2 (2014): 319–336.
Bisin, A., E. Patacchini, T. Verdier, and Y. Zenou. "Formation and persistence of oppositional identities." *European Economic Review* 55, no. 8 (2011): 1046–1071.
Bluhm, Richard, Christian Lessmann, and Paul Schaudt. "The political geography of cities." *CESifo Working Paper* no. 9376 (2021).
Bolt, Jutta and Jan Luiten van Zanden. "Maddison style estimates of the evolution of the world economy. A new 2020 update." *Maddison-Project Working Papers* WP-15 (2020). www.rug.nl/ggdc/historicaldevelopment/maddison/publications/wp15.pdf.
Bonney, Richard (ed.), "European State Finance Database." 2007. Accessed December 12, 2016.
Boone, Catherine. "Sons of the soil conflict in Africa: Institutional determinants of ethnic conflict over land." *World Development* 96 (2017): 276–293.
Borah, Woodrow. *Justice by Insurance*. University of California Press, 1982.
Borah, Woodrow. *New Spain's Century of Depression*. University of California Press, 1951.

Borah, Woodrow. "III. The New World." *The Americas* 12, no. 3 (1956): 246–257.
Botero Villegas, Luis Fernando. "Espacio, cuestión agraria y diferenciación cultural en Chimborazo, Ecuador. Una aproximación histórica." *Gazeta de Antropología* 24, no. 1 (2008). https://digibug.ugr.es/bitstream/handle/10481/7069/G24_08LuisFernando_Botero_Villegas.pdf.
Bridikhina, Eugenia. *Theatrum Mundi: entramados del poder en Charcas colonial*. Plural editores, La Paz, 2007.
Browning, Harley L. "Urbanization and modernization in Latin America: The demographic perspective." In *The Urban Explosion in Latin America*, edited by G. H. Beyer. Cornell University Press, 1967.
Bruhn, Miriam, and Francisco A. Gallego. "Good, bad, and ugly colonial activities: Do they matter for economic development?" *Review of Economics and Statistics* 94, no. 2 (2012): 433–461.
Bueno, Cosme. *Geografía del Perú Virreinal del Siglo XVIII*. Edited by Daniel Valcárcel. Azángaro, 1951.
Bulmer-Thomas, V. *The Economic History of Latin America since Independence*, 3rd ed. Cambridge University Press, 2014.
Burkholder, Mark A. *Administrators of Empire*. Routledge Press, 2018.
Burkholder, Mark A., and Dewitt S. Chandler. *Biographical Dictionary of Audiencia Ministers in the Americas, 1687–1821*. Greenwood Publishing Group, 1982.
Burkholder, Mark A., and Dewitt S. Chandler. "Creole appointments and the sale of audiencia positions in the Spanish Empire under the Early Bourbons, 1701–1750." *Journal of Latin American Studies* 4, no. 2 (1972): 187–206.
Burkholder, Mark A., and Dewitt S. Chandler. *From Impotence to Authority: The Spanish Crown and the American Audiencias, 1687–1808*. University of Missouri Press, 1977.
Campbell, Leon G. "A colonial establishment: Creole domination of the Audiencia of Lima during the late eighteenth century." *Hispanic American Historical Review* 52, no. 1 (1972): 1–25.
Carrillo Ureta, Gonzalo Alberto. "Las Redes de Sociabilidad de los Oidores de Lima: Cultura política, redes clientelares y gestión del poder en Lima virreinal (1745–1761)." PhD diss. Pontificia Universidad Católica del Perú, 2019.
Carter, Christopher. "Extraction, assimilation, and accommodation: The historical foundations of indigenous-state relations in Latin America." *American Political Science Association* 118, no. 1 (2023): 1–16.
Castro Flores, Nelson. "Estrategias Familiares, Práctica Jurídica y Comunidad de Memoria. Los Descendientes de Tito Alonso Atauchi y Viracocha Inca en Charcas, Siglos XVI-XVIII." *Estudios atacameños* 61 (2019): 177–198.
Cebrian Moreno, Alfredo. *El corregidor de indios y la economía peruana del siglo XVIII:(los repartos forzosos de mercancías)*. Editorial CSIC-CSIC Press, 1977.
Centeno, Miguel Angel. *Blood and Debt: War and the Nation-State in Latin America*. Penn State Press, 2002.
Challú, Amilcar. "The great decline: Biological well-being and living standards in Mexico, 1730–1840." In *Living Standards in Latin American History: Height, Welfare, and Development, 1750–2000*, edited by Ricardo D. Salvatore, John H. Coatsworth, and Amilcar E. Challú. Cambridge University Press, 2010.

Chhibber, Pradeep, and Irfan Nooruddin. "Do party systems count? The number of parties and government performance in the Indian states." *Comparative Political Studies* 37, no. 2 (2004): 152–187.

Chiovelli, Giorgio, Leopoldo Fergusson, Luis R. Martínez, Juan David Torres, and Felipe Valencia Caicedo. "Bourbon reforms and state capacity in the Spanish empire." *Documentos CEDE* 21106 (2024).

Clayton, Lawrence A. "Trade and navigation in the seventeenth-century viceroyalty of Peru." *Journal of Latin American Studies* 7, no. 1 (1975): 1–21.

Cleary, Matthew R. "Electoral competition, participation, and government responsiveness in Mexico." *American Journal of Political Science* 51, no. 2 (2007): 283–299.

Coatsworth, John H. "Inequality, institutions and economic growth in Latin America." *Journal of Latin American Studies* 40, no. 3 (2008): 545–569.

Coatsworth, John H. "La independencia latinoamericana: hipótesis sobre sus costes y beneficios." In *La independencia americana: consecuencias económicas*, edited by Salvucci, Richard J., and Linda K. Salvucci. Alianza, 1993.

Coatsworth, John H. "Obstacles to economic growth in nineteenth-century Mexico." *The American Historical Review* 83, no. 1 (1978): 80–100.

Coatsworth, John H. "Patterns of rural rebellion in Latin America: Mexico in comparative perspective." In *Riot, Rebellion, and Revolution: Rural Social Conflict in Mexico*, edited by Friedrich Katz. Princeton University Press, 1988.

Cobban, Alfred. *The Social Interpretation of the French Revolution*. Cambridge University Press, 1999.

Cole, Jeffrey A. "An abolitionism born of frustration: The Conde de Lemos and the Potosí Mita, 1667–73." *Hispanic American Historical Review* 63, no. 2 (1983): 307–333.

Collier, Paul, and Anke Hoeffler. "Greed and grievance in civil war." *Oxford Economic Papers* 56, no. 4 (2004): 563–595.

Cook, Edward R., and Paul J. Krusic. "The North American Drought Atlas." In *AGU Fall Meeting Abstracts*, vol. 2003, pp. GC52A-01. 2003.

Cook, Noble David, Alejandro Málaga Medina, and Therese Bouysse-Cassagne. *Tasa de la visita general de Francisco de Toledo*. Universidad Nacional Mayor de San Marcos, 1975.

Cook, Noble David. "The Corregidores of the Colca Valley, Perú: Imperial administration in an Andean region." *Anuario de estudios americanos* 60, no. 2 (2003): 413–439.

Cook, Sherburne F., and Woodrow W. Borah. *Essays in Population History: Mexico and the Caribbean*. University of California Press, 1971.

Cook, Sherburne F., and Lesley Byrd Simpson. *The Population of Central Mexico in the Sixteenth Century*. University of California Press, 1948.

Cuesta Alonso, Marcelino, and José Ramón Medina Moreno. "La prohibición de los repartimientos de mercancías a los indios en la subdelegación de Fresnillo a finales del siglo XVIII." *Temas Americanistas* 46 (2021): 119–141.

Curvale, Carolina and Przeworski, Adam. "Does politics explain the economic gap between the United States and Latin America." *Nueva York, New York University, mimeo* (2005).

Curvale, Carolina and Adam Przeworski. "Does politics explain the economic gap between the United States and Latin America?" In *Falling Behind: Explaining the Development Gap between Latin America and the United States*, edited by Francis Fukuyama. Oxford University Press, 2008.

De Corso, G. "El crecimiento económico de Venezuela, Desde la Oligarquía Conservadora Hasta La Revolucion Bolivariana: 1830–2012: Venezuelan economic growth from the conservative oligarchy to the Bolivarian revolution (1830–2012)." *Revista De Historia Económica/Journal of Iberian and Latin American Economic History* 31, no. 3 (2013): 321–357.

Dell, Melissa. "Path dependence in development: Evidence from the Mexican Revolution." Harvard University, 2012.

Dell, Melissa. "The persistent effects of Peru's mining mita." *Econometrica* 78, no. 6 (2010): 1863–1903.

Dessaint, Alain Y. "Effects of the hacienda and plantation systems on Guatemala's Indians." *América indígena* 22, no. 4 (1962): 323–354.

Díaz, J. B., Lüders, R., and G. Wagner. "Economía Chilena 1810–2000, Producto total y sectorial una nueva mirada." *Pontificia Universidad Católica de Chile, Instituto de Economía, Documento de Trabajo* no. 315, 2007.

Dincecco, Mark, and Mauricio Prado. "Warfare, fiscal capacity, and performance." *Journal of Economic Growth* 17, no. 3 (2012): 171–203.

Dincecco, Mark. *Political Transformations and Public Finances: Europe, 1650–1913*. Cambridge University Press, 2011.

Dobado-González, Rafael, and Héctor García-Montero. "Neither so low nor so short: Wages and heights in Bourbon Spanish America from an international comparative perspective." *Journal of Latin American Studies* 46, no. 2 (2014): 291–321.

Domínguez Ortiz, A. "Un virreinato en venta." *Mercurio Peruano* 453 (1965): 43–51.

Doyle, William. "The price of offices in pre-revolutionary France." *The Historical Journal* 27, no. 4 (1984): 831–860.

Doyle, William. *Venality: The Sale of Offices in Eighteenth-Century France*. Oxford University Press, 1996.

Drelichman, Mauricio. "All that glitters: Precious metals, rent seeking and the decline of Spain." *European Review of Economic History* 9, no. 3 (2005): 313–336.

Drelichman, Mauricio. "Spanish Finance, 1348–1700" in *Handbook of Key Global Financial Markets, Institutions, and Infrastructure*, edited by Gerard Caprio. Academic Press, 2012, 259–268.

Drelichman, Mauricio, and Hans-Joachim Voth. "The sustainable debts of Philip II: A Reconstruction of Castile's fiscal position, 1566–1596." *The Journal of Economic History* 70, no. 4 (2010): 813–842.

Eagle, Marc. "Portraits of bad officials: Malfeasance in visita sentences from seventeenth-century Santo Domingo." In *Corruption in the Iberian Empires: Greed, Custom, and Colonial Networks*, edited by Christoph Rosenmüller. University of New Mexico Press, 2017.

Easterly, William. "Can foreign aid buy growth?" *Journal of Economic Perspectives* 17, no. 3 (2003): 23–48.

Eissa-Barroso, Francisco A. "'Our delivery consists in appointing good ministers': Corruption and the dilemmas of appointing officials in early eighteenth-century

Spain." In *Corruption in the Iberian Empires: Greed, Custom, and Colonial Networks*, edited by Christoph Rosenmüller. University of New Mexico Press, 2017.
Elizalde, Aldo, Eduardo Hidalgo, and Nayeli Salgado. "Public good or public bad? Indigenous institutions and the demand for public goods." *QUCEH Working Papers*, no. 23–01. Queen's University Belfast, 2021.
Engerman, Stanley L. and Kenneth L. Sokoloff. "Factor Endowments, Inequality, and Paths of Development among New World Economics." NBER Working Paper Series, National Bureau of Economic Research, 2002.
Engerman, Stanley L. and Kenneth L. Sokoloff. "Factor endowments, institutions, and differential paths of growth among new world economies: A view from economic historians of the United States." In *How Latin America Fell Behind*, edited by Stephen Haber. Stanford University Press, 1997.
Faguet, Jean-Paul, Camilo Matajira, and Fabio Sánchez. "Is extraction bad? *Encomienda* and development in Colombia since 1560." *Documentos CEDE* no. 48 (2017).
Fearon, James. D., and David D. Laitin. "Explaining interethnic cooperation." *American Political Science Review* 90, no. 4 (1996): 715–735.
Fearon, James D., and David Laitin. "Does Contemporary Armed Conflict Have 'Deep Historical Roots'?" Available at SSRN 1922249 (2014).
Felstiner, Mary Lowenthal. "Kinship politics in the Chilean independence movement." *Hispanic American Historical Review* 56, no. 1 (1976): 58–80.
Fergusson, Leopoldo, Horacio Larreguy, and Juan Felipe Riaño. "Political competition and state capacity: evidence from a land allocation program in Mexico." *The Economic Journal* 132, no. 648 (2022): 2815–2834.
Fischer, Wolfram, and Peter Lundgreen. "The recruitment and training of administrative and technical personnel." In *The Formation of National States in Western Europe*, edited by Charles Tilly. Princeton University Press, 1975, pp. 456–561.
Fisman, Raymond, and Miriam A. Golden. *Corruption: What Everyone Needs to Know*. Oxford University Press, 2017.
Fouka, Vasiliki. "Backlash: The unintended effects of language prohibition in US schools after World War I." *The Review of Economic Studies* 87, no. 1 (2020): 204–239.
Fox, Jonathan. "The difficult transition from clientelism to citizenship: Lessons from Mexico." *World Politics* 46, no. 2 (1994): 151–184.
Franco-Vivanco, Edgar. "Justice as checks and balances: Indigenous claims in the courts of colonial Mexico." *World Politics* 73, no. 4 (2021): 712–773.
Freire Costa, Leonor, Susana Münch Miranda, and Pilar Nogues-Marco. *Early modern financial development in the Iberian Peninsula*. No. unige: 147492. 2021.
Fukuyama, Francis, ed. *Falling Behind: Explaining the Development Gap between Latin America and the United States*. Oxford University Press, 2008.
Gailmard, Sean. "Building a new imperial state: The strategic foundations of separation of powers in America." *American Political Science Review* 111, no. 4 (2017): 668–685.
Galeano, Eduardo. *Open Veins of Latin America: Five Centuries of the Pillage of a Continent*. Monthly Review Press, 1997.
Gallegos, Laura Machuca, and Álvaro Alcántara. "La Vigencia del Estudio de los Repartimientos en Época de Subdelegados." *Temas Americanistas* 46 (2021): 1–8.

García Fuentes, L. *El comercio español con América, 1650 a 1700*. Escuela de Estudios Hispano-Americanos, 1980.
Garfias, Francisco, and Emily A. Sellars. "When state building backfires: Elite coordination and popular grievance in rebellion." *American Journal of Political Science* 66, no. 4 (2022): 977–992.
Garfias, Francisco, and Emily A. Sellars. "From conquest to centralization: Domestic conflict and the transition to direct rule." *The Journal of Politics* 83, no. 3 (2021): 992–1009.
Garfias, Francisco, and Emily A. Sellars. "Epidemics, rent extraction, and the value of holding office." *Journal of Political Institutions and Political Economy* 1, no. 4 (2020): 559–583.
Gavira Márquez, María Concepción. "El Repartimiento de Mercancías y los Subdelegados en el Alto Perú. La Denuncia en 1785 del Subdelegado de Carangas, Juan Dionisio Marín." *Temas Americanistas* 46 (2021): 33–64.
Gelabert, Juan E. "Rasgos generales de la evolución de la Hacienda moderna en el reino de Castilla (siglo XVII)." *Iura Vasconiae. Revista de Derecho Histórico y Autonómico de Vasconia* 6 (2009): 47–68.
George, Lovell, W. and Lutz, Christopher H. "The historical demography of colonial central America." In *Yearbook (Conference of Latin Americanist Geographers)*. Conference of Latin Americanist Geographers, 1991.
Gergis, Joëlle L., and Anthony M. Fowler. "A history of ENSO events since AD 1525: Implications for future climate change." *Climatic Change* 92, no. 3 (2009): 343–387.
Gibson, Charles. *The Aztecs under Spanish rule: a history of the Indians of the Valley of Mexico, 1519-1810*. Stanford University Press, 1964.
Giraudy, Agustina. *Democrats and Autocrats: Pathways of Subnational Undemocratic Regime Continuity within Democratic Countries*. Oxford University Press, 2015.
Giraudy, Agustina. "Varieties of subnational undemocratic regimes: Evidence from Argentina and Mexico." *Studies in Comparative International Development* 48 (2013): 51–80.
Giraudy, Agustina. "The politics of subnational undemocratic regime reproduction in Argentina and Mexico." *Journal of Politics in Latin America* 2, no. 2 (2010): 53–84.
Glaeser, Edward L., and Joshua D. Gottlieb. "The Economics of Place-Making Policies." NBER Working Paper Series no. 14373, National Bureau of Economic Research, 2008.
Gölte, Jurgen. *Repartos y rebeliones. Túpac Amaru y las contradicciones de la economía colonial*. Instituto de Estudios Peruanos, 1980.
Gonzalez Casasnovas, Ignacio. "Las dudas de la corona: la política de repartimientos para la minería de Potosí (1680–1732)." *Editorial CSIC, Madrid* (2000).
Gonzalez Enciso, A. "A moderate and rational absolutism: Spanish fiscal policy in the first half of the eighteenth century." In *War, State and Development: Fiscal-Military States in the Eighteenth Century*. EUNSA Ediciones Universidad de Navarra, 2007, 109–132.
Grafe, Regina, and Maria Alejandra Irigoin. "A stakeholder empire: The political economy of Spanish imperial rule in America." *Economic History Review* 65, no. 2 (2012): 609–651.

Grafe, Regina, and Maria Alejandra Irigoin. "The Spanish empire and its legacy: Fiscal redistribution and political conflict in colonial and post-colonial Spanish America." *Journal of Global History* 65, no. 2 (2006): 241–267.

Grafe, Regina. *Distant Tyranny: Markets, Power, and Backwardness in Spain, 1650–1800*. Princeton University Press, 2011.

Grieshaber, Erwin. P. "Survival of Indian Communities in Nineteenth-Century Bolivia." PhD Dissertation. The University of North Carolina at Chapel Hill, 1977.

Grieshaber, Erwin P. "Survival of Indian communities in nineteenth-century Bolivia: a regional comparison." *Journal of Latin American Studies* 12, no. 2 (1980): 223–269.

Grossman, Guy, and Janet I. Lewis. "Administrative unit proliferation." *American Political Science Review* 108, no. 1 (2014): 196–217.

Guardado, Jenny. "Checks and balances in the colonial government of Peru: Evidence from office prices." In *Roots of Underdevelopment*, edited by Felipe Valencia Caicedo. Palgrave Macmillan, 2023.

Guardado, Jenny. "Hierarchical oversight and the value of public office: Evidence from colonial Peru." *The Journal of Politics* 84, no. 3 (2022): 1353–1369.

Guardado, Jenny. "Long-run economic legacies of colonialism." In *the Oxford Handbook of Historical Political Economy*, edited by Jared Rubin and Jeffery Jenkins. Oxford University Press, 2023.

Guardado, Jenny. "Office-selling, corruption, and long-term development in Peru." *American Political Science Review* 112, no. 4 (2018): 971–995.

Guardado, Jenny. "New Territories, Old Peoples: Revisiting State Formation in Spanish America" *Mimeo*, 2025.

Guardado, Jenny, and Edgar Franco-Vivanco. "Jurisdictional Havens: The Geography of Indigenous Identity in Mexico" *Mimeo*, 2024.

Haber, Stephen, ed. *How Latin America Fell Behind: Essays on the Economic Histories of Brazil and Mexico, 1800–1914*. Stanford University Press, 1997.

Hamilton, Earl. J. *El tesoro americano y la revolución de los precios en España, 1501–1650*. Editorial Crítica, 2000.

Hamilton, Earl J. "Revisions in Economic History: VIII – The Decline of Spain." *Economic History Review* (1938): 168–179.

Harbers, Imke. "Taxation and the unequal reach of the state: Mapping state capacity in Ecuador." *Governance* 28, no. 3 (2015): 373–391.

Haring, Clarence Henry. *The Spanish Empire in America*. Oxford University Press, 1947.

Herzog, Tamar. Ritos de control, prácticas de negociación: pesquisas, visitas y residencias y las relaciones entre Quito y Madrid. Fundación Hernando de Larramendi, 2000. https://core.ac.uk/download/pdf/71612412.pdf.

Herzog, Tamar. *Upholding Justice: Society, State, and the Penal System in Quito (1650–1750)*. University of Michigan Press, 2004.

Hidalgo Lehuede, Jorge. "Fases de la Rebelión Indígena de 1781 en el Corregimiento de Atacama y Esquema de la Inestabilidad Política que la Precede, 1749–1781." *Chungara: Revista de Antropología Chilena* (1982): 192–246.

Hill, Ruth. *Hierarchy, Commerce and Fraud in Bourbon Spanish America: A Postal Inspector's Expose*. Vanderbilt University Press, 2005.

Hollyer, J. R. Meritocracy or Patronage? The Choice of Bureaucratic Appointment Regimes. Working Paper, 2009. http://jameshollyer.com.

Huenchumil, Paula. "A dos años de la destrucción de monumentos coloniales ¿Qué pasó con estos símbolos?" Interferencia (2021). https://interferencia.cl/articulos/dos-anos-de-la-destruccion-de-monumentos-coloniales-que-paso-con-estos-simbolos.

Huillery, Elise. "History matters: The long-term impact of colonial public investments in French West Africa." *American Economic Journal: Applied Economics* 1, no. 2 (2009): 176–215.

Huillery, Elise. "The impact of European settlement within French West Africa: Did pre-colonial prosperous areas fall behind?" *Journal of African Economies* 20, no. 2 (2011): 263–311.

Irigoin, Maria Alejandra and Regina Grafe. "Bargaining for absolutism: A Spanish path to nation-state and empire building." *Hispanic American Historical Review* 88, no. 2 (2008): 173–209.

Irigoin, Maria Alejandra. "Representation without taxation, taxation without consent: The legacy of Spanish colonialism in America." *Revista de Historia Económica-Journal of Iberian and Latin American Economic History* 34, no. 2 (2016): 169–208.

Jia, R., M. Kudamatsu, and D. Seim. "Political selection in China: The complementary roles of connections and performance." *Journal of the European Economic Association* 13, no. 4 (2015): 631–668.

Jiménez Jiménez, Ismael. Poder y corrupción administrativa en el Perú colonial (1660-1705). PhD diss., *Mimeo*, 2016. https://idus.us.es/bitstream/handle/11441/39090/4/Image060416110925.pdf?sequence=1.

Johnson, N. D., and M. "Tax farming and the origins of state capacity in England and France." *Explorations in Economic History* 51 (2014): 1–20.

Juan, Jorge and Antonio de Ulloa. *Discourse and Political Reflections on the Kingdoms of Peru*, edited by John J. Tepaske. Translated by John J. Tepaske and Besse A. Clement. Norman: The University of Oklahoma Press, 1978.

Kahle, Louis G. "The Spanish colonial judiciary." *Southwestern Social Science Quarterly* 1 (1951): 26–37.

Kammann, Peter. *Movimientos campesinos en el Perú: 1900–1968*. Universidad Mayor de San Marcos, 1982.

Kaske, Elisabeth. "Fund-raising wars: Office selling and interprovincial finance in nineteenth-century China." *Harvard Journal of Asiatic Studies* 71, no. 1 (2011): 69–141.

Kaske, Elisabeth. "The price of an office: Venality, the individual and the state in 19th century China." In *Metals, Monies, and Markets in Early Modern Societies: East Asian and Global Perspectives*, Thomas Hirzel and Nanny Kim (eds.) Vol. 17 LIT Verlag Munster(2008): 281–308.

Keefer, Phil, and Carlos Scartascini. "Trust, social cohesion, and growth in Latin America and the Caribbean." *IDB Publications (Book Chapters)*, 2022. https://doi.org/10.18235/0003792.

Kim, Diana S. *Empires of Vice: The Rise of Opium Prohibition across Southeast Asia*. Vol. 11. Princeton University Press, 2021.

Klein, Herbert S. "Current debates about the colonial economy and government from the Spanish royal treasury records." *Hispanic American Historical Review* 104, no. 2 (2024): 213–242.

Klein, Herbert S. *The American Finances of the Spanish Empire: Royal Income and Expenditures in Colonial Mexico, Peru, and Bolivia, 1680–1809*. University of New Mexico Press, 1998.
Klein, Herbert S., and Sergio T. Serrano Hernández. "Was there a 17th century crisis in Spanish America?" *Revista de Historia Económica-Journal of Iberian and Latin American Economic History* 37, no. 1 (2019): 43–80.
Klein, Herbert S., and John J. TePaske. "The seventeenth-century crisis in New Spain: Myth or reality?" *Past and Present* 90 (1981): 116–135.
Knight, Alan. *The Mexican Revolution: Counter Revolution and Reconstruction*. Cambridge University Press, 1986.
Kurtz, Marcus J. *Latin American State Building in Comparative Perspective: Social Foundations of Institutional Order*. Cambridge University Press, 2013.
Langer, Erick D. "Bringing the economic back in: Andean Indians and the construction of the nation-state in nineteenth-century Bolivia." *Journal of Latin American Studies* 41, no. 3 (2009): 527–551.
Langer, Erick D. "Indigenous independence in Spanish South America" in *New Countries: Capitalism, Revolutions, and Nations in the Americas, 1750–1870*, edited by John Tutino. Duke University Press, 2016.
Lazear, Edward P. "Culture and language." *Journal of Political Economy* 107, no. 6 (1999): 95–126.
Lecoin, Sylvie. "Intercambios, movimientos de población y trabajo en la diócesis de Michoacán en el síglo XVI (un aspecto de las Relaciones Geográficas de 1580)." In *Movimientos de población en el Occidente de México*, edited by Thomas Calvo and Gustavo López. El Colegio de Michoacán/Centre d'Etudes Mexicaines et Centroamericaines, 1988.
Lee, Melissa M., and Nan Zhang. "Legibility and the informational foundations of state capacity." *The Journal of Politics* 79, no. 1 (2017): 118–132.
Lee, Melissa M., and Nan Zhang. State Capacity Scores, 2020. http://statecapacityscores.org/.
Lejonagoitia, Guillermo B. *Gobernar las Indias: venalidad y méritos en la provisión de cargos americanos, 1701–1746*. Vol. 19, Universidad Almería, 2015.
Lewis, Bernard. "Some reflections on the decline of the Ottoman empire." *Studia Islamica* 9 (1958): 111–127.
Libertad Digital. "Maduro crea una comisión para pedir reparaciones a España por la Conquista." Libertad Digital, January 27, 2022. www.libertaddigital.com/cultura/historia/2022-01-27/maduro-crea-una-comision-para-pedir-reparaciones-a-espana-por-la-conquista-6859220/.
Lohmann Villena, Guillermo. *El corregidor de indios en el Perú bajo los Austrias*. Pontificia Universidad Catolica del Peru, 1957.
Lohmann Villena, Guillermo. *Los ministros de la Audiencia de Lima en el reinado de los Borbones (1700–1821)*. Escuela de Estudios Hispano-Americanos, 1974.
López-Alves, F. *State Formation and Democracy in Latin America, 1810–1900*. Durham, NC: Duke University Press, 2000.
Lovell, W. George. *Conquest and Survival in Colonial Guatemala: A Historical Geography of the Cuchumatan Highlands, 1500–1821*. McGill-Queen's University Press, 2005.

Luna, Juan Pablo, and David Soifer Hillel. "Capturing sub-national variation in state capacity: A survey-based approach." *American Behavioral Scientist* 61, no. 8 (2017): 887–907.

Lynch, John. "The institutional framework of colonial Spanish America." *Journal of Latin American Studies* 24, no. S1 (1992): 69–81.

Macleod, Murdo J. "Some thoughts on the pax colonial, colonial violence, and perceptions of both." In *Native Resistance and the Pax Colonial in New Spain*, vol. 4, edited by Susan Schroeder. University of Nebraska Press, 1998.

Mahoney, James. *Colonialism and Postcolonial Development: Spanish America in Comparative Perspective*. Cambridge University Press, 2010.

Maloney, William F., and Felipe Valencia Caicedo. "The persistence of (subnational) fortune." *The Economic Journal* 126, no. 598 (2016): 2363–2401.

Martínez Peláez, Severo. *Motines de indios. La violencia colonial en Centroamérica y Chiapas*. 2nd ed., edited by Coralia Gutiérrez Álvarez and Ernesto Godoy Dárdano. Piedra Santa, 2021 [1985]. Kindle.

Mauro, Paolo. "Corruption and growth." *The Quarterly Journal of Economics* 110, no. 3 (1995): 681–712.

Mazzuca, Sebastian. *Latecomer State Formation: Political Geography and Capacity Failure in Latin America*. Yale University Press, 2021.

McClintock, Cynthia. *Revolutionary Movements in Latin America: El Salvador's FMLN & Perú's Shining Path*. US Institute of Peace Press, 1988.

McClintock, Cynthia. "Why peasants rebel: The Case of Peru's Sendero Luminoso." *World Politics* 37, no. 1 (1984): 48–84.

McCreery, David. *Rural Guatemala, 1760–1940*. Stanford University Press, 1994.

McFarlane, Anthony. "Breaking the Pax Hispanica: Collective Violence in Colonial Spanish." In *A Global History of Early Modern Violence*, edited by Erica Charters, Marie Houllemare, and Peter H. Wilson. Manchester University Press, 2021.

McFarlane, Anthony. "Cimarrones y palenques en Colombia: siglo XVIII." *Historia y Espacio* 14 (1990): 53–78.

McFarlane, Anthony. "Civil disorders and popular protests in Late Colonial New Granada." *Hispanic American Historical Review* 64, no. 1 (1984): 17–54.

McFarlane, Anthony. "Rebellions in late colonial Spanish America: A comparative perspective." *Bulletin of Latin American Research* 14, no. 3 (1995): 313–338.

Michelet, Dominique. "Apuntes para el Análisis de las Migraciones en el México prehispánico." In *Movimientos de población en el Occidente de México*, edited by Thomas Calvo and Gustavo López. El Colegio de Michoacán/Centre d'Etudes Mexicaines et Centroamericaines, 1988.

Minder, Raphael, and Elisabeth Malkin. "Mexican Call for Conquest Apology Ruffles Feathers in Spain and Mexico." New York Times, March 27, 2019. www.nytimes.com/2019/03/27/world/americas/mexico-spain-apology.html.

Mishra, Ajit. "Hierarchies, incentives and collusion in a model of enforcement." *Journal of Economic Behavior & Organization* 47, no. 2 (2002): 165–178.

Montesquieu, Charles de Secondat. *The Spirit of Laws*. Batoche Books, [1748] 2001.

Morales, Mariano S., Edward R. Cook, Jonathan Barichivich, Duncan A. Christie, Ricardo Villalba, Carlos LeQuesne, Ana M. Srur et al. "Six hundred years of South American tree rings reveal an increase in severe hydroclimatic events since mid-20th century." *Proceedings of the National Academy of Sciences* 117, no. 29 (2020): 16816–16823.

Moreno Cebrian, Alfredo. *El corregidor de indios y la economía peruana en el siglo XVIII: (los repartos forzosos de mercancías)*. Editorial CSIC-CSIC Press, 1977.

Moreno Yánez, Segundo E. *Sublevaciones indígenas en la audiencia de Quito*. La Pontificia Universidad Católica del Ecuador (EDIPUCE), 1985.

Moyo, Dambisa. *Dead Aid: Why Aid is Not Working and How there is a Better Way for Africa*. Macmillan, 2009.

Mukherjee, Shivaji. *Colonial Institutions and Civil War: Indirect Rule and Maoist Insurgency in India*. Cambridge University Press, 2021.

Mukherjee, Shivaji. "Historical legacies of colonial indirect rule: Princely states and maoist insurgency in central India." *World Development* 111 (2018): 113–129.

Naritomi, Joana, Rodrigo R. Soares, and Juliano J. Assunção. "Institutional development and colonial heritage within Brazil." *The Journal of Economic History* 72, no. 2 (2012): 393–422.

Naseemullah, Adnan. "Shades of sovereignty: Explaining political order and disorder in Pakistan's northwest." *Studies in Comparative International Development* 49 (2014): 501–522.

Navarrete, Carlos. "Documentos guatemaltecos, I: Un fichero sobre la participación indígena en revoluciones, asonadas, y motines de Guatemala y Chiapas, en el Archivo General de Centro América, Guatemala." *Tlalocan* 9 (1982): 313–338. https://doi.org/10.19130/iifl.tlalocan.1982.6.

Navarro Concepción, and Cannen Reuigóme. "La ordenanza de intendentes y las comunidades indígenas del virreinato peruano: una reforma insuficiente." *Revista complutense de historia de América* 19 (1993): 209–231.

Niedzwiecki, Sara. "Social policies, attribution of responsibility, and political alignments: A subnational analysis of Argentina and Brazil." *Comparative Political Studies* 49, no. 4 (2016): 457–498.

North, D. C., and B. R. Weingast, "Constitutions and commitment: The evolution of institutions governing public choice in seventeenth-century England." *The Journal of Economic History* 49, no. 4 (1989): 803–832.

Nunn, Nathan. "Historical legacies: A model linking Africa's past to its current underdevelopment." *Journal of Development Economics* 83, no. 1 (2007): 157–175.

O'Phelan Godoy, Scarlett. *Un siglo de rebeliones anticoloniales. Perú y Bolivia, 1700-1783*. Centro de Estudios Andinos Bartolomé de las Casas, 1988.

Oberem, Udo. "'Indios libres' e 'indios sujetos a haciendas' en la sierra ecuatoriana a fines de la colonia." In *Colección Pendoneros: Contribución a la etnohistoria ecuatoriana* 20, edited by Segundo Moreno Yánez and Udo Oberem. Instituto Otavaleño de Antropología, 1981.

Olken, Benjamin A., and Patrick Barron. "The simple economics of extortion: Evidence from trucking in Aceh." *Journal of Political Economy* 117, no. 3 (2009): 417–452.

Orellana-Sánchez, Juan Carlos De. "De la crítica a la reforma. Pensamiento político, económico y visión de reino en las denuncias indianas de corrupción (s. XVII)." *Historia y Memoria* 19 (2019): 67–120.

Ortiz de la Tabla Ducasse, Javier. "Obrajes y Obrajeros del Quito Colonial." *Anuario de estudios americanos* 39 (1982): 341–365.

Ortiz Escamilla, Juan. *Guerra y gobierno: Los pueblos y la independencia de México, 1808–1825.* Colegio de México, 2014.

Otero-Bahamón, Silvia. "When the State Minds the Gap: The politics of subnational inequality in Latin America." PhD diss., Northwestern University, 2016.

Ottinger, Sebastián, and Nico Voigtländer. "History's Masters: The Effect of European Monarchs on State Performance." *Econometrica* 93, no. 1 (2025): 95–128.

Paglayan, A. S. "Education or indoctrination? The violent origins of public school systems in an era of state-building." *American Political Science Review* 116, no. 4 (2022): 1242–1257.

Parry, John Horace. *The Sale of Public Office in the Spanish Indies under the Hapsburgs.* Vol. 37. University of California Press, 1953.

Pearce, Adrian John. "Early Bourbon Government in the Viceroyalty of Peru, 1700–1759." PhD diss., University of Liverpool, 1998.

Pelayo, Agueda J. "Funcionarios ante la justicia: Residencias de alcaldes mayores y corregidores ventiladas ante la audiencia de Guadalajara durante el siglo XVIII." *Estudios de historia novohispana* 40 (2009): 81–120.

Peng, Peng. "Governing the Empire: Threats to Manchu Rule Survival and Bureaucratic Appointments in Qing China, 1644—1799." PhD diss., Duke University. 2022. https://sites.duke.edu/hiscope/files/2022/04/Peng_Duke_HPE.pdf.

Peng, Peng. "War, Bureaucracy, and State Capacity: Evidence from Imperial China." Duke University, 2019. https://sites.duke.edu/statecapacity/files/2019/04/Peng-2019-War-Bureaucracy-State-Capacity-in-China.pdf.

Phelan, John Leddy. "Authority and flexibility in the Spanish imperial bureaucracy." *Administrative Science Quarterly* 5, no. 1 (1960): 47–65.

Phelan, John Leddy. *The Kingdom of Quito in the Seventeenth Century: Bureaucratic Politics in the Spanish Empire.* University of Wisconsin Press, 1967.

Phelan, John Leddy. *The People and the King: The Comunero Revolution in Colombia, 1781.* University of Wisconsin Press, 1978.

Pietschmann, Horst. "Alcaldes mayores, corregidores und subdelegados. Zum Problem der Distriktsbeamtenschaft im Vizekönigreich Neuspanien." *Jahrbuch für Geschichte Lateinamerikas* 9, no. 1 (1972): 173–270.

Pomeranz, Kenneth. "The great divergence: China, Europe, and the making of the modern world economy." In *The Great Divergence.* Princeton University Press, 2009.

Prado de la Escosura, Leandro. "Lost decades? Economic performance in post-independence Latin America." *Journal of Latin American Studies* 41, no. 2 (2009): 279–307.

Prado de la Escosura, Leandro. "The economic consequences of independence in Latin America." In *The Cambridge History of Latin America*, vol. 2, edited by Bethell, Leslie. Cambridge University Press, 2008.

Prado de la Escosura, Leandro. "When did Latin America fall behind?" In *The Decline of Latin American Economies: Growth, Institutions, and Crises*, edited by Sebastian Edwards, Gerardo Esquivel and Graciela Márquez. University of Chicago Press, 2007.

Prendergast, Canice, and Robert H. Topel. "Favoritism in organizations." *Journal of Political Economy* 104, no. 5 (1996): 958–978.

Queralt, Didac. "War, international finance, and fiscal capacity in the long run." *International Organization* 73, no. 4 (2019): 713–753.

Queralt, Didac. *Pawned States: State Building in the Era of International Finance.* Vol. 109. Princeton University Press, 2022.

Quiroz, Alfonso W. *Historia de la corrupción en el Perú.* Instituto de Estudios Peruanos, 2013.

Quiroz, Alfonso W. "Reassessing the role of credit in late colonial Peru: Censos, Escrituras, and Imposiciones." *Hispanic American Historical Review* 74, no. 2 (1994): 193–230.

Ramos Gomez, Luis J. *Las "Noticias Secretas" de América de Jorge Juan y Antonio de Ulloa (1735–1745).* Consejo Superior de Investigaciones Científicas, 1985.

Ramos-Toro, Diego. "Historical Conflict and Gender Disparities." *MPRA Paper* 85045, University Library of Munich, 2018.

Ravi Mumford, Jeremy. "Litigation as ethnography in sixteenth-century Peru: Polo de Ondegardo and the Mitimaes." *Hispanic American Historical Review* 88, no. 1 (2008): 5–40.

Reina, Leticia. *Las luchas populares en México en el siglo XIX.* Vol. 90. SEP, Cultura, Centro de Investigaciones y Estudios Superiores en Antropología Social, 1983.

Revilla Orías, Paola A. "Pasquines reformistas, pasquines sediciosos: aquellas hojas volanderas en Charcas (siglos XVIII-XIX)." *Revista Ciencia y Cultura* 22–23 (2009): 33–43.

Rivadeneira Acosta, Alexander P. "Essays in Economic Development." PhD diss., Arizona State University, 2019.

Robinson, David J. "Patrones de migración en Michoacán en el siglo XVIII: Datos y metodologías." In *Movimientos de población en el Occidente de México*, edited by Thomas Calvo and Gustavo López. El Colegío de Michoacán/Centre d'Etudes Mexicaines et Centroamericaines, 1988.

Roessler, Philip, Yannick Pengl, Robert Marty, Kyle Titlow, and Nicolas Van de Walle. "The Cash Crop Revolution, Colonialism and Legacies of Spatial Inequality: Evidence from Africa." *Centre for the Study of African Economies Working Paper Series* 2020–12 (2020).

Rojas, Beatriz. *Las ciudades novohispanas: siete ensayos: historia y territorio.* Instituto de Investigaciones Dr. José María Luis Mora, 2016.

Root, Hilton L. *The Fountain of Privilege: Political Foundations of Markets in Old Regime France and England.* University of California Press, 1994. http://ark.cdlib.org/ark:/13030/ft1779n74g/.

Root, Hilton L. "The redistributive role of government: Economic regulation in old regime France and England." *Comparative Studies in Society and History* 33, no. 2 (1991): 338–369.

Rosenmüller, Christoph. "'Corrupted by ambition': Justice and patronage in imperial New Spain and Spain, 1650–1755." *Hispanic American Historical Review* 96, no. 1 (2016): 1–37.

Rosenmüller, Christoph. "The Execrable Offense of Fraud or Bribery: Corrupt Judges and Common People in the Visita of Imperial Mexico (1715–1727)." In *Corruption in the Iberian Empires: Greed, Custom, and Colonial Networks*, edited by Christoph Rosenmüller. University of New Mexico Press, 2017a.

Rosenmüller, Christoph. *Corruption in the Iberian Empires: Greed, Custom, and Colonial Networks*. University of New Mexico Press, 2017b.

Rowe, John H. "The incas under Spanish colonial institutions." *The Hispanic American Historical Review* 37, no. 2 (1957): 155–199.

Saleh, Mohamed, and Jean Tirole. "Taxing identity: Theory and evidence from early Islam." *Econometrica* 89, no. 4 (2021): 1881–1919.

Saleh, Mohammed. "On the road to heaven: Taxation, conversions, and the Coptic-Muslim socioeconomic gap in medieval Egypt." *The Journal of Economic History* 78, no. 2 (2018): 394–434.

Salgado, Marcos. "Building Loyalty through Personal Connections: Evidence from the Spanish Empire." Working Paper, Stanford University, 2021.

Salvatore, Ricardo D., John H. Coatsworth, and Amílcar E. Challú (eds.). *Living standards in Latin American history: Height, welfare, and development, 1750–2000*. Harvard University Press, 2010.

Sánchez-Albornoz, N. *Indios y tributos en el Alto Perú*. Vol. 6. Instituto de Estudios Peruanos, 1978.

Sánchez-Alonso, Blanca. "The age of mass migration in Latin America." *The Economic History Review* 72, no. 1 (2019): 3–31.

Saffon Sanin, Maria Paula. *When Theft Becomes Grievance: Dispossessions as a Cause of Redistributive Land Claims in 20th Century Latin America*. Columbia University, 2015.

Sanz Tapia, Ángel. *¿Corrupción o necesidad?: la venta de cargos de gobierno americanos bajo Carlos II (1674-1700)*. Vol. 13. Editorial CSIC-CSIC Press, 2009.

Sanz Tapia, Angel. "Provisión, beneficio y venta de oficios americanos de Hacienda (1632–1700)/Purveyance, Purchase and Sale of Official Posts in the Treasury of the Spanish American Colonies (1632–1700)." *Revista Complutense de Historia de América* 37, (2011): 145–172.

Saylor, Ryan. *State Building in Boom Times: Commodities and Coalitions in Latin America and Africa*. Oxford University Press, 2014.

Schenoni, Luis L. "Bringing war back in: Victory and state formation in Latin America." *American Journal of Political Science* 65, no. 2 (2021): 405–421.

Schiaffino, Santiago Lorenzo. "El Corregidor chileno en el siglo XVIII." *Historia* 32 (1999): 131–139.

Schroeder, Susan, ed. *Native Resistance and the Pax Colonial in New Spain*. Vol. 4. University of Nebraska Press, 1998.

Scott, James. *The Art of Not Being Governed: An Anarchist History of Upland Southeast Asia*. Yale University Press, 2009.
Sellars, Emily A., and Jennifer Alix-García. "Labor scarcity, land tenure, and historical legacy: Evidence from Mexico." *Journal of Development Economics* 135 (2018): 504–516.
Seminario, B. *El Desarrollo de la Economía Peruana en la Era Moderna*. Universidad de Pacifico, 2015.
Sheikholeslami, A. Reza. "The sale of offices in Qajar Iran, 1858–1896." *Iranian Studies* 4, no. 2–3 (1971): 104–118.
Shleifer, Andrei, and Robert W. Vishny. "Corruption." *The Quarterly Journal of Economics* 108, no. 3 (1993): 599–617.
Soifer, Hillel David. "Regionalism, ethnic diversity, and variation in public good provision by National States." *Comparative Political Studies* 49, no. 10 (2016): 1341–1371.
Soifer, Hillel David. *State Building in Latin America*. Cambridge University Press, 2015.
Solórzano Fonseca, Juan Carlos. "Las comunidades indígenas de Guatemala, El Salvador y Chiapas durante el siglo XVIII: los mecanismos de la explotación económica." Anuario de Estudios Centroamericanos (1985): 93–130.
Stangl, Werner. "Data: Places gazetteer of Spanish America, 1701–1808." Harvard Dataverse, V2, UNF:6:LWLrwzItZ+LD7gDT2qY/AQ== [fileUNF], 2019a. https://doi.org/10.7910/DVN/FUSJD3.
Stangl, Werner. "Data: Routes of the flotas y galeones, 1564–1778." Harvard Dataverse, V1, 2019b. https://doi.org/10.7910/DVN/UGLWCR.
Stangl, Werner. "Data: Territorial gazetteer for Spanish America, 1701–1808." Harvard Dataverse, V4, 2019c. https://doi.org/10.7910/DVN/YPEU5E.
Stangl, Werner. "Demographic data, 1701–1808." Harvard Dataverse, V2, 2019d. https://doi.org/10.7910/DVN/QABIBG.
Stasavage, D. *States of Credit: Size, Power, and the Development of European Polities*. Vol. 35. Princeton University Press, 2011.
Stasavage, D. *Public Debt and the Birth of the Democratic State: France and Great Britain 1688–1789*. Cambridge University Press, 2003.
Stein, Stanley J. "Bureaucracy and business in the Spanish Empire, 1759–1804: Failure of a bourbon reform in Mexico and Peru." *Hispanic American Historical Review* 61, no. 1 (1981): 2–28.
Stern, Steve J. *Resistencia rebelión y conciencia campesina en los andes*. Instituto de Estudios Peruanos, 1990.
Stern, Steve J. ed. *Resistance, Rebellion, and Consciousness in the Andean Peasant World, 18th to 20th Centuries*. University of Wisconsin Press, 1987.
Summerhill, William. "Colonial Institutions, Slavery, Inequality, and Development: Evidence from São Paulo, Brazil." MPRA Paper 22162, University Library of Munich, 2010.
Swart, K. W. *Sale of Offices in the Seventeenth Century*. Martinus Nijhoff, 1949.
Tanck de Estrada, Dorothy. *Atlas ilustrado de los Pueblos Indígenas: Nueva España 1800. In Comisión de los Derechos Indígenas y Fomento Cultural Banamex*. El colegio de México/El colegio mexiquense, 2005.

Tandeter, Enrique, and Nathan Wachtel. "Precios y producción agraria. Potosí y Charcas en el siglo XVIII." *Desarrollo económico* 23, no. 90 (1983): 197–232.
Tannenbaum, Frank. *Mexican Agrarian Revolution*. Macmillan, 1929.
Taylor, William B. *Drinking, Homicide, and Rebellion in Colonial Mexican Villages*. Stanford University Press, 1979.
TePaske, John Jay, Herbert S. Klein, and Kendall W. Brown. *The Royal Treasuries of the Spanish Empire in America*. 3 volumes. Duke University Press, 1982.
Thies, Cameron G. "War, rivalry, and state building in Latin America." *American Journal of Political Science* 49, no. 3 (2005): 451–465.
Thornton, Jay David. "'Without him the Indians would leave and nothing would get done.' The changing relationship between the Caciques and the Audiencia of Charcas following Francisco de Toledo's reforms." *Bolivian Studies Journal* 18 (2011): 134–160.
Thorp, Rosemary, and Maritza Paredes. *La etnicidad y la persistencia de la desigualdad: el caso peruano*. Lima, Instituto de Estudios Peruanos 2011. https://hdl.handle.net/20.500.14660/602.
Tirole, Jean. "Hierarchies and bureaucracies: On the role of collusion in organizations." *Journal of Law Economics & Organization* 2, no. 2 (1986): 181–214.
Tomás y Valiente, Francisco. *La venta de oficios en Indias (1492–1606)*. Instituto de Estudios Administrativos, 1972.
Tutino, John. *From Insurrection to Revolution in Mexico: Social Bases of Agrarian Violence, 1750–1940*. Princeton University Press, 1986.
Tutino, John. "Rebelión indígena en Tehuantepec." *Cuadernos políticos* 24 (1980): 89–101.
Tutino, John. *The Mexican Heartland*. Princeton University Press, 2017.
Ucendo, José Ignacio Andrés, and Ramón Lanza García. "Estructura y evolución de los ingresos de la Real Hacienda de Castilla en el siglo XVII." *Studia Historica: Historia Moderna* 30 (2008): 147–190.
Van Young, Eric. *The Other Rebellion: Popular Violence, Ideology, and the Mexican Struggle for Independence, 1810–1821*. Stanford University Press, 2001.
Villalobos R, Sergio. "Contrabando francés en el Pacífico, 1700–1724." *Revista de Historia de América* 51 (1961): 49–80.
Villanueva Urteaga, Horacio. "*Cuzco 1689. Informes de los párrocos al obispo Mollinedo.*" *Economía y sociedad en el sur andino*. CERA Bartolomé de Las Casas. 1982.
Vollmer, Gunther. *Bevolkerungspolitik und Bevolkerungsstruktur im Vizekanigreich Peru zu Ende der Kolonialzeit (1741–1821)*. Verlag Gehlen, 1967.
von Grafenstein, Johanna, and Carlos Marichal. "Introduction" in *El secreto del imperio español: los situados coloniales en el siglo XVIII*, von Grafenstein, Johanna, and Carlos Marichal (eds.) El Colegio de México/Instituto de Investigaciones Dr. JML Mora (2012), pp. 9–31.
Voth, Joachim, and Guo Xu. "Discretion and Destruction: Promotions, performance, and patronage in the Royal Navy." *CEPR Discussion Paper* No. DP13963, 2020.
Weaver, Jeff. "Jobs for sale: Corruption and misallocation in hiring." *American Economic Review* 111, no. 10 (2021): 3093–3122.

Weber, M. *Economy and Society: An outline of Interpretive Sociology*. Vol. 1. University of California Press, 1978.

Weinstein, Jeremy. M. *Inside Rebellion: The Politics of Insurgent Violence*. Cambridge University Press, 2006.

Wimmer, Andreas, Lars-Erik Cederman, and Brian Min. "Ethnic politics and armed conflict: A configurational analysis of a new global data set." *American Sociological Review* 74, no. 2 (2009): 316–337.

Xu, Guo. "The colonial origins of fiscal capacity: Evidence from patronage governors." *Journal of Comparative Economics* 47, no. 2 (2019): 263–276.

Xu, Guo. "The costs of patronage: Evidence from the British Empire." *American Economic Review* 108, no. 11 (2018): 3170–3198.

Yashar, Deborah J. *Contesting Citizenship in Latin America: The Rise of Indigenous Movements and the Postliberal Challenge*. Cambridge University Press, 2005.

Zevallos, Juan Manuel Pérez. "El movimiento de población como estrategia de sobrevivencia de los indios en la Nueva España." *Estudios Ibero-Americanos* 25, no. 2 (1999): 39–60.

Zhang, Lawrence Lok Cheung. "Legacy of success: Office purchase and state-elite relations in Qing China." *Harvard Journal of Asiatic Studies* 73, no. 2 (2013): 259–297.

Zhang, Lawrence Lok Cheung. *Power for a Price: Office Purchase, Elite Families, and Status Maintenance in Qing China*. Harvard University Press, 2022.

Zhu, Jiangnan. "Why are offices for sale in China? A case study of the office-selling chain in Heilongjiang province." *Asian Survey* 48, no. 4 (2008): 558–579.

Index

administrative hierarchy, 2
administrative level 3, 2
  municipalities, 2
Africa, 2, 181
agency problems, 50, 64, 73
Alaska, 5, 24
alcabalas, 28, 135, 141
alcaldes. *See alcaldía mayor, alcaldes mayores*
alcaldía mayor
  alcaldes mayores, 5, 8, 11, 20, 22, 29, 33, 37, 41, 48, 52, 66, 68, 70, 73–75, 77, 83, 92–93, 95–96, 98–102, 108–109, 111, 121–124, 126–127, 129, 131–132, 136–138, 145–149, 153–156, 177, 180, 207, 214–215, 221, 223–225
  alcaldías mayores, 5–6, 9, 27, 30–31, 37, 40, 43, 49, 53, 60, 67–68, 70, 87, 96, 103, 106, 147, 162–163, 202, 206–207
alcaldías. See alcaldía mayor
Alcántara, *caballero de la orden*, 67, 87, 222–223
appointees, 11, 35, 65–66, 72, 74, 81, 83, 85–87, 115, 121, 135
Argentina, 5, 15–17, 24, 31, 112, 161, 164, 192, 202, 214
Asia, 2, 181, 213
audiencias, 5, 14–15, 19–20, 23–30, 32–34, 44, 49, 51, 59–62, 86–87, 95–102, 104, 106, 108–111, 115, 119, 121–124, 133–134, 136, 140, 146–147, 149, 156, 214, 224

Charcas, 25, 44, 61, 66, 94, 96, 98, 100, 106, 111–112, 115–116, 119–121, 134–135, 137, 143, 149, 190, 222, 224
Guadalajara, 24, 43, 66, 106, 139, 222, 224, 235
Guatemala, 24, 26, 62–63, 122, 126, 135–136, 147, 149
Lima, 25–26, 32, 36, 38, 42, 44, 61, 66, 75–76, 78, 84, 95–96, 98, 100–101, 106, 111–117, 119–121, 124, 129–130, 134–135, 137, 141, 149, 222, 224, 229–230
Manila, 25–26, 38, 96, 106, 140
Mexico, 15, 24, 26, 35, 44, 66, 134, 136–139, 141, 222
Panama, 24
Quito, 25, 91, 95, 98, 106, 111, 115, 121, 135, 149–150, 153
Santa Fe, 24, 63, 106, 112, 117, 122, 133–136, 146–147, 149, 152, 156
Santiago, 25–26, 96, 98, 101, 115, 119
Santo Domingo, 25, 62–63, 96, 120
authoritarian enclaves, 2–3, 199
autonomy, 13, 161, 166, 175, 177, 183, 185–187, 190, 212
ayuntamientos, 163, 177

Bentham, Jeremy, 7–8, 82–83
Biobío (river), 6
Bishop of Arequipa, 8, 95, 102, 129–130

261

Bolivia, 5, 7–8, 10–12, 19, 21, 24–25, 40–44, 61, 65–68, 86, 89, 94, 96, 98, 106, 111–112, 115–116, 119–120, 123, 125, 128–130, 133–134, 138–140, 142–144, 146–147, 154, 156, 158–159, 162, 166, 172–176, 187–192, 196–197, 199, 201–202, 204–205, 207–208, 210–211, 217, 229–230, 234–236, 238
  Sicasica, 190, 207–208
Bourbon
  dynasty, 4, 23, 37, 48, 120, 126, 214
  Reforms, 11–20, 61, 127–128, 135, 141, 148, 151–153, 182
Brazil, 2, 15–16
British, Empire, 2, 19, 24, 27, 62
Buen Retiro, Palace, 5, 58, 64, 106
Burkholder and Chandler (1977), 10, 19, 48, 65–67, 69, 78, 80, 85, 92, 97, 102, 115, 137

cabeceras, 32, 154, 156, 189, 206, 233
cabildos, 18, 32, 161–162, 177, 180, 192
caciques, 177
cajas (treasury), 5, 22, 27–28, 30, 32, 35–36, 40, 58–59, 64
  caja officials, 28–29, 33, 95
  fiscal positions, 48, 59, 70
cajas de la comunidad (indigenous), 40, 132
Calatrava, *caballero de la orden*, 67, 87, 222–223
California, Alta, 6
Cámara de Indias, 62, 216
Caribbean, 5, 25, 96, 105–106, 122, 202
Central America, 5, 14, 24
Chile, 1–2, 5–7, 15–17, 24–25, 31, 43, 64, 96, 106, 111, 115, 120–121, 123, 140, 161, 165, 202, 205, 217, 235
China, 8, 18, 20, 22, 47, 50, 64, 92, 213, 215–217
Church, Catholic, 27, 58, 130, 150, 161, 187
cochineal, 11, 41, 131, 167
coffee, 162, 166–169, 190
collusion, 12, 82, 95–96, 102, 108–111, 113, 120–121, 159, 215
Colombia, 5, 7, 16, 22, 24–25, 28, 43, 106, 112, 122, 126, 133–134, 140, 146–147, 152, 156, 161, 174, 181, 201–202, 204–205, 213, 217, 231–232, 235–236

colonial administration, 8–10, 21, 32, 39, 49, 60, 66–67, 69–70, 72–74, 84, 91, 93, 95–96, 98, 109, 111, 121–123, 125–126, 145, 165, 192, 194–195, 225
colonial governance, 72, 91, 136, 154, 158, 169, 172, 183, 199, 202, 204, 206–207
colonial jurisdictions, 2, 12, 202, 206, 208–209, 217
colonial officials, 3, 7–9, 11–12, 18–19, 21, 41, 44, 73, 75, 77, 81, 85, 89, 91, 118, 120, 126, 128, 134, 136, 145, 147–148, 153, 155–156, 158–159, 172, 212, 215, 219
comunas. See administrative level 3
concertaje, 162, 171–173
conflict, violent, 3, 160, 165, 191, 212, 220
  motines, 148–149
  political violence, 180
  rebellion, 5, 10, 60, 62, 78, 92, 106, 122, 126–128, 130, 133–136, 138, 141–145, 147–148, 150–153, 163, 180–183, 185, 216, 219
  subnational conflict, 165, 186, 193
  uprisings, 10, 13, 21, 62, 101, 124–130, 132–141, 143–145, 147–153, 158–160, 162–163, 180–181, 183–185, 193, 195, 215, 219, 229–230
conquest of Mexico, 1
core, 1–2, 15, 17, 192, 213–214
corregimiento
  corregidores, 5, 8, 11, 20, 22, 29, 32–33, 35, 37, 40, 43–44, 48, 52, 60–61, 66, 68, 73–75, 77, 83, 90, 92–96, 98–103, 108–109, 111, 113–114, 116–119, 121–127, 129–132, 135–136, 145–146, 150–151, 154, 172, 175–177, 180, 214–215, 218, 225
  corregimientos, 5–7, 9, 11, 19, 27, 29–31, 34, 37, 39–43, 49, 53, 58–59, 60–61, 64, 66–70, 72, 86–87, 96, 98, 102–103, 106, 108, 114, 116, 121, 123, 146–147, 149–150, 152–153, 162–164, 173, 178, 180, 182, 184, 194, 202, 206–208, 214, 234
corruption, 8–10, 48, 51, 73, 79, 86, 91, 112, 117, 154, 213–215, 217

Cortes of Cádiz, 160, 177
Costa Rica, 17
Council of Indies, 9, 23, 33, 40, 52, 60, 62–63, 67–68, 70, 72, 74, 76, 81–83, 85–86, 92, 97, 100, 104–105, 115, 131, 214
criollo, 20, 27, 40, 48, 51, 66, 72, 80, 102, 110, 112, 120, 122, 177, 217
criollo elites, 20, 122
Crown, Spanish, 3–10, 19–24, 27–30, 32–37, 40–41, 44, 46–52, 54–70, 72–75, 77–81, 83–91, 93–95, 98–99, 101–102, 104–106, 108, 111, 113–115, 117, 120–123, 128–129, 131–132, 135, 137–138, 141, 145, 147, 151–153, 158, 162–164, 171–172, 174, 177, 180, 187, 202, 213–215, 218–219, 225, 228
Cuba, 13, 27–28, 63, 125, 161, 192

debt peonage, 162, 167, 174
demographic collapse (Americas), 3
displacement (population), 10, 13, 21, 90, 124–125, 154, 156–160, 186–188, 190, 197–198, 215
distritos. *See* administrative level 3
doblones (currency), 22, 79, 218
drought, 10, 142–144, 158–159, 182, 184
Dutch, Empire, 2, 24

economic geography, 3, 10, 12–13, 17, 164
economic growth, 13, 49
economic surplus, 8, 57, 60, 65, 71, 85, 97, 122, 124, 127, 145, 154, 156, 159, 182, 215, 218
Ecuador, 2, 5, 7–8, 11–12, 21, 24–25, 43, 83, 98, 106, 111, 115, 117, 119–120, 123, 125, 133–134, 140, 147, 153, 156, 162, 166, 171–174, 187, 191–192, 202, 205, 207, 217, 231, 235
Quito, 111, 117–119, 126, 133–134, 151, 181, 231
El Niño, 10, 143, 145, 159
endowment (factor), 17–19, 206, 212
England, 22, 50, 63–64, 216
ethnic enclaves, 21
ethnic segregation, 3, 17, 158, 160, 165, 193, 212

Florida, 25, 27, 56, 62–63
Florida, La, 6
forced labor, 111, 116, 130, 148, 150, 154, 166, 171, 232
France, 7, 20, 22, 47, 50–52, 63, 104, 213, 215–217
French, Empire, 2, 24
fronteras, 5–6
futuras, 4, 34–35, 37, 92, 97, 127

geopolitical threat, 24, 104, 106, 123
gobernación, 5–6, 15, 29–30
gold, 116, 220
Guatemala, 7, 11–12, 21, 39–41, 43, 106, 133–134, 140, 146–148, 150, 153, 162, 166–168, 171, 173, 176, 187–192, 197–198, 201–202, 204–205, 207–211, 217, 231, 234–236, 238
Ciudad de, 149

Habsburg, dynasty, 4, 22, 48, 126, 214
haciendas, 40, 108, 111–112, 171–172, 187
Historical Geographical Information System of Las Indias, 14–15, 25
Honduras, 38
human capital, 181, 202, 225

illiteracy, rate, 209, 219
independence (from Spain), 1, 11, 13–14, 16, 20–21, 125, 134, 142, 148–149, 159–166, 173–182, 184, 187, 190–191, 194, 219
indigenous communities, 2, 131, 155–158, 161–163, 166, 169, 171, 174–175, 177, 180, 185–191, 195–198
indigenous population, 3, 9–10, 12, 19, 21, 23, 40–41, 57–58, 60–62, 64, 73, 80, 83, 91, 94–95, 100–101, 108, 111, 119–122, 124–125, 127, 129, 131–132, 138, 140, 148, 150–151, 153, 155–159, 161–163, 168–170, 172–173, 175, 177–180, 189–190, 194, 198–200, 202–203, 211, 218–220, 229–230, 233
indigenous segregation, 156, 171, 180, 191
inflation, 39, 59, 221
intendencias, 146–147
interest rate, 4
Iran, 213, 216–217

José Antonio Areche, visitador, 8, 129
José de Gálvez, visitador, 8, 129, 131
Juan and Ulloa, 8, 41, 43, 73, 81, 84, 95, 172
juicio de residencia, 95, 99

King. *See* King of Spain
King of Spain, 1, 3, 22, 124
    Charles II, 3–4, 22, 28, 33, 37, 47, 52, 158
    Charles III, 135
    Ferdinand VII, 160
    Philip IV, 23, 33
    Philip V, 37, 58, 73, 77
    Phillip II, 3
    Phillip VI, 1
kurakas, 177

labor coercion, 11–12, 21, 162, 166, 170, 190
Lima *Consulado*, 112
liquidity crises, 4
literacy, rate, 209–210
living standards, 3, 12, 127, 196–197, 201–204, 206–207
local elites, 40, 48, 51–52, 65–66, 71, 112, 122–123, 164–165, 177, 181, 191–192, 194
local governance, 3, 7, 12, 21, 128, 146, 157, 162, 200, 207, 217
"Lost Decades," 161
Louis XIV, King of France, 47, 51
loyalty (officials), 44, 63, 74, 79

malnutrition, 202–203, 217
Manuel de Guirior, Viceroy of Peru, 124, 130, 145
maravedís (currency), 223
marquis, 67
    of Villahermosa, 218
    of Villarias, 58
media anata, 57
merchants, 11, 28, 39, 42, 82, 112, 114, 121
merit, 7, 19, 33, 44, 51, 67–68, 72, 75, 77, 82, 86, 91, 94, 216
mestizo, 10, 130, 156–158
Mexico, 2–3, 5–8, 10–12, 14–16, 18, 21, 23–24, 28, 31, 34–35, 38–41, 43–44, 61–62, 64–68, 77–79, 86, 89, 99–101, 106, 108, 111–112, 122, 125, 128–129, 131–135, 138–140, 142–144, 146–147, 154–165, 173–174, 179–183, 186–190, 192–193, 197, 200, 202, 205, 207–211, 217, 224, 229–230, 233–236
Mexico City, 15, 17–18, 27, 34, 140
Palacio Nacional, 15
migration (population), 125–126, 154–155, 157, 164, 187, 191–192, 195, 197, 202
military governor, 5, 27–28, 31, 33, 37, 49, 53, 58–60, 62, 64
military governorships, 22, 28, 60
military title, 67, 78, 89, 222–223
mines, 41, 108, 111, 130, 135, 150, 154, 207, 211–212
mita, 40, 117, 132, 137, 150–152
Montesquieu, 7
municipality, 3, 18, 161, 165, 168–171, 178–179, 183–184, 188, 190, 197
municipios. *See* municipality

Nicaragua, 62–63
nobility title, 44, 75, 90, 218, 222–223
    nobility, 7, 9, 44, 46, 48, 52, 60, 66–68, 70, 72, 74–76, 78, 82, 86, 90, 100, 125, 177, 218, 221, 223
Nuevo León, 15
Nuevo México, 6

obrajes, 96, 111–112, 117–119, 150, 172
office prices, 9, 39, 41, 43, 46, 108–109, 130, 214, 228
    price spread, 139, 173, 205, 209, 229–230, 237–239
office-selling, 3–12, 17–21, 36–37, 47–58, 61, 64–68, 70, 72–75, 81, 83–85, 90–97, 102, 111–112, 114–115, 117, 121–128, 131–133, 135–136, 138–139, 145, 148, 152, 154, 158, 160, 180, 182, 184, 195, 207, 215–217, 219
oidor (*audiencia*), 94, 98, 101, 110, 112–113, 116, 119, 122, 225
oidores. *See* oidor (*audiencia*)
Ottoman Empire, 22, 47, 50, 216
oversight (supervision), 4, 26–27, 44, 67, 69, 93, 95, 98–99, 101–103, 108, 121–124, 136

Panama, 24–25, 28, 64, 96–97, 106, 112, 117, 122, 140, 202
Paraguay, 5, 17, 24, 27, 31, 161, 214

parroquias. See administrative level 3
pasquin, 9, 94–95
Patagonia, 5
patronage, 7, 19, 51, 68, 84, 92, 177, 219
Pax Hispannica, 10, 126–128, 135, 138, 147, 159, 180, 193
Pedro Castillo, 1
periphery, 156, 213–214
Peru, 1–2, 5, 7–8, 10–12, 14, 16–17, 19, 21, 25, 28, 32, 35–36, 39–44, 48, 61, 65–68, 75–76, 78, 83, 86, 89, 92, 95, 98, 106, 111, 113, 116–117, 119–120, 123, 128–130, 132–134, 138–140, 142–147, 154, 156–163, 167, 172–174, 178–179, 181–182, 184–190, 192–193, 197–199, 201–202, 204–205, 207–211, 214, 217–220, 229–230, 233–236
  Azángaro, 214
  Cuzco, 18, 25, 97, 116, 120, 132, 146, 154, 159
  Huamalíes, 218–220
  Lampa, 214
  Lima, 27, 38–39, 113–114, 140
pesos (currency), 6–8, 34–36, 38–39, 41–43, 46, 59, 103, 108, 113, 116, 137, 175, 207, 218, 221–222
Philippines, 5, 13, 25, 96, 106, 109, 125, 161
political representation, 3, 11, 13, 17, 21, 160, 162, 177, 180, 184, 191–194, 196, 199–200, 217, 219–220, 233–234
Portuguese, Empire, 2, 24
poverty, 3, 203, 208, 210–211, 220, 236
president of Mexico, 1
president of Venezuela, 1
profitability (offices), 37–38, 46, 74, 88–90, 93, 121, 223, 228
provinces, 2, 12, 18, 22, 27, 31–32, 37, 41–42, 44, 59, 66, 68, 78, 90, 92, 95, 99–100, 103, 113, 118, 126–127, 130, 132, 136, 138–140, 146–147, 150–151, 153, 158–159, 168–170, 173, 176–177, 180–181, 188–190, 192, 194, 197–198, 202, 204, 207, 210–211, 213–214, 219, 225, 234–235
public goods, 3, 12, 18, 21, 40, 158, 170–171, 190, 194, 196, 201, 204, 208–210, 212, 215
  public services, 2, 12, 203, 206

pueblos, 18, 155, 161, 188–189, 197, 207–208, 211
Puerto Rico, 13, 27–28, 62–63, 125
purchasers (office), 4–5, 8, 34, 37, 50, 60, 62, 64–66, 69–70, 72, 74, 81–83, 85–88, 90–94, 96–97, 102–103, 106, 108–110, 112, 115, 117–123, 136–138, 140, 172, 203, 213, 215–216, 218, 221, 224–225

Qing, dynasty, 8, 22, 47, 64, 215–216
Queen of Spain
  Queen Mariana, 33

regional disparities. *See* spatial inequalities
regional inequalities. *See* spatial inequalities
repartimiento, 11, 40–43, 84, 96, 99, 108, 111, 114, 116, 119, 121–122, 128–132, 136, 146, 148, 150, 172, 175–176, 219, 232
  repartimiento de indios, 40
  repartimiento del algodon, 41
  repartimientos de indios, 154
revenue (tax), 4, 10–11, 20, 28, 35, 40, 47–50, 52, 54–61, 64–65, 70, 72, 81, 121–122, 130, 141, 145, 165–166, 174, 187, 191, 215
royal treasury, 19, 28, 35–36, 77, 118, 121, 232

Santiago, *caballero de la orden*, 67, 78, 87, 222–223
secondary market, 4, 35, 114, 219
self-dealing, 7–8, 10, 73, 100, 108–111, 117, 123, 218
Shah (Iran), 216
silver, 23, 28, 41, 100, 116, 154, 220
situado, 23, 28, 165, 213
social status, 8–9, 27, 38, 46, 66, 69, 75–76, 78–79, 81, 86–87, 89–90, 92–93, 178, 221
sorting, 84–86, 88–90, 92, 121, 206
Spain, 2, 4–5, 14, 22, 27, 33–34, 37, 39, 42, 44, 46, 48, 50, 52–56, 59, 61, 65–66, 79, 87, 100–101, 107, 115–116, 120, 138, 160, 177, 203, 215, 220, 223
  Cádiz, 112
  Madrid, 10–12, 35, 52, 55, 64, 69, 90, 101–102, 106, 113, 127, 131, 137, 195

Spanish America, 1–4, 7–8, 10–12, 14, 20–21, 23, 39, 44, 52, 66, 83, 92, 106, 126–128, 133, 158, 160–162, 164–166, 175, 186, 191–195, 199, 201, 204–205, 213, 215–217
Spanish Empire, 2, 5, 7, 14, 17–19, 21, 23–25, 30, 46, 51, 75, 81, 92, 104, 123, 125, 133–134, 158, 160, 162, 193, 213–214, 217, 223
spatial inequalities, 3, 12, 193, 201–202, 212
state-building, 13, 158, 165–166, 191–192, 194
Strait of Magellan, 24
stunting (childhood), 12, 201–205, 217
subdelegaciones, 11, 146, 182
  subdelegados, 11, 121, 145–146
subnational authoritarianism, 12, 21, 196
subnational disparities. *See* spatial inequalities
subnational inequalities. *See* spatial inequalities
subsistence crises, 10, 128, 141–142, 144, 159, 230
Swart (1949), 4, 20, 22, 47–48, 50–52, 56, 216

tax rate, 2, 127–128, 172, 186
territorial organization, 5, 20, 179
tithe, 58, 121, 130, 150, 151, 232
trade monopoly, 2
tribunal de cuentas, 38
tributo, 28, 60, 148, 150–152, 162, 166, 172, 174–175, 188, 232
Túpac Amaru, 126, 130, 133–135, 143–144, 147, 180, 219
Tzetzal (rebellion), 126, 133–134

United States, 5, 15
Uruguay, 5, 15–17, 24, 31, 166, 192, 214

venal officials, 10, 21, 93, 158–159, 163, 194
  venal bureaucracy, 47

venality, 3, 10, 12–13, 19–21, 124, 127–128, 138–139, 141, 145, 147–148, 151–152, 156–160, 162–163, 165, 168–171, 173, 177–178, 180–186, 188–189, 191, 193–197, 202–203, 206, 210, 213–217, 230, 233–234
Venezuela, 3, 5, 16, 24–25, 62, 112, 146, 214
viceroy (Spanish Empire), 24, 27, 35, 42–43, 48, 177
viceroyalty of New Spain, 5, 22, 24, 62, 146
  New Spain, 63, 131
viceroyalty of Nueva Granada, 24, 133–134
viceroyalty of Peru, 5, 22, 24, 111, 130–131, 137, 146
viceroyalty of Rio de la Plata, 24, 112, 146
viceroys (Spanish Empire), 14–15, 24, 30, 52, 65, 67–69, 78, 98, 114, 127, 129

wages, 32, 37–38, 43, 69, 73, 83, 89, 127, 167, 184–185, 218, 228
wars involving Spain
  Anglo-Spanish War, 4, 52, 54, 62
  Franco-Dutch War, 4, 47, 52
  Nine Years' War, 4, 52, 53
  War of Devolution, 4, 47
  War of Jenkins' Ear, 4, 52–54
  War of the Austrian Succession, 4, 52, 106
  War of the Polish Succession, 4, 52
  War of the Quadruple Alliance, 4, 52
  War of the Reunions, 4, 52
  War of the Spanish Succession, 4, 52

Yucatán, 15, 139

zapadores, 167

Printed by Libri Plureos GmbH in Hamburg, Germany